Great Objectives

Great Objectives

An Inquiry into Secular Ethics

Robert Finch

Robert Finch

Library of Congress Control Number: 2016907963
ISBN: Hardcover   978-1-5245-0073-3
                Softcover   978-1-5245-0072-6
                eBook   978-1-5245-0071-9

Print information available on the last page.

Rev. date: 06/29/2016

To order additional copies of this book, contact:
Xlibris
1-888-795-4274
www.Xlibris.com
Orders@Xlibris.com
732192

Dedication

for my wife, Sheila Ann

Contents

List of Appendixes

List of Figures

Cover: The Statue of Liberty.

"Give me your tired, your poor, Your huddled masses yearning to breathe free," from Emma Lazarus' famous poem

1. Introduction

1. Introduction

1.1 Knowledge, Science, and Morality

The inspiration for this investigation struck me a decade ago when the new atheists came into vogue. The new atheists, of course, were Sam Harris, Richard Dawkins, Daniel Dennett, and Christopher Hitchens, all of whom had recently written books denying the existence of God. It occurred to me that a consequence of this spate of activity was that there would be a renewed need for books on nontheistic ethics. I had been writing a series of essays for our *Houston Humanist and Freethought Newsletter* on the very subject of ethics, and I am now turning these essays into a collection for publication. After a while, the news came out that Sam Harris had produced a new book *The Moral Landscape*, which seemed to confirm my prediction. There have also been several other new works on ethics published in recent months.

Why has it taken a decade to produce a draft for the book? One reason comes from the fact that ethics is such a wide subject. Consider the compendium edited by Peter Singer (1991). This massive work contains some forty-seven original essays covering the range that the discipline now encompasses. It is interesting to note that in an afterword to the volume, Singer asserts that "if ethics is a jigsaw puzzle, then we are at the stage where we have laid out all the pieces, and are beginning to see the outline of the picture. For ethics is *not* a meaningless series of different things to different people in different times and places. Rather, against a background of historically and culturally diverse approaches

1

to the question of how we ought to live, the degree of convergence is striking." Singer did not say how long he might estimate it would take to produce an authentic synopsis of his compendium. The second reason for the delay is that the material to be comprehended has been growing rapidly in several disciplines: in paleoanthropology, genetics, psychology, and philosophy. Many of the scientific advances are forcing revolutionary reinterpretations of the way we see the subject.

Ethics began as people learned to talk and began to ponder and question the way they behaved. Eventually, some of these discussions were recorded; and as a result, we have preserved the literary output of philosophers in Mesopotamia, India, and China. In Greece, we had Protagoras, Epicurus, Socrates, Plato, Aristotle, and many others. Modern humanist ethics began with the work of the Renaissance, the Enlightenment, Hume, and the utilitarians. Early humanist ethical systems stressed individual responsibility and the use of social principles. Our principles have evolved through the exercise of reason, scientific investigation, strategic planning, and sense of commitment. Humanism is to be found in a variety of institutions stressing different values, theories, and strategic plans. Furthermore, humanism is not a finished product so that the expanding circle of the membership contemplates an evolving set of principles, as well as continuing narratives of our progress. Everyone has a unique morality and ethology, and we conclude that there is no single quintessential humanist. To improve our definitions, manifestos, practices, reasoning, and narratives, we are obliged to evolve, to plan, and to respond as contingencies. Socrates began his discussions of ethics by asking questions, and we might do the same:

- Why should we be good?
- Is ethical behavior synonymous with altruism?
- How should we face death?
- How should we examine and plan our lives?
- How should we criticize others or offer constructive ideas?

Every generation of philosophers has tackled issues like these, sometimes adding new insights until the scope of the subject has gradually expanded to encompass nearly everything we do, say, think, plan, and learn. Plato, in his famous book *The Republic*, offered the first comprehensive treatise on ethics, asking who should rule and offering an interpretation on the world in which we live in his allegory of the cave. Aristotle is credited with giving us a start on systems theory with the comment that the whole is greater than the sum of its parts. His views on science, particularly biology, held sway for a thousand years or more.

Humanism is atheistic or Nietzschean rather than Christian. The nontheist's basis for ethical thinking does not include divine sanctions or supernatural revelations. The basis of our ethical knowledge is subjective emotion and meaning and our best understanding of the natural world, which we could call truth. Objective knowledge is what we can share with other people through language, reason, logic, and mathematics. Hence, we have built up natural science and cosmology, biology, psychology, and social theory. We use the same cognitive tools in art and in inventing systems for business and economics. Finally, we see ethics as part of the practical panoply of politics and law and of medicine and the engineered world.

We expand on humanist ethical thinking by considering possible behavior and situations in relation to our naturalist world view. Our individual lives are controlled by our brains. The subjective part of our behavior is governed by emotions. Plants do not have emotions. It is only members of the animal kingdom who need instinctive direction for their behavior. It was only a few hundred years ago that people still believed thought was centered in the heart. And even after the brain came to be recognized as important, people still believed in the existence of a soul, which they supposed departed the body at the time of death. We now know that our mental existence is the proper province of psychology and cognitive science. Our lifestances are governed by instinct, psychology, ethics, and individual management.

1.2 Systems, Basic Drives, and Evolution

Consider the complexities of the behavior of animals as they move around to satisfy needs for breathing, nutrition, reproduction, protection from danger, shelter, and so forth. Biologists tell us that animals have various urges based on chemical potentials associated with their primitive motivations. For most animals, presumably these urges are felt as elementary drives or emotions, and they do not require complex choices or deliberations for the animal to arrive at decisions. Sexual reproduction was an early improvement to animal biology. With the appearance in the world of vertebrates, and especially the large-brained mammals and primates, quite-complicated thinking evolved between stimulus and action. The additional sophistication in data processing permitted by the nervous system provided its possessor with more successful ways of coping with life together with a wider range and repertoire of emotions. The young had to respect parents. Male and female had to learn to care for their mates. Parents had to care for their young. Along the way, we acquired an aversion for snakes and bad smells and entrapment as well as a reluctance to kill our own kind. By the time we became human, many of us were seeking beauty and acting out of compassion for others.

Our brains are continuously bombarded with inputs from the five senses, our internal organs, the endocrine system, and the specialized modules of the brain itself. These sensations and emotions are subject to interpretations that tell us about the situation in the world around us as well as our own internal drives and conditions. It was Hume who first pointed out that the way this works is that the brain recognizes certain constancies. The constant categories underlie what we term *systems* in modern parlance. The word *system* has been in use since the time of the ancient Greeks, but the term *system theory* only became widespread during and after World War II, sometimes to describe the operation of hardware of interest or, sometimes, a process or method of performing some task. But once the term came into service, it was realized that a system or pattern was an object with a recognizable constancy and then it was appreciated that it could apply in a wide range of circumstances, e.g., all physical laws, physical structures, computers, programs, languages, organisms, organizations, sciences, and religions. Following Murray Gell-mann, we might introduce another term here, namely, the *schema* or that which encodes the constancy of a system (i.e., the essence of a pattern). Examples of schema include lexicons, grammars, rules, programs, algorithms, blueprints, plans, genomes, etc.

Systems may be simple or complex, usually depending on the amount of information needed to express the schema. The biological cell is an example of an open system whose constancy is determined by its genome. Organisms contain assemblies of cells that are built into functional parts called organs, which grow and reproduce according to programmed instructions. Animals are multicellular but are mobile and have nerve connections that permit learning and controlled behavior. The organisms and organs are further examples of systems. We humans are animals but with self-consciousness and knowledge of our knowledge, typically encoded using symbolic language. Finally, there are sociocultural organizations with multiple human members, ranging from families to nations, all of which are systems.

Now let us introduce the idea of *adaptive* systems, i.e., ones in which the constancy changes, usually by a small amount. This gives us a precise way to define evolution as the changing expression of adaptive systems. Biological evolution may be defined as the usually gradual process by which an organism changes into a different and usually more complex form. The changing form leaves a trail of paleontological or genetic evidence, which enables us to construct treelike structures to trace the system's ancestry. In the biological case, for example, the variation occurs in the genome or its epigenetic control. Ethics is a part of human culture, and it also evolves. To that extent, it is inspired by Charles Darwin, Julian Huxley, and Edward O. Wilson. Ethics is part of ethology or the study of animal behavior. Several authors, most notably Philip Kitcher, have emphasized that ethics is a product of evolution and have introduced the term *ethical project* to focus attention on its tentative and incomplete nature.

There is a theory by Marc Hauser that we have an instinctive moral system that operates in a way similar to language. This built on the theory, due to Noam Chomsky, that language is a complex adaptive system put in place genetically as generalized equipment that enables the process of language acquisition to begin. We may think of the brain as similar to computer hardware. In the early years of life, an operating system is laid down by our learning a set of parameters, which encode the grammatical rules for our particular language. The underlying universal grammar has to permit the wide variety of human languages.

A baby can learn any one of the family of languages, but new language acquisition becomes increasingly difficult as the person grows older. The theory posits that there exists a universal grammar underlying our moral system and that the codes for the various different moral cultures are laid down as sets of parameters we learn in youthful instruction.

1.3 Becoming Human

There was a major transition in our development when we became human. A number of biological characteristics were involved in the process from bipedal walking and manual dexterity as well as mental activities such as talking and thinking. Some theories associate the transition with climate in the southern end of the living range of the African apes, forcing the hominins out of the forest and onto the open savannah. We know now that these changes resulted in a growth in volume of the human brain by a factor of two to three times in a relatively short period of evolutionary time. A theory has taken hold starting with Darwin's 1872 publication that the evolutionary driver for the transition has been sexual selection. Over the century since Darwin wrote, there has been an accumulation of evidence that speech, moral development, and the wide variety of human culture and art all resulted from the growth of the brain size in men and women. This evidence is presented well in Geoffrey Miller's (2000) volume *The Mating Mind*.

1.4 Values, Virtues, and Utility

The next features of our moral repertoire, which we must mention, involve values, virtues, and utility, which are verbal constructions to assist our ethical thinking. The fundamental importance of emotion to ethics was reemphasized by Spinoza and by Hume during the period of the Enlightenment. Hume's book on human nature (1748 and 1777) is credited with being the first modern psychology text, and his emphasis on emotion is now accepted by all psychologists. Emotions are felt directly by the person experiencing them, and we say that they are subjective. On the other hand, there are many situations in which phenomena are observable to the general public; and in this case, they are said to be objective. Reports on evaluations of ethical and moral behavior are thus objective. Science has progressed by concentrating its deliberations on objective phenomena.

In respect of sensation and emotion, the human brain is basically the same as that of our animal forebears. One of the most important attributes evolution gave to the human species was a great enhancement of the power of reasoning. In the cerebral cortex, we have additional neuronal layers in which we are able to store memories, which enable us to perform further analysis of the information we receive. We are able to recognize the constant characteristics of the various systems that we encounter. Humans are able to use symbols to stand for objects and actions and to use these symbols in associations that model the world in expressions of language and art. We are the only species that thinks deeply, employing long chains of reasoning based on simple syllogisms. We can use the cerebral cortex to enable us to imagine the consequences of our actions. We may use language and words in these recognition processes and indeed designate certain combinations of sensations and emotions as systems of a higher level, which we call *values*. It appears that hunter-gatherers had already developed systems of values reflecting the virtues that enhanced their lives: strength, bravery, loyalty, love, and so on. By the time of the ancient civilizations, the desirable virtues reflected the ideals of urban living: honesty, industriousness, knowledge, wisdom, benevolence, freedom, and justice. Because they involve the use of language, values may be shared with other humans and are thus objective. We are able to compare the degree of value in various circumstances, a process we actually term *evaluation*. This includes the basis of the economic activity of bartering and determining market prices.

Our recognition of constancies enables us to respond in definite ways and develop what we call habits. These are what provide the structure to our everyday behavior. A person may develop habits quite privately but is much more likely to do so in interaction with others. We all incorporate specific values in what we do, and the aggregate of those values are what we recognize as our individual characters. Good character traits are said to be *virtues*, and their study has been a facet of ethics since the earliest times. We understand now that well-established habits may actually be reinforced in the brain by the growth of new neurons and that there is a plethora of neurotransmitters that can strengthen the interneuronal synapses.

Over the years, beginning in ancient Greece and continuing to the present, nontheists have worked to develop values to which whole groups may aspire. These are the so-called humanist values:

- Truth
- Rationalism
- Objective knowledge
- Science and Enlightenment
- Civilization
- Beauty
- Equality
- Compassion
- Democracy and tolerance
- Equality and justice
- Freedom and liberty
- Optimism
- Commitment
- Responsibilities

Various philosophers have written on particular values at some length. Kant, for example, stressed the importance of reason in our deliberations. Truth is at the heart of scientific investigation, and so is of concern to philosophers of science. We think of Popper in this connection. Equality and justice are pivotal to legal systems, and then we think of John Rawls. Benevolence was one of Hume's favorite values, and *On Liberty* was the title of a celebrated essay by John Stuart Mill. Paul Kurtz has written extensively on an ethic of responsibility.

There is, however, a problem with using such values individually, which is that they can often lead to contradictory results. For example, should a doctor tell a cancer patient the *truth* of his condition or try to be *compassionate* by withholding a diagnosis? It takes further thinking to resolve the dilemma. Problems of this sort gave ethicists of the nineteenth century, such as Henry Sidgwick, much pause for thought. The modern position, reflecting John Dewey, is that these value systems are nonetheless useful by providing *measures* to assess our plans and situations. To find the best way forward in a given situation, we need to propose plans and theories and then test them out as best we can. How should we do this? The answer to the dilemma is the assessment of utility, a value first proposed by Hume and then developed by Bentham and Mill. This was followed by more complex procedures that might be termed *system processes*.

1.5 System Processes

The flowchart in the figure 1 helps us resolve moral or ethical dilemmas. We begin by assessing the situation we are in. We think about it and come to a tentative decision on what to do. If we take action or propose to do so, then we can assess or predict the result. We evaluate this result in terms of the emotions and values we hold, and the evaluation feeds back into our situational assessment. Our memories of these results and evaluations will then be part of our "database" for the future. The figure also shows an idea due to Habermas whereby the inputs of morals and ethics operate in two separate branches of the feedback. We might find this a useful concept if we wish to think of morality as the instinctive or a priori part of our ethology and ethicity as putative proposals or theories. Figure 1 is also useful in modeling the making of choices, as we explain next.

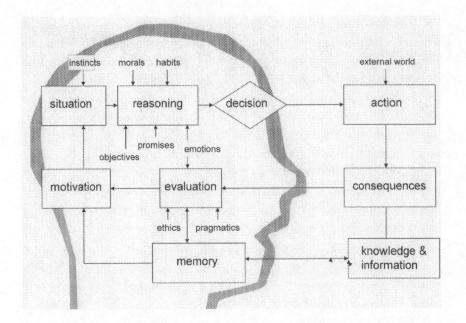

Fig. 1 Processes of Human Thought

Remember that the controversy over "free will" has been a persistent difficulty in the treatment of ethics. The rationalist approach to cognitive science is based on the assumption that there is a cause for every event. This so-called deterministic stance seems to belie our ability to choose freely between alternatives. That this is not the case, however, may be demonstrated by the following argument. Suppose a course of action is considered. Then its likely physical results can be predicted from reasoning and from memories of similar circumstances. These results may be then evaluated on the basis of the sensations and emotions likely to be caused by said physical events. The outcome of this evaluation may be compared with that from some other possible course of action. The one with the highest figure of merit can then be selected. But this is precisely the process by which computers are programmed to make choices, the computer being well-known to be a thoroughly deterministic machine. Our choices may, of course, be far more complex than in the foregoing simple case, but they can always be reduced to a simple situation. Thus, we see that human beings have the ability to make choices.

Figure 1 is also useful to show where subjective and objective processes take place. The point here is that the thinking goes on inside our heads and is then purely subjective. But sometimes our thinking takes in events that occur in the external world, and if these events are observable to other people, we have the possibility of forming objective assessments. It is also possible that speech or writing could be involved. This would then give us a basis for scientific observation and testing.

1.6 Social Systems and Great Objectives

Serious efforts to study social systems in a scientific manner started in the nineteenth century with the work of Auguste Comte who is often regarded as the first Western sociologist. Karl Marx was working at about the same time and formulating his theory of the economic determinism of society. Marx maintained that ethics was, in turn, decided as a subset of the economic system. Marxism became very influential in the twentieth century, and there were many studies to focus on its weaknesses. One of these was the work of Karl Popper who argued that Marx really did not understand the methods of science very well. A later study by Jürgen Habermas substituted a social mechanism based on communicative action (rather than economics) as the driving force of human life. Habermas separated morality and ethics into two parts of human ethology. John Dewey also wrote on the links between social theory and personal ethics.

Talcott Parsons was a professor of sociology at Harvard who proposed a system theory for the differentiation of society. He propounded the idea that the evolution of generalized adaptive capacity was involved in the interaction of small groups of people resulting in the appearance of subsystems for culture, the economy, the polity, and the overall societal community. This is a theory for the development of a more extensive social system. There are, of course, numerous major social subsystems including language, science, literature, governance, capitalism, justice, and so on. Each of these areas has an extensive literature, and there are university departments devoted to teaching and further research in each one. Furthermore, there are star performers in them all, and one might take it as an objective to emulate such a star.

John Stuart Mill wrote extensively on utilitarianism, liberty, and
subjugation of women. These were major contributions to the literature
on ethics. He saw utility as measured by happiness, reminding us of
Aristotle. It is in his book on utilitarianism that Mill mentions the
"great objects" of human life and cites as examples money, fame, and
power. Any one of the great objects can become an end in itself and a
source of happiness. Then he points out that virtue can be just as much
an end objective as the others. It was this reference to great objects
that inspired the title of the present work. Some people choose a single
objective in life while others choose two or more. Each choice has its
problems, and one really needs several objectives for a balanced life.
There is an old adage that a human being should aim to be happy,
wealthy, and wise. These great objectives constitute parts of a complete
ethic. We may recollect Aristotle again to remember that he thought
that the main objective of life was happiness.

1.7 Humanist Principles

The same divisional procedures can be applied to personal systems.
Stephen R. Covey, who died recently, wrote several books along these
lines, which are recommended for humanist reading. Covey showed
how personal life may be divided into a number of domains (each of
which can be thought of as systems), as follows: self, spouse, family,
money, work, possessions, pleasure, friends, enemies, and church. The
same humanist principles can then be applied to all these subsystems.

Let us recapitulate some humanist principles:

Truth and knowledge. We should base our conduct on the best
available knowledge of the natural world, in which people and their
minds have evolved, and on our human-made systems.

Rationality. The systems of the human mind, based in the natural
world, enable us to think and be creative agents and are the source of
personal freedom, dignity, and responsibility.

Emotions. We have to recognize that emotions are the driving force of our behavior. We need to provide the loving relationships of a family for the security of young and old.

Values. People are able to share emotions and refine their values through the various arts.

Ethics. We should use our emotions, values, and rationality in building ethical theories and systems to live by.

Pragmatism. We should uphold the methods of social systems that have proven to be successful in the past, including the law, science, and good practice, while working for their improvement.

Commitment. We need to belong to the organizations that foster our world view and enable it to be tested and improved.

Destiny. We believe that humanism should offer visions of the future that will inspire the individual and guide the policies of society.

1.8 Examined Lives and Future Plans

These principles could be thought of as moral rules for the construction of a humanist ethic, but there is another whole side to such an exercise that we might think of as objectives and planning. We may also trace this back to Aristotle who proposed that the goal of human life was happiness. Socrates thought our goal was to be good and that the unexamined life was not worth living. Taking off from this statement, Robert Nozick wrote an excellent book titled *The Examined Life*. When we make plans for the day, week, month, year, and five years, we first examine how well we met objectives for the preceding period and then try to envisage how we might make rational extensions for the succeeding period. Developmental stages in life have been recognized by poets, from William Shakespeare onward. Kohlberg has written about the periods of moral development in people's lives, and many psychologists have taken up the theme.

There was another Socratic philosophical movement of the twentieth century that also derived from the work of Hegel, as did that of Marx, and that also started by repudiation of Marx, as was done by Popper. This was the so-called Frankfurt school, founded by Max Horkheimer and his pupil Theodor Adorno and later joined by Adorno's pupil

Jürgen Habermas. They left Nazi Germany and eventually settled in the United States. It was in the United States that Horkheimer (1937) published *Traditional and Critical Theory*. Although the group returned to Germany after the war, the seeds planted by Horkheimer's work led to the development of critical theory in the United States as well as in Germany in the 1960s and 1970s. A magnum opus of democratic humanism, see Habermas (1984), produced from this same source, was styled "The Theory of Communicative Action."

Peter Drucker has written extensively on the application of planning to businesses of many varieties. We remind everyone that the American Humanist Association itself conducted a five-year planning process finishing in 2007. Ethics dictate that the AHA should assess how well or otherwise it has met its objectives from that time and where its directions should lie now for the next five-year period. Perhaps we will now see the way forward in terms of education and research. We began extending outreach to other organizations (atheists, freethinkers, academics, and political parties) and need to continue this. But we also need to start working for the moral order of all peoples in science, justice, prosperity, polity, and religion. Perhaps the objective of our work should be to define a worldwide humanist civilization.

Even though we cannot predict the precise outcome of human efforts beyond a few years into the future, surely, we could aspire to a destiny in which all people might have the best possible life on this Earth and try to define what that might be and how it might come about. Among the moral imperatives we have faced in recent times, we have demanded an end to slavery. We continue to press for equal rights for women and equality of opportunity for all people. Should we not continue to explore the known universe and continue to search for other intelligent life? We need to understand the nature of the dark matter and energy that constitute the majority of the universe. Should we not try to build a civilization throughout our galaxy? Should we not continue to try to understand what might be accomplished in the universe? We continue to seek beauty in music, literature, and art. All these great objectives are there in front of us. As Jaap van Praag (1982) has told us, it is the meaning inherent in them all that we seek and that which continues to urge us onward.

References

There is a literature of hundreds if not thousands of books and papers on ethics, some of the best of which are listed here and in the humanist bibliography of appendix 5.

Aristotle "The Nicomachean Ethics" in "Introduction to Aristotle" Modern Library Ed., (1992)

Compte-Sponville, Andre (1996) "A Small Treatise on the Great Virtues", Metropolitan Books.

Darwin, Charles, (1859), "On the origin of species by means of natural selection", John Murray. (Reprinted in 1964 by Harvard University Press.)

Darwin, Charles, (1872) "The Expression of the Emotions in Man and Animals" and "The Descent of Man, and Selection in Relation to Sex" (1871) in "From So Simple a Beginning: The Four Great Books of Charles Darwin" Ed., Edward O. Wilson, W.W. Norton, 2006.

Dewey, John, (1932) "Ethics", reprinted in John Dewey: The Later Works, 1925-1953, Ed. Jo Ann Boydston, Southern Illinois University Press.

Dewey, John, (1922) "Human Nature and Conduct" Barnes & Noble Ed., 2008.

Fromm, Erich, (1947) "Man for Himself: An Enquiry into the Psychology of Ethics", Owl Book Edition, 1990.

Grayling, A.C. (2003), "What is Good? The Search for the Best Way to Live" Weidenfeld & Nicholson.

Habermas, Jürgen (1981), The Theory of Communicative Action, vols 1 and 2, Beacon Press.

Horkheimer, Max (1937), "Traditional and Critical Theory"

Hume, David, (1777) "An Enquiry Concerning The Principles of Morals" in "Enquiries", Edited by L.A. Selby-Bigge, Third Edition with notes by P.H. Nidditch, Clarendon Press,1975

Huxley, Julian, (1964) "Evolutionary Humanism" Prometheus Books Ed, 1992

Kitcher, Philip, (2011) "The Ethical Project", Harvard University Press.

Kohlberg, Lawrence (1981) "Essays on Moral Development, Vol. I: The Philosophy of Moral Development." Harper & Row.

Kurtz, Paul (1988) "Forbidden Fruit: the Ethics of Humanism," Prometheus Books.

Mackie, J.L., (1977) "Ethics: Inventing Right and Wrong", Penguin Books.

Maslow, Abraham H., (1971) "The Farther Reaches of Human Nature", Viking.

Mill, John Stuart, (1859) "On Liberty", Everyman's Library, 1910.

Mill, John Stuart, (1861) "Utilitarianism".

Mill, John Stuart, and Harriet Taylor (1869) "The Subjection of Women".

Miller, Geoffrey, (2000) "The Mating Mind: How Sexual Choice Shaped the Evolution of Human Nature", Anchor Books.

Nozick, Robert, (1989) "The Examined Life: Philosophical Meditations", Simon & Schuster.

Nietzsche, Friedrich (1887), "The Birth of Tragedy" and "The Genealogy of Morals", Anchor Books edition, 1956

Rachels, James, and Stuart Rachels (2007) "The Elements of Moral Philosophy", 5th Ed., McGraw-Hill.

Russell, Bertrand, (1929) "Marriage and Morals" Liveright Paperbound Ed. 1970

Shermer, Michael (2004) "The Science of Good and Evil", Owl Books.

Sidgwick, Henry, (1874) "The Methods of Ethics", 7th edition 1907, republished by Hackett Publishing Co., 1981

Singer, Peter, (1993), "How Are We to Live?" Prometheus Books.

van Praag, J.P. (1982), "Foundations of Humanism", Prometheus Books

Wilson, Edward O. (2012), "The Social Conquest of Earth", W.W. Norton & Co.

2. History and Nature of Ethics

Outline

2. History and Nature of Ethics

2.1 Science and the Origins of Ethics

In introducing the subject of ethics, it is difficult to decide if one should follow the historical order in which ethical principles have developed or set out the subject matter of those principles. The difficulty is compounded because historical attention has switched back and forth as new methods have arisen, particularly so in the recent past. One very important new insight that has occurred is the illumination provided by evolutionary psychology. There are expositions of this recent development by Leda Cosmides and John Tooby (1992, 1997). But it is one that informs us about our oldest instinctive behavior. There are similar examples in the areas of paleoanthropology and neuroscience. Anthropology has also provided us with new insights on the ethical behavior of hunter-gatherers. We are learning more about all the human attributes from disciplines that have blossomed in recent decades: genetics and studies of comparative anatomy of ape species. All these disciplines continue to speed along at the present time, and the literature describing it all struggles to keep up. The following books were found to be helpful in writing this and the next chapter: on genetics, *Before the Dawn* by Nicholas Wade (2006); on altruism and its antecedents, *The Ethical Project* by Philip Kitcher (2011); on paleoanthropology, *Lucy's Legacy* by Donald C. Johansen (2009), *Becoming Human* by Ian Tattersall (1998), *The Complete World of Human Evolution* by Chris Stringer and Peter Andrews (2005), "Ardipithecus ramidus" special issue of *Science* (vol. 326); on comparative anatomy, *Bonobo the Forgotten Ape* by Frans de Waal and Frans Lanting (1997); on business and bartering *The Rational Optimist: How Prosperity Evolves* by Matt Ridley (2010); on religion, *The Faith Instinct* by Nicholas Wade (2009); and, finally, as a general summary, *The Theory of Communicative Action* by Jürgen Habermas (1981).

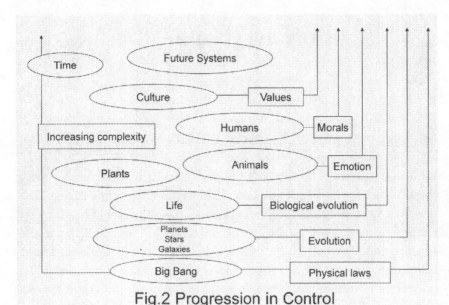

Fig.2 Progression in Control

Fig. 2 Progression in Control

The ethics found in nature are written in the human genetic code, not in the laws of physics. We have already remarked that Hume recognized the prevalence of instinctive ethics and we have only to ask where these instincts came from to answer our own question. Darwin (1872) was the first to see that evolution will favor those behaviors that improve the chances of an animal species' survival. Figure 2 is a representation on the sequence of events in the progression of behavioral control. The universe is about 13.7 billion years old and thus much older than Earth, which is 4.55 billion years old. Life—and, in particular, animal life—came into existence only after Earth had itself evolved to some degree. Animal behavior is controlled by instinctive emotion starting with simple mechanisms in unicellular creatures to govern feeding, avoidance of danger, etc., and then evolving to more sophisticated systems in higher animals. Instinctive morality dates from the time that animals first appeared and is thus much younger than the laws of physics. As animals added functional capabilities, so these systems became more complex. Finally, with the appearance of humans, eight to five million years ago, a whole new suite of abilities came into existence, including bipedalism, toolmaking, and speech, these being the means that enabled cultural evolution to take place. Our consciousness of instinctive morality dates from the same period and is also much younger than the physical laws. But ethics itself, i.e., the discussion of morality and planning for future actions, presumably did not truly arise until after the growth of culture and speech.

We learn from this biology that some of our modern-day human behavior dates back to times far in our evolutionary past. Hume (1777) stated clearly that such instinctive behaviors were "taught by nature itself." The operation of an instinctive control is experienced as an emotion. In the case of the human animal, some of these emotions are said to be morals. Darwin (1871, 1872) believed in this origin of morality and, of course, saw evolution by natural and sexual selection as the means by which nature did its teaching. There are certain modes of conduct that clearly have survival value, for example, pairing between male and female and empathy and caring for others. Such behaviors are passed on to succeeding generations, and some of them have become part of our moral heritage. The theory has recently been celebrated again by E. O. Wilson in his writings on consilience (1998) and sociobiology (1980). Although we still do not have a complete understanding of the mechanisms whereby this instinctive moral behavior is inherited, Wilson suggests that the explanation lies in the realm of epigenetic phenomena. Sam Harris (2004), one of the new atheists, has also published some research in the area of biological determinants of belief, and we will be studying the topic of the genetic basis of morality in more detail in a later chapter.

2.2 The Naturalist Tradition

Humanists have a cosmology by which we mean a theory of the universe and the place of humanity in it. We see the universe as one great system whose many parts interact with one another and where we ourselves are just one of those interacting parts. *Nature* is simply another name for the *universe*, the sum total of all things in time and space, as *Webster's Dictionary* puts it. We accept the theories of the origin of the universe propounded by physics: the big bang followed by condensation of elementary particles and then atoms and molecules, a story told in books such as *Cosmos* by Carl Sagan (1980) and *A Short History of Nearly Everything* by Bill Bryson (2005). Primordial dust accumulated into clouds from which stars and galaxies were formed. We believe that there is just this one reality, the world of nature, and we reject concepts such as a separate world of the spirit inhabited by disembodied gods and demons. Thanks to Darwin and Mendel, we now have a convincing explanation of the evolution of life driven by the mechanism of natural selection and recorded by the genetic material encoded on DNA. The reader may find modern accounts of evolution in books by Richard Dawkins (1976, 2004) and Ursula Goodenough (1998). Old ideas of mind-body duality are being replaced by a naturalistic explanation of mental phenomena, as expounded in such works as Richard Restak's (1984) *The Brain*, Patricia Churchland's *Neurophilosophy* (1986), and Michael Gazzaniga's *Human* (2008). We are approaching the point when a full explanation for consciousness and awareness will be forthcoming on a naturalistic basis.

Among the earliest contributors to the scientific and naturalist traditions was Thales of Miletus who attempted to explain natural phenomena without reference to mythology as early as 600 BC. Thales thought everything was composed of water, which we now know to be incorrect, but his basic idea that all of nature can be explained by simple underlying theories caught on and has been extremely successful. Democritus, who was born about 460 BC, was the originator of the atomic theory. He maintained that everything consists of invisible particles of matter that existed in empty space and that this is all that exists. Democritus thought that the atoms themselves were indestructible but could be combined into material bodies including plants, animals, and human beings. The great champion of naturalism among the Greek philosophers was Epicurus, who lived from 341 to 271 BC and wrote a book *On Nature*, which contained his exposition of the subject built on the earlier theories of Democritus. Epicurus presented the world with a philosophical system that was an alternative to the mystical and dualistic concepts of Plato and Aristotle. There is an introduction to Epicurus's thought and some selected writings in the publication by Inwood, Gerson, and Hutchinson (1994). Epicurus saw death simply as the cessation of feeling and the dissolution of the atoms in the body. "Death is nothing to us," he said. His key to good health was to take pleasures in moderation, contrary to the caricatures of his philosophy often made. In the communities established in Epicurus's name, women and slaves were accepted on an equal basis, which probably did not enhance his popularity. His work was expounded in the Roman empire by Lucretius (95–52 BC) whose poem "De Rerum Natura" is recognized as one of the masterpieces of Latin literature. The naturalist tradition lived on until it was almost eclipsed by the coming of Christianity whose practitioners found that the works of Plato and Aristotle better suited their doctrines. It took the work of the physical and chemical scientists of the Enlightenment to revive the concepts of natural science and the atomic theory and the attention of skeptics such as Hume to reestablish naturalism as a guiding ethical principle.

E. O. Wilson (1998) gave an account of the growth of physical science in his book *Consilience*. Scientific methods have been refined and improved over the centuries to make them into the sophisticated tools that they are today. We use what is called Occam's razor whereby the simplest theory that fits the facts is the one to choose. Francis Bacon first explained the process of theory formulation and correction as the way to approach the truth. It was Hume who pointed out that we recognize constancy in establishing physical law and in defining systems, including artificial ones. Natural science has advanced as if by connecting chunks of a jigsaw puzzle together. Thus, Newton found that the same force of gravity that endows objects with weight close to Earth's surface is responsible for the rotation of the planets around the sun. Electricity and magnetism turned out to be different aspects of the same phenomenon, and Maxwell showed that light was an electromagnetic wave motion. Chemistry was joined to the unified theory through the quantum mechanical theory of bonding. Natural science has grown enormously in scope since the time of Democritus and Epicurus whose simple atoms have been isolated and studied and shown to be composed of even more elementary particles. But ultimately, we expect all scientific knowledge to be connected through a unified theory as Einstein, Weyl, and Wilson, to mention just a few, have all anticipated. This has to be the case if everything is, in fact, one unified system. This then is the world of nature or, as Popper (1972) called it, world one.

One of the most basic facts about human existence is that it is finite. We come into existence at conception, we are born, and eventually we die. The denial of death is a feature of most religions, and we may each need some psychological counseling to cope with the actual reality, and this is discussed again in later chapters. Religions have invented the concept of our each having an eternal soul as part of the web of denial. There are many other implications of the scientific theory of nature. For example, there is the problem of understanding how mental phenomena (or world two, as Popper referred to them) could be explained in terms of the natural world. We will elaborate on the growth of cognitive science in the next chapter; but for now, we will simply say that it has always seemed that subjective sensations, emotions, thoughts, awareness, and consciousness were something apart from the physical world. This is why the idea of the soul was so appealing. It was only a few hundred years ago that it was finally realized that it is the brain that is the seat of mental activity (as opposed to the heart). Of course, as Restak (1984) recounts, the progress has been rapid since then. Although we still do not have an explanation of qualia (the actual experience of mental activity), it seems that hypotheses for consciousness are beginning to take shape, as Dennett (1991) has explained. Another phenomenon that is difficult to understand is free will or volition. Here Dennett (2003) proposes that we can grasp what goes on as a process of decision making or making choices as a part of the data processing that goes on in the brain. The related riddles of selfish versus altruistic choices have been thoroughly explored by now, and it is clear that we can indeed be altruistic, as detailed by Kitcher (2011) among others.

2.3 Natural and Artificial Systems

There is a vital aspect of human thinking concerned with the recognition of constancies, which seems to have first been commented on by Hume (1777). We define associations of constant elements to be "systems" as pointed out by Anatol Rapoport (1986). Thus, we came to recognize the laws of physics by their constant effects in similar situations. We also apply the same methods in dealing with recurrent situations of interest in our personal lives, and we call these situations and the techniques for dealing with them artificial systems. In an earlier essay (Finch, 1992), I proposed that ethics and morality can be described in terms of systems. One of the first artificial systems to be invented was toolmaking such as the shaping of flints and other stones for use in knife blades, spears, and arrowheads. *Homo sapiens* in Africa is credited with the development of the spear thrower, which made the hunting of large game a much safer process for the hunter. Speech may have advanced as an aid to coordination during hunting. Trade may have begun as humans developed "theories of mind," enabling them to realize that other members of the species, even strangers, could share similar needs and wants. Thus, one group might have been able to barter for stone, such as obsidian, uncommon in their native area. Once it had begun to flourish, speech could have been used for many purposes, including storytelling, thus opening up a method of transmitting information over time and space. This ability would have complemented the human improvement in memory. In its turn, memory was the necessary prerequisite to recognize constancies.

The Human Spark is the title for a television series narrated by Alan Alda in which he discusses the abilities possessed by humans that distinguish us from other animals. There are several traits involved, and all of them have to be present for us to have made the transition to humanity. Many of these characteristics have only been elucidated in the past century. One discovery that dates to the time of the acquisition of the human spark is the law of cause and effect. In other words, we found that every happening and event was the result of a cause. However, from time to time, our ancestors could not identify the cause of a phenomenon; and then they were prone to call up spirits, demons and gods, or other supernatural phenomena to serve as explanations. Our religious proclivities seem to have derived from these beginnings.

Popper invented the term *world three* for the man-made or "artificial" realm of culture, language, artifacts, theories, values, knowledge, industries and companies, religions, and cosmologies such as humanism and naturalism. All these things have been of interest to thinkers since the start of civilization, but it was not until the time of Charles Darwin and Herbert Spencer that it was realized that they all evolve. They are all created by human beings in the process of living. Simon (1969) referred to them as the sciences of the artificial in his discussion of systems theory. In everyday speech, the term *artificial* is sometimes used as a synonym for *unnatural*, and we must contradict this impression to make the point that all the man-made systems are as much a part of the natural world as the humans who created them. Many of the man-made systems have lives that are much longer than those of their human inventors and participants. They may serve to immortalize their founders and members and influence the lives of subsequent generations. Of particular interest to us in connection with the present topic is the fact that ethical systems and indeed the whole subject of ethics are also among the inhabitants of world three.

There has been considerable confusion over the years about the nature of ethics and its relationship to nature. Some of the confusion may have arisen because we use the same word *law* to describe physical principles and ethical or moral rules. Some of the confusion probably lingers on from the time when people thought that morality was laid out in the "laws of God." When eventually thinkers such as Hobbes and Voltaire realized that there was no evidence to support a belief in God, religious apologists proposed that moral laws were to be found in the physical laws of nature itself. This was contradicted by Hume in his book *A Treatise of Human Nature* with a careful introspective argument on the difference between moral and cognitive thinking. In the case of animals, all their behavior is based on instinctive urges. Human behavior is similarly basically driven by emotion, but we may additionally bring reasoning into action through the use of deliberation or habits. Hume contended that morality is based on our feelings of virtue and vice. In another place, he states that reason is the slave of the emotions. On the other hand, our reasoning is based purely on facts that we ascertain from sensations and not emotions. Thus, he reasoned that facts and emotions are different phenomena. The situation is summarized by the canard "you can't get ought from is" often ascribed to Hume himself. Mary Warnock's book (2004) is of interest in this regard with a chapter entitled "Where Ethics Comes From." Earlier in the work, she has some remarks on G. E. Moore, an influential British ethicist at the turn of the twentieth century who had written an imposing work titled *Principia Ethica*, which purported to be to ethics what Newton's *Principia* had been to physics. Warnock feels that Moore's approach amounts to claiming to know what is good in advance of ethical investigation. Moore had famously accused John Stuart Mill of committing the "naturalistic fallacy" of deducing ethical rules from the physical world. So it appears that the naturalist fallacy is another instance of trying to deduce "ought" from "is." Perhaps we should say in Moore's defense that he was writing before the recent work on evolutionary psychology, which, in effect, shows that we do indeed have at least some innate ethical principles. So where then does ethics come from?

2.4 Science and Instinctive Morality

We have learned something of our history before the separation from our present-day relatives—the chimpanzees, bonobos, gorillas, and orangs—by studying the apes and assuming that they have changed much less than ourselves. Then there was a period in human development after *Australopithecus* left the forest and ventured onto the savannah about five million years ago and before we settled in villages and began to record our history using writing about ten thousand years ago. During this time, we lived as hunters and gatherers. A source of much of our information on what happened to the bands of proto-humans after the separation comes from the anthropologists who study hunter-gatherers in various parts of the world. It is remarkable how many of these groups are still to be found living lives that have scarcely changed in the tens of thousands of years. The *National Geographic* is a good source in this regard. The issue of June 1963 featured two articles on the Bushmen of the Kalahari and their art treasures. In

July 1975 there was an account of the Last Andaman Islanders. Those two articles were written before the recent discoveries in genetics that revealed the close and ancient relationships between these groups, which were revealed in an article titled "The Greatest Journey" in the issue of March 2006. Some other ancient hunter-gatherers have been featured since then. For example, see the recent article on Shamans (December 2012) and the one on modern aboriginals (June 2013). There is further informative work on research on hunter-gatherers in Nicholas Wade's *The Faith Instinct* (2009). Collectively, these sources give us a means of looking back on the life of our own ancestors. An important point is that the time span involved has been sufficient for biological evolution to record the changes that have occurred. Another thought comes when we realize that these people have repeatedly exercised an ethic to explore our planet further.

2.5 The Use of Philosophy

As human beings, we have to decide for ourselves how best to live our lives. The humanist movement has been developed to put human values at the center of our belief system; and there are now a number of books that explore the general outlines of our philosophy, as in Blackham (1968), Lamont (1949), Wine (1995), Grayling (2003), and Epstein (2009). Atheism, meaning solely a nonbelief in God, is not enough. The gods who were at the center of the old religions need to be replaced by human beings. We are not in any way proposing to worship human beings: there are certainly human beings who have done many evil things. The point is, as Alda or Grayling might have put it, we have to use our human faculties, employing that human spark, in a search for the best way to live, a new ethos based on human values.

Ethics is conventionally viewed as a part of philosophy. There are authors—see Roe (1980), for example—who see ethics as the most important part of philosophy. Unfortunately, philosophy is often seen nowadays as outdated and even frivolous, having been superseded by science and having relapsed into largely irrelevant niceties. So it seems appropriate to discuss this relationship between ethics and philosophy and emphasize why both are, in fact, important to our study. This will take us back in time to the very beginning of human thinking when our ancestors started to ask questions and wonder about the phenomena of nature. There were many occurrences that were at first explained as the actions of spirits and gods and many shamans and witch doctors who claimed to intercede for them. The first philosophers were people who tried to base their assertions about the world on reasoned arguments.

Philosophical thinking seems to have started in India around 1000 BC. There is an account of this in *Wikipedia*, which states that competition and integration among the various schools of Hindu philosophy was intense during their formative years, especially between 800 BC and AD 200. There are six orthodox schools of Hindu philosophy and three Heterodox, including Jain, Buddhist, and the materialist Carvaka. Future humanist researchers will doubtless be studying the early Hindu and other eastern philosophies more fully. Greek philosophy began soon afterward with a group of thinkers, of whom the most prominent was Thales of Miletus (circa 624 BC–546 BC). Thales is also credited with being the father of science. He was believed to have been of Phoenician descent and almost certainly had exposure to Egyptian mythology, astronomy, and mathematics. He was not solely a thinker but was also involved in business and politics. One story recounts that he predicted the weather and rented all the olive presses in Miletus after foreseeing a good harvest for a certain year. One version of the story is that he did this to show his fellow Milesians that he could use his intelligence to enrich himself.

Thales tried to find naturalistic explanations for the world. He explained earthquakes by imagining that Earth floats on water and that quakes occur when Earth is rocked by waves. Herodotus cites him as having predicted the solar eclipse of 585 BC, which put an end to fighting between the Lydians and the Medes. Thales's most famous theory was that the world originated from water. He is also credited with discoveries in mathematics. The early Greek period is often referred to as the pre-Socratic and of being characterized by an emphasis on studying physical and natural phenomena as opposed to the human studies, as preferred by Socrates.

2.6 Philosophical Methods

The study of method in philosophy often starts with Socrates (469–399 BC) and his pupil Plato (424–348 BC). Socrates would first present his views in an everyday conversation. When his companion showed interest, Socrates would point out a philosophical concept that needed to be analyzed. Then he would ask the companion for his opinion on the matter. Socrates would analyze the answer and ask questions to expose weaknesses or errors. The companion would then provide another definition revised to be clearer, and Socrates would repeat the process until the clearest definition was obtained. This would point out ignorance to the companion. Sometimes Socrates would use a reductio ad absurdum form of the argument. The fact that he used the same approach repeatedly was why we say he was using the Socratic method.

Aristotle advanced the use of methodological proceedings by developing and using what is called the syllogism in relation to his work in philosophy. This is a species of logical argument in which one proposition (the conclusion) is inferred from two other propositions (the premises). We may use the syllogism many times in succession in developing a lengthy argument, and the result can then be regarded as an established proposition. The Euclidean proofs in geometry would be an example of such a use in which we infer conclusions from established facts (or axioms) in mathematics. These proofs could then be regarded as either mathematics or philosophy, and the record of the proceedings is what went into the mathematical textbooks. Philosophical arguments were said to be negated when inconsistencies were found. The syllogism was used throughout the Middle Ages and beyond with some refinements and became a foundation of logic in the nineteenth century. There have been a number of developments in philosophical methods in recent years, and we will go into these later. But we may say now that these techniques all produce results as a consequence of logical operations. The work can be said to be scientific if the premises are established facts. Aristotle wrote a number of books, including titles on ethics, politics, and physics. He started the university method of specialization and served as tutor to Alexander the Great.

2.7 Queen of the Sciences

Philosophy has grown from its inception until the present day and now has a massive literature. Students are recommended to read any of a number of summary works such as Will Durant's *The Story of Philosophy: The Lives and Opinions of the Greater Philosophers* (1926), Antony Flew's *An Introduction to Western Philosophy* (1971), Konstantin Kolenda's *Philosophy's Journey* (1990), Bryan Magee's *The Story of Philosophy* (1998), and Bertrand Russell's *A History of Western Philosophy* (1945). We can remind readers of the scope of philosophy by citing some of the topics mentioned in the texts above. The Greeks were responsible for initiating the ethical schools of Epicureanism and stoicism. There was considerable interaction between philosophy and early Christianity, and Saint Augustine was responsible for drawing the two together. The beginnings of science with Nicolaus Copernicus, Sir Isaac Newton, Niccolo Machiavelli, Francis Bacon, and Thomas Hobbes were all thought of as part of philosophy at the time they were written. Then came the rationalists including Rene Descartes, Baruch Spinoza, and Gottfried Wilhelm Leibniz. It was about this time that philosophy became known as the queen of the sciences. It is only fair, however, to point out that several other disciplines were awarded this regal title, including mathematics. Philosophy accommodated itself to empiricism with the work of John Locke, George Berkeley, and David Hume. The revolutionary French thinkers Francois Marie Arouet (or Voltaire), Denis Diderot, and Jean-Jacques Rousseau were followed by a century of German writers, including Immanuel Kant, Arthur Schopenhauer, Georg Wilhelm Friedrich Hegel, Karl Marx, and Friedrich Nietzsche. Philosophy had its greatest influence on politics through the work of Locke, John Stuart Mill, and the American pragmatists. The twentieth century saw Gottlob Frege and his work in logic and then Bertrand Russell, Ludwig Wittgenstein, Sir Karl Popper, the existentialists and the critical theorists.

2.8 Karl Popper and Cosmology

Sir Karl Popper compared the accomplishments of philosophy unfavorably with those of science a half century ago. His preface to the 1934 edition of his famous work *The Logic of Scientific Discovery* begins: "A scientist engaged in a piece of research, say in physics, can attack his problem straight away. He can go at once to the heart of the matter: to the heart, that is, of an organized structure. For a structure of scientific doctrines is already in existence; and with it, a generally accepted problem-situation. This is why he may leave it to others to fit his contribution into the framework of scientific knowledge. The philosopher finds himself in a different position. He does not face an organized structure, but rather something resembling a heap of ruins."

A little further on in the same book, Popper maintained: "There is at least one philosophical problem in which all thinking men are interested. It is the problem of cosmology, i.e. the problem of understanding the world—including ourselves, and our knowledge, as part of the world." Popper added that "all science is cosmology." Popper was writing at a time when philosophy was preoccupied with linguistic analysis and he was at some pains in the same passages to stress that although understanding the functions of language is an important part of philosophy, explaining away our scientific problems as merely linguistic "puzzles" is not. Popper had a dispute with Wittgenstein over this, which is told in *Wittgenstein's Poker* by David Edmonds and John Eidinow (2001). Popper continued with some remarks on the methods of philosophy. There is, according to him, a method that might be described as the "one method of philosophy." It is the one method of all rational discussion and therefore of the natural sciences as well as of philosophy. This is the method of stating one's problem clearly and of examining its various proposed solutions critically. Popper believed that there are any number of different methods a philosopher might use.

2.9 Metaphilosophy

In recent years, there has been an interest in studying the nature, aims, and methods of philosophy. For example, there is an interesting article on this in *Wikipedia*. I was attracted to a book by M. F. H. Roe (1990) because of its title, *Ethics Issues*. The book starts with a discussion of the purpose of philosophy, and I discovered that Roe had written an earlier work (1975) all about this. He starts by pointing out the vagueness and imprecision of the word *philosophy*. Love of wisdom can mean whatever we choose it to mean, he explains. This tends to foster doubt as to philosophy's value to the general public. What is philosophy about? Roe (1975) seems to echo Popper when he says as science went from strength to strength, philosophy became subject to growing doubt. "Science took its verification from experiment and not from any a priori principles supplied by philosophy." He continues, "Despite its cult of truth, philosophy makes a virtue of leaving questions open and subject to debate. Thus science advances while philosophy seems to mark time. The idea that philosophy could discover truths about the nature of being could no longer be held." According to Roe (1975), philosophy is powerless to formulate a purpose. It also seems to have no bearing on action. He goes on to examine the four main branches of philosophy: logic, epistemology, ontology, and axiology. He explains that axiology contains both aesthetics and ethics. He then argues that it is ethics that is the real core of philosophy because that is the subject that contains values. He maintains that this restores philosophy to the position of queen of the sciences: "In sum, it is ethical quality or general evaluation considered in ethical terms, an interest which is unique to it, and socially even urgent, which must characterize its purpose." Another recent book by Michael Dummett *The Nature and Future of Philosophy* (2010) contends that philosophy can clarify our vision of the world and provide exciting ways to interpret it. But it seems to this author that philosophy, in fact, rests upon logical inferences and that such exercises must be valid if their premises are such. Philosophy has lost much credibility through the way its constructions have either hung together or failed to do so. There is, after all, substantial use of logic in science and mathematics.

2.10 Ethics and the Academic Disciplines

Dewey defined ethics as the study of behavior as it pertains to right and wrong. How ought we to live and behave? Humanism is a pragmatic approach to life in which we employ all the arts and sciences. However, when it comes to matters of the individual's lifestance, there are certain subjects that are the most relevant, namely, ethics, philosophy, psychology, management, and increasingly these days the biological and medical sciences. Ethics, the first of these areas, began as a systematic discipline in the time of the ancient Greeks while the subject of management was only recognized as an academic discipline in the twentieth century when schools of business finally won acceptance on American campuses. Thus, we are constantly learning. But precisely because we are in a period of rapid learning, ethics remains a difficult and mysterious domain. I believe that more emphasis should be placed on Hume's assertion of the primacy of emotion in determining human behavior. He maintained that it is our emotions (or passions as he called them) that drive our behavior. The problems of free will and egoism may be related to this issue of the primacy of emotions, and as humanists, we need to get a clear understanding of the issues. We may moderate our behavior using our reason or use it to investigate the consequences of actions, even using long chains of reasoning in the process, but the bottom line (or what Hume calls the last sentence) is some act of evaluation. In another place Hume refers to reason as being the slave of the passions. Psychology, the study of human behavior, as it actually occurs, has demonstrated that we are able to modify our emotionally driven behavior when and if we acquire experience in growing older. Knowledge of a given topic acquired in different disciplines should be consistent so that there should be a unity overall. Furthermore, we should be able to summarize and understand it. And finally, we should aim for wisdom in its use.

There is an interesting argument that goes on sometimes as to what sort of discipline ethics is. Is it a science, an art, a practice, a philosophy? Different authors have chosen various of these designations to classify the subject, and it is hard to say that any particular choice is wrong. One may view ethics as a science of humanity so that it is comparable to engineering or technology or law. We face a similar problem when we try to classify humanism, and here again, my personal inclination is to think of it as a science of humanity, or we may use the modern term *project* to describe either one.

2.11 Ethics and Morality

We need to define the two terms *ethics* and *morality*. The two words are often used as synonyms, and in much of everyday conversation, there is really no problem with this. We follow Habermas in the belief that there is, in fact, a difference between the two. As he sees it, morality is a set of rules (norms) that exists in a person's mind. Morality is recognized as feelings or emotions that tell us if certain actions are acceptable or repugnant. Ethics, on the other hand, is an academic discipline, a branch of philosophy, in which we study the acceptability of human behavior. It is comprised of certain factual knowledge and the conclusions that can logically be derived from it. Again, we recognize ethical conduct through a related feeling of "oughtness." One reason for making the distinction is to clarify the history of the two. The contention is that morality is much older than ethics. There are many animals that show various moral behaviors, and primitive men and women are also to be credited with morality. But in these cases, it is generally agreed that the behaviors are instinctive. The understanding of this prehistoric morality has increased with the study of evolutionary development and the genome, and we will examine this in more detail later. As Said (2004) has pointed out, once humankind was able to tell and write stories, we began to celebrate desirable behavior. Some of the earliest writings we have are about the times in which we were hunters and gatherers. Manly features at that time included physical strength; and commendable behavior included courage, fortitude, and fearlessness. As Stearns (1990) has pointed out, the hunting society was still prevalent in Europe when the Christian conversion began and the hunting ethos still persists in many of the traditions of the Western aristocracy and military to this day. The word *virtue* is, in fact, derived from the Latin *vir* (*a man*). Once the wanderers had settled down in farms, villages, and towns, the leading virtues became those of the civilized life: justice, goodness, honesty, and compassion.

Ethics, as a philosophical discipline, did not arrive on the scene until the coming of civilization. There are a number of excellent historical accounts of the classical ethical systems including Sidgwick's *Outlines of the History of Ethics* (1902), Rachel's *The Elements of Moral Philosophy* (2007), and Grayling's *What is Good? The Search for the Best Way to*

Live (2003); and the reader is referred to these for further details. Certain historical events support the thesis of a systems interpretation of the subject. The earliest Greek philosophers including Thales and Democritus were more concerned with the nature of the physical world, and it was not until the time of Protagoras and Socrates that attention focused on human behavior. They are credited with the famous aphorism "Good people in a good society." The question became how to define the good. Plato was much moved by Socrates's death from drinking hemlock, and he recorded most of what we know about Socrates's thinking in his famous work *The Republic*, the first text devoted to ethics and political philosophy. *The Republic* is divided into ten books, each of considerable sophistication, covering such subjects as who should rule. It turns out that the philosopher is the one designated (of course). There is an allegory on some prisoners in a cave who are chained up and can only see the shadows of objects carried past. This illustrates our difficulty in understanding the natural world. Another book concerns the ring of Gyges, which supposedly makes its wearer invisible and thus able to commit immoral acts without being observed. This is a lead into a discussion of why we should be good. There is also a treatment of the nature of justice. Plato himself had suffered greatly from the excesses of democratic rule by the untutored successors of Pericles, and he (i.e. Plato) advocated an authoritarian system of rule by an aristocracy. In turn, Plato's student, Aristotle (1992) reverted to a belief in democracy. In Aristotle's system, the aim of life is to secure happiness, and this is to be done by living a life of virtue. In the years following Aristotle, Greek ethics developed a number of divergent paths that continued to develop under the Roman empire. Epicurus advocated a life in which happiness came from responding to the emotional drives with which nature has endowed us. The stoic school, on the other hand, as represented by Epictetus and the emperor Marcus Aurelius, stressed the importance of doing one's duty.

2.12 Religious Connections

Animals clearly show the basics of moral behavior as exemplified by care and sacrifice by parents for the young. Modern apes show altruism toward others of their kind although it is not clear if this behavior predated the separation of apes and humans. It is even possible that there was some rudimentary religious behavior before the split occurred. But what is becoming increasingly clear is that religion became a major influence in the lives of *Homo* during the hunter-gatherer period. Anthropologists have now made many studies of hunter-gatherer groups all over the world and have found religious practices in them all. Wade (2009) summarizes the common elements of the oldest such societies (the !Kung, the Andamanese, and the Australian aborigines). These primitive religions are primarily focused on dance, ritual, and music. They have no shamans or priests, and it is inferred that this is the way in which religion began. Again, we learn from anthropology that there was a further transformation in religion that occurred after the people settled into village life and took up agriculture. Specialized careers became common, and it was then that shamans and priests began to take over the practice of religion. Theism flourished; life after death became a common belief; gods and spirits were invented; and religions, including Hinduism, Judaism, and many others, developed and evolved in different ways. Philosophy and humanistic practices arose contemporaneously with the evolution of religion, and they all influenced one another. Wade also gives an excellent summary of these later developments.

The final years of the Roman empire saw the triumph of Christianity, and the humanistic Epicurean and stoic movements were eclipsed for a millennium until the revival of classical learning in the Renaissance. Much of the early instruction in ethics was carried out by shamans and priests who in the Middle East and Europe found it expeditious to label their teachings as divine commandments. Their ethical views fitted in with their ideas of the soul and the supernatural, which, in turn, were adopted by the Greeks. These same ideas were introduced into early Christianity by Saint Paul. Aristotle believed everything in nature had a purpose (teeth were there for chewing, etc.), and the later Christian philosophers (such as Saint Thomas Aquinas) argued that it was God who had created nature and all natural objects for various purposes. They believed in the existence of a natural law that specified how things (including humans) should behave. There are still adherents of natural law within the Catholic Church.

We are fortunate that there were people such as Voltaire with the courage to confront the irrational ideas put about by the church. In *Candide* (1759), for example, he mocked the notion that the present was the best of all possible worlds. Our principal disagreement with religion concerns its cavalier attitude toward facts: belief in miracles and belief in immortality. The belief in miracles was examined in some detail by Hume (1737), and the illusion of immortality has been dealt with by Lamont (1990). Nevertheless, religion continues to exert great influence in human society and continues to provide comfort to millions of adherents throughout the world. Dealing with this pernicious influence is one of the major challenges before humanism today.

Religion has continued to evolve and has had a great influence on our behavior. A whole class of people have been brought into its service as priests and bishops; and eventually, by bolstering the power of the political rulers, it became part of the fabric of society. It persists to this day, and in the USA, it seems to be approaching a pinnacle of influence. This is the reason that nonbelievers have given so much attention lately to atheism with a spate of new books on the subject, such as those by Harris (2004), Dawkins (2006), and Hitchens (2007). The conclusion from these new books, as also from all the old books on the subject, is that there is no evidence that God exists, i.e., there is no proof that a supernatural agent, omniscient and all-powerful, either created the universe in the first place or subsequently guides events. No one has been able to explain who created God if, in fact, he exists. To many people brought up in the Abrahamic religions (Judaism, Christianity, and Islam), this comes as a profound shock. They believe they might have to contemplate forsaking their birthrights and that their lives will no longer be centered on the worship of God, deriving ethical precepts from ancient scriptures and priestly liturgies and with all the cultural contrivances of religion. The Christian religion dominated Europe for a millennium, suppressing rational inquiry and generating controversy and war mongering between its various followers.

2.13 Enlightenment

With the Renaissance, there came a revival of interest in classical Greek thinking in Europe, and philosophers and scientists began to build a picture of the natural world free of superstition and supernaturalism. Stephen Greenblatt's work *The Swerve* (2011) is an account of how Lucretius's poem "On the Nature of Things," which was the definitive classical account of the physics of nature, was rediscovered in 1417, thus starting off the Renaissance. Trade had begun to flourish in the Middle Ages with the help of bankers and early capitalists such as the Medici family. There is an account of *The Rise and Fall of the House of Medici* by Christopher Hibbert (1974). Artists began to experiment with new styles and techniques. Philosophers began to consider the question of how we should behave in the absence of the Christian assumptions of divine commandments. Rationalism flourished due to Descartes and entered ethics and politics with Spinoza whose books heralded the modern age. Spinoza shared with Hume the conviction that emotion has the primacy in ethical assessment. He offended his Jewish brethren with his questioning of traditional beliefs including the concept of God. He was ostracized by the synagogue and forced to make his living by grinding lenses. But in this work, he had a fine reputation among the great scientists of his day who were exploring the big and the small with telescope and microscope. Galileo and Newton were leaders in the development of physics. One of the first of the new philosophers was Thomas Hobbes who lived through the time of the religious and civil strife in England in the seventeenth century and served as a tutor to the future King Charles II. Hobbes was a materialist and an atheist and wanted to find a theory on which to base ethical and political behavior. He started by considering "the state of nature." By this, he meant a time before the institution of law and government by man. According to Hobbes, the lives of men at that time were "nasty, short and brutish." He proposed that men got together and made a "social contract" whereby they agreed to follow certain rules, which were to be enforced by the state, with the king as its representative. Hobbes was followed by John Locke who also presupposed a "state of nature" but reintroduced the Almighty into the scheme of things to provide the ultimate sanction for the king's authority. In some ways, Locke improved on Hobbes's ideas by being the first in the English-speaking world to introduce the concepts of the "separation of church and state" and "separation of powers." The French philosopher Jean-Jacques Rousseau also took up the idea of a "state of nature"; but in his system, it was supposed to be an idyllic state of affairs, a "golden age."

The ethical implications of this new world view were best understood by David Hume who realized that these concepts of the state of nature and the golden age were both, in fact, "philosophical fictions." Hume observed that men are necessarily born in a family society (Hume 1777, para. 151) and based his own theory of morality and ethics on observable facts. Hume's skepticism was profound enough that he laid the ground both for modern physics and the connectionist approach to the theory of the brain. Hume's theory of cognition was presented in his *Enquiry Concerning Human Understanding* (1748, see Finch, 2007), which is an integral part of his overall scheme of human nature. The major points in that essay were firstly Hume's vision of philosophy as encompassing all human knowledge and ideas. The next plank in Hume's platform was his theory of the association of ideas. He ascribes great importance to habits and customs in our thinking process. He pointed out that animals as well as human infants have a repertoire of instinctive behaviors. But perhaps the most important aspect of this part of Hume's philosophy is his anticipation of systems theory by two hundred years or so as will be described later.

2.14 Utilitarianism

True to his program of examining which personal attributes make men objects of either esteem or contempt, Hume begins by considering the social virtues of benevolence. He points out that the epithets sociable, good-natured, humane, merciful, grateful, friendly, generous, beneficent, or their equivalents are known in all languages. He quotes Pericles, Cicero, and Juvenal, all of whom extolled benevolence in people of high station. He finds no quality more entitled to the general goodwill and approbation of mankind than beneficence and humanity (140). In the next paragraph (141), he stresses the benefits that accrue to society from a man's beneficence to his family, friends and employees, and society at large if he is a man of high station. He points out how monks and inquisitors are enraged when we treat their orders as useless or pernicious to society. The strongest praise for a profession such as merchandising or manufacturing is to observe the advantages it procures to society. Thus follows the connection between the individual's ethic of benevolence and his utility to society. Hume maintained that no attribute "can bestow more merit on any human creature than the sentiment of benevolence in an eminent degree" (144). This evaluation of ethics based on its societal benefits is termed utilitarianism, and several prominent philosophers including Jeremy Bentham, the Mills (father and son) and Henry Sidgwick followed Hume in its further development.

The version of utilitarianism propounded by Bentham (1789) was a very practical subject amenable to engineers and businesspeople, and this was the philosophy passed on to John Stuart Mill by his father, James, who had become a disciple of Bentham. Mill felt that the emotions admitted by Bentham should be broadened to include the aesthetic. The background for this was his own revival from a youthful despondency through reading the poetry of William Wordsworth. Mill argued further that the driving emotions of Bentham's utilitarianism should include all the varieties known to psychology and that it is in their satisfaction that we experience the state we call "happiness" following Aristotle's lead. In turn, this led on to the extensive literature of psychology in the twentieth century. It is also the starting point for later writers, including Kitcher, who seek to base morality on altruism.

2.15 The Impact of Evolution

The idea of biological evolution had been around since the time of the Greeks, but it was not until Charles Darwin published *On the Origin of Species* in 1859, two years before the Civil War began in America, that the implications began to sink in with the general public. Darwin was a naturalist and not a philosopher, and his book was seen as a biology text and received little attention at first. Eventually, it became clear that the theory completely upset the established thinking on biology, geology, and paleontology. It was realized that Earth was millions of years old and that natural selection and gradual adaptation could account for the great variety of life-forms. As the story gradually became clear—that man had evolved from apes, who came from primitive mammals—so it was realized that life might have arisen from nonliving antecedents. We did not need to hypothesize a supernatural god or other agency to explain our existence. Gregor Mendel's discoveries in genetics supplied a mechanism, and finally, Crick and Watson showed that the key to the operation of that mechanism was the DNA molecule. Thus, the schema of a biological system (a plant or animal) is written on the amino acids of the double helix. The gradual changes of the evolving organisms are due to the usually slight changes in genetic material, and the gradual changes of the expressed system are then said to have evolved.

But there can be evolutionary changes in nonbiological systems such as the linguistic, social, governmental, and technical systems invented by humans. This general evolutionary landscape was first envisaged by Herbert Spencer (1862) who wrote extensively on the subject and coined the phrase *survival of the fittest*. It fell to Herbert Spencer to expound on what evolution said about human behavior and about society. It was Spencer who explained the universality of evolution not only in nature but also in humans and their society, behavior, morals, history, and ideas. Spencer advocated what became known as social Darwinism. "Every man is free to do that which he wills, provided he infringes not the equal freedom of any other man". Werth, in his book *Banquet at Delmonicos* (2009), tells how Spencer influenced a number of prominent Americans and so helped shape a newly emergent post–Civil War intellectual climate by expanding the theory into a far-reaching cosmology in which evolution came to be seen as a factor in sociology, politics, and ethics. In the 1890s, industrial capitalism overtook the United States, and the theory of evolution set the terms for the larger debate over what America is. "Survival of the fittest" was seen to be a justification for unscrupulous capitalism. One of Spencer's leading followers was Andrew Carnegie whose *Gospel of Wealth* argued that the rich must be the stewards for society (although in other places Carnegie supported socialism). It is interesting that this commended evolution to the business community where it is still used and respected, although we now see pragmatism and management science as more reasonable interpretations of its implications. Similar ideas were used later to justify the political expansionism of the Nazis. We need to understand why those ideas were wrong and set out a better picture of evolutionary morality.

August Weismann (1893) posited the new mechanism for inheritance through the germ line (i.e., eggs and sperm), thus denying Lamarckian transmission of acquired characteristics. This led Spencer to write four essays defending "use inheritance." Mendel's thirty-year-old findings were rediscovered in 1900, thus putting Weismann's theory on a firm footing. Finally, we should mention that there seems to be some hope of a Spencer revival at least in respect of seeing evolution as being a much wider principle than its limited application in biology alone. Evolution has to be recognized as basic in psychology, ethics, sociology and politics, as Spencer taught.

2.16 Theory of Communicative Action

Immanuel Kant was the other of the two great philosophers at the end of the eighteenth century besides Hume. In fact, he helped Hume get established by declaring that Hume's work had served to awaken him from his dogmatic slumbers. Kant was one of the first to propose a world government. He was also a physicist of some repute and put forward a theory of planetary formation that was widely accepted for a while and helped to explain how the solar system could have come into existence without the need to invoke divine agency. So he had a number of claims to fame, and he is definitely someone we should respect. Kant wrote a famous book on ethics titled the *Metaphysics of Morals* (1785). He claims that we have a number of ends, which are rather like Plato's eternal forms. In the book, he claimed that we experience moral influences called imperatives, which can be either absolute or undeniable, in which case they were called categorical imperatives, or optional, in which case they were "hypothetical imperatives." If we do not believe in the existence of objective morals, then categorical imperatives have to be rejected. Mackie (1977) makes this plain when he states that "my thesis that there are no objective values is specifically the denial that any such categorically imperative element is objectively valid." Unfortunately, Kant was so much attached to his categorical imperatives that he maintained that they must be of divine origin. So it is sometimes said that Kant showed God out of the front door, only to let him back in again through the back door.

Kant was the first of a series of continental (i.e., European) philosophers including Hegel, Schopenhauer, Nietzsche, Kierkegaard, Marx, Husserl, Heidegger, Sartre, Camus, Horkheimer, Adorno, and Habermas. Hegel saw the fundamental basis of existence as something he called the geist. This German word has a connotation midway between *spirit* and *mind*. Hegel became famous for his recognition of the importance of history in human affairs. He proposed out that at any one time there was something like a "spirit of the age," which he called the zeitgeist. In a way, these men of the European continent have followed a path that has parallels to that of the Anglo-American writers. Thus, Hegel and Frege in Germany were pioneering in logic at about the same time that it was being studied by Peirce and Dewey in America. Another of Hegel's important contributions was to recognize the way in which philosophy progressed as a sort of conversation, which he called the dialectic. It was the geist which got modified as thesis and antithesis were exchanged between people. One of the remarkable things about Hegel was that he was admired by both the left and right wings of the political spectrum. Karl Marx was one of the first to realize the importance of economic influences on society. He made the geist into a material medium and called his theory dialectical materialism. Later, on Max Horkheimer, Theodor Adorno, and Jürgen Habermas converted the substance of Hegel's ideas into a new social theory based on the exchange of human communication. Horkheimer and Adorno had to leave Nazi Germany because of their Jewish ancestry. They were so shocked by the revelations about the Holocaust they came to believe that no social theory could be any longer be sustained. Habermas was somewhat more optimistic and went on to formulate the theory of communicative action (1984). There is an interesting account of this work by David Held (1980). In English, it is said to be a critical theory and is associated with critical thinking that flourishes today in American universities.

2.17 Evolutionary Humanism and Evolutionary Ethics

Another influential continental philosopher was Friedrich Nietzsche who built on Schopenhauer's legacy and famously declared "God is dead," which set the European tradition on an atheistic path. Many of the continentals are included in the existentialist movement. Kierkegaard explored the importance of choice and decision making in ethics. Husserl was the originator of the theory of phenomenology, which was built on the idea that reality consists of the impressions that physical stimuli evoke in our minds. We will say more about these theories later. In Britain, in the middle of the twentieth century, humanism was greatly influenced by Nietzsche and the existentialists through the work of Blackham (1952, 1953, and 1968). In the United States, the leading lights were the pragmatists and John Dewey (1934).

The argument over social Darwinism extended throughout the twentieth century and is perhaps not fully resolved even now. My contention is that some parts of Spencer's thesis were correct even as some parts were wrong. The problem has been that Spencer has been disregarded in some quarters, and even those parts of his theories that do merit attention have been neglected. Perhaps, therefore, we need to refocus on the valid parts of his works. Spencer was incorrect in his support for Lamarkian evolution in biology and in his belief that evolution necessarily supported unscrupulous behavior as in laisser-faire capitalism and in racist opinions of the superiority of whites, especially Anglo-Americans. But he was correct to emphasize the extension of evolution to cultural and social systems. There is, in fact, an enormity in this claim. The pragmatic methods expounded by James and Dewey are clearly extensions of evolutionary techniques to cultural and societal systems. They may be seen as scientific methods generalized to the whole of living. Drucker's excursion into management sciences made it clear that business planning could be approached in the same way.

Finally, we must realize that science is itself a major part of our culture, and the philosophy of science has been a major issue in the past century. It was Popper and his work on falsification and the evolution of science, who is most clearly associated with this. Hume (1748) was the first to question the assumption that if an experimental result was consistent with a hypothesis, then the theory could be considered to be confirmed. He insisted that the process of induction can never have the logical certainty of deduction. It was left first to Peirce (1896) and then independently to Popper (1934) to point out that a hypothesis was certainly wrong if a deduction based upon it was ever shown to be false. Peirce introduced the term *fallibilism* while Popper chose the word *falsifiability*. Popper saw false results as "problems," which might be around for years, and he went further by pointing out that the formulation of hypotheses is not a rational process but a creative one comparable to the aesthetic act of creating a work of art. He also realized that the gathering of a set of facts was usually followed by a scientist already having some ideas in mind before precisely formulating a hypothesis. These ideas might even arise from innate or unconscious knowledge. Thus, he proposed that science is an endlessly repeating cycle of the following:

- Problems being posed
- Tentative theories being proposed to solve the problems
- The deduction of testable propositions from the theories
- The testing of the propositions
- Elimination of errors from the theories
- The posing of new problems

In Popper's view, a scientific theory is successful if it works and unsuccessful if it does not work. Only successful theories survive; and thus the growth of science, through this survival of successful theories, is actually an integral part of the process of evolution. Popper has shown how the concept of falsifiability leads on to the evolution of science in several books including *Realism and the Aim of Science* (1956), *Conjectures and Refutations: The Growth of Scientific Knowledge* (1963), and *Objective Knowledge: An Evolutionary Approach* (1972). We may interpret the growth of knowledge in fields other than natural science in evolutionary terms. Languages have obviously evolved over time as is evidenced by the tree of linguistics. Engineering artifacts have also evolved over time as has been described by Basalla (1988). And finally, we are claiming here that it is evolution that is the essential key to humanism and human ethics. This idea was first advanced by Julian Huxley in his 1947 book *Religion without Revelation* and expanded upon in the 1964 *Evolutionary Humanism*. That ethics is also evolutionary was implicit in these writings. As Rifkin (2008) has recently pointed out, Huxley's proposition was immediately greeted with derision by the sociologists for a variety of reasons, probably as an echo of the old quarrel over social Darwinism. Hopefully, the intervening half century will have served to put that episode behind us so that Spencer's ideas might have another chance to receive an airing.

2.18 The Present Situation

I gave a paper based on an early version of this work at a conference and was challenged as to why there was no mention of women or Eastern philosophy in the presentation. This short summary of the history of ethics cannot do full justice to all the philosophers and scientists who have contributed to the contemporary discipline. In particular, we have concentrated on the thinking in the West to the exclusion of that in the Middle and Far East. But we are coming to realize that the thinkers of ancient India and China actually followed somewhat similar courses to those in the Western world. There are many similarities between Western humanist thought and Buddhist philosophy, Confucianism, and other Oriental schools. We have also passed over the work of the many women who managed to rise above their enforced second-class status to make marks in their respective disciplines. It is not difficult to understand why women have been reluctant to get involved in philosophy when we remember the story of Hypatia, who lived in Alexandria following her father as a philosopher, mathematician, and astronomer. Hypatia earned an excellent reputation among philosophers of the ancient world who came from all over the Roman empire to visit with her. She wore scholar's rather than women's clothes and used to drive her own chariot—an action no woman who "knew her place" would have undertaken lightly. Unfortunately, she ran afoul of the Christian bishop Cyril who incited a mob, which seized her from her chariot one day in 415 CE, dragged her down, stripped, and killed her. Cyril, however, was made a saint. There were other women of note in ancient times including Aspasia, the courtesan who was associated with the Athenian statesman Pericles for twenty years and was regarded as his equal. In modern times, Elena Cornaro Piscopia was the first woman to earn a doctor's degree in 1678. Mary Wollstonecraft was a pioneer of women's rights; and in the past century, there were Ayn Rand, Simone Weil, Hannah Arendt, Simone de Beauvoir, Angela Davis, and Gloria Steinem. We need to integrate feminism and humanism.

In recent years, humanist philosophy and ethics have been dominated by Paul Kurtz, Peter Singer, and Jürgen Habermas; and we will say more about each of these when we come to expand upon and discuss their ideas as later chapters unfold. Singer, for example, has been very influential with his books on *Animal Liberation* (1975) and *The Expanding Circle* (1981). There has been much progress in philosophy and ethics, but it is clear that there is much work still to be done. One way in which the effort is moving forward is through the growth of specifically humanist institutions such as the American Humanist Association (AHA), the British Humanist Association (BHA), numerous other national organizations, and the International Humanist and Ethical Union. In the USA there has recently been a growing collaboration between atheist, free-thought, and humanist groups under the title of secularism. There are now all sorts of annual conferences and publications of books, magazines, and journals. Most of the national groups sponsor local groups and activities including sections catering to women, minorities, and youth. We should mention the growth of service organizations dedicated to charity and helping both the existing secular community and members of the general public. Finally, we must understand that part of our work must be directed toward the future. There are also a number of university level research groups devoted to extending the theory and science of humanism. Space travel and exploration, robotics, genetic engineering, and extension of the human lifespan all pose existential choices for our civilization. Secular ethics has grown in an evolutionary fashion and faces a challenging future as human wealth and technology continue to advance.

3. Science and Instincts

Outline

3. Science and Instincts

3.1 Hunter-Gatherers

We described in the preceding chapter how at certain times the progress of ethics was advanced by people who did not regard themselves primarily as either ethicists or philosophers. Scientists investigating times from the start of the mammalian age came to be called paleontologists and biologists. In one sense, we might argue that these people studied different records of the past: the paleontologists literally unearthed the fossil record, and the biologists studied the human genome. Another source of knowledge came from the anthropologists who studied the primitive humans of the African bush and the shoreline of the Eurasian landmass. In later chapters, we will be meeting the psychologists who studied humankind in its later civilized development. In this section, we concentrate on the hunter-gatherers who were the earliest hominins.

We still do not know the full story of why some of the apes split off from their brothers in the forests of the Congo in a migration toward the south, but there are some plausible theories. One is that there was a climate change that turned their habitat into savannah. Here, they would have encountered various predators and would also have been forced to hunt for their own food. Being able to stand erect and run on two legs while carrying children and food in their arms would have had survival value. Toolmaking, initially the shaping of stones to produce knives, then arrowheads, and finally spears would have added to their engineering repertoire. Growth of the brain and its memory capacity would also have been highly advantageous. Successful hunter-gatherer existence calls for considerable knowledge of plants and animals and of the weather. It was pointed out by Michael Finkel (2013) that to absorb the full breadth of aboriginal knowledge at the present time takes thirty to forty years. The ability to communicate through language would have come with the improvement of memory, thus enabling members of a social group to share information and concepts. Nicholas Wade (2009) points out that the instinctive morality of the forest-dwelling apes would have had to be modified by the change of environment to savannah living. There would have been the emergence of special skills: baby minding, toolmaking, hunting, gathering, storytelling, and so on. There is a strong egalitarian instinct among hunter-gatherers that would represent a great change from the hierarchical social structure of alpha-male-dominated bands. This change had to result if the skilled hunters were not to be the sole survivors of life on the grassland.

Wade discusses the evidence that these various human innovations were embedded in genetic modifications. Speech, for instance, is articulated by several neural and muscular skills governed by the FOXP2 gene discovered in 2001. Chomsky (1965) had researched the way in which language is passed on to children through a genetically coded syntax or grammar, which is receptive to training in the native language of the adults. Hauser (2006) has proposed that behavior and morality is stored and handed on through a similar grammatical system of rules. Following on the growth of language, storytelling and morality came what Wade indicates was the greatest change of all: the evolution of religion. Wade is at pains to show that there is a clear survival advantage to having religion. He argues that religion belongs to a community, and it is thus to the benefit to that community that its value accrues: it is a matter of group selection. Wade continues that the quality of a society—its cohesiveness; freedom from crime; members' willingness to help others; and the rarity of lying, cheating, and freeloading—is shaped by its morality and people's adherence to community standards.

Wade understands that practical morality is not universal. Compassion and forgiveness are owed to one's in-group, but not to an out-group and certainly not to an enemy. Human behavior is, as Wade puts it, "steely, implacable and often genocidal toward other societies."

Religion has been involved in warfare, from the time of the apes until this very day, because it is invoked by leaders to justify aggression, sustain morale, and spur soldiers to the ultimate sacrifice. But here again we see its evolutionary advantage.

3.2 Religion and Anthropology

With this perspective, one can begin to see how religion may be crucial to a society's survival. Emile Durkheim, a founder of anthropology, wrote in his 1921 book *The Elementary Forms of Religion* about religion as a system of ideas by means of which individuals imagine the society of which they are members and the relations they have with it. He pointed out that religious beliefs are shared and bind together those that hold them. This then would have given the religious group the survival advantage by allowing it to produce more children. Wade (2009) followed Durkheim with a recent book *The Faith Instinct: How Religion Evolved and Why It Endures.* He cites the work of a number of anthropologists who have lived among the groups they studied for months or years, learned the languages of their groups, and witnessed everyday living and morality as well as religious practices. To make his case, Wade selects three groups who are among the oldest survivors of the migration that started from Africa about fifty thousand years ago: the!Kung, the Andaman Islanders, and the Australian aborigines. These three have religions with many common characteristics. None of them have priesthoods; but they all express their religion in dance, chant, and trance. The dances may last for hours, for all day or night. They have ceremonies that may last for months. The participants in these dances and trances experience intense emotional states similar to hypnosis, and these extreme experiences are never forgotten. Wade argues that these common features must define what he calls the ancestral religion, and this is how it came to bind the groups together. The religion of these groups is, in fact, a central defining schema in the system of their lives.

Wade opens his book with these words: "For the last 50,000 years, and probably for much longer, people have practiced religion. With dance and chants and sacred words, they have ritually marked the cycles of the season and the passages of life, from birth to adolescence, to marriage and to death . . . Religions point to the realm of the supernatural, assuring people that they are not alone in the world. Most religions teach that there is an afterlife and some promise a better existence there, often for lives lived correctly in this world or to compensate for its misfortunes . . . In religion's name, people have fed the hungry, cared for the sick, founded charities and hospitals. Religion creates circles of trust whose members may support one another in calamity or find hosts and trading partners in distant cities. In societies throughout the world, religious rites are intimately associated with the communal activities of music and dance . . . Religion above all, embodies the moral rules that members of a community observe toward one another . . . It sustains the quality of the social fabric . . . It binds people together for collective action." He continues that it can unite people to the extent that they can define their cause by religion. But he does point out the darker side of religion, drawn from the excesses of the fierce loyalty it inspires. It has been routinely used to justify and sustain wars between Christian and Muslim, Protestant and Catholic, Shi'a and Sunni. He mentions the atrocious wars of the Aztec empire and its ravenous search for victims who were sacrificed every day, sometimes by the thousands in a single ceremony, so that the stream of their blood could nourish the sun god.

From a philosophical point of view, we may ask: what is religion? There are a number of definitions that have been offered by various authors from Durkheim (1921) to Boyer (2001). It is generally described as a social system with some sort of faith or set of beliefs in the supernatural, often including one or more gods. Other characteristics may include a philosophy or cosmology consistent with these supernatural beliefs. There is an organized community of adherents of the faith, with a culture of rituals and practices, frequently with singing and symbols. There are usually traditions for celebrating life events and a priesthood who may intercede with the gods. Wade states that the new evolutionary approach to religion promotes the idea that religion evolved because it conferred essential benefits on ancient societies and their successors. Biological drives for all functions essential to survival are embedded in the human brain, and he argues that it surely is no scandal that an instinct for religious behavior is one of those necessities. Religion can be the source of some of the deepest emotions, such as awe, exaltation, or transcendence. But it may also be the source of fears of punishment.

Wade points out that fears of omnipresent supervision could be of great value to a group that lacks courts or police forces.

Wade explains that there was a major transformation in religion between about fifteen and ten thousand years ago when the hunter-gatherers settled down in villages and began to practice agriculture. The egalitarian stance of the hunter-gatherer society faded away as kings and military appeared. It was only then that shamans and priests took over the ministrations of religion and began to record the ancient narratives, liturgies, and laws in writing. The priesthood assumed an authoritative role, often as a branch of tribal government. Wade explores this extension of religious evolution at some length with detailed accounts of the history of Judaism, Christianity, and Islam. He also discusses the long conflict between the priestly churches and the remnants of the old ecstatic regions. These religious developments are too complex to enter into here and will be taken up elsewhere.

3.3 Altruism

At first, many opponents of the theory of evolution claimed that there was no way that altruism could have been favored because they thought that each individual would seek to follow his own self-interests. But it eventually became clear that there had to be instances where a behavior could favor the selection of a group. Parents will go to great lengths to protect their offspring, even so far as to place their own lives at risk. But it is only in the past decade or so that any real advance has been made over Hume's picture of the role of instinct in ethical development. We may explain matters in the following way. In scientific observation, some sensations are apprehended and interpreted as facts of some kind. These facts are then "explained" as a theory. In moral observations, emotions (virtues or vices) are apprehended and then reported as facts, which are then "explained" as an ethical theory. So we may conceive that an ethical science can be built up on the reported facts of virtues and vices. What has been discovered is that ethical or moral facts of instinctual behavior can be found by testing people with fictional moral scenarios. Partly, this has come about through the realization that some of our behavior is hereditary or at least that we have predispositions to behave in certain ways that are genetically determined.

Once this was understood, we could envisage how evolution could influence the suite of behavioral genes to select those which favor our survival. Credit for this partly rests with E. O. Wilson in his expansion of the concepts of sociobiology. Some apparently unrelated research was done in the field of linguistics by Noam Chomsky who was puzzled by the remarkable way in which babies acquire speech. Chomsky (1957) came to the conclusion that human children must be born with an innate sense of grammar in order to be able to gain proficiency as rapidly as they do. The connection between linguistics and morality genetics was supplied by John Rawls (1971) who realized that a grammar is essentially a set of rules that governs the permissible ordering of words in a language. If there can be a set of rules governing acceptable word order, then Rawls proposed that there could be a set of rules governing acceptable behavior. Hauser (2006) has summarized what we know in both fields and has amassed an impressive assemblage of similarities and parallels to which he has added some original research of his own. This work is detailed in his book *Moral Minds*, which concentrates mainly on work done in psychological testing. A recent work by Sam Harris (2010) covers much the same area of ethical science and instinctive morality. Harris stresses that it is possible to ask questions about moral issues that have right or wrong answers, thus making morality a science. The critical criterion according to Harris is whether the given answer leads to an improvement in human welfare or otherwise. He stresses how religion has regularly obfuscated such inquiries.

3.4 Instinctive Morality

Monkeys and apes show empathy and a sense of reciprocity. Humans would have inherited these building blocks from our apelike ancestors and developed them into moral instincts. Morality has been wired into the genetic circuitry of our minds by evolution, as proposed by Wilson in sociobiology. Spinoza and Hume were among the first to propose that morality sprang from emotion, not reason. But Kant thought otherwise and that morals should be based on universal laws.

Wilson said this made no sense. Nevertheless, Piaget followed Kant and Kohlberg followed Piaget. B. F. Skinner was likewise a follower of Kant. The logjam was broken in 2001 by Haidt who was studying the emotion of disgust. Haidt told people disgusting stories, for example, of a family who ate their pet dog. Haidt formed the opinion that there are two kinds of moral decision: (1) moral intuition where an instantaneous decision comes from the unconscious mind and (2) moral reasoning, which is used to find justification for judgments already made. Why are there two psychological processes? An answer to this question is that the two processes emerged from different stages of evolution. Intuition is the more ancient—from before we had the power of reasoning or language. Snap judgments occur and are delivered to consciousness, which then takes over and acts like a lawyer to rationalize and justify the individual's actions to himself and others.

Haidt argues that moral intuition is partly genetic and partly cultural. People learn the moral values of their society early in life, according to the psychologist Jerome Kagan. By age two, they already have a list of prohibited actions. Between three and six years, they show guilt (see Jerome Kagan, *Morality and Its Development*, 2001). Children everywhere follow the same stages, which suggests that there is a genetic program like vision or language. Damage to the prefrontal cortex, as in the case of Phineas Gage, can disturb this programming. Patients with Huntington's disease become very utilitarian (i.e., they ignore social taboos and consider only the consequences). Huntingdon's patients will eat chocolate candy in the shape of a dog turd. There seem to be neural circuits both for morality and for disgust since specific damage can cause a loss in either behavior. Both behaviors are heavily influenced by culture. Because of cultural differences, societies may vary widely in actions they consider morally permissible. Nancy Howell (1979), in *Demography of the Dobe!Kung*, explains that among the!Kung San, hunter-gatherers of the Kalahari Desert, it is the mother's duty to kill after birth any deformed infant or one of a pair of twins. The reason for this is that a!Kung mother has to carry her infant with her wherever she goes, for maybe five thousand miles, before the child learns to walk. The mother also has to carry food, water, and possessions and therefore cannot carry twins. This should be regarded as a shaping of human moral intuitions to circumstances, not as a moral deficiency.

In aboriginal Australia and neighboring Melanesia, conception is not regarded as dependent on the father's sperm, and men are less jealous of sexual access to their partners. At sporting events, a tug-of-war has men and women on opposite sides. The winners deride the vanquished, assail their prostrate opponents, and have sex in public. Commonalities in morality are more striking than the variations. The golden rule is found in all societies, as are prohibitions against murder, theft, and incest.

3.5 Research on Morality

Hauser uses cartoons to depict what he calls Humean, Kantian, and Rawlsian creatures, which are supposed to think according to the human cognitive system as understood by these three famous philosophers. In point of fact, Hauser's creatures are three caricatures of what the philosophers actually believed. Hauser's Humean creature, for instance, thinks with nothing but emotions, whereas if we read Hume's work, we learn that although he saw the emotions (passions he called them) as the primary driver of people's behavior, he clearly recognized the moderating influence of reason in our mental processes. Hume's viewpoint was anticipated by his near contemporary Spinoza and in ancient times by Epicurus. One of Hauser's most telling instances is in his description of the working of the brain. He gets into this with an account of United Airlines Flight 93 on September 11, 2001. The passengers on this flight certainly had a plan of action, instigated by several of them having been alerted to the earlier attacks on the World Trade Center. They must have decided that it was permissible to risk the lives of their fellow passengers to save an even greater number of people, but "their emotions must have been abuzz." Hauser continues as David Hume intuited and as the neuroscientist Antonio Damasio (1994) has emphasized more recently that "rational thought often relies on an intimate handshake with the emotions." It is, in fact, not clear that we have any experiences without emotions. Empathy is based on our ability to replicate the emotions being felt by another human, and the golden rule instructs us to use our empathy before we do something to someone else.

One of the primary areas for the operation of instinctive morality is our sense of fairness. Much of the research work has been done using scenarios written by investigators and evaluated by test subjects who are often graduate students. Here are two examples:

1. Sports Car. A man is driving his new sports car when he sees a child on the side of the road with a bloody leg. Should the driver take her to a nearby hospital even if it costs $200 to clean blood off the car seat?
2. Charity. A man gets a letter from UNICEF's child health care division requesting a $50 contribution that could save the lives of twenty-five children by providing oral rehydration salts. Should the man contribute to the charity?

Something pushes most of us to answer yes in case one while a much smaller number say yes in case two. After a lengthy analysis, the investigators arrived at the principle behind the responses: if we can directly prevent, with a high degree of certainty, something bad without sacrificing anything of comparable significance, we are obliged to do it. A number of rules of this sort have been uncovered using scenarios inspired by Rawls. One of the best known is the aphorism "Do no harm" frequently quoted to students in medical school. Subjects are frequently unaware of specific moral principles in making their evaluations and may arrive at their verdicts very quickly. Most subjects agreed with Rawls on two central principles: (a) all members of society have equal rights and (b) the distribution of goods should be set to benefit the least advantaged. There have also been some studies of how people play games such as "survivor." Hauser comments that in this case ordinary people behaved as if they had studied pages from Jane Goodall's chimpanzee diaries. Economists have studied how people allocate resources in games. The actions are frequently irrational, and it transpires that this arises from a deep sense of fairness. In repeated games, the reputations of other players are frequently the basis of strategic decisions. The need to punish cheaters becomes an important consideration, and subjects are prepared to go to considerable personal costs to ensure that punishment is administered. But there were also some cases in which it was demonstrated that non-Rawlsian principles were preferred as in preferences to maximize the overall resources of a group. Groups also did better with principles they had themselves voted to approve.

3.6 Instinctive Killing and Violence: Trolley Problems

Most ethical codes prohibit killing, but there are exceptions. In wartime, killing of enemy combatants is encouraged, and even killing of noncombatants is condoned. Suicide is mostly condemned, but there are approximately one million suicides per year. There are about five thousand deaths each year, mostly of women, in so-called honor killings mainly in Muslim countries (see Jimmy Carter, 2014). In some cultures, such as that of the Semai of the Malaysian rainforest, physical and verbal aggression is forbidden whereas in others, such as that of the Yanomamo of South America, extreme violence is regarded as a virtue. Hauser investigated the circumstances under which killing is permissible. Catholics and Protestants killed heretics and Satan worshipers for centuries. The Bible permitted abortion and infanticide. Hauser recounts a particularly horrific case of an honor killing that occurred in Jerusalem in 2001 in which a family invited guests to witness the murder of their own pregnant daughter by the father. Women are still regarded as property in many cultures. Although this moral intuitional system is inaccessible to the conscious mind, it can be traced by the use of the moral exercises known as trolley problems, invented by Philippa Foot. To test people's distinction between killing and letting die, which lies at the core of many bioethical decisions, it is supposed that a trolley is bearing down on five people walking on the track. The trolley can be switched onto a side track, but there is a person walking on that side track. Is it permissible to make the switch and kill one person, or should the five people be left to die? There are several variations of this scenario from which it emerges that the rule most of us would use is that it is not permissible to cause an intentional harm even if that harm is used as a means to a greater good. Killing in self-defense or under extreme provocation is viewed as permissible. Impulsive actions as opposed to premeditated ones are often condoned. Hauser concludes that there are hidden parameters underlying people's intuitions about these cases. The subjects themselves are hopeless at justifying their intuitions.

3.7 Common Sense

Contrary to the assertion that humans are born as "blank slates," there is mounting evidence that we each have a certain amount of innate knowledge or common sense. This knowledge resides in our brains and includes some moral strictures for which reason Hauser speaks of the brain as the "moral organ." Newborn babies, no more than an hour old, can imitate the facial expressions of adults, say, by sticking out the tongue. Young babies learn to label objects verbally. Hauser argues that something about the human brain allows us to acquire a system of moral norms. But the dogs and cats that grow up with us never acquire these norms. This is not to say that there are no cross-cultural variations or that social conventions cannot change with time. But when an individual breaks with expectations, they are considered to have done wrong and may be punished. Such conventions upheld the institution of slavery for hundreds of years. The violation of expectations is usually accompanied by negative emotions. We also have an innate sense of physics embedded in our common sense. For example, common sense tells us that two solid objects cannot both occupy the same space. In programming robots, such laws have to be encoded in the machine's software. The psychologist Piaget discovered that for very young children, out of sight means out of existence. Only experience teaches us that we can still reach for hidden objects. Hauser details a number of principles held in common sense such as that objects moving on their own are animated. We infer that moving objects, which change direction in response to environmental stimuli, are rational. We also have the capacity to perceive events as parts of meaningful sequences. We have a sense of self and senses of self-control, self-confidence, and self-esteem. Identical twins are in many ways remarkably similar but differ in other ways. We infer that genes control our basic attributes and characters but that personal preferences for foods, activities, and friends are influenced by environmental factors. Some of these abilities of the self seem to depend on very prescribed modules. Prosopagnosics are people who suffer from the inability to recognize their own faces in a mirror or the faces of familiar people. Sufferers from Capgras delusion can recognize faces but then believe they are mistaken. It is inferred that these persons have a breakdown in the circuitry of feeling what it is like to be in the presence of the familiar. Then we are reminded of the case of Phineas Gage who was a model citizen until he suffered a horrendous accident in which a mining stake shot through his frontal lobes, miraculously leaving him unimpaired in all functions except for a deficit in moral control. It appears that in psychopaths there are deficits in the normal control mechanisms for which treatment has so far been quite ineffective.

3.8 Moral Development

There was a well-known study of moral development by Kohlberg (1981) who found that we typically move through a number of stages. The control of our urges and inhibitions begins with the baby whose demands the parent has to balance in her own interest as well as that of other children. Baby flashes manipulative smiles and adds crying and tears if that is not enough to secure his wants. The same signals are to be seen from kittens and puppies. This hereditary morality dictates our behavior on matters from nursing to abortion and infanticide. As technology advances, we encounter problems our human psychology did not evolve to cope with. John Rawls, E. O. Wilson, and Richard Dawkins all foresaw the problem of reconciling Darwinian selfishness with rational moral systems. Thinking on the subject started with Sidgwick (1874). The interest was revived a century later in Trivers's theory of reciprocity and then advanced to systems in which we keep count of favors using our arithmetical capabilities. But we have also to account for the difficult problem of detecting cheaters. Cosmides and Tooby (2000) showed that we possess specialized modules for that purpose. Extensive testing of infants' sense of fairness confirmed that such systems are actually in place. This work has been extended into studies of pretend play and thinking on alternative realities and the legal issues of when children realize that lying is an offense. It appears that children acquire a theory-of-mind module, which enables them to recognize that others have false beliefs at about four years of age.

Another interesting development of recent years concerns the role of certain emotions whose evolutionary purpose was not previously clear. Envy and jealousy are now believed to play a key part in survival by motivating achievement, serving conscience, and alerting us to inequities. Experimental economists have tested for envy as a catalyst in reducing inequities. There are advantages to feeling good about cooperation. Selfishness drives us to defect; but positive emotions (joy, interest, and contentment) act to stabilize cooperation. These views were first propounded by Frank (1988) in his book *Passions within Reason*. Hauser argues that all societies have two norms for altruistic behavior: "Help people who can't help themselves" and "Return favors to those who have given help in the past." Patterns of helping change with development: possibly our moral faculty is on a slowly maturing time course, as proposed by Maslow (1971). Alternatively, we may have a grammar of social norms, as argued by some sociologists. There is a disagreement over social rules at present. One school argues for an all-purpose inference engine. The other side maintains there are distinct principles and parameters in a taxonomy including moral, conventional permission and personal rules. Natural selection suggests the mind has specialized reasoning abilities for different problems such as social exchange and precautionary rules. There is some evidence in support of this from brain damaged patients. Hauser points out that theorizing on the topic goes all the way back to Aristotle who argued that our virtues arise from nature but are made perfect by habit. Similar thoughts were expressed by Hume: "Nature must furnish the materials and give us notion of moral distinctions." The human mind has some innate capabilities chimps, dolphins, and parrots do not. So there must be something about our DNA that causes these psychological differences and the acquisition of the unique signatures of our cultures. Hauser contends that the mind has evolved reasoning abilities for different problems and maintains that the way to resolve the dispute is to return to the model espoused by Aristotle, Hume, and Rawls: a general learning mechanism and a suite of principles.

3.9 Human Systems

Hauser's thought is that we have an instinctive moral system that operates in a way similar to the language system. Chomsky's (1957) theory of language posits that it depends on a complex adaptive system, which is put in place genetically as universal equipment, which enables the process of language acquisition to begin. We may think of this as computer hardware. In the early years of life, an operating system is laid down by our learning a set of parameters that encodes the grammatical rules for our particular language. The underlying universal grammar has to permit the wide variety of human languages. A baby can learn any one of the family of languages but new language acquisition becomes increasingly difficult as the person grows older. Hauser believes that there exists a universal "grammar" that underlies our moral system and that the codes for the various different moral cultures are laid down as sets of parameters which we learn in youthful instruction. He points out that these two are not the only complex adaptive systems we possess but that there are, in fact, countless biological processes that operate in the same way. The immune system works in principle in the same way. In our early years, the immune system is exposed to a suite of molecules, viruses, and bacteria that fill the environment in which we live; and the system develops antibodies to combat these particular threats. We also have universal aesthetic systems of symmetry in the visual arts and consonance in music. The moral intuitions that drive our judgments often conflict with the dictates of law and religion. This is especially the case in battles over euthanasia and abortion.

The evidence suggests that there were several emigrations of *Homo* from Africa, including ones by *H. erectus* and *H. neanderthalensis*. A recently published book by Matt Ridley (2010) is interesting from the point of view of the use of genetic information as well as Ridley's speculations. The central theme of the work is that *Homo sapiens* migration from Africa of five hundred thousand years ago resulted eventually in the elimination of the Neanderthals. The later Africans had learned many other skills as well as the value of barter with other tribes. This led to the use of materials, manufactures, ideas, and inventions from hundreds or thousands miles distant. They also had to deal with potentially hostile neighbors that demanded the use of fair play, a potential source for the development of good manners. Neanderthal sites, on the other hand, only used materials from less than a one-hundred-mile radius. Ridley argues that it was the great success of this strategy of peaceful coexistence that was the basis of the optimistic and rational outlook of the Africans.

It also appears that much of our sexual conduct owes its origins to evolutionary inheritance as argued compellingly by Geoffrey Miller (2000). Here there is evidence from the study of other living primates—orangs, gorillas, chimpanzees, and bonobos—as well as paleontological evidence from such fossils as Lucy and Ardi. Each of the great ape species has its own characteristic division of labor and sexual roles, and these patterns are preserved to this day. Women are the child minders and gatherers while men are the hunters, fighters, and barterers. Chimpanzees, orangs, and gorillas all treat their females as subordinates while it is only humans and bonobos who permit some measure of equality between the sexes. Possibly, it is the deep commitment of the woman to childbearing and rearing that leads to her greater need for reassurance from her mate.

3.10 Ethical Science and Psychology

Recollect that Hume believed that our morality was built on two foundations: instinct and experience. We come now to the subject of experience as a source of ethical behavior. In other words, we are now considering the modifications to human behavior after our emergence with full human capacities. Up to that point, we had lived as animals, guided by instinct alone. But once we emerged as humans, our enhanced cerebral capabilities came into play. Perhaps the most fundamental change we experienced was the improvement in our memories. We would have been able to record experiences and learn about successful strategies. It would have been necessary to recognize similarities in situations and the events leading up to them and the consequences of any actions we might have taken in dealing with them. Simple toolmaking would have fitted into this picture. Then, of course, we learned the value of using symbols in our thinking, and art and language would have developed. Each of these new abilities could be thought of as new ethics, e.g., use memory and knowledge, use symbols and language, recognize constancies and systems, and, use tools and stratagems. It seems so simple when cataloged in this way but realize that this was what Hume saw as the history of the human race and the experience of each individual person. It encompasses the vast panoply of psychological phenomena that have been studied since Hume first wrote his monumental Treatise. We will discuss psychological findings in greater detail in chapter 4, the central theme of which will be to emphasize that the most successful humans are those whose behavior is allowed to evolve and use the virtues that have been developed over the millennia. There are persuasive expositions of these psychological approaches in works by Maslow (1971) and Butler and Hope (1995) and in advocates of the sciences of virtue and happiness, and we will have to let this suffice for the moment.

Generations of teachers have influenced the shape of ethical beliefs, and the ethical codes themselves can be modified by the people who use and teach them. We can examine our lives using time-honored values. The instinctive morals we inherit can be overridden when necessary and new habits can be developed, which have all the moral imperative of instinctive rules. We can use our powers of reasoning to evaluate instinctive, as well as newly acquired morality. One way to do this is by using principles acquired from thinking and experience. Such principles include utilitarianism—as propounded by Hume, Bentham, and Mills—and Singer's concept of the expanding circle. We also have the ability to make plans that might extend over long periods.

3.11 Instinctive Ethics and Humanism

What can be learned from this discussion of instinctive ethics that is relevant to the humanism of the twenty-first century? The first lesson comes from remembering Wade's admonition that if the ethics and the ancestral religion of the hunter-gatherers can be included in their evolutionary heritage to us, then we should be able to identify their evolutionary advantage. Wade argued that this evolutionary advantage is easier to see for the ancestral religion than for its modern descendant. He documents how the religions of a number of ancient groups (the!Kung, the Andamanese, and the Australian aborigines) all express these traits and how their adherents enter a psychological state resembling hypnosis. His contention is that these ecstatic religions of music, dance, and trance serve to bind their adherents together in unison and promote a sense of common purpose. This common purpose is a clear evolutionary benefit even when the group becomes bent on the extermination of a neighboring tribe. Since the ancient groups shared ecstatic religion, he presumes that it was a defining characteristic of the common ancestor of all *Homo*. When people began to settle down and pursue agriculture for a living, their religion had to change to an orientation based on the annual cycle of planting and harvesting. The practice of religion became the province of shamans and priests who undertook to intercede with the gods and instruct the populace accordingly. This was when writing began to be used to record traditional narratives, liturgies, and moralities. Wade relates stories of the early Jews, Christians, and Muslims and the origins of their sacred scriptures. Religion became more complicated, but it still had the function of embodying the morality and sense of purpose of its membership.

The modern humanist might even take the viewpoint that humanism should supply a modern version of religion. But the problem then is that we have no reason to believe in the existence of gods or the supernatural. Of course, we might then opt for a religion without god or the supernatural, a position that was argued by Paul Kurtz at one time in one of his columns. Humanism could then be seen as an equivalent to religion. And it could be that some religions are evolving toward that very destination. The unitarians might be an example of such a development. However, there is another approach in which we take a secular academic stance. We could then ask ourselves what history tells us about our origins. We could then ask how we should behave in order to formulate a modern ethics. Finally, we have to peer into the future to see where we are going. We could thus benefit from the knowledge of what philosophers, scientists, and artists have written in answer to these questions. This is, in fact, the purpose of the remainder of this book. It is sad to see the way in which primitive people have lost their sense of purpose, overcome by alcoholism and despair when confronted by our modern juggernaut of a civilization. Perhaps we could help such groups. Perhaps we could see it as part of our purpose to extend a helping hand to those many of our own contemporaries who have fallen into confusion if not despair over the conflicting pulls of the modern world.

Although we claim that ethics is naturalistic, we have to explain that at the present time, there is only one agency we know of that can generate ethical systems, and that is the human being. We use our human emotions, instincts, and rationalities to invent new systems and then to evaluate and modify existing ones. Thus, we might just as well describe our ethics as being humanistic as being naturalistic. The humanist tradition is as old as naturalism; and recently, several authors have begun to explore the relationships between the two as, for example, Eller (2004), Carrier (2005), and Kurzweil (2005). Eller has adopted an anthropological approach in his book and appears to regard science as just one of various world views. Carrier explores the implications of the multiuniverse theories of physics but seems to neglect the vast technological changes that could be brought about in the time scales of the universe we live in. Finally, we must commend the remarkable work of Ray Kurzweil (2005) whose detailed procedures are based on knowledge of systems in general and medicine and technology in particular. Kurzweil's visions of the future may prove to be the most valuable to us. Advanced cultural systems are already with us, and we may anticipate the future advances they may bring. Robotic devices are likewise already being employed and may soon exceed human capabilities. They may be used to extend human lifespan and augment our abilities as cyborgs. These are some of the topics for chapters 9 and 10.

We are becoming increasingly adept at shaping our own evolution, both within the biological domain and in engineering, cultural, commercial, and political systems. Our actions may affect others directly and also indirectly via effects on the environment in which we all live. So we have to adopt an attitude of responsibility toward the world we live in. In fact, our responsibilities extend to nature as a whole or the universe in its entirety. This is an exciting time because we may get answers to the question of the existence of extraterrestrial life in the near future. We even may encounter other intelligent life-forms with evolved emotional and instinctive ethical systems. If and when this happens, the impact may be even more dramatic than it is depicted in science fiction, and we may have to learn rapidly how to live with other intelligent agencies.

4 Psychology and Neural Science

4.1 Methods and History

A Late-Developing Science
Introspection
Behaviorism
Theoretics
Neuroscience

4.2 Basic Mental Experience

Sensation
Perception
Memory
Instinct

4.3 Emotions and Motivation

Negative: Disgust, Hatred
Positive: Love, Compassion, Joy
Emotional Intelligence
Sex

4.4 Cognition and the Emergence of Humanity

Intelligence
Reasoning and Creativity
Personality

4.5 Communication, Language, and Death

Symbols
Origins of Language
Consciousness
Awareness of Death

4. Psychology and Neural Science

4.1 Methods and History

It is surprising that modern humans existed in their present genetic incarnation for hundreds of thousands of years before any systematic scientific study of the workings of their brains and associated behaviors got under way. This subject, psychology, is the background for the present chapter. Our memories, our present sensations, our emotions, our hopes, our knowledge, our powers of reasoning, our beliefs, our loves, our wills, our self-consciousness—these things are the stuff of our minds. These are the things that make us our selves. When I was a boy, I used to wonder what the world was like before I existed. What would it be like to sense directly the working of another mind? Robert Burns wrote: "Wad some Pow'r the giftie gie us to see oursels as others see us!" Josef Popper-Lynkeus once said that every time a man dies, a whole universe is destroyed. Kant put it that human beings are ends in themselves. Although my knowledge of my own mind is of necessity a private affair, I make the assumption that others have minds similar to mine so that it would be valuable to me to share the experience of others. What do we know of this amazing phenomenon of the mind? This is the subject whose methods and history we must remind ourselves about now.

Three hundred years ago, psychology, the study of the mind, was regarded as a branch of philosophy. Two thousand years ago, Aristotle thought that it was the heart that was the seat of cognition, and it was not until the time of Leonardo da Vinci that the idea appeared that it was, in fact, the brain that played that role. John Locke and David Hume speculated on the way in which sensation and perception were our window onto the external world. The first observations in psychology by Hume and others were based on introspection, and this was the leading method of the new subject until the nineteenth century. It was the work of the physiologist Weber and the physicist Fechner that established the logarithmic relationship between the perceived intensity of a sensation and the magnitude of its physical stimulus that first suggested that psychology might be treated as a branch of natural science. The beginning of psychology as an experimental science may be dated to 1879 with the founding of Wundt's laboratory at the University of Leipzig. One of Wundt's students was the American William James who wrote a celebrated review of the subject *Principles of Psychology* (1890). James Watson and B. F. Skinner led a new school of thought, behaviorism, which advocated restricting psychological study to externally viewed activity. Modern textbooks in general psychology owe much to James's work and may be consulted for the latest developments. I have relied upon two such volumes, namely, Norman Munn's *Introduction to Psychology* (1956) and Henry Gleitman's *Psychology* (1986).

4.2 Basic Mental Experience

Wundt's school was characterized by the use of experimental introspection, the attempt to provide a description of the structure of consciousness through observation of mental experience in process. Wundt concentrated on sensations, perceptions, and motor reactions to stimuli. The first work on memory, by Ebbinghaus, required that learners repeat verses and nonsense syllables. This then was an observation of behavior rather than an introspection. Experiments with animals and children were obviously limited to observations on behavior; and around 1920, there arose a school, chiefly associated with James Watson, called behaviorism, which eschewed any information from introspection.

Another important school in the history of psychology was started by Sigmund Freud, whose methods of treating the neurotic were known as psychoanalysis. From the use of hypnosis, Feud discovered that behavior could be influenced by events, desires, and fears of which patients might be unconscious when awake. He found that childhood experiences could be particularly influential in this regard, and he placed a heavy emphasis on repressed memories and desires of sexual experience. Not all psychoanalysts agree with this emphasis and instead see importance in any form of childhood frustration and insecurity. Freud formulated a theory of the mind according to which there are three important systems: the id, the most primitive part of the mind and the earliest to appear in childhood; the ego, which reconciles the drives of the id with external reality; and finally the superego, the voice of conscience that represents the commands of parents and society.

Our human brains entail such functions as sensation, perception, memory, and instinct, which date to our remote evolutionary past and are consequently said to comprise our lizard brain. The mind is constantly bombarded with information from the senses (sight, hearing, taste, smell, and the tactile senses of pressure and heat together with the sense of muscular tension and movement). Work on the detailed understanding of the mechanisms whereby physical stimuli give rise to sensations and then perceptions is still proceeding. There is a well-known passage in which Russell describes the many various presentations that could be afforded by a physical object such as a table. All these have to be recognized as belonging to the particular object, which may be just one of a multitude of different types of table. The continuous stream of data has to be sorted into symbolic representations by the perceptual mechanisms of the mind. The realization of the extent of this preprocessing or pattern recognition was one of the early achievements of experimental psychology. The same challenges are confronted in the design of robotic vision. Chomsky has described the problems of understanding speech containing ambiguous sentences. Popper has stressed that perception is "theory soaked" by which he might have meant such theories as this set of sensations are caused by a dangerous predator. The mechanisms of the lizard brain have been understood by psychologists for some time in terms of action potentials.

On the other hand, the operations of memory as well as its mechanisms are still challenges to psychology. We have short -and long-term memories. Some people have eidetic or photographic memories. Unpleasant memories may be repressed or temporarily forgotten. There is evidence that memories are forgotten more readily with the presence of interfering activity. One of the major challenges to physiologists is to explain these various well-known aspects of memory. It seems clear that there has to be some form of "trace" or "neurogram" left in the brain after a mental event. Speech and language may be involved in the process. However, even without language, children and animals evidence memory by the repetition of motor performances or by relearning of habits with a saving in time. The most promising theories of memory involve concepts of signal processing and microbiology.

We have discussed the role of instinct in the previous chapter where we emphasized that much of our behavior is essentially the same as in our animal cousins. When our survival is threatened, for instance, by deprivation of oxygen in suffocation or drowning, all thoughts are driven from the mind but the primitive urge to breathe. Other life-threatening situations provoke similar reactions. In terms of urgency, our next priorities seem to be procuring food and shelter. Then come the sexual drives and other emotions such as the love of mother and child. Instinctive behavior patterns not only involve sensations and emotions, they also embody responses so that they may be regarded as being feedback loops. As we remarked earlier, the fact that these instincts comprise a foundation for human behavior was not lost on Darwin, who believed that this was consistent with evolution having built on previously existing structures.

4.3 Emotions and Motivation

Animals, including humans, are driven to action by what is called motivation. Gleitman (1986) devotes a whole chapter on this subject. We have already mentioned that the most primitive and basic motivations are those concerned with breathing, feeding, survival, shelter, sex, care of the young, sleep, etc. These motivations also serve to direct our behavior toward specific goals. The motivations are caused physically by electropotentials. We are able to sense our motivations, and the experience is then said to be an emotion. In addition to the instinctive motivations already mentioned, which are felt by individual humans, there are other cultural motivations we acquire by virtue of our being members of a social species. In this class, Munn (1956) lists gregariousness, the tendency to imitate, and the tendency to appeal to stronger individuals when our own resources are inadequate. Some of these motives may arise from the extreme dependency of the human infant. Another motivation may be the desire to communicate. And there are motivations that vary with the particular society in which the individual lives. In most societies, there is an emphasis on achievement, self-assertion, and mastery. Another motivation common in some societies is aggressiveness.

Most personal goals appear to be rooted in cultural motivation (education at home and at school, in economic and religious institutions), but there is a wide variety of individual variation that perhaps depends on the relative balance of influence in our lives from different people and groups. Furthermore, these influences are assimilated in different ways and assessed differently by each individual in accordance with his or her own aptitudes. For example, there may be a number of influences that cause us to choose a particular career. Consider the astute Dale Carnegie (1936) in his book *How to Win Friends and Influence People*. To the primitive motivations already mentioned, Carnegie adds that every normal adult wants money and the things that money will buy: life in the hereafter, the well-being of their children, and a feeling of importance. As time goes by, the relative balance of personal motivation usually changes. Interests and attitudes are determined by the state of our motivation.

Emotions are states of mind that reflect our motivations. Munn (1956) proposes that there is a continuum of emotional states in the mind comprising a relatively low-level background or mood associated with everything we do and a number of high-level peaks that constitute the recognized emotions, such as fear, disgust, anger, jealousy, sympathy, joy, elation, affection, and love. The emotions may be divided into the pleasant and the unpleasant, and human motivation consists of seeking pleasure and avoiding the unpleasant.

Our sexual urges are one of our strongest drivers. They are also very ancient, having started their evolutionary development before the differentiation between plants and animals. Sexual reproduction has significant advantages over the asexual variety. The apes show a variety of strategies in conjugal life. Orangs and gorillas show a sexual dimorphism with alpha males cast in the leading role. Chimpanzees, bonobos, and humans are much closer in size although only the bonobos seem to use sex for multipurpose social interactions. The female bonobo is frequently a social leader. Homosexuality also seems to predate the evolutionary separations. The invention of language and various cultural enhancements have served to improve our sexual repertoire, but the basic sexual strategy of the species does not seem to have changed significantly with our having become human. Many of the differences in personality between men and women can be traced to the greater commitment to childbirth and rearing on the part of the woman. Since these traits are a part of the female's instinctive legacy, it is clearly not feasible to try to override them by fiat. We discuss these issues more fully in chapter 12.

4.4 Cognition and the Emergence of Humanity

After the appearance of *Australopithecus*, the evolution of the hominid line was marked by increasing intelligence, reasoning, and creativity. Paleoanthropologists classify these advanced creatures as hominins and regard them as the first humans or the vanguard of humanity. Munn defined intelligence as the ability to learn and to utilize what has been learned in adjusting to new situations and solving new problems. In this sense, even earthworms have intelligence in that they can be trained to take one branch of a T-shaped maze. It is interesting that there is considerable variation in the length of time taken by different animals to learn the correct path, so it may be said that some earthworms are more intelligent than others. Rats are clearly more intelligent than earthworms since much more complicated mazes can be used to demonstrate their abilities. Humans are not significantly better than rats in learning to run mazes by trial and error. Human intelligence clearly excels, however, in our ability to invent symbols and use them to reason and verbalize. Many tests to demonstrate this ability in humans have been devised and have been shown to produce a wide spread in abilities among test subjects. Suffice it to say that the ability of humans to think is clearly superior to that of animals, varies among individuals, and can be measured to some degree by standard tests.

The term *stream of consciousness* was invented to describe the constant mental activity in the waking brain. In common parlance, we might simply call it cognition or thinking. There seems to be an analogy between thinking and the processes of visualization in which colors are perceived over and above light intensity (or brightness). In the analogy, there is a level of thought perceived as pure logic underlying emotional content. It is hard to say that thinking is ever completely free of emotional content since we may still call up an emotional response when "checking" logical analysis by using more than one line of analysis to arrive at a final conclusion. There are several types of cognitive activity that fall under the general heading of thinking. Firstly, there is the recollection or recall of past events. Then there is the state in which we allow the thoughts to run freely from one to another in a reverie or free association. Fantasies or daydreams are mental constructions whereby we see in imagination the fulfillment of wishes. Sometimes these arise from the subconscious and are similar to the dreaming of the sleeping mind. The last activity is reasoning, which we define as the process of manipulation of symbols so as to find realistic solutions to problems. Reasoning ability has been demonstrated in rats, monkeys, chimpanzees, and other animals. Munn states that three things are necessary for reasoning: retention, recall, and recombination of what is recalled. He remarks that so-called thinking machines (of the 1950s) have such processes built into them, but he adds that their computing is dependent upon a detailed programming of routines to be followed.

When faced with a new problem, we form inferences or hypotheses about its cause or nature based on our prior knowledge or experience. We then evaluate the inferences using further thought or by testing them in the actual world. Our initial inferences are often limited by the associations determined by the manner in which the problem is posed. Sometimes we become set on one particular inference and need to take deliberate steps to approach the problem from "another angle."

Much human thought involves subvocal talking or other forms of kinesthetic activity, but it has been shown that thinking still proceeds even during complete paralysis. People who have been deaf and dumb since birth show that they can still think. Part of the reasoning process involves conceptualization, i.e., the "discrimination of common properties of different objects." Beyond this, there is the process of generalization and symbolic representation. Higher phases of the reasoning process involve the use of grammar and logic, i.e., the meaningful manipulation of symbols.

We may define personality as the most characteristic integration of an individual's mind and behavior, especially from the standpoint of adjustment in social situations. There is disagreement among psychologists as to how to approach the assessment of personality. Some advocate the measurement of so-called personality traits. However, there is no general agreement on which traits should be selected. One study, by Thurstone, determined that there are seven primary personality traits: general activity or drive, masculinity-femininity, impulsiveness, dominance-submission, emotional stability, sociability, and reflectiveness. Certain aspects of the personality contribute most heavily to the way in which others see us, namely, how well we get along with others, how susceptible we are to irritation by what others say and do, how we dress, our manners, and how our behavior is measured to be moral or good. There are a number of tests that attempt to measure personality traits, with results being presented in the form of a profile.

There are a number of classifications of people into simple categories. For instance, Jung invented the designations "introvert" and "extrovert." Another classification divided people according to body build (endomorphs, mesomorphs, ectomorphs, and normal). Such schemes appear to be oversimplifications and not very useful. Another approach to assessing personality involves holistic testing in which the entire personality is evaluated at the same time. This might be necessary in selecting a job applicant or selecting service personnel for specific assignments. The evaluation might be in the form an interview or of some sort of test such as the ink-blot test devised by Rorschach. But most of the personality traits mentioned above are superficial. Freud did much to make it clear that there are deeper factors in personality which are based on underlying urges, desires, and aspirations. He described the personality of the individual in terms of the three systems: the id, the ego, and the superego. The id comprises the primitive instinctive urges. According to Freud, the id "contains everything that is inherited, that is present at birth, that is fixed in the constitution." As a child grows, he begins to learn to modify the biological urges to conform with the demands of his environment. Freud says the ego arises to act as an intermediary between the id and the external world. Eventually, there is added the superego, or conscience, which consists of the moral or ethical precepts passed down to us by our parents. It has been maintained that we all have multiple personalities to some extent. But psychotics and those with severe cases of multiple personalities, including schizophrenics, have extreme personality disorders with physiological causes. Such people require medication and/or psychotherapy.

4.5 Communication, Language, and Death

Most animals communicate, but it is only among humans that there is an extensive use of symbolic communication or language. Beyond the reception of sensory data and the perceptual organization of this data, there appears to be a process in the mind whereby symbols are assigned to the various batches of data. Various sounds or inscriptions, since they occur in the physical world, are available to other humans. If the processes of symbolic representation are similar in the minds of different individuals (as seems reasonable), then they may be used to transfer thoughts from one to another. This ability has obviously enabled us to pass on knowledge of the physical and man-made worlds that individuals could not possibly acquire by themselves in their own lifetimes. The acquisition of oral and written language skills is essential to children's development. The way in which we see the world may be enhanced by the use of language. For example, in the realm of ethics, we may recognize that certain complexes of motives, emotions, and actions could be designated by words. Thus emotions, which are essentially in the private domain of an individual, could become associated with an objective and social measure we designate as a value. It has been argued that one's very concept of the self is, in fact, something that depends upon language, i.e., that consciousness itself is something learned. It might be argued that our awareness of the approach of death would also be heightened by consciousness of our spoken language and interaction with others. This, in turn, might have led us into fearful apprehension of the hereafter and acceptance of religious narratives promising deliverance from the unknown.

4.6 Learning

We argued in the previous chapter that at least some of our behavior is instinctive and automatic. So much has been made of the recent work by Hauser and Harris to uncover the instinctive nature of morality that it is important to realize that not all our repertoire is inherited in this way. Some of the most dramatic evidence of just how inhuman we can be is provided by the remarkable stories of children raised by animals and of children raised in isolation, without normal learning in human environments. There are accounts of both varieties given by Gleitman (1986).

There are some thirty to forty stories of wild children of which the best known were Kamala and Amala who were found in a wolf den in 1920. Kamala was about eight, and Amala was only one and one-half. They were thoroughly wolfish in appearance and behavior. Hard calluses had developed on their knees and palms from going on all fours. Eating and drinking were accomplished by lowering their mouths to the plate. They ate raw meat. At night they prowled and sometimes howled. They had no speech.

In 1976 another young boy was discovered in India who also appears to have been raised by wolves. He was named Ramu, and Gleitman (1986) has photos of him. Again, he was deformed and could not walk. He had no speech, and his favorite food was raw meat. He eventually learned to bathe and dress himself but never learned to speak. He died in 1985. Gleitman also recounts cases of children raised in almost unimaginable isolation by parents who were either vicious or deranged.

The retardation of these children was severe, and depending on their ages when rescued, they could not always be rehabilitated.

Gleitman also gives an account of the scientific studies of learning. Pavlov was the first to realize that new modes of behavior can be acquired through conditioning of reflexes. Pavlov believed that habits are nothing but a long chain of conditioned reflexes. Such habitual behavior as walking, talking, writing, and numerous personal and professional skills free the higher parts of the mind from conscious attention to certain stimuli. Studies of the learning process emphasize the importance of motivation with incentives, reinforcement, and optimum timing. In summary, Gleitman states that the simplest of all forms of learning is habituation.

The other form of learning at which we humans excel is the cognitive variety. This refers to the information coming from our senses (sight, hearing, taste and smell, touch, and kinesthetic feeling) and our inbuilt ways of interpreting the world called common sense, our interactions with other people assuming they have minds like our own as well as motives similar to ours. Finally, we have the ability to perform original analysis and synthesis. Creative thinking might be defined as the formation of totally original hypotheses or works by people such as artists, scientists, or inventors. Analysis of creative thinking by the thinkers themselves and by others has led to the conclusion that there are four stages in the process: (1) preparation, or the gathering of relevant information; (2) incubation or a period of relative inactivity; (3) inspiration or a relatively sudden insight or illumination; and (4) verification or the testing of the new idea. We build on these observations and assumptions to interpret the world around us and guide our own behavior. Collectively, we have developed a vast store of knowledge of the universe and our own environment in an increasingly sophisticated way, which is said to be scientific. We will discuss this important part of the modern world in greater detail in later chapters. The development of scientific theories and knowledge is paralleled by the work of artists, poets, and novelists who create the scenes, stories, and images of the fictional worlds of film and literature. We will expand on these hugely important works of both fiction and nonfiction in later chapters.

4.7 Volition

One clear distinction between computers of the 1950s and human beings is that the computers performed only as programmed by a human being whereas human beings have a will or volition of their own, i.e., they select their own course of action without the intervention of any externally controlling agent. This aspect of the human mind is mentioned variously by different psychologists. James, for instance, discusses volition at some length and is at pains to show that possible courses of action as they are reviewed mentally are rehearsals of movements based on kinesthetic memories. Robots or automata, on the other hand, are built with simple motivations, which may then be regarded as equivalent to the human volition. Dennett (2004) has a discussion of free will and concludes that we do have volition although it is operated by means of choice. Other writers see the will as a superego moderating the conflicting desires of the persona and devolving on the action to be taken. James writes of the fiat, i.e., the final resolution to pursue a given course, which sets in motion the motor nerves, and in turn, the muscles. We will return later to the question of whether it would be possible to build a computer with a will and the related issue of whether will is truly free of external constraint or whether our behavior is in some way predetermined. James reviews other interesting issues, such as the difference between impulsive and deliberate decision making and the feeling of effort that may be involved in exercise of the will. These phenomena are not discussed very much nowadays, but I believe them to be real and worth more attention. It is important to realize how much we live in worlds created by human volition as it is exercised in politics and law, arts, engineering, and technology and just everyday life.

4.8 Developmental Psychology

Psychologists have devoted much effort to studying the development of children. Many interesting questions have been illuminated in this way. The issue of nature versus nurture, i.e., the relative importance of genetic versus environmental influences on the mind can be evaluated from studies of identical twins. It has been clearly established that babies need affection and stimulation for healthy development. This has been clearly demonstrated by the horrific accounts of the results of isolation of babies in orphanages in Romania and other places. Children seem to start from a single type of emotion, one of generalized excitement. A distinguishable emotion associated with unpleasantness comes later, as do distinguishably pleasant emotions. We have learned that emotional trauma in childhood can leave profound mental scars for life. Personality traits seem to grow as the child matures. There are definite stages in the acquisition of language and the other habits necessary for successful growth. The influence of social pressure to conform to the peer group seems to be greater during childhood than during any other stage of life. Then there come the enormous mental consequences of adolescence.

We spend a great portion of our lives in the process of change. Shakespeare speaks of the seven ages of man: the infant, the schoolboy, the lover, the soldier, the justice, the old man, and the dotard. Fromm (1947) pointed out that ethics can be a potent force in the lives of individuals. Such periods of life have been the subject of study by Daniel Levinson (1978), who points out that there is a transition between each period that can be a time of crisis and emotional upheaval as the individual seeks to realign his or her priorities and goals. Kohlberg (1981) made one of the most detailed studies of ethical development in the psychology of individuals. Maslow (1971) showed how the ethics of the individual tend to become increasingly sophisticated and selfless as people grow in experience. Singer (1981) proposed that the ethical development of the individual results in an expanding circle of social concern, which he believes should include animals. Most psychologists regard death as the final stage in the life cycle; and several humanists including, notably, Corliss Lamont (1990), have elaborated on this. We will return to the topic in chapter 8.

4.9 Under the Skull: Neuroscience

In the same way that we can drive an automobile without understanding how the engine works, we can live our lives without understanding the brain. But we know now that ongoing work is changing our conception of how the brain functions and holds great promise for the treatment of mental disorders. It may be now that the fastest ethical progress will be made in the area of brain physiology. The challenge is then be to provide explanatory mechanisms for the established findings of the psychologists. This effort is bringing us to grips with issues of practical as well as profound philosophical importance. How do sleep and consciousness work? What is the nature of the qualia (colors, sounds, smells, pains, emotions, etc) that flood our minds? We know that our ability to ask questions is fundamental to our research programs, but what, after all, is a question?

From the time of Locke, Hume, and Kant, ethical philosophers all made presumptions about the way in which the brain (mind) dealt with sensations, emotions, and feelings. How does the brain work to give us a picture of the world around us? The study of the mind and behavior can proceed independently of the issue of the relationship to physiology and hence to chemistry and physics. In fact, the two subjects of psychology and brain physiology have proceeded on somewhat independent paths, pursued by workers in different disciplines. The physiological connections of the mind are not obvious. As we have already mentioned, Aristotle believed that the heart was the seat of human thought and emotions. Leonardo da Vinci believed the brain to have that role, and Vesalius in 1543 published a book describing the nervous system as comprising the brain, the spinal cord, and the peripheral nerves. The first accurate description of the brain's physiology was given by Willis and illustrated by Sir Christopher Wren. Since that time, evidence has been accumulating to link various parts of the brain to specific functions of the mind. Accounts of the status of brain research have been given by Restak (1984), Popper and Eccles (1977), and Churchland (1986). The reader may wish to remind him- or herself of the main features of the brain: the lizard brain (cerebellum, amygdala, hippocampus, and thalamus) and the two hemispheres of the cerebrum (frontal, precentral, and parietal regions).

In the late eighteenth century came the discovery by Galvani of the involvement of electricity in the action of the nerves. It was at the beginning of the twentieth century that Santiago Ramon y Cajal was responsible for the first accurate representation of the histology of brain cells or neurons. He found that each cell comprised a body containing the nucleus, a long fiber called the axon, and a large number of fibers called dendrites, which extend toward other cells. At the end of each dendrite, there is a small gap to the dendrite of the next cell. These gaps are called synapses. There are between ten billion and one hundred billion neurons in the human brain, each with over a thousand synapses and in some cases approaching two hundred thousand. We have learned that the synapse itself has an important influence on the transmission of nerve impulses. In 1921 Loewi performed some experiments on frogs, which showed that the impulse was conducted across the gap by a chemical known as a neurotransmitter. Acetylcholine and adrenaline were two of these, and Loewi found that they could slow down and speed up heart rate respectively. Since that time, it has been found that there are at least sixty such neurotransmitters.

4.10 Artificial Intelligence

Whether or not we will be able to build machines with intelligence is one of the great questions of our age. The debate over whether machines can be equipped with minds ranges such great intellects as Turing, who believed that we will be able to construct such machines against Karl Popper who believed that if we ever do succeed in that endeavor, we will need to create life first. There is a long way to go, from the standpoint of the objective science of world one, in explaining the phenomenon of mind in terms of the functioning of the brain.

Popper and Eccles (1977) have explored the relationship between mind and brain in their book *The Self and Its Brain*. In the early chapters of the book, Popper outlines some of the variations of what he calls physicalism. He defines this as the belief that the theories of physics will eventually provide an explanation for all the phenomena observed by humans. Extreme or radical physicalists, who include Quine, according to Popper, are inclined to deny the very existence of the phenomenon of mind. Since Quine was regarded as a leader by many professional philosophers, Popper took some trouble to dispute his position. He viewed Quine as being as extreme a physicalist as Bishop Berkeley was an extreme idealist, who argued that the physical world consisted of mental constructions. Popper's refutation of the physicalist position, as I understand it, is similar to the argument for rejecting Berkeley's idealism. It is simply mind-boggling to think that one has invented the whole world. Similarly, it is unbelievable that every action one takes and that every other human takes, or has taken or will take, not to mention the whole evolutionary history of the rest of the universe and every creature in it can all be traced back through long chains of cause and effect to a set of initial conditions at the time of the big bang, or at least some instant in the remote past. It seems simpler to suppose that that the actions we take result from our own volition.

Popper and Eccles advanced a viewpoint they term interactionism, i.e., a belief that worlds one, two, and three interact with one another. The implication is that physical processes at work in the brain influence the mind but do not wholly determine its workings. The mind is seen as the cause of certain physical effects in the brain. These are then the starting points for finite "downward" chains of causation, which provide simple explanations for our actions.

4.11 Behavioral Choices

Perhaps psychologists have paid more attention to the mentally ill than the mentally healthy. What is to be found in the works of respected psychologists for the guidance of lay people is frequently rather brief. There is, however, a large body of literature, which might be described as "self-improvement." Perhaps the first of this genre was Samuel Smiles's *Self Help*. (1859) Smiles saw the key to success in education, and he cited a number of people who raised themselves by self-education. Shaffer and Shoben in *The Psychology of Adjustment* offer the following principles of mental health: good physical health, accepting yourself, accepting other people, maintaining a confidential relationship with someone with whom you can discuss your problems, assuming a positive attitude toward difficulties, participating in social activities, finding a satisfactory line of work, finding enjoyment in creative undertakings, and using the scientific approach to the solution of personal problems. A very practical book with psychological insights is Mursell's *How to Make and Break Habits* (1953). The basic premise is that habituation is the machinery of living. We need to understand our habits, which have histories. He discusses habits of anger, fear, eating, and drinking alcohol. Habits can be in conflict and can grow and spread. We can develop habits in dealing with people. Mursell suggests methods for studying habits and how to control them for effective living. He contends that friendship should be seen as a business we need to work at by maintaining correspondence, visiting and caring. We need to be on the lookout for friends and to learn to trust people. Mursell summarizes his advice by recommending development of the following habits: (1) reflection about one's own intimate personal problems, especially of impulsiveness and feelings that seem beyond the range of reason; (2) acting intelligently and according to plan especially where one is inclined to impulsiveness due to unthinking emotion; (3) exchange of psychological reassurances with others (4) giving service to some cause, institution, or group; (5) and pursuing interests such as hobbies, studies or recreations.

4.12 Managing the Mind

Fig. 3 is a flowchart for a behavioral control system or what might be labeled "managing the mind." We should think of this as an illustration of the method by which an individual person controls his or her interactions with the world. It is in effect a feedback loop containing both what are called morals (in the feed forward mode) and ethical evaluations (in the return mode). There are a number of interesting corollaries of the picture. Firstly, we might note that some of the boxes in the diagram represent mental processes such as reasoning, decision making, evaluation, memory, and the individual's situation as he or she perceives it. His motivation, as also represented in the flowchart, stands for the various psychological drives he experiences. Some other boxes represent events or features in the individual's external environment, including actions, the consequences of those actions and external aids to memory such as records, notes, and books. Other influences on behavior such as instincts, emotions, knowledge, and information may be brought to bear on the process and are represented by inputs as shown. These inputs may arise from within the person's own brain or be partly external in their origin. Finally, there are inputs such as morals, habits, objectives, promises, pragmatics, and ethics all of which the agent has committed him- or herself to from time to time and which are mainly internal as regards their influences on the ethological system. Some modern clinicians such as Butler and Hope (1995) have started to emphasize management concepts.

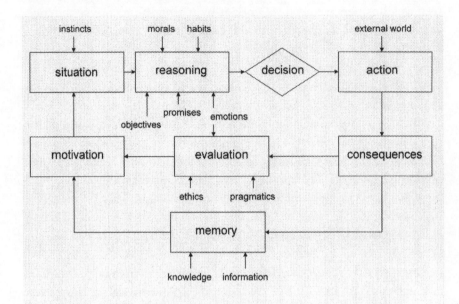

Fig.3 : Flow Chart for a Behavioral Control System

Figure 3 illustrates the process of learning. Some of the inputs may have been developed by multiple repetitions of the thinking process, perhaps extending over many years, perhaps even a lifetime. Of course, we know that human mental activity really takes place over vast assemblies of neurons and synapses, and we have to use our knowledge of equivalent circuits from electrical engineering to justify this representation of these huge collections of components as "black boxes." Parts of the pathways we would describe as logical or rational and other parts would be emotional or affectional, and it might be very difficult to separate them out. Figure 3 is clearly a simplification of the actual mental process, and the branch of knowledge that deals with it is called neurophysiology.

Let us illustrate the use of this depiction by looking again into the old question of subjective and objective processes, where *subjective* means of, affected by, or produced by the mind and *objective* means independent of the mind. Subjective processes are therefore something resulting from the feelings or temperament of a single subject or thinking person. Objects and objective processes, on the other hand, can be observed by more than one person. The question of whether ethology is subjective or objective has become an extension of the issue of theist versus atheist morality, through the claim that ethics and morality are absolute (and not man-made). Barnhart (2005) has written of morality having both subjective and objective poles. To clarify matters in figure 3, we have divided the boxes of our ethological system into those that are subjective, i.e., occurring in the mind or, in other words, in the brain or under the skull, and those that occur in the external world, which are objective. To be consistent with what Epicurus, Hume, and the Utilitarians taught us, the processes of evaluation, which depend on comparison with emotions, have to be events that happen in the head. Mackie (1977) presented the clearest exposition of the subjective-versus-objective debate and was adamant that ethics should be evaluated emotionally. Evaluation is then a subjective process. But the results of evaluation can be transmitted to the external world through speech or sound or by gesture and/or recorded by external devices such as books or film and thus can be accessed by other people *and are objective*. In this way, ethology (both morals and ethics) can be discussed by the whole community. This is the viewpoint first expressed by Sidgwick (1874) in the nineteenth century and more recently by Habermas (see Finlayson, 2005). The ethological systems, which are developed by a community are, what we have called values (see chapter 5), where we point out that values are considered basic to sociology.

4.13 Contributions from Electrical Engineering: Pattern Recognition

One of the most prolific of the electrical engineers contributing to neuroscience is Ray Kurzweil. Kurzweil's first book, *The Age of Intelligent Machines*, was published in 1990. The nonfiction work discusses the history of computer AI and also makes forecasts regarding future developments. Other experts in the field of AI contribute heavily to the work in the form of essays. Next, Kurzweil published a book on nutrition in 1993 called *The 10% Solution for a Healthy Life*. In 1999, Kurzweil published *The Age of Spiritual Machines*, which focuses heavily on further elucidating his theories regarding the future of technology, which themselves stem from his analysis of long-term trends in biological and technological evolution. Much focus goes into examining the likely course of AI development, along with the future of computer architecture. *The Singularity Is Near* was published in 2005. The book was made into a movie starring Pauley Perrette.

Kurzweil has some very important engineering accomplishments to his name. The first of these was his development of an optical text reader. He started a company in 1973 called Kurzweil Computer Products, now known as Nuance Speech Technologies, which eventually mastered the recognition of printed characters. The company spent years training a set of research computers to recognize printed letters, but after forty years, the evolved patterns can be downloaded in the form of software. By connecting this machine to a speech pronunciation device, he developed the first machine for reading to the blind. In the 1980s, Nuance started work on speech recognition and developed a system known as Siri, which is now seeing service as an assistant to the iPhone. In his book, Kurzweil relates the tribulations of his speech recognition efforts. It should be noted that at the time he started, speech recognition was still considered to be a remote and difficult objective. He began by using the standard acoustical engineering approach of making a spectral analysis and attempting to compare the results with a template of phonemes. The outcome was only partially successful. However, there was a breakthrough when the company incorporated Markov modeling in their program. This is a technique in which the program is "trained" as if there were a filter available with the actual response of a human ear. The filter is constructed by adjusting the unknown response to duplicate a series of known speech samples.

Kurzweil's several books pointed out that there has been such rapid growth in the complexity of computers and such progress in their miniaturization that by 2040 we might expect a PC to be able to duplicate the computational capacity of the human brain. In the latest work, Kurzweil explains how simple neural nets can serve as pattern recognition devices, i.e., as circuits capable of taking inputs from a system and either accepting or rejecting those inputs as having originated from a specific system. As examples of such systems, he cites printed-type written letters, particular phonemes (sounds), or human faces. He explains further that patterns might be grouped together to make more complex patterns and that whole hierarchies of patterns might be recognized. The human brain has evolved by wrapping the lizard brain in a crumpled sheet of neurons, thus comprising the neocortex. It was the American neuroscientist Vernon Mountcastle who in 1957 discovered that the cortex was comprised throughout of the same "Lego block" basic elements. Kurzweil is proposing that these elements are pattern recognizers. His research suggests that these pattern recognizers each contain about one hundred neurons. Thus, the human neocortex, which is just six layers thick, contains some thirty to fifty million repetitions of the same basic structure. According to this theory, our memories are stored using these pattern recognizers and our superior intelligence comes from our abilities to recognize the patterns. Memories are stored using sequences of patterns. We need to read the sequences in the correct order if we are to recall a memory correctly. We learn the alphabet from A to Z and find it difficult to recite it backward without first writing it down. We need to embed events in stories to remember them exactly. The patterns or systems are recursive, i.e., they can be fitted together to make new patterns and then the new patterns can be built up to make yet further patterns in hierarchical structures. A pattern may be recognized even when parts of it are missing, which is often referred to as autoassociation. A pattern may still be recognized even when some feature(s) of it are transformed, which is referred to as feature invariance.

4.14 Artificial Neural Nets

One of the attractions of Kurzweil's approach is his references to "patterns." The introduction to Kurweil's book is virtually a synopsis of systems theory. There is a vital aspect of human thinking concerned with the recognition of constancies, which seems to have first been commented on by Hume (1777). We define associations of constant elements to be "systems" as pointed out by Anatol Rapoport (1986). Thus, we came to recognize the laws of physics by their constant effects in similar situations. We also apply the same methods in dealing with recurrent situations of interest in our personal lives, and we call these situations and the techniques for dealing with them artificial systems. Now the crucial test of this pattern recognition theory comes with the construction of computers having ever-increasing capacity for pattern recognition. Thus, Deep Blue—the computer that defeated Garry Kasparov, the world chess champion, in 1997—was capable of analyzing two hundred million board positions every second. Humans (Garry Kasparovs at any rate) are therefore able to match this performance after training in pattern recognition. The ultimate objective of psychology is to understand how the brain works, that is, to explain on the basis of physics and chemistry, how the brain functions to produce the mind. How are we able to see and hear and to have experiences such as hunger, fear, lust, and love? How are we able to think, talk, read, and conceive of plans of action? Why do we need to sleep and experience altered states such as hypnosis? There have been a number of books published on neuroscience recently, and for a good overview, I recommend *Human: The Science Behind What Makes Us Unique* by Michael S. Gazzaniga (2008). Gazzaniga mentions some work by Jeff Hawkins, an electrical engineer well-known for his invention of the Palm Pilot. In collaboration with Sandra Blakeslee, Hawkins published a book titled *On Intelligence* (2004), which introduces us to the burgeoning field of artificial neural networks. This was followed by Ray Kurzweil's *How to Create a Mind* (2012), which goes beyond Hawkins's claims with a complete theory of how the brain works, followed by descriptions of plans to build computers that will be able to simulate human thinking.

Kurzweil points out that the evolution of the neocortex has enabled us to vastly speed up the learning process. In the future, we can speed up further the learning process by turning to nonbiological intelligence. Doctoral student David Dalrymple at Harvard is planning a simulation of the brain of a nematode (roundworm). This consists of about three hundred neurons. It will be tested as a virtual nematode in a virtual world. Henry Markram, a Swiss neuroscientist, is running a project called Blue Brain, which will simulate a complete rat brain in 2014 and a complete human brain by 2023.

4.15 Systems Theory

In an earlier essay (Finch, 1992), I proposed that ethics and morality can be described in terms of systems. One of the first artificial systems to be invented was toolmaking such as the shaping of flints and other stones for use in knife blades, spears, and arrowheads. *Homo sapiens* in Africa is credited with the development of the spear thrower, which made the hunting of large game a much safer process for the hunter. Speech may have advanced as an aid to coordination during hunting. Trade may have begun as humans developed "theories of mind," enabling them to realize that other members of the species, even strangers, could share similar needs and wants. Thus, one group might have been able to barter for stone, such as obsidian, uncommon in their native area. Once it had begun to flourish, speech could have been used for many purposes, including storytelling, thus opening up a method of transmitting information over time and space. This ability would have complemented the human improvement in memory. In its turn, memory was the necessary prerequisite to recognize constancies.

Popper invented the term "world three" for the man-made or "artificial" realm of culture, language, artifacts, theories, values, knowledge, industries and companies, religions, and cosmologies such as humanism and naturalism. All these things have been of interest to thinkers since the start of civilization, but it was not until the time of Charles Darwin and Herbert Spencer that it was realized that they all evolve. They are all created by human beings in the process of living. Simon (1969) referred to them as the sciences of the artificial in his discussion of systems theory. In everyday speech, the term *artificial* is sometimes used as a synonym for *unnatural*, and we must contradict this impression to make the point that all the man-made systems are as much a part of the natural world as the humans who created them. Many of the man-made systems have lives that are much longer than those of their human inventors and participants. They may serve to immortalize their founders and members and influence the lives of subsequent generations.

4.16 Consciousness and Free Will

Kurzweil has some good sections on perennial philosophical topics. One such is consciousness. How can we explain consciousness on a scientific or naturalistic basis? Every night, when we go to sleep, we lose consciousness until waking again. Of course, we may dream and then we exist in another mental state, experiencing undirected thoughts, but this state is also hard to understand. When we die, again we lose consciousness and so revert to our condition before birth. Kurzweil discusses all this and the related issue of explaining "qualia"—that is to say the fabric of our mental experiences, such as colors and sounds. Certainly, there are some natural correlates of colors: red is associated with the six thousand angstrom wavelength of electromagnetic radiation, but we still cannot explain why that wavelength should be red and not, say, blue. There is a somewhat similar problem with our understanding of volition. This problem came about following our grasping the law of cause and effect. This law is the finding that every happening and event was the result of a cause. If everything was due to something else, then it seemed that there was no room for us to have started anything. Dennett has a good exposition on this, and indeed, Kurzweil does refer to Dennett, but he also summarizes some arguments by Stephen Wolfram in a book titled *A New Kind of Science* (2002), detailing results on cellular automata. Although these follow strict rules, there are some of the ilk that produce results that are completely unpredictable. It seems we still have work to do on this problem, but as Kurzweil himself says, we can make a leap of faith that we do have a facility at least similar to free will.

Nevertheless, it is clear that much of the brain's activity proceeds at an unconscious level. It is possible to monitor this using an electroencephalograph. There have been extensive studies of sleep patterns done in this way. It has been found that bodily activities such as walking or even driving an automobile may be pursued while the subject is entirely unconscious. There was even a famous murder carried out while the perpetrator was unconscious. Some of these incidents have been investigated in the law courts and may eventually lead to changes in the laws themselves, as discussed by Eagelman (2015).

It follows that if the brain is a system composed of parts with specific functions, then it should be possible to replace any given part of the brain with an artificial part provided the replacement has the identical function of the original. By a similar argument, we may reason that if a certain part is defective while the rest of the brain has a normal function, then it should be possible to replace the defective part with an equivalent prosthesis having a normal response. Operations of this variety have been performed to replace the cochlear and restore hearing to patients who were profoundly deaf. Other similar procedures have restored vision with artificial retinas implanted in the blind. Operations to correct epileptic seizures have been performed by removal of an entire hemisphere. Information on such surgery has been offered by Gazzaniga (2008) and more recently by Eagleman (2015). There is another type of procedure being contemplated by scientists in Switzerland that is parallel in concept but in which all the connections from particular brain cells are removed and replaced. This then is a replacement of an actual part of the brain and is referred to as a connectome. It will be a more faithful reproduction of brain tissue than the simulations represented by the prostheses previously mentioned. There is discussion of the possibility of downloading the information stored in a biological brain onto some inanimate platform, thus permitting the brain function to be stored and preserved, or uploaded as it is described. The proponents of this idea imagine that the stored brain could then be reactivated as a duplicate of the original or even as a survivor in the event of the death of the original. The complexities of these procedures are so challenging that we have to wonder if they are really within the bounds of the possible.

4.17 Happiness: Ancient and Modern

Previous chapters have given a sketch of the beginnings of ethics with gradually more sophisticated approaches culminating in the watershed work of Hume. Early philosophy was much concerned with establishing the correct use of simple logic in argumentation and logical, linguistic, and mathematical frameworks. Ethics has profited from several kinds of interaction with philosophy, both in its broader sense of all of knowledge including science and law as well as in its narrower sense of providing something for argumentation and discussion. But there is one more important consideration we have not yet mentioned, and that is the human ability to make predictions of the future. Our animal ancestors were strictly or completely limited in this respect. Plato and Aristotle believed that every object existed for a purpose, and they saw the ends or goals of our human activities as the guiding light of ethics. Although we no longer accept the idea of every object having an essential meaning or a preordained purpose, Aristotle's concept of an "end" for our ethical purposes still has meaning for us in terms of our subjective vision of a desirable future state. Aristotle discussed the ends to which humans should be committed and arrived at the conclusion that our goal should be to seek "happiness." Trying to define and grasp the nature of happiness became an enterprise, which extended from Aristotle's time to the present as is related in McCready (2001). In this chapter, we pick up the threads of this ancient discussion, which will lead, as we shall see, to some very modern insights.

It is clear that happiness is a variety of emotion we experience when events meet our expectations. We say we are happy when our basic needs for food, drink, sex, and security are met; but the feelings then are examples of bliss, euphoria, ecstasy, or transient satisfactions. We sometimes use the word *hedonism* to describe these short-duration forms of happiness. There are other feelings such as well-being or comfort, which can also be described as happiness but which are usually of longer duration. Aristotle did not believe that "true" happiness is simply hedonism, but rather, he used the word *eudaimonia*, which is perhaps best translated as *flourishing*, meaning a sense of ongoing activity rather than just fleeting emotion. The Greeks associated happiness in general with the achievement of the "good." The stoics believed that true happiness resulted from doing the will of the gods. In Indian philosophy and religion, happiness was found in the concept of Nirvana; and in China, there were descriptions of it in Tao, Confucianism, and Buddhism. Modern psychologists, including Martin Seligman (2002) and Jonathan Haidt (2006), use the word *happiness* as an overarching term to refer to all positive emotions. But Seligman also introduces some further distinctions by dividing the positive emotions into past, present, or future orientations. Thus, he sees past positive emotions as exemplified by satisfaction, contentment, pride, and serenity. On the other hand, future positive emotions are exemplified by optimism, hope, confidence, trust, and faith.

In the middle of the twentieth century, there developed a school of thought known as humanistic psychology whose leading members were Erich Fromm (1947) and Abraham Maslow (1971). These workers believe that *happiness* is a word whose meaning is a general sense of well-being. They discuss the concept of "peak experience," which occurs when everything is going well and is evidently similar to a certain variety of religious experience, as described by William James (1902). The experiences are clearly emotional states, but Fromm and Maslow expect us to use what might be variously described as thought or reasoning or cognitive skills in arriving at the peak moments. Maslow sees our progress as cyclic, meaning that we move through periods of activity ruled by reason between peak experiences. He also describes a hierarchy of psychological needs (basic, security, social, egoistic, and culminating in actualization). Simpson (2002 and 2005) has described Maslow's scheme and discussed how a humanist might follow it. There are excellent discussions of the science of happiness in articles by Livingston (2006) and in the book edited by McCready (2001). The concept of happiness is clearly related to our emotions and is thus consistent with Hume's (1739–40) outlook. By making happiness a goal of our ethical system, Aristotle recognized the need for us to relate present actions to their future consequences. We can use our reason to find the *means* to such ends. It is tempting to associate "ends" purely with emotions and "means" purely with cognition, but as Dewey (1908) pointed out, things are not that simple and both mental processes are usually involved with means and ends. Nevertheless, we can still say that means-ends analysis presents us with a method of deriving an ethical system that is an alternative to the construction of pluralistic values. It is probably best to view both methods as complementary. The writings of Kurtz (1983, 1988, 1989) and Lamont (1982) exemplify how the humanist movement has attempted to develop theories and systems that will be of real utility to the individual and society.

4.18 Anatomy of Consciousness

One of the upshots of research related to happiness was the discovery of "flow" by Mike Csikszentmihalyi (1990), who became curious as to why some people after World War II, deprived of their former situations, collapsed into helplessness and despondence whereas others radiated integrity, good cheer, and purpose. Incidentally, Csikszentmihalyi is pronounced "cheeks sent me high." His insight into happiness came from thinking about the flow of conscious activity, which we have already alluded to in discussing the flowchart (figure 3). We saw that in passing around this circuit, activity could be interrupted or intercepted by all sorts of inputs, some internal, such as instincts, habits, or memories, and some external, such as social cues or physical effects. There are circumstances where such interruptions can be so distracting as to completely prevent us from continuing our work. On the other hand, there are conditions where the extraneous inputs are not even registered and the "flow" of activity continues uninterrupted. Csikszentmihalyi studied the conditions under which flow occurred. He found that many people in all sorts of occupations from assembly-line workers to ballerinas could find great gratification in their work if skill was needed and they concentrated on clear goals, with immediate feedback, where they had a deep involvement and a sense of control. Under these conditions, their sense of self vanishes and time seems to stop. As a young researcher, Seligman became interested in a similar phenomenon, "learned helplessness," wherein an animal or a human being learns to be helpless when confronted with a situation that they cannot change. What is puzzling is that some subjects give up trying to do anything even when later they are provided with the means to alter matters.

4.19 Hope and Optimism

Seligman's (2002) early experimentation led him on to studies of hope and optimism in children and adults. He cites examples of people whose whole attitude to life can be described as cheerful or optimistic. Such folk often have what is described as a Duchenne smile (after its discoverer Guillaume Duchenne). Studies have been made of large groups of yearbook photographs. Years after the pictures were taken, those subjects with the Duchenne smiles were found to be still cheerful and indeed to have lived longer than their cohorts. Other measures of cheerful dispositions show the benefits of optimism. To quote Seligman, optimism and hope cause better resistance to depression when bad events strike; they show better performance at work, particularly in challenging jobs, and better physical health. Seligman has devised tests that can be used to measure optimism. In general, people who give up easily believe the causes of bad events that happen to them are permanent, i.e., those causes will always be there to affect their lives. The more optimistic people, on the other hand, believe the causes of bad events are temporary and therefore may go away in time. Permanence is a measure in time, and there is an equivalent measure of explanations applied to space, which Seligman labels "pervasiveness." Thus, pessimists accept universal explanations for their failures (e.g., all teachers are unfair) whereas optimists settle for specific explanations (e.g., Professor Finch is unfair). There is a very similar division between hopelessness and hopefulness as there is between pessimism and optimism. Seligman presents techniques developed to teach hopefulness and optimism to those who lack them. These feature methods to first recognize, and then to dispute, the self-given arguments that lead to bad feelings.

At the start of his term as president of the American Psychological Association, Seligman took stock of the field of psychology, an account that is also recounted in his book (2002). He pointed out that in 1947 none of the major mental illnesses were treatable whereas by 1997 sixteen were yielding to psychotherapy, psychopharmacology, or both. This was largely the result of research funded by the US government and aimed at curing specific mental illnesses, but the science of the subject had lagged. Seligman and a few others, including Csikszentmihalyi, aimed to correct this imbalance by calling for a new "positive psychology" aimed at investigating "that which makes life worth living." One of the mainstays of the new field is the study of positive emotions: joy, contentment, gratitude, and love, as has been described by Barbara L. Fredrickson (2003). The positive emotions contrast with such negative ones as anger, anxiety, and sadness, all of which feature in mental illnesses. Researchers began to explore the then largely uncharted terrain of human strengths and the sources of happiness. One of the problems in studying positive emotions was that they are relatively undifferentiated and except for a few signals, such as the Duchenne smile, not easily recognized. The negative emotions such as anger, fear, and disgust have intuitively obvious adaptive value, which would have promoted survival behavior in our ancestors. It took a while for researchers to realize that the positive emotions solve problems concerning positive growth and development. Fredrickson (2003) argues that the positive emotions help people to see the big picture and help them prepare for later hard times. They help people to acquire intellectual resources including problem-solving skills such as resilience and optimism and to learn new information. There are some hints that the positive emotions help to undo the physiological damage caused by the effects of negative emotions on the cardiovascular system. This may explain the effects on longevity mentioned earlier. There are also some indications that meditation can be used as an entry to positive emotion.

4.20 Life, Death, and Pollyanna

Now there are situations in which positive emotions do not belong. Extreme suffering or imprisonment, for example, could not be described as happy circumstances. Optimism cannot counter all the facts of human existence, and if we act cheerfully in the face of extreme trouble, the effect is "Pollyanna-ish." The implication of the naturalist philosophy for the life of the individual is the inevitability of death. The doctrine that the mind or soul has an existence separate from flesh and blood was part of many ancient cosmologies. One of the important corollaries of the humanist belief expressed by Corliss Lamont (2001) that the "mind is indivisibly conjoined with the functioning of the brain" and the mind ceases to exist when the body dies. Lamont argues that there is no possibility that the human consciousness can survive the shock and disintegration of death, with its memory and awareness of self-identity intact. Humans are mortal, and we need to find meaning and satisfaction in this life. Lamont puts great emphasis on the distinction between Christianity and humanism as regards a belief in immortality. People who have been brought up to believe that the rewards for this life lie in another one beyond the grave will have to completely rethink their attitudes and goals. The humanist comes to the conclusion that this life is all and enough. Perhaps it was the superstitions put about by religion that were responsible for the fear of death. Old religious attitudes to death persist today even among educated people despite the fact that ethicists and humanists such as Lamont (1977, 1990, and 2001) and Jane Wynne Willson (1995) have helped readers come to terms with death in sensitive, sensible ways. Memorials should be conducted for the living: in sympathy for grief but also in appreciation of the life stories and achievements of the departed. Humanistic funerals, which celebrate the life of the departed, have, in fact, become the norm not only in organized humanism but also increasingly among Christians. Beyond a certain point living can become a burden of unending suffering and humanists such as Derek Humphry (1996) have been among the forefront of those seeking to legalize suicide. People of great courage can adapt to extreme situations as exemplified by Viktor Frankl (1984) who showed us how to maintain personal dignity even while imprisoned in a Nazi concentration camp. The naturalist understands that advances in medical science have extended the lifespan by emphasizing healthy living and by conquering disease. The naturalist understands that the human lifespan is probably determined genetically and may ultimately be brought under our own control.

4.21 Meaning and Purpose

It would be depressing to finish the chapter with a section on life and death, and we might be forgiven if we wonder if death is the final culmination of life. Do our lives have some lasting meaning and significance? Such meaning is important for us, and in fact, it may be the most important aspect of our whole lives. Seligman puts forward the viewpoint that we need an attachment to something bigger than ourselves to find meaning in our lives. The religiously inclined call the most important things sacred and associate them with God. Seligman (2002) had told us of his own and other psychologists' metaphysical doubts, so I was interested in the final chapter of his book on meaning and purpose. He leads into the topic with an account of a meeting at the home of Sir John Templeton, the billionaire with a passionate interest in religion. The occasion was a chance to hear a talk by Robert Wright on his own work, *Non-Zero*, which turns out to be a prophecy that the world will eventually come together around a destiny of win-win beliefs shared by all major religions and philosophies. Seligman appears to endorse Wright's views and sees the situation as the emergence of a nonsupernatural god who ultimately acquires omnipotence, omniscience, and goodness.

My own conclusion is that humanists also need an attachment to some belief in things bigger than our own lives, our own secular version of the sacred but not a personal God. We are the ones striving toward omnipotence, omniscience, and goodness. My feeling is that our approach to such goals will be an evolutionary process and will involve us working together in legislation, science, engineering, and art. Our individual lives will have meaning if we can each contribute to the broad purpose. For the humanist meaning and purpose are not injected into life by belief in gods or by religion—they are created by our own thinking and efforts. Happiness is an emotional state that accompanies our cognition and evolves along with our world view. Although there are psychological techniques that have been developed to enhance happiness, there are limits to the effectiveness of these methods. Lasting happiness can only be achieved by cognitive understanding of our situation. Humanists spend their lives searching for the best way to live. After a while, we all learn a good way forward and should then feel a need to pass on the good news to others. We will investigate the evolution of these cognitive and ethical ends and means in subsequent chapters.

4.22 Future Minds

There has been an argument going on ever since computers were first introduced as to whether the brain is a computer. Kurzweil argues that this is akin to saying that "computers are not word processors." But a computer can become a word processor if it is running word processing software. Thus, he argues that a computer can become a brain if it is running brain software. The human brain runs a specific set of algorithms. A general-purpose computer was, by definition, capable of running any algorithm. Claude Shannon showed that you can create accurate communication using even the most unreliable channels if you transmit the message multiple times and then average the results. Digital data can be transmitted as many times as necessary using Shannon's theorem; and this is how CDs, DVDs, and program disks can continue to provide reliable results even after being dropped on the floor and scratched.

The other important idea on which the information age depends is the Turing machine, which was not an actual machine but a thought experiment. Turing's machine consists of an infinitely long memory tape with a one or a zero in each square. Input to the machine is stored on the tape, and the tape can read one square at a time. The machine also contains a stored program. Each instruction in the program puts the machine into a definite state. Each instruction specifies one action if the square being read is a zero and a different action if the current square is a one. Possible actions include writing a zero or a one on the tape, moving the tape one square to the right or left or halting. Each state will then specify the number of the next state that the machine should be in. The input is presented to the machine on the tape. The program runs, and when the machine halts, it has completed its algorithm and the output of the process is left on the tape.

In 1939 Turing designed an electronic calculator called Bombe that helped decode messages encrypted by the Nazi Enigma coding machine. By 1943, an engineering team influenced by Turing completed what was arguably the first digital computer, the Colossus, enabling the Allies to continue decoding more sophisticated versions of Enigma. On these foundations, John von Neumann created the architecture of the modern computer. This was intended to create a feasible concept for a computational machine, and in fact, it has been the core structure of every computer ever since. The von Neumann model includes a central processing unit (CPU), a memory where program and data are stored; mass storage; a program counter; and input/output channels. The stored program, one of von Neumann's ideas, was what made it possible for the computer to serve as a universal device as opposed to limiting it to a specific task.

There was one genuine forerunner to von Neumann's concept from a full century earlier, which was the design of the Analytical Engine by Charles Babbage, which featured a program stored on punched cards borrowed from the Jacquard loom. Unfortunately, the technical requirements were beyond the capability of machine shops at that time, and the Analytical Engine was not completed. The work was rediscovered after the development of the modern electronic machines; and recently, as a historical venture, an Analytical Engine was finally assembled. Babbage was assisted by Ada Byron, Countess Lovelace, the only legitimate child of the poet Lord Byron. Countess Lovelace wrote the first computer programs.

In 1956 von Neumann began preparing a series of papers to be delivered as a lecture series at Yale. He did not complete the work because of the ravages of cancer, but Kurzweil credits it with being the first serious inquiry into the human brain, and it was published posthumously as *The Computer and the Brain* in 1958. It brought the fields of computer science and neuroscience together. Von Neumann pointed out that the output of neurons was digital: they either fired or they did not. This was far from obvious at the time since the neurons might have been producing analog signals. The processing in the dendrites leading into the neurons, however, was analogue. He described this calculation as a weighted sum of inputs with a threshold. This model was the basis of a spate of research activity known as connectionism, which followed and which we have already referred to in connection with neural nets. He explains that a general-purpose computer can simulate the brain but that the brain itself is not a von Neumann machine since it does not have the facility of storing a program.

Kurzweil became famous in his original books by drawing attention to the growth of computing capabilities. The best known of these is called Moore's law, which can be expressed by the observation that, over the history of computing hardware, the number of transistors on integrated circuits doubles approximately every two years. The period often quoted as eighteen months is due to Intel executive David House, who predicted that period for a doubling in chip performance (being a combination of the effect of more transistors and their being faster). The law is named after Intel cofounder Gordon E. Moore, who described the trend in a 1965 paper. Kurzweil argues that many other technical parameters (e.g., global Internet data traffic) are also showing exponential growth rates. Associated unit costs are declining in proportion. He points out that similar trends are now observed in neuroscience. He cites the growth of DNA sequence data and the decline in the cost of sequencing a human genome. The bottom line in his argument is that we are rapidly approaching a singularity in our affairs when information processing will become almost instantaneous. One suspects that Kurweil deliberately presented this concept to have a shock effect. But his latest work adds gravitas when he points out that it was von Neumann was actually the first to propose in the 1950s that "the ever accelerating progress of technology and changes in the mode of human life give the appearance of approaching some essential singularity in the history of the race beyond which human affairs, as we know them, could not continue." The effects of the singularity are clearly potentially earth shaking. We may, for instance, be able to use biological information to extend life indefinitely. We might be able to assemble replacements for entire artificial brains. These then could become the controllers of very efficient robots. We might be able to build brains with wide geographical distribution, useful for space travel or for monitoring of the performance of remote installations. We should be able to build brains not only to beat the world's best chess players but also to surpass all manner of human specialists in every conceivable science and engineering, mathematics, and all manner of professions and arts. We may all become infinitely rich. We may be able to control the universe.

5 Values and Virtues

5.1 Recapitulation

Honor Codes
Good Manners and the Golden Rule

5.2 Values as Systems

Elements of Value Systems
Motivation

5.3 Benevolence, Altruism, and Utility
5.4 Humanistic Psychology
5.5 Somatic Nature of Emotion
5.6 Liberty

Choice

5.7 Situation
5.8 Individual Virtues and Happiness
5.9 Societal Values
5.10 Deliberation
5.11 Kant's Theories
5.12 Dennett on Decisions

Zoological Control Systems
Can-Do

5.13 Action, Results, and Evaluation
5.14 Memory and Moral Development
5.15 Common Moral Decencies
5.16 Sidgwick and His Ethical Theories

5.17 Existentialism

Philosophy as a Way of Life
Becoming an Individual
Humanism and Existentialism
Authenticity, Choice, and Commitment
Existential and Social Thought

5.18 Summary and Outlook

5. Values and Virtues

5.1 Recapitulation

In the first and second chapters, we discussed a historical outline of ethics and the contributors, predominantly philosophers, who were responsible for it. In chapter 3, we asserted that an important part of our behavior dates from before our evolution as humans and then from the period of our early human phase. We are still governed by such remanent influences through what is known as instinct. Our knowledge of instinctive morality has largely been acquired from scientific inquiry in paleoanthropology, genetics, and comparative zoology. This knowledge has been supplemented recently by uncovering behavioral traits by questioning subjects on their reactions to various moral scenarios. In the fourth chapter, we went on to study our behavior in the later period of our evolution as humans in so far as that behavior is manifested by the study of the human mind in psychology. Hume followed Descartes in regarding the organism as a machine with a nervous system that receives stimuli and transmits information to the brain where a response is evoked and a reaction is transmitted to muscles. These feedback responses are termed *conditioned reflexes*. Since Hume's time, we have learned many more details of the physiology of the brain and how it supports the mind, and we may see how far we have traveled by reviewing modern texts on the subject such as the ones by Gleitman (1986), Gazzaniga (2008), and Kurzweil (2012). We now know that nerve impulses are transmitted by neurons. From neuron to neuron, contacts are made at synapses by means of numerous chemicals called neurotransmitters.

In addition, there is another means of communication in the body through the endocrine glands such as the pancreas, the adrenals, and the pituitary, which release hormones directly into the bloodstream. These mechanisms control some of the simple motives we share with other animals and are associated with primitive emotions such as thirst, hunger, fear, sexual arousal, and so on. We are now able to image brain activity as it occurs using fMRI and other means. In addition, we have learned much which is relevant to understanding the brain through the development of computers and automatons. Of course, the various domains of knowledge overlap to some extent, and in particular, it is not always clear where the cognitive activities of human beings are completely within the bounds of psychology and where they begin to fall within philosophy and, specifically, the ethics of values and virtues. In the fourth chapter, we discussed Kurzweil's theory on the importance of pattern recognition in neuroscience. We can apply this to the building of systems based on emotions. These are the topics we wish to take up in the present chapter.

5.1.1 Honor Codes

To make the transition, we will first discuss some borderline areas between psychology and ethics. Consider first the subject of honor codes. Here, I am not sure that we have any thorough scientific study to guide us and will propose some recourse to speculation to sketch some ideas. It seems to me that honor codes are strongly linked to the emotions of shame, and it is codes of shame that caught the interest of Lee Harris (2006) in his book *The Suicide of Reason: Radical Islam's Threat to the West.* Certain types of behavior are regarded as honorable, but failure to follow them results in emotions of shame, which can be very strong in certain situations. These codes are especially linked with sexual conduct. There are powerful emotions involved with sexual behavior between individual men and women, but there are also attendant social taboos and rituals called up by family and religion. Honor codes depend on the society under consideration; and although they involve emotions felt universally, the exact nature of the actions and taboos called up are different in different countries, religions, and societies. Killings in response to violations of honor codes have become a severe problem with Muslim immigration to the West. Some bizarre and shocking instances have been recorded in the books by Sam Harris (2010) and Lee Harris (2007). We have argued that the general format of our sexual conduct goes back to our animal ancestry, and so the primitive emotional underpinnings of the honor codes involved must be comparably ancient. Lee Harris states that they predate our acquisition of speech but doubtless there have been at least minor modifications as evolution has continued on.

5.1.2 Good Manners and the Golden Rule

Another borderline example of conduct is that of "good manners." In his work on Virtues, Comte-Sponville starts by discussing good manners, which he views as a preliminary to ethics. Although most people would regard good manners as a desirable characteristic, we do not generally regard the topic with the same seriousness as the full-blown treatment of ethics. It is interesting, therefore, to note that Matt Ridley (2010) has advanced a new theory on the origin of good manners which shows them to be of some considerable importance. Ridley's thesis is that *Homo sapiens* discovered the great advantages of barter and trade and then extended commercial transactions beyond the boundaries of his immediate tribe. This permitted the exchange of goods with other tribes who had access to materials and products unavailable at home. But since most humans up until that time had been antagonistic to foreigners, it was necessary to find ways of conducting affairs with at least a modicum of civility. This then was the origin of virtue and trust among our ancient forbears. According to Ridley, these new codes were, in fact, the distinguishing asset of *Homo sapiens*, which gave us the advantage over the Neanderthals. Research on neurophysiology has suggested that humans have a brain module that enables us to posit a theory of mind in other people. In other words, we are able to imagine ourselves in the other man's place and to envisage what he might want at a given time and place. Such a module for reciprocity would clearly be an advantage to people seeking to act with a modicum of civility. It is only a short step further to the invention of an ethic that one should treat others as one would wish to be treated oneself. But this is exactly what we call the golden rule, one of the most basic of morals and one that is incorporated in all religions and cultures. The fact that the golden rule is of such widespread provenance by itself suggests that it must be of ancient evolutionary origin, and of course, the suggestion we have just made would be consistent with great antiquity. Codes of etiquette have evolved considerably since their ancient beginnings and where they are explicit about including the golden rule they have become quite sophisticated, although they may differ considerably in different times and places. Two books that cover the subject are *Ethics and the Golden Rule* by Harry J. Gensler (2013) and *Freedom and Reason* by R. M. Hare (1963).

5.2 Values as Systems

We continue our investigation of the themes involved in ethics by pointing out that Hume made another important contribution by saying that much of our behavior relies on constancies. In more modern parlance, we might use the word *system* to describe such a mental process. Hume singled out benevolence and justice as two important examples of values, but they are not the only ones by any means. In chapter 1, we already listed a number of values: truth, honesty, fidelity, love, etc. Many books have been written about the various values that have been posited down the ages. Many of these values have become the basis of social systems—in some cases, systems of great complexity. In Finch (2000), I attempted to provide a description of such a process. *Language* itself serves to bond groups from tribes to nations and is frequently associated with complex rules, vast lexicons, and literatures. We use language to embody *knowledge* of the humanities, sciences, and practices. *Trade, commerce, and finance* are all built on *economic values* and again are associated with complex systems of rules and practices. There are all sorts of *commercial organizations* from farms to market places to companies to banks each with their own rules and values. *Legal systems* are connected with *governments* and with all the agencies and ramifications of government. The *arts* embody aesthetic values. How these values and their systemic infrastructures have evolved reveal some fascinating questions for philosophers, psychologists, and sociologists. These studies are components of the humanist curriculum. An account of the history of knowledge would list some of the important works that have moved us forward in the various areas from Plato's Republic to modern times. We have already mentioned Hume but would be remiss to neglect Bentham and the Mills (father and son) who took up his ideas on utilitarianism. I believe that Hume and his followers understood how the great human systems were formed in the mind even if they did not elaborate on all the details of the process.

5.2.1 Elements of Value Systems

Systems contain components such as instincts, habits, and customs; and most importantly Hume saw that the impetus driving any such system is emotional. When we come to analyze our behavior more closely, we realize that we repeatedly employ certain systems, which could be termed *values*. The codes we have just been examining are simple value systems, and if our speculations are correct, then they must be among the oldest of human values. We could distinguish their use from purely animal behavior because they involve at least some element of socially influenced cognitive deliberation, which later on in evolution might involve language. The elements of the process are represented in Fig. 4.1. It is important to realize that both virtues and values can be described using this flowchart. A virtue is a character trait of a particular human being whereas a value is usually shared among a community of people (see Brinkerhoff and White, 1985).

As Rachels (2007) and others have pointed out, emotions are essentially subjective. Hume's knowledge of psychology was derived from introspection, and he was followed in this approach by many investigators, including William James (1890). But introspection was always suspect, and it gave way in psychology to other more objective techniques including behaviorism and psychoanalysis. One of the more fruitful departures was known as humanistic psychology, which combined both subjective and objective aspects. The state of the art in humanistic psychology through about 1940 has been well portrayed by Fromm (1947). Values are open to many humans and are thus objective. Fromm equates these experiences with happiness and sees this state as the realization of all our values, the summum bonum, as Aristotle called it. The humanistic psychologists have continued to study people's development and the influences that shape it. Lyle Simpson (2003 and

2005) has given reviews of the work of Maslow (1971) who realized that people, in fact, attempt to integrate ethics into their private lives and that there is a developmental cycle with an upward spiral, which can culminate in what he describes as peak experience. There are several works based on the principles of happiness, which are discussed in chapter 6.

5.2.2 Motivation

Ethics did not develop in an analytical matter. It might have been convenient from the educator's point of view had that happened, but historically, we did not acquire our various emotions in some neat, orderly sequence. In compiling this synopsis, I have referred to Gleitman's *Psychology* (1986) and to the article on emotion in *Wikipedia*. Primitive animals needed several urges: to breathe, to feed, to drink, to avoid danger and to reproduce, etc. These elementals were present in our earliest unicellular ancestors and as time went on and our nervous systems developed they eventually became the bases of emotions. At first, these motivating urges, ultimately based on simple chemical potentials, would have been subconscious and only became manifest as emotions when consciousness itself evolved in zoological nervous systems. Different combinations of emotions would be called for in different situations. Psychologists have recognized the distinction between "primary" and "secondary" emotions. The process of combination of emotions might be similar to the way in which primary colors are combined in the working of color vision. Specific situations must recur innumerable times in the lives of any one animal and then in more and more complex variations as evolution continued. Emotional states and instinctive reactions of greater complexity would have appeared with the progress of time. Eventually, animals acquired cognitive abilities, which would have enabled them to respond quickly with an understanding of the situations confronting them at any particular time. The workings of logic, to extend the earlier analogy, might be similar to our perception of black-and-white in vision. These cognitive abilities were enhanced even further in the human brain, and then we added memory and the powers of speech and narrative to our repertoire. Narratives could have been the start of knowledge acquisition, that characteristic of the human animal that enabled her to gain ascendancy over the natural world. Seen in this light, reasoning is a process that involves both emotion and logical analysis. This idea has been elaborated on in the book *Passion within Reason* by Frank (1988) and has been reemphasized recently by David Brooks (2011).

5.3 Benevolence, Altruism, and Utility

Hume saw benevolence (or altruism) and justice as being the primary motivations in ethics. The pursuit of justice led to the development of the system of law and became a factor in government: two topics we will dwell upon at some length in chapter 16. The question of benevolence, however, demands our immediate attention. We have already noted that Hume believed that morality derived from emotions and depends on taste and sentiment. It is different from mathematics and science, which require only the cool assent of the understanding. It is different from what is honorable, fair, becoming, or generous, which all take possession of the heart. Morality is not practical if we extinguish warm feelings for virtue or disgust and aversion to vice. The bottom line depends on some internal sense or feeling. Hume's method is to identify those mental qualities that we call personal merit. We should verify that we would like to have those feelings ourselves. This is how we first arrive at the social values of benevolence and justice.

We may continue by following Hume's exposition: Benevolence or softer affections are estimable. They engage the approbation and goodwill. They call up such epithets as sociable, good-natured, humane, merciful, grateful, friendly, generous, beneficent. If they are accompanied at birth by power and eminent abilities and displayed in good government or useful instruction, they raise the possessor above human nature and approach the divine. Only by doing good can a man truly enjoy the advantages of being eminent. When we recommend even an animal or plant as useful or beneficial we are endorsing it. The eye is pleased with the prospect of fields of corn, loaded with vineyards.

"We praise the advantages of certain professions to society. But is not a monk and inquisitor enraged when we treat his order as useless or pernicious to mankind." Utility is thus seen as the basis of ethical behavior. Section 3 of Hume's essay argues that public utility is the sole foundation of the merit of justice, and section 4 posits the same for political society. Utility, or the greatest good for the greatest number, was explored further as a basis for a social theory by Jeremy Bentham (1789) J. S. Mill (1859), and Henry Sidgwick (1874).

A problem arose later when considering benevolence or altruism in the context of evolutionary theory in that it might appear that actions that benefit others could mitigate against the actor's own interests, thus seeming to deny his evolutionary advantage. But Darwin himself supplied an answer to this conundrum in that the benefit could be seen to redound to a group to which both benefactor and beneficiary belong.

5.4 Humanistic Psychology

The term *humanist psychology* acquired a certain meaning in the middle years of the twentieth century, which distinguished it not only from theism but also from Freudian and Adlerian psychology. The humanistic viewpoint was amplified in the writings of Ellis (1961) and Maslow (1971). It became associated with the self-esteem movement, partly arising as a reaction to theistic and other restrictive influences. It seems to be a descendant of Epicureanism and the teaching of Aristotle, and it expressed the ideal of self-love or what Sidgwick had called egoistic hedonism. Incidentally, this is not the same as selfishness, which is an unbalanced concern with one's own welfare. Fromm equates these experiences with happiness and sees this state as the realization of all our values, the summum bonum, as Aristotle called it. Simpson (2003 and 2005) has given reviews of the work of Maslow (1971) who realized that people, in fact, attempt to integrate ethics into their private lives and that there is a developmental cycle with an upward spiral, which can culminate in what he describes as peak experience. Livingston (2006) has given an excellent contemporary review of work on happiness. These lessons in psychology are among the most important of our humanist messages, and we shall have more to say about them in the next chapter.

There are many mental and physiological states that are described as emotions including many feelings, thoughts, and behaviors. Emotions may be fleeting and last for just moments or they may persist for years. Emotions may result directly in certain behaviors such as crying, fighting, or fleeing; but overt behavior is not always the outcome of an emotional state. There is still much controversy about how emotions are defined and classified, and research on quite basic aspects of the subject is still going on. Some features are generally agreed upon, however. At least, some part of an emotion is a subjective "feeling." It is generally recognized that there are "negative" and "positive" emotions where the former have inhibitory effects on behavior while the latter promote certain actions. Anger, fear, and disgust are examples of negative emotions; and they can usually be understood as evolutionary adaptations to life-threatening situations. It was not clear to psychologists why positive emotions such as joy, serenity, and gratitude had any evolutionary benefit until the work of Seligman and others made it clear that these feelings resulted in increased longevity for those who experienced them regularly. These ideas are supported by the development of evolutionary psychology as also are the explanations of moral emotions, such as altruism and attraction between the sexes. Several authors including Hauser (2006) and Wright (1994) have written recently on the evolutionary origins of various instinctive behaviors and the physiological mechanisms by which they are expressed. It has also been well documented that emotion plays an important role in learning.

5.5 Somatic Nature of Emotion

Some theories of emotion stress their "somatic" nature, i.e., their connection or causation by certain bodily states, such as hunger, thirst, sexual arousal, etc. Other theories emphasize the role of "cognition," the thinking process, as in the process of understanding the meaning of certain observed situations. Our ability to detach behavior from emotions is regarded as important in distinguishing between the validity of such theories. It also has led to the development of a "component process model" in which emotions are seen to involve the synchronization of many different bodily and cognitive processes. The compound theory is very important in understanding the nature of social interactions and the sociology of emotions. The effectiveness of cognitive processes must have been vastly improved with the introduction of speech to human relations. The further addition of art and literature to the panoply of human abilities must have increased our transmissions of both thoughts and emotions between one another. One may speculate that the natures of thought and emotion still have to be finally clarified. But it is still clear that sociology is very important in ethology, and we need to bring this into account, regardless of the precise underlying mechanism of the interaction of emotion and cognition.

It is hard to believe that morality and ethics could have begun as conscious activities before speech and narrative powers had reached a certain level of sophistication. But over the millennia, the two modalities have tended to progress in comparative isolation. Even today the subjects of ethics and morality are frequently treated separately, as systems of rules or laws governing behavior, on the one hand, and as the analysis of purpose in some aspect of life or business, on the other. It is only recently that philosophers such as Habermas have begun to compare the two and to stress the relatedness of the two. It might be better to refer to our subject by a single word such as *ethomorality*, which would be a new coinage. Alternatively, we might use the word *ethology*, which already exists in the dictionary, being defined as the science of behavior that includes both ethics and morality. Such feedback loops could have been the generators of behavioral systems long before we understood what we were doing.

Ethology, the study of animal behavior, consequently includes both the morals and ethics of the human animal. This book concerns the question of how we might optimize our ethology in the broadest sense in order to live in the best possible way. Assuming we are nontheists, then the question becomes how we might construct an ethology based on human reason and serving our human motivations or, in other words, a humanist ethology. In a previous essay (Finch 2008), I argued the case that ethics and morality should be considered as two aspects of our behavioral control system. Each of these two modalities was developed as separate approaches to the philosophy of behavior, but it seems that both are needed as parts of a unified system. In section 4.2, we reviewed the general status of human nature as it is known in psychology and cognitive science and then showed how system theory permits one to summarize and represent this knowledge succinctly, for instance, using flowcharts (see figure 3).

5.6 Liberty

The concept of individual liberty has undergone considerable change over the centuries: it has evolved as Dennett suggested. When humans first settled down in agricultural communities as opposed to living isolated lives in small tribal groups, we might suppose that certain social constraints came into being to enable people to live together. As time went on, some people were reduced to slavery by the social leaders, and so we might suppose that the concept of liberty or freedom was invented to denote the relaxation of the constraints which bound people to society. In this sense, freedom is a social concept. There is an essay on *Positive and Negative Liberty* (2009) in the *Stanford Encyclopedia of Philosophy* on the Internet, which goes into many of the ramifications of the discussion of the social concept of freedom. A key idea, which was defended by Isaiah Berlin, is that of negative freedom, i.e., freedom defined by the absence of certain constraints. The flags of liberty and freedom were used as calls to arms in both the American and French Revolutions, as in Tom Paine's (1791) *Rights of Man*. It is interesting to reflect that the idea of "rights" evolved in the political arena. A right is surely a piece of political machinery engineered to protect citizens from tyranny and guarantee their property, speech, and participation in government and the law.

5.6.1 Choice

John Stuart Mill's famous essay (1859) *On Liberty* opened the door to another line of thinking, namely, about individual choice. There were other philosophers interested in freedom at about the time Mill was writing. One of the most famous was Kierkegaard whose book *Either/Or* elaborated on the importance of choice in our mental lives. It was pointed out by a group of philosophers and literati known as the existentialists that it is the choices we make that do more to determine the character of our existence than anything else. There is an account of existentialism in a recent book by Flynn (2006) who devotes a chapter to the discussion started by Sartre on whether or not existentialism and humanism are synonymous. The verdict seems to be that there is a strong humanistic thread in existentialism through the individual's pursuit of identity and meaning.

5.7 Situation

Which values are brought to attention depends on the situation in which we find ourselves. The main division in this case is whether we are acting alone or in a social setting. Let us start by considering the ethics of an individual. Plato and Aristotle were among the first to approach the subject of ethics from the point of view of virtue, i.e., by assessing the various qualities of a man's character. As Hume himself points out, this way of approaching ethics goes all the way back to Homer. These characteristics are reflections of the habits men have cultivated, and the habits are, in turn, reflections of values. Hume (1777) has a most interesting section in the *Enquiry Concerning the Principles of Morals*, which perhaps reveals his own character. This is in section 7 titled "Of Qualities useful to Ourselves." He starts by pointing out some habits that are clearly prejudicial to the possessor: indolence, negligence, want of order or method, obstinacy, fickleness, rashness and credulity. But then, he points out that no quality is absolutely blamable or absolutely praiseworthy. He takes "celerity" as an example. Dispatch in business is commendable, but too much speed leads to mistakes. There is a happy medium with most of these systems. We think of the person who can strike such a balance in terms of happiness, joy, success, and prosperity. Hume states that "the quality most necessary for the execution of any useful enterprise, is discretion." This is a rather surprising first choice until we remember that Hume was a man who was condemned for his skepticism and classified as an atheist at a time not long removed from the age when nonbelievers were hanged and burned at the stake. He was denied a professorship for being an atheist although he never said he was one. Even today in the Middle East and parts of the USA,

Hume's advice should be well heeded. But it is an open question as to whether discretion or honesty or tolerance or kindness or some other concept is really the most important value. In certain systems of belief, especially religions, there are objects and concepts that exceed all others in value, and these are said to be sacred. It would appear that there is not necessarily any supernatural association involved with the sacred, so there may be sacred aspects to humanism as well.

5.8 Individual Virtues and Happiness

Hume argued that we do not need to prove the advantages of industry in the acquisition of power or riches or in raising a fortune. He admires frugality, which is a happy medium between avarice and prodigality. One of the most intriguing remarks that he makes is that qualities often stem from complicated sources. Thus, honesty, fidelity, and truth promote the interests of society but once established on that basis are also considered advantageous to the person himself as a source of trust and confidence. He argues the case for sticking to our general resolutions for the long haul if we wish to ensure happiness and honor. We all need self-esteem, but if we are wise, we back it up with experience and knowledge since no one needs the imputation of ignorance and stupidity. Different qualities suit particular customs, manners, and situations. Qualities that are meritorious at various times include temperance, sobriety, patience, constancy, perseverance, forethought, considerateness, secrecy (by which I presume that Hume meant the holding of confidences); presence of mind; quickness of conception; and facility of expression. There are modern expositions of virtues as in Bennett's *Book of Virtues*, which has a Christian outlook. Comte-Sponville's *Small Treatise on the Great Virtues* (1996) is more illuminating to the humanist. He covers eighteen virtues: love, politeness, fidelity, prudence, temperance, justice, generosity, compassion, mercy, courage, gratitude, humility, simplicity, tolerance, purity, gentleness, good faith, and humor. Each one of these virtues could be the basis of an essay in itself with plenty to discuss in the way of qualifications, caveats, and exceptions.

5.9 Societal Values

We need to say something about values and society. Aristotle himself viewed ethics as a part of politics. Politics must be a part of ethics because it concerns our behavior in groups and societies ranging from the nuclear family to the United Nations. Human beings are social animals who evolved from ancestors who lived in families, groups, and tribes. All manner of societies have evolved since humans first appeared in Africa. Consider some of the social values, which Hume lists: maternal love, sexual bonds of lust and love, benevolence, justice, war, honesty, freedom. As our societies developed and technological knowledge expanded, so also did our institutions and associated values: government, law, democracy, political parties, and education generally. As Hume has pointed out, some of the virtues of individual humans derive from social values. Some of the most contentious issues in society today revolve around the values held by different philosophers and groups, and clarifying our priorities among these is, in fact, a major part of the work of the modern humanist movement. There are political philosophies that seem to be based on certain limited values, and these might be described as ideologies. The libertarian movement appears to put its priority on the liberty or freedom of the individual, as expressed in the writings of Ayn Rand (1963) and others. Freedom, however, is a difficult concept in philosophy, and we would be well advised to study a work such as Dennett's *Freedom Evolves* (2003) to grasp its meaning or a political assessment such as Lamont's *Freedom is as Freedom Does* (1990). Another approach is based on the concept of justice, as propounded by Rawls (1963).

5.10 Deliberation

There is clearly emotional content in any one of these value systems, but there is also a cognitive or conceptual framework that enables emotional evaluation to take place. This thinking or deliberation is often called cognition nowadays. We make choices among possible behaviors by reaching a bottom line approbation or disapproval (i.e., distinguishing the good or the bad). We often describe the concepts behind the systems in terms of laws or rules. Hume investigates at some length the possibility that we follow these rules and systems simply for our own selfish benefit. But he finds numerous counterexamples of behaviors of which we approve that cannot be ascribed to our direct self-interest. Sympathy and empathy are examples in this regard. Hume's explanation for our approbation in these cases is simply that the behaviors have utility. It is clearly only a short step further to see that utility (or usefulness) has survival value and is thus consistent with Darwinian evolution. It is possible that Hume, in fact, held ideas about evolution, including moral evolution, a hundred years ahead of Darwin. Darwin certainly read Hume's work.

5.11 Kant's Theories

Kant's work on *The Critique of Pure Reason* (1949) is, according to Friedrich, an exposition of the limits of reason and natural science. Kant gave us a summary of his arguments in the *Prolegomena* (1783). He basically agreed with Hume about the working of human rationality and the motivational force of emotion. In a subsequent book *The Critique of Pure Practical Reason*, Kant further explicates his view that, whereas the world of science is deterministic, when it comes to human affairs, there is freedom. Kant believed that our morality is based on duty as expounded further in *The Metaphysics of Morals* (1785). Sidgwick realized that the many different values embodied in common sense can be in conflict and thus understood Kant's efforts to find rational principles on which to make final choices. Sidgwick shows how many of the common-sense values can be derived from Kant's maxim of universality, meaning that such maxims should apply to all men. Kant also offered a sophisticated dissertation on aesthetics in *The Critique of Judgment* (1790). He maintained that the mark of genius in artistic work is originality. But perhaps the most important point for humanists that Friedrich has to make is that Kant was driven by an overriding passion for peace. Kant was a scholarly man who lived all his life in the Kingdom of Prussia—a realm more devoted to the glory of warfare it is difficult to imagine. Kant was out of favor with the authorities for much of his life because of his liberal religious views. But the pinnacle of his disrepute surely came with publication of his last book *On Eternal*

Peace in which he expanded his belief in ethical universality into a plea for world government.

Although he made great progress in escaping from the shackles of religious ideology, Kant still made some serious errors in that regard. He claimed that we could have no direct knowledge of God and therefore had no physical evidence for theistic beliefs. However, in his later work, he supposed that there had to be a God to support our morality. He was said to have pushed God out of the front door but then let him in through the back door. He believed in the subordination of wives to their husbands and in the exclusion of women from intellectual pursuits and political rights. He was a racist and a white supremacist. Sterba points out that modern adherents of Kant's philosophy try to make corrections for his deficiencies.

5.12 Dennett on Decisions

There is still a great deal of ancient thinking around when it comes to understanding how the brain works, and Dennett expounds on this in *Freedom Evolves* (2003). Primitive people used to believe that we had an immortal soul that animated our bodies during our lives. Thanks to advances in the sciences, that idea has been largely rejected. But this leaves some people despondent, feeling robbed of their free will. Dennett maintains that we still have something like the old idea of free will, but it is nothing other than being able to draw on the "can-do" of learned responses as described below. A crucial idea in the book is that the modern interpretation of free will involves our ability to make choices in life. It was often supposed that there must be indeterminist aspects of our thinking to account for free will. This viewpoint persists even today, and Dennett devotes a chapter to expounding and denouncing it. There is a telling discussion about chess-playing computer programs. The computer is just about the most determined object we encounter, but it can make choices. Since the choices made depend on the computer's capacity to search in databases, there can be variability in the decisions made in a finite time. Humans must have similar variances. Dennett also argues that our natures cannot be fixed even if the universe is determined since we can learn from our experience.

5.12.1 Zoological Control Systems

To prove his points, Dennett traces the evolution of zoological control systems. Starting with simple switch-like mechanisms, animals have multiplied their degrees of freedom, finally producing brains as controllers. The brain has progressed from situation-action machine to choice machine. It was the open minds of *Homo*, which contrived the great ramifying families of families of families of cultural entities. Chief among these cultural symbionts are languages. It is on the transmission and mutation of these "memes" that Dennett bases his theory of cultural evolution.

5.12.2 Can-Do

The whole of human history might be seen as the search for better knowledge of how to do the things we want to do. Freedom, in other words, is the primary value in the humanist ethology as described in the previous three chapters of this book. Freedom is a good example of a value system. It is clearly driven by multiple motives, including both basic biological drives and the whole panoply of economic goods and services. There are several suites of "can-do" measures that can be called upon to make the system function: communication through speech, writing and graphic arts, all the infrastructure of agriculture and the built world, as well as all the apparatus of engineering. We would have to list every one of the arrangements of society and government including the capitalisms of the various nations all as parts of the system of freedom. In other words, the view of ethics becomes broadened into a complete social theory as proposed by Habermas among others.

5.13 Action, Results, and Evaluation

When the human takes action, the results of the deliberation and decision making finally assume concrete form and shape. But what exactly will transpire depends on the situation in the physical and social worlds. Most of the time, the actor will have sufficient experience to anticipate the final consequence of the chain of events he has set in motion; but of course, there will be circumstances when he cannot anticipate what these results may be. It was John Dewey (1939) who first proposed that value systems should be regarded as instruments for measurement of the effectiveness of ethical action. Thus, we can ask how our habits and procedures are leading to good lives and health for ourselves and our families, giving us freedom to do what we want. After we assess these consequences, we may wish to modify our ways.

5.14 Memory and Moral Development

Dewey (1932) describes a way in which moral habits may come about: "We commence life under the influence of appetites and impulses, and of direct response to immediate stimuli of heat and cold, comfort and pain, light, noise, etc. The hungry child snatches at food. To him the act is innocent and natural. But he brings down reproach upon himself; he is told that he is unmannerly, inconsiderate, greedy; that he should wait till he is served, till his turn comes. He is made aware that his act has other connections than the one he had assigned to it: the immediate satisfaction of hunger. He learns to look at single acts not as single but as related links in a chain. Thus the idea of a series, an idea which is the essence of conduct, gradually takes the place of a mere succession of disconnected acts." So the child acquires the habits of good manners, consideration for others, and restraint and an associated set of values. Dewey goes on to discuss the importance of distinguishing between the thought of an act before it is done and as it is experienced afterward. We need to institute connections between causes and effects, and in that way, we establish consistency in our character and our deeds. In common with other writers, Dewey maintained that there are three approaches to ethics: (1) to seek the good and happiness as its reward; (2) to stress the importance of law and regulation, which leads us to the supremacy of the concepts of duty and the right; and (3) to use praise and blame as the primary moral facts, thereby making the concepts of virtue and vice the central issues.

5.15 Common Moral Decencies

Whatever the details of the process, it seems that there are certain aspects of our moral behavior to which we have biological predispositions. There is clearly a need for these innate tendencies to be brought out by instruction and emulation of our parents at an early age. So we see that both nature and nurture have a place in our moral development. This level of morality is the same the world over, among people of all religions and persuasions, humanists included. Paul Kurtz (1988), one of the leading humanist ethicists, introduced the term *common moral decencies* to describe this foundation of our behavioral experience. Kidder (1995) claims that the principles found in ethical codes the most frequently are:

- telling the truth
- being loyal
- being compassionate
- being fair (or just)

The first of these involves personal integrity, being honest and sincere and keeping our promises. The second encompasses trustworthiness, dependability, and responsibility. The third covers the need to be kind, sympathetic, and benevolent to others. We should follow the golden rule of doing to others as we would have them do to us. This appears to be an innate predisposition resulting from our ability to imagine ourselves doing the same actions we observe being performed by other people. We should avoid harming others, stealing their property, or being vengeful or malicious. The fourth principle involves the concept of equality, accountability for our actions, and tolerance of others over matters of opinion. Kidder makes the point that our most painful moral dilemmas arise when we find moral principles in conflict (e.g., when a child has cancer do we tell her the truth or lie out of compassion?). We are forced to reexamine the applicability of the principles in these circumstances.

5.16 Sidgwick and His Ethical Theories

Henry Sidgwick lived in the period after Hume and Kant and into the twentieth century. He included Bertrand Russell among his pupils.

His magnum opus was *The Methods of Ethics* (1907), which went to seven editions. Sidgwick was impressed by the way different values led to conflicts. He explained that he was at first a follower of John Stuart Mill whose beliefs might be summarized in two principles: firstly that men should follow their own passions and secondly that our conduct should produce the greatest good for the greatest number. But Sidgwick found these two principles incompatible and turned to Kant who advocated the idea that individual morality included a certain number of instinctive "categorical imperatives" to do good for the benefit of others. Sidgwick realized that Darwin's theory of evolution contained the explanation of these instinctive urges to act in altruistic ways. They may seem like absolutes to us, but in fact, they are really well-reinforced emotions. There were three methods by which men could arrive at reasoned ethical stances according to Sidgwick: hedonism, intuitionism, and utilitarianism. These were the methods referred to in the title of his book. Sidgwick's lifelong devotion to the study of ethics has been said to have left us with probably the most closely and carefully reasoned presentation on the subject up to his time. His work has provided a background for later writers such as Rawls (*Theory of Justice*) and Peter Singer (theory of the expanding circle of our involvement). Justice and law, politics and democracy, art, beauty and aesthetics, knowledge, science and truth, economics, and freedom are all values and parts of the humanist curriculum. Studies of these various values and systems have taken on lives of their own, but they cannot be completely divorced from one another. How we treat them in our individual lives comprises our ideologies. We should recognize that oversimplified ideologies are not just cramping in style but positively dangerous. Sidgwick draws attention to what he terms the morality of common sense, which includes all the various values that have been accumulated in history. He points out that these values may be in conflict with one another. If we wish to resolve the difficulties, Sidgwick proposes that we must find more basic principles such as Kant's stipulation on universality. We might say that Kant and Sidgwick between them took us beyond values. We have to accommodate many different values and become pluralistic as Isaiah Berlin was inclined to say. Sidgwick did not think that evolution had any relevance to ethics.

5.17 Existentialism

I first heard about existentialism when I was a student at university and later read Fromm's book *Man for Himself* (1947) and *Six Existentialist Thinkers* by H. J. Blackham (1952), the doyen of British humanism. I read Sartre's *Is Existentialism a Humanism*, and finally, I studied a book by Thomas R. Flynn titled *Existentialism: A Very Short Introduction* (2006). I no longer have any doubts that existentialism and humanism are closely related, and in fact, they seem to me now to be like the two sides of the proverbial coin.

5.17.1 Philosophy as a Way of Life

There has been a long tradition of philosophy being a way of life and the study of self-conduct, going all the way back to Socrates who lived a life in harmony with his teaching. The Epicureans and stoics were more interested in moral than scientific truth. Flynn portrays the modern existentialist movement as being started by Kierkegaard and Nietzsche both of whom were searching for a truth to live and die for. Nietzsche proclaimed God is dead and proposed a radical new theory of the origin of religion in his *Genealogy of Morals* (1887). Kierkegaard was a Danish writer whose main accomplishment was the realization that our lives are shaped by the choices we make. His most famous book had the title of *Either/Or* (1843). He attacked the three forces of conformity in the Copenhagen of his day: the popular press, the state church, and the reigning philosophy of Hegel. Although Nietzsche was an atheist, Kierkegaard remained Christian, but they both shared a desire to shake up their bourgeois contemporaries. It was Jaspers who originally proposed a philosophy of existence and first discussed Nietzsche and Kierkegaard as a pair. Jaspers was courageously anti-Nazi and was stripped of his professorship as a result. Husserl, the inventor of phenomenology, a very important contribution to existentialism, was also removed from a professorship by the Nazis.

The existentialist movement has never been a tight-knit organization but rather a loose grouping of literary and philosophical writers who have shared certain thoughts and values and worked on similar themes. Flynn lists the main themes that characterize the movement:

1) Existence precedes essence, i.e., what you are (your essence) is a result of your choices (your existence) rather than the reverse. You are what you make of yourself.
2) Time is of the essence. We are fundamentally time-bound beings, who are born into this world and later die.
3) Existentialism, like humanism, is a person-centered philosophy. Though not antiscientific, its focus is primarily on the individual's pursuit of identity in the midst of a mass society.
4) Freedom and responsibility: Existentialism is a philosophy of freedom. But we have to be as responsible as we are free.
5) Ethical considerations are paramount. The underlying concern is to make us examine the authenticity of our personal lives and of our society.

5.17.2 Becoming an Individual

Kierkegaard's epitaph was *That Single Individual,* and much of his writing was focused on the need to achieve one's individuality. He contended that individuals can go through three stages: the aesthetic, the ethical, and the religious. Don Juan was a model for the aesthetic, Socrates for the ethical, and Abraham for the religious. Some people may only reach the first stage, which is governed by the sensual satisfaction of the present moment. The ethical stage is governed by the choices we make. The first choice is whether or not to play the game, i.e., to choose between good and evil. The religious stage is entered by a leap of faith, which is beyond good and evil. Flynn speculates if this choice is the move into situation ethics, and he stresses how Sartre and others had to choose whether or not to stay in Nazi occupied France. Nietzsche was concerned with the will to power and thus was for freedom although not for everyone. His "free spirits" had to escape from the confines of Jewish-Christian morality. The later existentialists, most notably Sartre, elaborated on this theme of the freedom and responsibility of the individual. The concern was for everyone to discover their true selves by using reason and emotion, thus becoming authentic individuals.

5.17.3 Humanism and Existentialism

Is Existentialism a Humanism? was the title of a famous lecture given by Sartre in October 1945 given to an overflow crowd and rapidly to become the talk of the left-bank cafes, then all of Paris and Europe. The talk started by proclaiming "existence precedes essence," which meant, he explained, that individuals create their own values because there is no moral order in the universe. This freedom is the ultimate value. The talk went on echoing his book *Being and Nothingness*. He gave the lecture to answer his critics among the Communists and Catholics. He needed to present a viable and relevant social philosophy in order to stand comparison with these two groups. He based his appeal on Kant's ethic of universal principles. He continued by arguing that we need a sense of responsibility for other people and for society as a whole (which was different from his previous contentions). In asserting that existentialism is a humanism, Sartre means that it places the human being at the center of its attention and at the apex of its value hierarchy. Our ultimate goal should be to foster the freedom of the individual. This highest value should not be sacrificed to Marxist class or religious gods. Sartre's existentialists echoed Nietzsche's free spirits as in *Human, All Too Human*.

But there is a problem with this freedom we humanists have, namely, that we are obliged to reformulate our goals and over and over as the situation changes. Camus viewed this freedom as a source of anguish and considered our situation to be absurd. He compared our situation to the myth of Sisyphus who was obliged to roll a stone up a hill only to have it roll down again over and over. But Sisyphus found happiness in the absurd situation by making a deliberate choice to roll the stone as often as needed. Camus counseled that our only hope is to acknowledge that there is no ultimate hope. Flynn believes that like the stoics, we must limit our expectations because of our mortality.

5.17.4 Authenticity, Choice, and Commitment

Flynn quotes Hume's insight that no statements of fact can justify a statement of obligation or in other words that the "ought" of moral value cannot be derived from the "is" of factual description. There has to be grounding in one's own emotions and values by being true to oneself. It was actually Heidegger who first used the term *authenticity*, but it came to be seen as the central existentialist virtue. It was taken up by Sartre who wrote "the choice of authenticity appears to be a moral decision." Ethical considerations are paramount for existentialists. Sartre claimed that Camus's stubborn humanism reaffirmed the existence of moral fact against the Machiavellians and amoral "realists" of his day. Sartre's prescription for authenticity was that we should each own up to our self-defining choices, make them our own, and consequently become selves by acknowledging what we are. The inauthentic person is one living a lie.

Now the existential truth of our condition is that we all have a being-in-situation. We are an integral part of the universe and the cultural world. Our situation is an ambiguous mixture of facticity and transcendence. We come onto the scene not with a blank slate because we already have a past. But it is the future that is most important, for as Sartre said, "You can always make something out of what you've been made into." We are fundamentally a work in progress, and to deny this is to be in bad faith. We become authentic when we have made our fundamental choices. This is what gives unifying meaning and direction to our lives. De Beauvoir says that as people face freedom from the strict moral categories of religion or philosophical traditions, they may end up rejecting all values—the position of nihilism. But those who feel the joy of existence will weather the storm of nihilism. She argues that we must work to enhance the freedom of others.

Kierkegaard used the word *truth* as a forerunner for what Sartre called commitment (l'engagement) in the next century. The existentialists made repeated reference to the commitment made by authentic people as individuals and to society. But Kierkegaard saw Don Juan the seducer as a human without commitment. For it is only in the later ethical stage of life that commitments are recognized. He has the judge in *Either/Or* speak of the midnight hour when everyone has to throw off their masks and admit to what they are. We are authentic if we have made commitments. Sartre maintained that it is these commitments that bind us to society and that which, as time goes by, should become more and more like political engagement.

5.17.5 Existential and Social Thought

Flynn's section on social thought is headed "a chastened individualism." This interesting title conveys very well the realization that came upon Sartre that he had social responsibilities to attend to after World War II when the French public obviously came to be very receptive to his message. In one of his earlier plays, Sartre wrote the infamous line "Hell is other people." But the resistance fighter who had become so well-known now had to develop a social theory in a hurry. He was criticized by both the Catholics and the communists for his apparently narcissistic ethic of authenticity. In fact, the existentialist movement had been opposed to bourgeois society from its beginning with Kierkegaard and Nietzsche. The European intellectuals at that time were worried by both the Bolshevik Marxists and the crass materialism and technologism of America. Heidegger wrote of Mitsein, our being thrown together into a cultural world where we are in thrall to public opinion. But Heidegger fell under the sway of Nazi influence in a way that indicates his ethical deficiencies. Habermas said of both Heidegger and Sartre that by making the individual the focal point of their philosophies, they overlooked the intersubjective and social aspect of human life. The end of World War II left Heidegger in disgrace while Jaspers occupied the high ground. Jaspers had lost his professorship by withstanding the Nazis but was reinstated in 1945. He wrote *The Question of German Guilt* (1947) in which he postulated four forms of guilt. Twelve years later, Sartre wrote *The Condemned of Altona*, which categorized French guilt in repressing the Algerian revolution. Jaspers argued that we have to change ourselves especially after the development of the atom bomb.

One of the major contributions of existentialist social thought is to show how social forces affect the individual. Thus, the abstraction of fighting the enemy is played out against the concrete reality of World War I trench warfare in the novel and film *All Quiet on the Western Front* by Erich Maria Remarque, a German veteran. This illustrates the existentialist theme that the political situation puts large numbers of people into a state of abasement and alienation. Sartre, Camus, and Merleau-Ponty were part of the French conscience during the Algerian War. Camus wrote *The Outsider* echoing a similar theme and was awarded the Nobel Prize for Literature in 1957. Sartre and Merleau-Ponty were both involved with communism, and both eventually parted company with it, Merleau-Ponty over Korea and Sartre over Czechoslovakia.

But perhaps the biggest social contribution was Simone de Beauvoir's existentialist feminism. De Beauvoir, like Sartre and Merleau-Ponty, was a graduate of the Ecole Normal Superior. She went on to teach high school. She never married but was Sartre's partner most of their lives. Her major achievement was the publication of *The Second Sex* in 1949. It is still perhaps the most important philosophy text in the feminist movement. The premise of the second sex is that human reality exists "in-situation," which is ambiguous and unstable. She develops the role played by gender and its social construction. She writes: one is not born a woman, one becomes one. Sex is not gender. Sex is a biological fact; gender is a social construction. A large part of the study concerns the secondary role of women in patriarchal societies. She debunks the myth of a feminine essence of passivity and unapproachable purity versus a masculine essence of activity and subjectivity. De Beauvoir argues that what has been socially constructed can be socially and politically dismantled. Above all, her book is an attack on patriarchal power structures and a call to raze them.

5.18 Summary and Outlook

In coming to the close of this chapter on virtues and values, it might be appropriate to summarize what we have learned and to relate it to the larger enterprise of our foray into ethics. My contention has been that both virtues and values are systems driven by human urges and, in fact, that they may both be represented by the same flowchart. By calling on various faculties established by earlier evolution, we have been able to assemble numerous systems useful to individuals (when the systems are called virtues) or useful to social groups (when the systems are called values). Existential philosophers have shown us that some of the choices we make are true life changers. In subsequent chapters, we will review lessons to be learned from other approaches to ethics, including the seeking of happiness and the study of duty and obligations. This then will lead us into issues of the politics of large and small societies, including law and economics. Finally, we will look at some long-range future scenarios, combining the theories of the Anglo-American, the European continental and the Eastern philosophical schools, and the definition of meaning and purpose.

6 Reason

6.1 Synopsis:

Instinct, Emotion, Values, and Reasoning

6.2 Socrates:

Logic and Questions
Gods and the Good

6.3 Plato's Republic

Who Should Rule?
Politics, Democracy

6.4 Aristotle: Logic, Philosophy, and Happiness

The Ethical Project
Syllogisms
Logic, Philosophy, and Happiness
Stoicism (Duty) and Epicureanism (Goodness)

6.5 Emotion and Cognition

Hume and Kant: Emotion and Cognition
Induction, Systems, Human Nature
Utilitarianism: Bentham, Mill, and Dewey
Social Theories: Hegel, Marx, and Habermas

6.6 Great Objectives

Mill and Culture
Healthy, Wealthy, and Wise
Three Factors in Morals

6. Reason

6.1 Synopsis

To summarize the previous chapter, we argued that the behavior of primitive animals was driven by instinct, which must have been felt in the form of emotions. As human evolution progressed, these emotions became the basis for various virtues and values. We argued that both are systems, driven by human urges and emotions. Once we acquired language, we argued that they may both be represented by the same logical flowchart (see figure 4.1). By calling on various faculties established by earlier evolution, we have been able to assemble numerous systems useful to individuals, when the systems are called virtues, or useful to social groups, when the systems are called values. Existential philosophers have shown us that some of the choices we make are true life changers. Progress in the ethics of values has largely been advanced by narratives and by expositions setting out the benefits of new value systems. But in subsequent sections, we will review lessons to be learned from other approaches to ethics, including the use of reason in debating and argumentation. The developments mentioned in the previous chapter are all heavily dependent on emotion. Although some of the later human systems involve the use of reason, it is taken for granted that it is subservient to emotion (or passions as Hume called them). The purpose of the present chapter is to focus on reason itself.

But where do we start studying reason? Do we learn any more by studying it than by using it? The issue is similar to asking if we learn more by studying artificial intelligence than by using a computer or if we can learn more by studying musical acoustics than by singing or playing an instrument. I believe we can learn more in depth about reason. The use of reason began when *Australopithecus* started talking and toolmaking. But it was not until the beginning of civilization that philosophers began thinking about the use of reason in ethics. This then led us into issues of the politics of large and small societies, including law and economics. It was much later that scientists and philosophers such as Locke, Hume, and Kant began to ask how human beings were able to reason. Finally, we will look at some long-range future scenarios, combining the theories of the neuroscientists, psychologists, and sociologists as well as the Anglo-American, the European continental, and the Eastern philosophical schools. This is where our advanced knowledge may be applicable.

6.2 Socrates

Socrates was a master of the use of questions to open up philosophical discourse. The discipline of philosophy has proceeded from his time with the growth of an ever expanding literature. Many questions have been explored although it is unusual for any issue to be completely resolved. Philosophy and the subsection of it we call ethics have recently been described as "projects," meaning that they are seen as ongoing undertakings. It is interesting that the literature of ethics, i.e., the academic writing that focuses on the actual reality of our behavior, has tended to progress on a path that is somewhat disengaged from, and behindhand, to what we actually do. We can recall the spirit of Socrates by asking: what is a question? Take a minute to try to answer this question. I must admit that I had difficulty with this until I found this answer in *Wikipedia*: a question is a linguistic expression used to make a request for information. It was Socrates who said that the unexamined life was not worth living, and Nozick (1989) who called on us all to examine our lives. Another powerful example of the use of reasoning was Plato's dialogue on the ineffectiveness of the gods in ethics. Socrates explains to Euthyphro that the good is not good because the gods approve it, but the gods approve it because it is good (see Plato, 1961).

6.3 Plato's Republic

Let us recollect some of the great ethical milestones by recalling the major works of the philosophical discipline aimed at truly penetrating the theoretical bases of morality. Some of these references will be expanded upon in later sections. Suffice it to say that perhaps the most outstanding work of this kind was *The Republic*, which started as Plato's reprise of Socrates's thinking but then went on to present Plato's own developing philosophy. Plato, who lived half a millennium before the common era, was the first great rationalist, believing that reason led to the truth. *The Republic* contains a number of dialogues, which laid out a wide cosmology including Plato's theory of physical reality (in the allegory of the cave). His ideas on who should rule the city reflect his sad experiences with democracy in the hands of uneducated men. These included those who condemned Socrates to drink hemlock at a punishment for corrupting the youth of Athens. *The Republic* is so startlingly original and impressive that it is still often used to introduce students to philosophy even today. *The Republic* is all about justice. Justice is described as a peculiar excellence or virtue of the soul. Plato and Socrates have high standards for the rulers (or guardians) of their republic. These people have to be philosophers who are well aware of the theory and forms of justice. They should not seek their own advantage but that of their subjects. They must be wise and good. Training of the guardians included music and athletics. Plato believed that women would make good rulers.

6.4 Aristotle: Logic, Philosophy, and Happiness

Plato's student Aristotle was another giant of early ethical discourse. It was Aristotle who introduced us to the concept of eudaimonia (usually translated as happiness or flourishing) as a goal for living. Aristotle set out the framework for philosophical discussion known as the syllogism in his work the *Organum*, delineating the conditions for valid deductions from various premises. The basis of scientific theories using induction, or generalizations, was also established through Aristotle's work. His work on logic and science stood for a thousand years as a touchstone of excellence. The philosophy of the age of Plato and Aristotle eventually gave rise to several schools of thought. The Epicureans and the stoics had become the leading groups before the Romans adopted Christianity. This, of course, was the prelude to a thousand-year dark age when reason was suppressed in favor of religious domination and mysticism. It was not until the time of the Renaissance that we find philosophers who could really challenge and improve upon the ideas of the Greek cosmologists with new inventions.

6.5 Emotion and Cognition

Reason came back into prominence in the time of Hume and Kant who began again in the period of the Enlightenment to explore the structure of the human mind and offer pictures of how emotion and cognition operate in the working of our morality. Bentham took up Hume's theory of Utilitarianism using reasoning to apply it in many legal situations. The Mills, father and son, extended this work further. John Stuart Mill wrote a book on the subject (1861) showing that there was a need to include poetry in the theory of morality after being moved by the work of Wordsworth. On the continent of Europe, a series of mainly German and French philosophers, starting notably with Hegel and his theory of history, launched a program of social theorizing. Karl Marx gave us one of the first ethical theories based on sociology which he claimed was determined by economics. Many philosophers took up the work, and by the time of the twentieth century, we have such giants as Dewey and Habermas expounding pragmatism and the theory of communicative action. Most recently, we have Singer and the expanding circle, pointing out that our morality must extend to other sentient beings who can experience suffering. Paul Kurtz (1988) has shown us the relevance of an ethic of responsibility to our lives as humanists. Philip Kitcher (2011) has shown how ethics is a project that must incorporate the findings of archeology, primatology, anthropology, history, and psychology.

6.6 Great Objectives

In his book *Utilitarianism*, John Stuart Mill (1861) refers to the great objects of human life. We may assume that that what Mill calls an "object" is the same as an "objective" in modern parlance. The examples of great objectives that Mill cites include power, fame, and money. One wonders how seriously Mill was actually endorsing such aims to be the overarching objectives of living or whether he was simply expressing his finding that many people actually do take such aims as these for their lives. My contention is that Mill was indeed recognizing that people do choose such goals in life. After all, happiness has been recognized as an objective of life at least since the time of Aristotle, and virtue has a similarly ancient pedigree. It is quite common for ordinary people to adopt such mottos as "Healthy, wealthy, and wise" as aims for life. We know that having more than one such value can lead to conflicts, which had been a concern to Sidgwick (1834). A resolution to the problem was found by the time of the twentieth century when it was realized that we should not try to achieve definite objectives but instead look to some other consequentialist procedure, such as a variety of evolution, to shape our objectives. In that case, we make plans and evaluate them as we proceed. We should use our values, as Dewey recommended, for guideposts and be prepared to modify our goals when we encounter problems.

I have been enthusiastic to cite the work of J. S. Mill and John Dewey in this section on great objectives. But I have to add some comments of my own before closing it out. Dewey (1930) wrote a paper entitled *Three Independent Factors in Morals*. In the paper, Dewey mentions the uncertainty that makes morality difficulty. The first two of Dewey's factors were goodness and duty. These have been recognized from antiquity and feature in Plato's *Republic*. The third factor, added by Dewey, is approbation or its negative. Presumably, this thinking was a preliminary to the sections on morals in his 1932 book. But my point is that any item to be included in any one of these three factors is based on some form of approbation. For the first category, we certainly approve of goodness (or value) of all sorts of materials, manufactures, and ideas.

We invented the word *goods* as a general term for anything in that class. The second category is duty, which includes justice and law and all varieties of rights, obligations, promises, and habits and human systems. These can similarly be multiplied indefinitely. Adding approbation or its negative as a third category makes the task of classifying any one item with certainty even more difficult. How we actually do our counting depends on our convenience and the circumstances we are in. My suggestion is that we should either cease to try classifying at all or be prepared to recognize many more than the canonical three categories. Perhaps Dewey included the word *independent* to limit the infinite number of possibilities to just his chosen three, but he does not elaborate on this. Thus, in the rest of this book, we examine a number of objectives or systems that might be encountered in life. Each of these can be seen as having a systems structure with a defined end or objective. The grand objective can then be composed of their sum total. We might argue (following Kitcher) that the overarching objective is altruism.

6.7 Dewey: Means and Ends

One of the most prominent philosophers of the early twentieth century was John Dewey who had a great influence on humanists and the intellectual community. He was a prolific author with several publications on moral and ethical topics (1908, 1932, 1939). There is a recent and helpful review of his moral philosophy by Elizabeth Anderson (2014) in the *Stanford Philosophical Series* on the Internet. Dewey saw value judgments as tools for redirecting conduct as opposed to using fixed moral goals and principles. He was clearly well aware of the relevant work in psychology, and Anderson starts with a summary of impulsive and habitual reactions, particularly in children. When habits and impulses are blocked, we are forced to reflect on intelligent conduct for the situation. There is discussion of the differences between valuing and evaluation; and this leads us into investigation of desires, interests, and tastes. Anderson suggests that Dewey's term *desires* is closer to the recent usage of *purpose* or even *plan*. Dewey saw value judgments as means. Anderson reviews the criticism of Dewey and then defends him for his concern with means and ends.

The review continues with Dewey's description of the variety of ethical theories: teleological (seeking a supreme end or good), deontological (looking for laws of morality), and virtuous (taking approval or disapproval as fundamental). Dewey was clearly aware of the contradictions that might occur between theories of the good, but he formulated a modified approach to their use in his theory of value. His reasoning was that these theories still had usefulness if employed as instruments or as means to final ends. Anderson claims that Dewey offered a critique of the three types of goodness theory dominant today: hedonism, ideal theories, and informed desire theories. Deontological theories tend to identify the right with fixed laws of conduct such as the Ten Commandments or with a single supreme principle of morality such as the categorical imperative. Virtue theories rest on approval or disapproval as a fundamental basis, and Dewey saw in this a connection to British utilitarianism. Anderson's review concludes with a discussion of Dewey's application of his ethical thinking to art, to aesthetics and social studies, and, in particular, to education.

6.8 Systems and Evolution

Among the most important contributions of reasoning to the ethical project was the clarification of the concept of a system invented by Aristotle and used in his biological researches. This was revived by Hume at the time of the Enlightenment, with an emphasis on finding constancies in our observation of nature and human affairs. But it was Darwin who realized that biological evolution could be described as gradual changes occurring in constant systems. Eventually, such changes were explained as mutations in the genetic code of species. It took some decades for these ideas to be fully appreciated, and it is only now that we are learning how to engineer genetic material to cure cancer and to produce new plants and animals. The theory of evolution has been slow to influence ethics effectively. Probably, a major holdup came from the work of Herbert Spencer who invented the phrase *survival of the fittest*. This slogan was actually adopted by Darwin himself for a while, but it unfortunately came to be interpreted as a justification for powerful people to do whatever they pleased in furthering their own aims. It might be paraphrased as "might makes right," and this was the slogan associated with a movement known as social Darwinism, which grew up at the end of the nineteenth century. But Darwin wrote a book *The Expression of the Emotions in Man and Animals* (1872), which contained an argument explaining how group selection could result in favoring altruistic behavior contrary to the expectations of the social Darwinists. There was also a very telling essay by Thomas Huxley to the effect that since it is impossible to predict the result of evolutionary change, there is no way to predict what is "right" for survival and thus to know who are the fittest at any one time. Social Darwinism went into decline around 1900. The theory of biological evolution was strengthened by its unification with Mendelian genetics, and social Darwinism faded away. Biological evolution came back into favor as an important predictor of individual and social behavior.

One relevant discussion is due to Daniel C. Dennett (2003), who introduced the term *can-do* to denote our ability to do the things that we want to do. Can-do is equivalent to practical knowledge, which is related in this way to "freedom," which, in turn, depends on our knowledge of particular situations. So we might say that *can-do* is roughly equivalent to *know-how*. Dennett's thesis is that freedom is not a God-given power: it is a human creation like music or money. Humans are the end product of a long history of biological evolution, which led to behavior with increasingly complex decision-making capacity. The more options there are available to us, the greater is our repertoire of can-do, including learned routines, habits and skills, machines, systems and social arrangements; and the greater is our freedom. Van Doren's *A History of Knowledge* (1991) is a recital of our progress in knowledge over last few millennia.

Dennett's book also shows how the concept of liberty as a system can also be applied to the life of the individual. Memes for personal morality are a part of Dennett's cultural thesis. It was difficult at first for evolutionists to understand cooperation. Many competing molecular systems had to be reconciled to enable cells to function. Then came the great revolution involved in the appearance of eukaryotic (multicellular organisms) posing more cooperative challenges. The immune system started as a co-option of foreign cells, which became slaves committed to the summum bonum of the body. Theorists demonstrate altruism and morality by using simulations of the evolutionary process based on game theory. As the conditions of the simulations are made more realistic and complex, the results get better. When the agents are programmed to learn from experience, cooperators start to punish defectors. But treating the welfare of others as an end in itself only occurs when agents make positive commitments and in addition convince others that they have done so by earning a good reputation. And how do we earn a good reputation? The best way is by actually being good. This is Dennett's way of describing how we build up trust in our associates.

Dennett has echoed Kierkegaard's theme in his claims. Choice machines were a great improvement on trial and error, and finally, communication was invented, requiring self-monitoring. The situation was thus similar to that faced by computer software writers in our own age who simplified control to click and drag, sound effects, and icons. Similar R&D was required to interface-talking people. The centerpiece was an icon called the self, which enabled us to keep track of emotions, answer inquiries, ask questions, and grasp reasons. The conscious will came about as a mechanism to control the language-using parts of the brain. This fits in with Dennett's theory of consciousness as explained in his earlier book (1991). Dennett refers to Hume who pointed out that our natural motives constitute the basis on which, with the use of reason, we build virtuous behavior and concepts such as justice. He saw ethics as a kind of technology. We derive ethical theories, political ideologies, and systems of justice. Each individual is involved in psychic engineering, and our lives are an arms race of rationality. We are the only species that can anticipate the future, and this we should do if we are to be morally responsible.

What is the answer to our puzzlement over the failure of the philosophical community to frame ethics in the context of evolution and systems theory? Sidgwick himself bore some of the responsibility for the lack of impact of evolution on ethics. In 1876 he wrote a paper on the subject, which was published in the first issue of Mind. This was seventeen years after the publication of *On the Origin of Species*. Sidgwick paid much attention to Herbert Spencer and comparatively little to Darwin, whose thoughts on altruism first appeared in the *Descent of Man* (1871) and then in *The Expression of the Emotions in*

Man and Animals. Sidgwick pronounced that the theory of evolution "as widely understood, has little or no bearing upon ethics." The ideas of systems theory came to fruition during and after World War II but not in such a way that there was a coherent body of knowledge anywhere near as well-known as the basics of physical science. In particular, the idea of recognizing a system from its constancy, which can be traced to Hume, himself a giant of moral theory, should have been a cornerstone in the understanding of ethics as systems. Finlayson's book (2005) is of some interest because it is in Habermas's combination of philosophical and social theoretic expertise that we might expect to find systems concepts best understood. In subsequent chapters, we will discuss how as humanists we can best bring together our individual lives with our social behavior to serve such goals as expanding knowledge, preserving the physical environment, contributing and upholding the world of aesthetics, and pursuing justice and a more benevolent society. Our aims should be centered on pluralistic systems; and we should be committed to work for them as professionals, scientists, leaders, artists, lovers, parents, and children. The humanist movement should be an attempt to develop theories and systems that will be of real utility as described in the writings of Kurtz (1983, 1988, 1989), Storer (1980), and Lamont (1982).

6.9 Science, Technology, and the Future

Reasoning has always played a major role in science and technology. In a sense, language and thinking are a part of, or at least an antecedent to, the technical areas. All through human history, from the earliest stone tools and primitive weapons up to the latest supercollider and computer, reasoning has kept pace with technology. In later chapters, we will discuss work by Daniel Dennett and by Ray Kurweil, two leading reasoners extraordinaire on science and technology. One of the key points here is the ability of the human brain to anticipate the future. We have reached the point now where there are predictions of robots designing robots to make improvements without human intervention. Of course, this calls for regulation and control (presumably by yet more robots). There are worries that we humans will be relegated to the trash heaps and equally strong contradictions. As science advances, we look further into the future. We are very concerned about climate change on Earth in this century and where evolving systems, from nanorobots to superorganisms will take us.

Predictions of the future by their nature are speculations of varying degrees. They are examples of reasoning based on assumptions, and the further ahead are the conclusions reached, the greater are the implicit uncertainties. E. O. Wilson (2014) has criticized philosophy for its unscientific stance, and yet in his latest book, *The Meaning of Human Existence*, he makes a number of predictions based on reasoning about subjects ranging from exoplanets to our species' long-range prospects. He finishes his book, as we will finish this chapter, by claiming that we are alone but free to make godlike choices in the universe.

7. Methods of Ethics

7.1 Introduction

Retrospect
Utility
Bentham's Theory: Law
Mill's Theory
Kitcher's Theory: Altruism

7.2 Liberty

Freedom of Development
Freedom of Speech
Tolerance
Individuality
Dennett's Theory

7.3 Equality

Slavery
Subjection of Women
Angels in the House
Women's Suffrage
Expanding Circles

7.4 Theories

Bacon, Hume, and Sidgwick
Recent Developments in Philosophy
Williams and Ethical Theories
Methodology of Moral Theory
Ethical Knowledge

7.5 Situational Ethics

Constancy and Unpredictability
Situational Analysis
System Determinants
Fletcher's Principles
Varieties of Systems

7.6 Organization and Objectives

Storer: Humanism and the Academy
Various Approaches
Finding Agreement: Translations
Responsibility
Means and Ends

7.7 Humanist Declarations

Manifestos
Universal Declaration of Human Rights
Symposia

7.8 Consequentialist Theories: Planning and Learning

State of Nature
Management by Objectives
Systematization
Future Prospects

7. Methods of Ethics

7.1 Introduction

How do we bring the lessons of these previous six chapters together in humanist theories of ethics? We saw in chapters 2 and 5 that historically ethics began with the development of virtues appropriate to hunter-gatherer societies. Even today a person might use these values and virtues as the basis of an ethical theory, and in chapters 3 and 6, we argued that such values are based on rational constructions supported by emotions as well as many instinctive morals. Values and their embodiments as virtues are, in effect, theories for living although they were not originally thought of as such. Early theories valued brave and strong individualists; and with the growth of civilization based on agriculture, traits useful in city life (the polis) such as altruism, benevolence, and fairness began to be appreciated. We concluded that a modern viewpoint is that all and any of the values are useful and that we live pluralistic lives. The Greeks Protagoras and Socrates adopted the slogan "good people in a good society." This is a neat encapsulation of the humanist philosophy. But among the later Greek thinkers, as we saw in chapter 2, it was the stoics and Epicureans with their naturalistic ideas who were the closest to modern humanism, which clearly excludes any supernaturalist beliefs such as were held by Plato and in the Christian and some Eastern religions. When Christianity triumphed in the Roman empire, it was the thinking of Plato and Aristotle that grew into theories with a theological basis such as those of Saint Augustine and Saint Thomas Aquinas.

When philosophers began to question the theological theories, they had to explain how order was maintained in society without the authority of a God. It was then that they began to see clearly that these theistic conceptions were indeed artificial theories. Hobbes invented the idea of a social contract: an agreement between men to accept the rule of a monarch. Hobbes was an atheist, and his purported social contract was certainly an arrangement between humans. Some version of the idea held sway until Hume applied the power of a skeptical examination to it, arguing instead that there had always been some sort of government which had grown gradually more complex with time. According to Hume, it was the growth of the system of laws that provided the state with its continuity and the emphasis on duty and obligation was what carried over into the ethics of the individual. Not very long after Hume's time, Marx produced a theory of society wherein the driving influence was economic: the means of production, as he phrased it. In chapter 5, we discussed theories that focus on some future end such as happiness.

Utilitarianism is a central philosophical doctrine of humanism. Its antecedents go back to Epicurus and Aristotle in ancient Greece, and its modern resurrection started with David Hume. The next great advocate of its concepts was Jeremy Bentham whose version of the philosophy was given in *Introduction to Principles of Morals and Legislation* (1789). Bentham believed that it was possible to calculate a number that would be the sum of all the benefits in a system minus its disadvantages. This number was then the utility. He used the concept to evaluate a wide variety of laws. If a system was applied to a number of people, then the calculation was made by summing the utilities for all the individuals. Bentham later came to equate utility with happiness and extended the theory until it became a complete ethical system. Bentham was credited with reforming the legal and prison systems in Britain. He was also the author of a plan for policing the River Thames in 1798, which, in turn, served as the model for Sir Robert Peel's 1829 organization of the London Police Force.

James Mill became a utilitarian through his friendship with Bentham, and it was he who introduced his son, John Stuart Mill, to the work in 1821. John immediately became an enthusiast and felt that the philosophy gave him a creed for his own thinking. His own version of the theory was first published in 1861. Mill starts by dealing with the ignorant blunder by which utility is opposed to pleasure. Another of the common charges against utility equates it to the grossest forms of pleasure. Critics complain that the theory is too dry when the word *utility* precedes the word *pleasure* and that the theory is too voluptuous when the word *pleasure* precedes the word *utility*. He says that everyone from Epicurus to Bentham knows that in the theory utility stands for pleasure itself. It might also stand for agreeable or ornamental or beauty or amusement. It does not necessarily imply superiority to frivolity or pleasures of the moment. The principle of utility or greatest happiness holds that actions are right in proportion as they tend to promote happiness, wrong as they tend to promote the reverse of happiness. The theory of life on which this theory of morality is grounded claims that pleasure and freedom from pain are the only things desirable as ends. Mill made it clear that the theory covered poetry, music, and fine arts not just simple pleasures and desires. He himself suffered a breakdown from which he eventually recovered with the help of the poetry of William Wordsworth. Eventually, both Bentham and Mill were convinced that utility was to be equated to the greatest happiness, which Aristotle had identified as the summum bonum.

There is an interesting aspect of Hume's work: in one place he writes of *benevolence* as an important value in ethics and, in another place, of *sympathy*. Clearly, these two words have different etymologies and different dictionary definitions. However, it is also clear that they both represent very similar emotions. I had been reading Philip Kitcher's book *The Ethical Project* in which he emphasizes altruism as the most crucial human emotion. I then attended a lecture by Frans de Waal in which he described empathy as the critical emotion. He also stresses the importance of empathy in his recent book *The Bonobo and the Atheist* (2013). When I asked de Waal about this, he indicated that the two words were in the same general area (I do not remember his exact words). My thought is that perhaps they are both associated with the same (or very similar) neurotransmitters (or neurotransmission paths) in the brain. Maybe that is what de Waal meant. To conclude, the suggestion is that all such words as utility, happiness, and pleasure involve a similar neurological response and words such as *benevolence*, *sympathy*, and *altruism* refer to a state where the emotion(s) called up by the former group are directed toward other people.

7.2 Liberty

A major contribution that John Stuart Mill made was his essay *On Liberty*. This was, according to Mill, the expression of a single truth, the importance of "giving full freedom to human nature to expand itself in innumerable and conflicting directions." I have quoted from Mill's powerful prose at some length in the following. He says his subject is "the nature and limits of the power which can be legitimately exercised by society over the individual." He defends the absolute freedom of individuals to engage in conduct not harmful to others and the near-absolute freedom of individuals to express opinions of all kinds. This results in the recognition of a variety of individual characters and views. In modern parlance, we might say that the book is about freedom and, in particular, of speech. Mill paints a dismal picture of a society in which the individual has been suppressed or kept down by the weight of unexamined customs. These people fail to exercise the human capacity of making a choice and developing qualities of "perception, judgment, discriminative feeling, mental activity and even moral preference." They only have the faculty of "apelike imitation." Mill believed there would be benefits for all when society allows persons the freedom to develop themselves.

Mill saw social progress and individual well-being in terms of the "free development of individuality itself, and as one of the principal ingredients of human happiness." New and enlightened forms of conduct will be discovered by the few original thinkers, "the salt of the earth." These compare with the "collective mediocrity" of the masses. He saw freedom as something of "intrinsic worth" not only as an element of civilization, instruction, education, and culture but as a part of all these. He maintained that, if a person possesses any tolerable amount of common sense and experience, his own mode of laying out his existence is the best. However, even those who spurn self-development have claims not to be subjected to the enlightened coercion of original thinkers. Mill stresses both the instrumental and intrinsic values of freedom of discussion. He points out that freedom of discussion is the best means to the discovery of true beliefs. This makes it the main tool of philosophy. We also need institutional arrangements for the expression of a diversity of views, including universities granting academic freedom to teachers and researchers. We must have constraints on the ownership of the media of communication. Concentration of such media in too few hands represents serious dangers.

Mill's instrumental arguments for freedom of discussion would cut no ice with those, especially religious people, who believe they have infallible sources of knowledge. They claim to have infallible holy books. The case for religious toleration must rest on the right of people to be guided by their own religious convictions even if wrong. If only one man held an opinion contrary to all the rest of mankind, mankind would not be justified in silencing him. But the instrumental argument is only a part of Mill's case for freedom of discussion. A more important part stresses the value of freedom even when we are sure we have true beliefs. Errors are fruitful to understand true beliefs. Mill aims to know the truth. This involves having an open mind to whatever objections can be raised against one's opinions and conduct. "All silencing of discussion is an assumption of infallibility." "Complete liberty of contradicting and disproving our opinion is the condition which justifies us in assuming its truth for the purposes of action." Even if a person knows the truth, they are not entitled to believe it. The importance of this in a changing world cannot be overestimated, e.g., consider persons, religious, or otherwise who believe they have shortcuts to the truth, bypassing free discussion. They typically claim to have access to general principles, but these need to be applied to various circumstances. Unless they understand the rationale and proper basis, they would be unable to apply them to new cases and situations.

Mill argued that individuality has a close connection to this defense of freedom of discussion. A clash of opinions and freedom to engage in conduct not harmful to others will generate the variety to challenge custom-induced uniformity. Ordinary people are the most vulnerable to the "despotism of custom" and the most likely not to develop individuality. But great thinkers can survive even in an oppressive environment. It is mainly to promote flourishing among "average human beings" that Mill pleads for freedom of discussion. To be truly free, we have to live in a free society with free institutions and tolerance of diversity and dissent. He does, however, set some limits to freedom of expression. He says you can't express the opinion that "corn-dealers are starvers of the poor" before an excited mob outside the corn dealer's house, i.e., where the expression is a positive instigation to some mischievous act.

There is a similar absoluteness in the freedom Mill extends to the conduct of individuals. He makes a distinction between self-regarding and other-regarding conduct. The former has absolute freedom but not the latter. The reason, according to Mill, is that self-regarding conduct has no adverse effect on others. The only purpose for which power can be rightfully exercised over an individual is to prevent harm to others. This is sometimes known as the harm principle and is probably the most widely quoted of Mill's writings. Interference with a man for his own good is not a sufficient warrant. Many take as an injury to themselves, conduct for which they have a distaste. But there is no parity between the feelings of a person for his own opinion and the feelings of another who is offended at his holding it. Persons should be free to develop their individualities without the paternalistic and moralistic interference of others. But when there is harm to others, then balancing the costs and benefits of intervention is appropriate.

Mill claims that his case for liberty does not rest on "the idea of abstract right, as a thing independent of utility." He sees utility as the ultimate appeal on all ethical questions. But he argues that it must be utility "in the largest sense." He was appalled by the Mormon institution of polygamy, which he called a retrograde step in civilization. But he tolerated it on the assumption that the women participated voluntarily. Parents should not have absolute power over children. Husbands should not have "almost despotic power" over their wives. He opposed all those who seek to control the lives of family, in the name of religion, culture, or deep moral principles.

Liberty or freedom have been the rallying cries for various political causes throughout history, and we take this up again in a later chapter. In addition, there have been other fundamental developments around the theme as in Daniel Dennett's *Freedom Evolves* (2003). The point there is that we cannot be free to do what we do not know how to do or if we do not have the means to implement our plans. Again we defer attention to the details of the arguments to later chapters.

7.3 Equality

Of course, the most flagrant violation of freedom was in the institution of slavery, the abolition of which was one of the greatest moral changes to have occurred comparatively recently in the Western world. Slavery was abolished in the British empire in 1833 due largely to the influence of William Wilberforce, but the struggle to overcome it was much more protracted in America. Although the ownership of one human being by another had been accepted since the early days of civilization, in the eighteenth century, revulsion at the practice finally grew so strong that it was abandoned throughout much of the world. There were many different concepts to distinguish those who might be enslaved from those who might not be. Each of these ideas drew its own counterarguments. As late as 1852, Mary Eastman wrote a response to *Uncle Tom's Cabin*, which assembled many of these arguments: Africans are descendants of Ham, cursed by God, with traits of character requiring firm discipline by wiser (and benevolent) people of European ancestry; slaves are no more appropriate bearers of freedom and self-government than wayward children. Even Voltaire and Hume believed in African inferiority, and Thomas Jefferson wrote disparagingly of Negroes. How did the transition from a patently ethical wrong take place?

A collection of counterarguments systematically dismantled the justificatory attempts of the apologists. They dissected the evidence for a biblical curse. They proposed other ways of bringing the African soul to grace than the ocean passage, slave auction, unremitting toil, sexual abuse, and lash. They displayed the accomplishments of individual slaves whose words and works refute theses of innate racial difference. A pioneering abolitionist was John Woolman who was troubled by the conflict between the institution and his Christian duty. He wrote a book *Some Considerations on the Keeping of Negroes* first published in 1754 in which he argued that *Negroes are our Fellow Creatures*. Kitcher (2011) has studied this work very carefully. Woolman first mentioned concern about slavery when he was asked to write a bill of sale for a female slave. He did not know that the women would not be maltreated. Kitcher admires Woolman's eventual rejection of slavery but stresses that his reasons are not those of any contemporary secular ethical framework. Progress was not achieved through any clear new ethical insight. The course of the change in attitude, and consequent growth in sympathy for slaves was unsteady and incomplete. It took lengthy wrestlings with conscience for Americans to see the suffering of slaves as those of real people.

Kitcher should be commended for associating the changes in the moral climate that occurred in Europe and America with the repudiation of slavery. But if anything, Kitcher has underreported the enormity of the transition involved. Consider the events in America as recounted for instance by Bacon (1991). There were many people who came to understand the immorality of the institution in the hundred years or so before its final rejection. It was Harriet Beecher Stowe (1852) who wrote the novel *Uncle Tom's Cabin*, which, according to Phillip Bacon's (1991) history of the United States, did more than anything else to turn people in the north against slavery. There were preachers such as Sojourner Truth who went up and down the country preaching freedom for all slaves. Frederick Douglass was born a slave on a Maryland plantation but eventually after teaching himself to read and write escaped to freedom in New York City. Thereafter, he lectured and started a newspaper on the privations of slavery. But there was also a major political aspect to slavery that had become a divisive difference between the northern and Southern states. The invention of the cotton gin made cotton growing a profitable occupation and slavery provided the plantation owners with the means to great wealth. The division between the free states of the north and the slave-owning states of the South became increasingly bitter as new states sought to join the Union. But perhaps the most eloquent appeal for freedom came from John Stuart Mill in England his work *On Liberty* (1859). By 1860 there were nearly four million slaves in the USA, and the price of a good field hand had risen to a thousand dollars. There was a network of safe places along the route to Canada, which was known as the Underground Railroad, and there were famous people who served as guides (known as conductors) along the route. One such person was Harriet Tubman, an escaped slave from Maryland who guided three hundred people to freedom. Abraham Lincoln was elected president in 1860 on the Republican platform, which stood against the extension of slavery and denying states the right to secede from the Union. Several slave states voted to secede and form what became known as the Confederacy.

The Civil War, which followed, lasted four years, and cost the lives of approximately 620,000 soldiers who died from combat, accident, starvation, and disease. The slaves were freed in 1863 by Lincoln's Emancipation Proclamation. Black soldiers fought for the first time on the Union side. Rifle muskets were introduced for the first time. Lincoln made the celebrated Gettysburg Address in 1863 in which he claimed that thousands had died so that "government of the people, by the people, for the people shall not perish from the earth." Lincoln's assassination occurred in 1865. Historians of the Civil War have long argued about its causes. It has been claimed to be due to economics, political (over state rights), and slavery. In recent years, it has been seen primarily as a moral war. Harry S. Stout has written *Upon the Altar of the Nation: A Moral History of the Civil War.* Now, of course, this goes well beyond Kitcher's presentation, but he is surely to be commended for realizing that, in fact, warfare is a moral issue. The repercussions of the Civil War and the aftermath of slavery are still being felt. But perhaps this account will have exemplified the nature of moral change as clearly as any. There was a growing awareness of the repugnance of the former situation followed by emotional reactions and persuasion and finally a period of combat as the new order came into being as the entire community became irreversibly persuaded.

For the last part of his life, Mill devoted himself to justice for women, for which reason Richard Reeves (2008) called him the father of feminism. His book *The Subjection of Women* (1869) spelled out the argument for equality. Mill summarized the argument in the first paragraph. It was "that the principle which regulates the existing social relations between the two sexes—the legal subordination of one sex to the other—is wrong in itself, and now one of the chief hindrances to human improvement; and that it ought to be replaced by a principle of perfect equality, admitting no power or privilege on the one side, nor disability on the other." He tackled head-on the view that women were not up to gender equality. He did not deny that women at that time were less well equipped for public life than men but insisted this was the result of their subjection rather than its cause. "What is now called the nature of women is an eminently artificial thing—the result of forced repression in some directions, unnatural stimulation in others."

It was also undeniable that women did not feature on the list of pioneering artists or scholars, but it was eminently deniable that this was due to inherent inferiority. Mill wrote, "Institutions, books, education and society all go on training human beings for the old, long after the new has come." Mill's most dangerous opponents were not the open misogynists but the men and women who romanticized women's delicate domestic nature, seeing them as "Angels in the House" after the 1854 poem by Coventry Patmore. Seventy-five years later, Virginia Woolf declared that killing the "Angel in the House" was part of the occupation of a woman writer. Even Dickens earned Mill's opprobrium by pillorying women's rights in *Bleak House*. Mrs. Beeton's feminine ideal was in stark contrast to the sort of women Mill spent time with. In 1892 William Gladstone based his opposition to women's suffrage on his "fear . . . lest he should invite her unwittingly to trespass upon the delicacy, the purity, the refinement, the elevation of her own nature, which are the present sources of its power." Such attitudes toward women were the real causes of their oppression, Mill believed. He compared women's second-class status with the domestic slavery practiced by the Greeks. One of the ways women were kept in the cold was through their exclusion from higher education. Mill bequeathed about half of his estate to women in higher education. He pointed out the absurd traditional custom in the Middle East of seeing it as the height of indecency for women to be seen in the streets unveiled. In *The Subjection of Women*, Mill covered the whole history of women's oppression, but he was convinced that the key to unlocking the door for women was getting them the vote. He based his argument on the fact that women paid taxes. Women's interests were not necessarily safe in the hands of fathers, husbands, and brothers since these men were frequently the most brutal abusers. Men were short-changing themselves by lowering the quality of their life companions. For Mill, being around a passive, meekly, subservient creature was not good for the soul. For him, equality was a necessary condition for liberty, and the virtue of human beings is fitness to live together as equals, claiming nothing for themselves but what they freely concede to everyone else.

We should be mentioning Hypatia, Wollstonecraft, Friedan, de Beauvoir, Gilligan, Held, Noddings, Ruddick, Rand, and many other women writers. There is an excellent review of feminist ethics on the *Internet in the Stanford Encyclopedia of Philosophy*. The ethics of caring feature prominently in these works, and we know that women are greatly interested in the humanities and the psychology of relationships. If we were to explore these subjects with the same zeal males give to justice, rationality, and hard science, we might begin to realize that women do, in fact, have abilities equal to those of the male. Surely, we should welcome women's contributions to their own salvation. We have only just started to investigate the psychology, neuroscience, and biology of reproduction.

7.4 Theories

Bernard Williams (1996), in a "second look" at contemporary philosophy, argues that if philosophers are to have a claim to attention, they should be prepared to offer *ethical theories*. He maintains that there are three basic types of such theories, which are sometimes called consequentialist, deontological, and virtue theories. The second category puts an emphasis on duty or obligation. We might suppose that the theorists are essentially political philosophers of liberal to libertarian views. Presumably, although Williams does not call them out, the group might include writers from Plato and Aristotle through Aquinas, Hobbes, Marx, Rawls, Nozick and Habermas, to name a few. Williams's calling for ethical *theories* seems to me to be one step closer to systems theory. Had he called for making the objective of ethicists the construction of complex pluralistic and adaptive systems, I could have been sure we were in complete agreement. At one point, he writes of *schema* (a term used in systems theory) rather than *theories*. But Williams is concerned that the impact of ethical theories on moral philosophy is very dubious. Perhaps the difficulty comes from the use of the word *theory*, which is usually reserved for explanations in natural science. Human arrangements do not have the exactness of laws of physics. To describe ourselves and our societies, we have to think in terms of systems governed by schema. But such schema could incorporate values such as truth, justice, benevolence, and so forth. They could be expressed in terms of behavioral rules and carry emotional connotations, be expressed in analytic terms, and be tested by evaluation as applied in the lives of social groups *or individuals*.

7.5 Situation Ethics

What are the contexts in which ethical reasoning is applied? As we pointed out in chapter 3, there is a substantial portion of our morality, which is instinctively guided. The only control we may exercise on this biological component of morality is to refrain from actions which our reason may deem to be inappropriate in modern life. Then there is a class of action we acquire by habit as we first discussed in chapter 2 in describing Hume's contributions to ethics. Bertrand Russell is one of the few philosophers who followed Hume's lead in praising the benefits of our habitual behavior. Once a habit has been acquired, we are saved the bother of having to think. Now there is an aspect of habitual behavior that would have been obvious to Hume but not perhaps to the many philosophers who overlooked it and that is that for a habit to develop there must be a repetition of the situation to which the habit applies. There must in other words be a *constancy* in the situation. Hume saw this human ability to recognize constancy as a very important human ability. Rapoport (1986) realized that the constancy in a situation is what defines a system. Let us take a while to reflect on the tremendous variety of such systems and constancies we recognize in the course of our lives. To start with, there are a large number of kinetic memory systems we use to get around: balance, standing, crawling, walking, running. Then there are all the skills we use in the process of feeding: chewing, swallowing, drinking. These were followed historically by the skills of hunting, baby care, fire making, the making of simple tools, and cooking. Somewhere along the line, we started to talk, then to use symbols. Other prehistoric innovations included agriculture, domestication of animals, building, and writing. All these behaviors and systems involved extensive learning all of it remembered through the use of habits. In the previous chapter, we discussed some specifically humanist ethical theories such as the various values, especially truth, benevolence, and justice, and then responsibility and the evolutionary ethic. But we have not so far written much about the effect of the situation on our ethical thinking.

This important refinement was introduced into the picture by Joseph Fletcher through his book *Situation Ethics: The New Morality* (1966). Fletcher argued that there were three approaches to ethical decision making: (1) the legalistic; (2) the antinomian—the opposite of the legalistic, i.e., a lawless or unprincipled approach; and (3) the situational. The legalistic approach uses rules to define our habits, and in Western morality, it was by far the most common. In the Jewish Talmudic law and Christian traditions, the rules were supposedly absolute and interpreted as directives to be followed. Secular law in the Western world started out in the same way. In some systems, there were rules to cover every contingency sometimes in extremely convoluted ways. These rules were woven into webs so complicated and hairsplitting that the adherents began to rebel and throw them off, as Fletcher explained. That is how the antinomian approach got started, as a reaction, with some groups such as the Gnostics of early Christianity and later with some Anabaptists and even some Puritan and Wesleyan sects. In the secular world, people who wish to jettison all rules and law are termed anarchists, a group who achieved some notoriety in the early years of the twentieth century. Fletcher advocated that the situational approach be used so that the rules useful in particular circumstances could be identified so as to avoid the inhumane results of trying to force one absolute system of rules to fit every case. One important change, which Fletcher proposed, was to make the rules somewhat fuzzy by the use of "maxims" or "principles" to provide guidance rather than the rigid directives, which could lead to conflicts.

The word *situation* has a variety of meanings besides its basic sense of location. But even locational situation is relevant to ethics as in rural versus urban settings or in reference to living in the third world versus living in the USA. Our situation may reflect limitations on freedom, on time, on property and financial resources, or on our knowledge and understanding. It may depend on our practical knowledge of technology, medicine, or law. Situation analysis is obviously applicable in our personal lives. Adults have to take responsibility for the lives of children, although difficulties often arise in allowing them increasing measures of self-control as they become teenagers. Sometimes situations arise when we may have to take responsibility for another who is elderly or infirm. Men and women differ in their instinctive behavioral habits and morality: we might say they differ in their genomic situations. For instance, there is considerable evidence that homosexuality is genetically based. All individuals differ in their aptitudes and interests and thus in the correct choices of education and careers. All these are cases where Fletcher's articulation of situation ethics is very helpful. In addition, there is a wide variety of situations in the life of a given person for which different rules or principles and even different values are appropriate. Taking care of the house is clearly a different situation from activity in the workplace or attending school. Shopping, saving and investing, visiting the family, or planning a vacation are all quite different situations. In each of these cases, we learn from experience, and it is useful to think in terms of separate systems of behavior as was pointed out by Covey (1991). Situation analysis may sometimes be equivalent to what other writers have termed *relativism*. Simon Blackburn (2001) lists relativism as one of the seven threats to ethics. He explains that many people think that because different morals are accepted in different systems that anything goes. He then explains that this is not, in fact, the case as we will investigate more fully in chapter 9.

One aspect of Fletcher's thesis, which I believe is mistaken, is his failure to appreciate some refinements of system theory. Although he correctly objects to the building of monolithic ethical systems, he fails to understand the role of subsystems should the situation warrant their being brought into play (as in if-then). The areas that Covey calls life centers, e.g., work, pleasure, friends, enemies, spouse, family, self, church, possessions, money, etc., could all be thought of as subsystems. They are also examples of what Mill termed *great objects of human life*. There are also systems that can respond to different and independent stimuli, for example, an automaton that could be sensitive to both light and pressure. This is the case with animal (including human) motivations. Apes have a limited number of primary emotions. In the case of the human, however, with our large and complex brains, there is a repertoire of additional emotions, which may be activated by "logic circuits" and which are not experienced by apes. These then are the "values" we cherish as measuring tools in complex situations.

We have already pointed out that Fletcher advocated the use of principles or maxims as a part of his theory of situational ethics. For a long time, I have been interested in the question of finding some principles, which could be used as a basis for humanist ethical theory. I have made several attempts to formulate such as, for example, in describing the humanist heritage in Finch (1998 and 2006). One of the reasons I was attracted to Covey's (1991) book was that he advocates an approach, which is "principle centered," although he never actually states what these principles might be, apart from a vague invocation of "natural laws and governing social values." Fletcher was much more specific and listed four principles, which he saw as presuppositions of situational analysis: (1) pragmatism of the same variety expounded by the American philosophers Peirce, James, and Dewey; (2) relativism, as described in the preceding paragraph; (3) positivism, or a basis in knowledge (unfortunately Fletcher took this to be theological knowledge so that humanists will need to substitute scientific and logical positivism); and (4) personalism, which appears to mean something equivalent to Hume's emotion-based psychology. As a Christian, Fletcher maintained that the ultimate value is that form of love, which the Greeks call agape. Fletcher explains that *agape* has the sense of goodwill at work in partnership with reason. It seems that agape is equivalent to Hume's benevolence or Kitcher's altruism. Love or agape is certainly a variety of emotion that would fit in well with Hume's concept of the ethical driver. But Fletcher tries to reduce other forms of value, such as justice, to a form of agape. He did, however, allow that a humanist might want to substitute some form of the sumum bonum (happiness? personal realization?) in the place of agape in resolving conflicts between principles.

7.6 Organization and Objectives

Thus far, we have said virtually nothing that would be out of place in any elementary college course on ethics. The various chapters of our book constitute, in effect, a short *academic* course on *ethics*. So what is special about *humanist ethics*? Nearly forty years ago, a number of humanist ethicists produced a symposium on this very topic edited by Storer (1980). The first observation to be made about that work is that, in fact, it argues a very close relationship exists between humanist and academic ethics. Storer made the point that university faculty members are predominantly humanist. The reason given for the symposium was that with all the trouble in the world at that time there was a great need for the health and harmony that might be supplied by moral thinking. But Storer was concerned that humanists were at odds about morality. Many of the leading humanist ethicists of that time contributed to the proceedings with ideas on how a greater morality might improve the world. Prof. Konstantin Kolenda (of Rice University and Humanists of Houston) proposed that a start might be made by building a consensus on international affairs. Another prominent contributor was a young Dr. Paul Kurtz who argued that humanism has, or should have, an ethic of responsibility. Kurtz's article presented a masterly summary of the lessons of our earlier chapters. He stressed that there are several humanist theories, all free of divine commandments but differing on meta and normative issues: existentialism, emotivism, pragmatism, and utilitarianism being the main examples. Existentialism, which is largely the product of philosophers of the European continent, seems to be following a parallel path to Anglo-American humanism. Humanists differ over any number of concrete issues: capital punishment, euthanasia, abortion, sexual mores, etc. We may have liberal or radical approaches, be socialist or capitalist. We may be libertarian or devoted to a cause or be committed to "humanity as a whole." Kurtz stated that "the truth is that humanism has attracted many diverse tendencies in the world under its banner and it may be impossible to find agreement among all those who claim identity with the humanist banner." He also cautioned that even if someone is identified as a humanist, there is no assurance that he or she will be moral.

Despite his apparent pessimism, Kurtz continued on to propose an ethic under which the freedoms and rights of the individual are to be balanced with responsibilities. In a later work, Kurtz (1988) he expounded the ethic of responsibility in greater detail setting out responsibilities to the self and the family, including a warm accolade to his own extended family, extending all the way to our membership in the world community. In effect, he carried us beyond the confines of personal value theory to a recognition that we must include others in our ethical thinking. Kurtz emphasized the need for moral education at some length. Other articles in the same volume included one by Markovic on *Historical Praxis as the Ground for Morality* and another by Radest on *Relativism and Responsibility*, both of which seem to hint at management approaches. The ironic thing is that despite his pessimism, Kurtz himself went on to establish a very successful humanist organization. Kurtz became recognized as one of the leading thinkers on humanism. It would be interesting to know what he and the other participants of Storer's symposium would think of the situation now. How would they assess progress? Would they now, after the appearance of "evolutionary psychology," be more receptive of systems theory and adaptive change in ethics and in human behavior? Kurtz's presentation of responsibility is primarily normative (descriptive) and does not say much about the "meta" aspects of the theory. *Responsibility* has become a general term for ethics and morality and conveys what in another place we have termed *ethology*. Another problem with Kurtz's ethic of responsibility is that it does not explicitly state how we are to decide on the ends to be pursued to benefit everyone. Are we, the exercisers of the ethic, to be the deciders, or are the beneficiaries to have a say in the ends to be pursued? Additionally, there is little guidance in the simple statements of the ethic as to the methods that are appropriate to the decision-making process.

7.7 Humanist Declarations

We have already pointed out that another important ethical consideration is the human ability to make predictions of the future. Aristotle believed that every object existed for a purpose, and although we no longer accept the idea of such essential meaning or preordained purposes, this concept of an "end" for our ethical purposes still has meaning for us in terms of our subjective vision of a desirable future state. We discussed how this led to the idea that our goal should be to seek happiness. By making happiness a goal of our ethical system, Aristotle recognized the need for us to relate present actions to their future consequences. We can use our reason to find the *means* to the ends. Means-ends analysis presents us with a method of deriving an ethical system that is an alternative to the construction of pluralistic values. Virtue theories posit future goals and values and the means or ends for achieving them. Over the years, such theories have grown from simple statements of our aim of achieving knowledge and wisdom, freedom and benevolence, and all the other virtues as listed by Comte-Sponville and others.

In the USA, the humanist movement has been represented by a succession of summary statements called manifestos. Humanism and Its Aspirations, subtitled Humanist Manifesto III, a successor to the Humanist Manifesto of 1933, was published in 2003 by the AHA, which wrote it by committee with a final approval by the board of directors and a membership vote. The new document was the successor to the previous ones, and the name Humanist Manifesto is the property of the American Humanist Association. The newest one is deliberately much shorter, listing six primary beliefs that echo themes from its predecessors:

- Knowledge of the world is derived by observation, experimentation, and rational analysis.
- Humans are an integral part of nature, the result of unguided evolutionary change.
- Ethical values are derived from human need and interest as tested by experience.
- Life's fulfillment emerges from individual participation in the service of humane ideals.
- Humans are social by nature and find meaning in relationships.
- Working to benefit society maximizes individual happiness.

The signatories of Manifesto III included 21 Nobel laureates.

Another important document is the Universal Declaration of Human Rights which is reproduced in appendix 4. This UN charter committed all member states to promote "universal respect for, and observance of, human rights and fundamental freedoms for all without distinction as to race, sex, language, or religion." Former first lady Eleanor Roosevelt led the American delegation and chaired the organization, which produced the thirty articles that comprise the charter.

There have been several earlier summary statements of our essential humanist beliefs such as the Humanist Manifestos I and II, Corliss Lamont's *Central Propositions of Humanism* (1982), Paul Kurtz's *Secular Humanist Declaration* (1983), and Fred Edwords's *The Humanist Philosophy in Perspective* (1984). We can see in these the changes of emphasis to reflect changing times. One way to approach the problem of formulating our basic principles is by working backward from the various fields of knowledge, summarizing what we know and abstracting the methods that have led us to our present status. This seems to be the method used by Corliss Lamont. As our knowledge grows in different areas and the literature in humanist libraries accumulates, we should expect to revise our basic statements; and they, in turn, will influence the future growth of our knowledge. A willingness to adapt and change should be a characteristic of humanism to distinguish it from dogmatic and inflexible religion. We would not expect every adherent of the humanist movement to subscribe completely to every one of the principles. Some of our members are more knowledgeable than others and may be leaders in the process of expansion and improvement.

7.8 Consequentialist Theories: Planning and Learning

A consequentialist theory is one that is evaluated on its results. All the preceding humanist manifestos and statements are intended to be consequentialist, but in addition, there are some other forms that need to be mentioned, in particular the various forms of planning. Any group of humans brought together for the first time and needing to find some common course of action may find themselves in the precarious position that Hobbes described as a state of nature. Their interaction is likely to be nasty, short, and brutish, like that of the citizens of revolutionary France who instigated the terror or the fictional schoolboys in *The Lord of the Flies*. Planning is the process of thinking about possible courses of action and is probably the only way to remove doubts and contention. Having a set of values will not by itself achieve this end: we must also have a theory or schema to follow. Unfortunately, humanists have to work through such situations quite frequently when a new group comes together. But some groups have understood the dangers and successfully formulated plans. Here we have emphasized the use of planning by groups, but it also can be used by individuals, and is so, advisedly.

In the twentieth century, some techniques were developed for the management of business. One of the leading advocates of these developments was Peter Drucker who was the author of a well-known text on management (1973) in which he advanced the concept of "management by objectives." Since Drucker was a professor of philosophy for some years, it is tempting to speculate that he might have derived the concept from Aristotle's original writing. After his ideas won acceptance in business circles, Drucker (1990) showed that the techniques could also be applied in not-for-profit organizations including schools, civic groups, and churches. It is not clear why ethicists should not have recognized that "management by objectives" is essentially the same thing as means-ends analysis and an important tool in ethics. In fact, it is nothing other than the exercise of corporate planning. It was Drucker who invented the "mission statement" as the means of getting an organization to focus on its goals and purposes. Every organization needs to assess its situation from time to time and then articulate a vision for the future. By reiterating its values and then applying them to current problems, the organization can arrive at strategic decisions for future policies. We will discuss planning methods more fully in the next chapter.

Once a plan has been formulated, the challenge is to implement it in a sensible manner. Nothing ever proceeds precisely according to plan. The assumption behind any plan is that there will be some constancy going forward. This, after all, is the definition of a system. The problem boils down to finding ways to deal with the variations that life engenders. We usually do this by creating an organization of people charged with handling specific tasks. If we are fortunate, there was some earlier form of organization in place before the new plan was formulated. In that case, the plan unfolds as an evolution from the earlier form. If we are unfortunate, events can completely disrupt the assumptions of planning as well as the prior organization resulting in collapse into chaos. On the other hand, if the plan is well conceived and allowed a suitable time to come to fruition (five years commonly), it could be the most ethical way to proceed.

The promise of the evolutionary ethic is that it will produce a change from an older to an emerging new form of humanism. We hope the new order will encompass all the traditional values as well as realize ethics of responsibility and show us a promising future in the twenty-first century. A most interesting article on Habermas by Jeffery Tate (2007) seems to indicate that there are indeed modern philosophers pursuing these ideas. Habermas himself is probably the leading champion of the Enlightenment Project, which he calls the theory of modernity. He is an optimist and is hopeful that Enlightenment thinking will prevail. Isaiah Berlin was a leading advocate of the importance of pluralistic approaches, and we need to pay attention to his writings.

8. Examining Life and Death

Outline

8.1 Constancy and Evolution

Sociobiology of Behavior
Systems of Ethics and Morality
Human Habits and Culture
Paradigms
Managing the Mind
Values and Behavior

8.2 Death Confronted

What the Living Know
Do No Harm
Final Exit

8.3 Ethical Communities

Philosophy and Knowledge
A Survey of Evolutionary Scientists
Evolution and Social Cohesion
Small Groups
Organizational Commitment
Educational Institutions

8.4 Planning and the Future

From Religion to Humanism
Strategic Decisions
Aims for Humanist Groups
Humanism in Florida
The Five-Year Plan of the American Humanist Association
Humanists of Houston Five-Year Plan
Humanist Purpose and the Future

8. Examining Life and Death

8.1 Constancy and Evolution

Let us briefly recapitulate our discussion in earlier chapters of how we tend to anchor our thinking on the constancies we find in nature and on the constancies we build and design into our lives. We are indebted to Hume (1748) for these important observations. The constancies we find in nature are the laws of physics, chemistry, and biology. Since early in the twentieth century and especially since World War Two, the constancies we employ in our own lives have become the subject matter of systems theory: the bases of knowledge, language, and practice (of law, medicine, engineering, etc). Both sorts of constancies are governed by simple mathematical statements Gell-Mann termed *schema*. In the case of a fundamental particle, such as the quark, the schema is a true constant and the quark does not change. But with a more complex system such as a jaguar, the schema resides in the animal's DNA; and this may show adaptations, which as generations pass, could result in evolutionary changes in the animal's physique. We saw, in chapter 4, that the human systems with which we populate our culture can be represented by flow charts showing how we can call on our memories, our emotions and evaluations, reasoning, and imagination in the process of decision making.

Sociobiology of Behavior

If we ask ourselves what is the purpose of a humanist life, the first response from biology has to be that it is basically the same as the purpose of any human life. Surely, the first human beings, apes with bipedal locomotion, such as Lucy and the Australopithecines were concerned with simply staying alive, finding food, reproducing, and caring for their young. Skills were added to the human behavioral repertoire, and if these conferred an advantage through natural selection, they eventually were made into instincts passed on to later generations through expression of the genome. Rudimentary ethics and morals presumably got started in the same way. We know that much animal (and that includes human) behavior is quite automatic and subconscious. We have the ability to make choices, and these may be influenced by strong predispositions, which we feel as emotions such as fear, hunger, and sex drive. In addition to these primitives, which we share with most animal species, we humans have a number of instinctive morals such as empathy and a certain amount of altruism, which are also felt emotionally. But biology has provided humans with brains of advanced cognitive capabilities. We can recognize natural systems, invent new ones, and, simultaneously, be conscious of what we are doing. It is these systems we have invented that give us a framework for living and that provide our social cohesion.

Systems of Ethics and Morality

Perhaps one of the most interesting aspects of the presentation in James Gordon Finlayson's (2005) exposition on Habermas's philosophy was the distinction made between morality and ethics. Early in his career, Habermas used *morality* and *ethics* interchangeably. But in his revised program of the 1990s, he drew a triple distinction among moral, ethical, and pragmatic discourse. The two terms *ethics* and *morality* actually represent different traditions of thinking although they are both varieties of pragmatism. Habermas's concept of ethical discourse, going back to Aristotle, is that it is teleological, i.e., involved with the choice of ends. It evaluates ends by the question "What is good for me?" Morality deals with right and wrong, which Habermas follows Kant in believing should be universally valid. However, "good" pertains to the individual's life history or the collective life of the community. The table below summarizes the difference between ethical and moral discourse in Habermas's scheme.

Table 8.1. Habermas's Division of Ethics and Morality

	Ethics	Morality
Basic Concept	Good/bad	Right/Wrong Just/Unjust
Basic Unit	Values	Norms
Basic Question	What is good for me? Or for us?	What is just? What ought I to do and why?
Validity	Relative and conditional	Absolute and unconditional
Type of theory	Prudential, teleological	Deontological
Aims	Advice, judgment Preference ranking	Establishing valid norms, Discovering duties

Human Habits and Culture

Much of our morality and many of our pragmatic human systems are rule based. Habermas employs the word *norm* as an equivalent to *rule*. We learn many of these rules when we are children. They are typically of the "thou shalt" or "thou shalt not" variety. They apply in certain situations whose constancy we recognize. As we grow older, we start making rules and habits for ourselves and begin to generalize the rules we already have into wider ranging categories. We discover that rules can be subsumed under more general rules and conversely that some rules can be broken down to serve us in different categories. In appendix 1, we listed a highly aggregated set of humanist principles, which are supposed to contain the main lessons of our intellectual history. Discourse may result in rules followed by an entire family. Eventually, as families grow into tribes, we may find that rules constitute important parts of a culture. The tribal rules and cultures were taken over by religious institutions and eventually by civic authorities, giving rise to the legal systems of the modern state. Kant was much concerned with the similarity between the exercise of rules and the law and the workings of logical rationality. He distinguished between categorical imperatives and hypothetical imperatives. In Habermas's terminology, perhaps these correspond to moral and ethical concepts. Hume recognized the importance of both rationality and emotion in the working of habits and culture. There are important emotions such as the feelings of obligation and loyalty, which are generally attached to the operation of moral and rule-based systems. The role of discourse in the establishment of both moral norms and ethical values is an important part of Habermas's philosophy. He stresses, following Kant, that the rules of discourse should apply universally, to women as well as men, and to all social classes, ethnicities, and races. Following the rules of rational discourse is one of the great benefits of humanism. Belief in the supernatural is not rational, but many religions are burdened in this way. Perhaps as such beliefs are overcome, religions might be able to progress.

Managing the Mind

According to Plato, Socrates affirmed that the "unexamined life was not worth living." This is a famous quotation, and the fact that it was Socrates who said it has lent it the force of a moral precept. It is so well-known and so apposite that Robert Nozick chose it for the title of his 1989 overview of philosophy, *The Examined Life*. It tells us that all the considerations we have made thus far are still not enough. Socrates says we have to examine the actual lives we have lived to date. All the instincts we have, all the values we have learned, and all the principles we have accepted still do not tell us if we are living good lives. It is worth repeating some of the points Nozick made in his introduction. Firstly, he notes that we tend to live on automatic pilot, following the habits we acquired early in life, with only minor adjustments. Happiness is not the only aspect of our lives with importance. He asks, "How has the Holocaust changed humanity?" He points out that we need to assess vignettes from different times and situations in our lives to get a total picture of ourselves. He points out that there are very few books that set out what a mature person can believe and that even with these we cannot simply accept everything that is said. He feels that Socrates is unnecessarily harsh in completely rejecting the unexamined life but puts it rather well when he says, "When we guide our lives by our own pondered thoughts, then it is *our* life that we are living, not someone else's, and in that sense the unexamined life is not lived as fully." Nozick's concern is with the whole of our beings—the three parts: the rational, the courageous, and the emotional. His aim is to find the harmonious union of the three. It is impossible to consider the ethics of individuals in isolation from other people, humans being social animals. The ethics of groups have, in turn, influenced the way individuals think. For instance, the ideas behind figure 3 were first developed for groups and only later realized to be valuable for individuals.

Values and Behavior

Humanism has always been committed to the great progressive values of truth, altruism, freedom, and equality. Humanism has always stood in the forefront of the social struggle for democracy, abolition of slavery, women's rights, and international brotherhood. We could attempt to reform religion by getting it to drop its bad features. Another approach was discussed by Paul Kurtz (2006) who asked if, as humanists, we can create secular alternatives to religion. We see philosophy as the embodiment of all knowledge so that humanism could be a species of philosophy informed by all the other disciplines and used as the cognitive basis for our alternative to religion. When we look back over time, we realize that it was our ability to learn, and the accumulation of knowledge, that has contributed to a major part of our species' advance, comprising the heritage we humanists wish to pass on. The invention of spoken language was followed by writing and then the development of books and libraries, the tools that made culture possible. We should be proud of our institutional inventions: schools, universities and academic societies, and research laboratories, which have enabled succeeding generations to absorb the stories to date and then to permit the growth of knowledge. Today we live longer, healthier, more interesting lives as a consequence of these advances. Education is the foundation of it all. Education is the process of learning and is not exclusively conducted in the style of the university lecture. We can learn in many different ways: reading books, browsing the Internet, viewing films or television, conducting experiments, visiting museums, and participating in discussions or debates or discourse. Kurtz (2006) lists the following conditions that need to be satisfied by our alternative to religion:

- A direct confrontation of the basic existential questions on the meaning of life, from suffering to death
- Development of ethical values and principles grounded in human experience
- Appeal to the heart as well as the head
- Use of the arts to create new narratives and to celebrate life and the march of reason
- Development of communities of people committed to science and reason

8.2 Death Confronted

What the Living Know

Death is a fact of life for living creatures. As the Bible says, the living know that they shall die, but the dead know not anything. This arrangement is probably a necessity of evolution. We have to recognize that we have just the one life to live and make the most of it. And that life is so precious that our laws forbid killing in most circumstances. But most of the time we act so as to preserve our lives by avoiding dangerous situations. If our normal lifespan is cut short by accident, violent confrontation, or disease, then it is a matter of grief for our friends and relatives. The community can be expected to offer comfort for the grieving, and we may suppose that this was the situation exploited by the primitive shamans who introduced our ancestors to the concepts of spirits and gods. Presumably, this was the origin of religious beliefs in the existence of the soul that many religious people still think inhabits the human body during life, and that departs upon our death to continue on forever in the afterlife. There is a whole mystique that has been spun around this myth in many different cultures. Fortunately, we have an excellent expose of the whole sham in Corliss Lamont's *The Illusion of Immortality* (1990).

The subject of death and the issues associated with it, probably because of the intense fear that drives us to preserve our lives, has become a major issue in ethical and moral theories. We are all aware of the biblical injunction thou shalt not kill. This has become a part of secular law. However, it is understood that killing is allowed in most societies, in warfare or in self-defense, or in situations calling for the death penalty. One circumstance of great concern is the issue of suicide and assisted suicide or euthanasia. Here most nonreligious people differ with the theists. There is a comprehensive thesis on the questions involved here in Derek Humphry's *Final Exit* (1991). There is growing support for legalizing suicide and/or assisted suicide or euthanasia for people who are dying and suffering. There is also a growing awareness of the exploitation of grieving persons by the funeral home industry and of the advantages of cremation versus burial. Humanists prefer simple memorial services in which family and friends reflect on the life of the departed.

Our understanding of the biology of death has been growing considerably since Darwin's time and life expectancy has been increasing. If any living species could live without any predetermined limitation to its lifespan, it would probably succumb by accident or by predation or through limitation of resources. If such a species encountered competition from another that did have a predetermined lifespan limitation, then the latter would likely be able to develop evolutionary mutations, which would enable it to kill or take away resources from the former. This is probably the reason that all living species have limited lifespans. The mechanism by which this seems to work is by the incorporation of a certain "clock" in the genome of each species. The clock eventually runs out on the repair to damage to the rest of the genome. In the case of humans, the clock seems to be the telomeres, which are eventually "used up" as cells divide and multiply throughout the life cycle. There is a good description of this process in an article on *Wikipedia* headed "DNA damage theory of aging." It is possible that we may be able to considerably extend the human lifespan in the not-so-distant future in which case it is clear that we will face a whole raft of ethical dilemmas. It would behoove us to start exploring these issues before they overcome us.

8.3 Ethical Communities

There is an aspect of ethics that we have only tacitly brought into the picture in our first seven chapters, namely, the interaction between humans that goes on during the real process of decision making. Up to this point, any thinking that occurs has been assumed to have taken place in the mind of a single individual. Any reasoning and evaluation could be described as a monolog. The seriousness of ethics was first realized when Socrates was forced to take hemlock and later when Plato, contrary to Socrates's inclinations, felt impelled to write the story down. We all know that some of the most important relationships are developed between pairs of individuals: the male and female couple and the parent and child. The essential male-female relationship was determined at a time when we still lived in trees. The superior physical strength of the male cast him in the role of hunter while the woman became the domestic and care giver. The lifelong commitment between human mates also dates from this prehistoric time. The helpless human infant required nursing and carrying around, both of which functions probably were facilitated by bipedal locomotion. There are various theories on the origin of language, but it may well have started with "motherese" communication between mothers and children and/or calling between males on the hunt. All the skills of humanity have to be passed on to infants, and the parents get the responsibility of doing the education.

Philosophy and Knowledge

To ask what is the purpose of life required a sophisticated human being—a philosopher—and it is interesting that such people appeared in several parts of the world where civilization had started to flourish at about the same time: in Greece, India, and China. The philosophers displaced the established religious and tribal leaders whose concepts were frequently inaccurate or lacking in other ways. They were the questioners who probed the established understanding of nature, society, religion, and the state. Frequently, as a result of their inquiries, they rewrote the books in various fields. In some cases, the accounts they gave became the established paradigms for hundreds or even thousands of years. Many of Aristotle's opinions were still accepted as truth until recent times. But as time went on, political powers improved their leadership through the development of democratic processes and philosophers had to specialize into science and mathematics to produce improved paradigms. At the same time, pragmatists, from engineers to medical doctors, businessmen, and lawyers, all came to the fore from time to time through evolution of their own disciplines. In each field, there was a paradigm that the specialists in that area had to grasp in order to be competent with the state of the art. The human race developed as many paradigms as were necessary for all the specialists to be fully employed. It is clear that there is no one paradigm that will guarantee intellectual leadership to philosophy or any other discipline. Although philosophy may still offer useful general summaries of all knowledge, it is not clear that executives with general responsibilities would not be served quite well with educations starting in almost any field. It is not clear how the curriculum for philosophy is determined in the modern age. The postmodern movement can be interpreted as a rebellion on the part of philosophers against the success and predominance of science and indeed of rationalism in general. When Richard Rorty used his own preeminent position to heap praises on Martin Heidegger as a way of deflating science and rationalism and when Paul Edwards (2004) had to write a book about it, then it is clear that philosophy has lost its sense of direction. We should note that Habermas played an important part in standing up to the postmodern juggernaut when, in 1980, he was awarded the Adorno prize and delivered a speech "Modernity—an Unfinished Project." He made it clear that he thought that the Enlightenment was an unfinished project, which had already yielded great benefits, and should be finished. He may have saved philosophy from itself. Postmodernists are not the only enemies we have: humanists and all modernists need to take the initiative in forging new intellectual paradigms for self-defense in the face of Islamo-fascists, Christian evangelicals, and other assorted anti-intellectuals.

A Survey of Evolutionary Scientists

Graffin and Provine (2007) present the results of a survey of scientists. Polls of *leading* scientists on their religious beliefs have been conducted for nearly a century, finding, for example, that the number who believe in the existence of a god has been declining from about one-third to just a few percent. This, of course, is no surprise, but Graffin and Provine instead polled *evolutionary* scientists with a variety of questions. They started out with a concern over the distinction between theism (personal God who intervenes in human life) and deism (impersonal God who starts the universe but does not intervene). They discovered that the evolutionary scientists really do not believe in either. But what they did find surprising was that the substantial majority of their respondents (72 percent) see religion as an adaptation and a part of evolution. In other words, "the tenets of religion should be seen as a labile [unstable] social adaptation subject to change and reinterpretation." Only 8 percent of the respondents agreed with Stephen Jay Gould's position that religion and our biological heritage should be regarded as nonoverlapping magisteria (NOMA). Graffin and Provine found another surprise in the very small support for a third choice—that evolution and religion are mutually exclusive and separated by a gulf that cannot be bridged. This was the answer chosen by Richard Dawkins who has a strong reputation for declaring that science has much better answers for human society than does religion. The position taken by Dawkins and the other new atheists is that they see no benefits whatsoever in religion. Only 3 percent of respondents believed that evolution and religion are "totally harmonious," i.e., that evolution is a way to elucidate the evidence of God's designs. Graffin and Provine continued the discussion of the implications of their poll by stating that eminent evolutionists currently see religion as subsumed under sociological evolution or what is now known as sociobiology. The evolutionists are worried that the American public's association of evolution with atheism or at least with nonreligion will hurt evolutionary biology, perhaps impeding its funding or acceptance.

Evolution and Social Cohesion

If there were no benefits to religion, real or perceived, then it might be expected to fade away as indeed was predicted for many years. This viewpoint, however, seems to overlook several facets of religion, which adherents find to be of benefit. Paul Kurtz (2006) points out that "religious creeds have provided important support systems, and they have cultivated charitable efforts and the bonds of moral cohesion . . . Where mainline religious denominations have built what were in fact secular communities of friends, they have satisfied important psychological-sociological needs, often without imposing authoritarian overlays. Secular humanists can learn much from the denominations about the need to build communities." Many observers recognize that religion does not simply provide an explanation for the universe and man's place in it but also provides a social structure for the individual, an idea propounded by Michael Shermer (2005) who states that there is a "twofold purpose that religions serve . . . (1) explanation and (2) social cohesion." He continues on, "Never have so many—professed a belief in a deity. Although explanations for this remarkable trend are as varied as the theorists proffering them, a general causal vector can be found in the second purpose of religion, that is, its social mode." A similar point can be derived from the philosophy of Jürgen Habermas, which has been ably summarized recently by Finlayson (2006). Habermas has advanced the thesis that what makes the coherence of human society possible is our extensive and continuous discourse. He has expounded this viewpoint in his magnum opus *The Theory of Communicative Action* (1984). Habermas sees ethical and moral discourse as a part of the theory of society, i.e., we cannot understand the one without the other. Perhaps we should ask what sociobiology can tell us about the evolution of human behavior and culture.

Small Groups

The nuclear family grows; and eventually, children find their own mates, thus bringing new members and then grandchildren into the community. In a few generations, an extended family becomes a tribe. Even in the times of the hunter-gatherers, people would band together for security, for hunting, and for many other purposes. People have always congregated together to tell stories, to dance and sing, to argue, and to discuss and worship. With the coming of civilization, all sorts of associations grew to cooperate for agriculture, for animal husbandry, for manufacture, for trade and so on. All these are what we might term *small groups*, and within each group, there is a culture of acceptable behavior. Bringing the story up-to-date, we find many innovations in the ways these groups are organized, from schools to political cells, and in the ways people communicate including radio, telephone, and the Internet. But they all use language in the form of words and dialogue to establish cultures of values, morals, and ethics to govern their interactions.

Organizational Commitment

What is of interest in the present context is the organizational commitment, which members feel toward their groups. It is quite clear that people brought together by random circumstances and having no cultural affinities or common interests soon wind up in conflict. Wars and natural disasters can produce such circumstances. Any group of humans brought together for the first time and needing to find some common course of action may find themselves in the precarious position that Hobbes described as a state of nature. Their interaction is likely to be "nasty, short, and brutish." Humanists have to work through such situations when a new group comes together. But some humanist groups have understood the dangers and successfully formulated plans. Within the nuclear family, if it functions well, we find love and support. Unfortunately, within a dysfunctional family, it might take lawyers, police, and psychiatrists to sort matters out. Usually, within the extended family, there are strong ties and affinities, and we often speak of tribal loyalty to describe such a commitment. But there are many other organizations that engender powerful loyalties. Religions are specially noted for the strength of commitment, which they engender and the antagonisms between rival religions. Catholics and Protestants went to war for a hundred years or more in seventeenth-century Europe, and there are still recurrences in places such as Northern Ireland today. For hair-raising accounts of religious atrocities, one has only to consult the works of Dawkins (2006), Dennett (2006), Harris (2004), and

Hitchens (2007). But political movements can be just as bad as religion, if not worse, in their abilities to enthrall people and then lead them on to evil behavior. Here the reader is referred to Hannah Arendt's *The Origins of Totalitarianism* (1951) or Eric Hoffer's *The True Believer* (1951). *The Lucifer Effect* by Philip Zimbardo (2007) describes the infamous mock-prison experiment in Stanford University's psychology building in 1971. A prison is, of course, another example of a small group, and Zimbardo analyzes its potential for generating both good or evil behavior.

Educational Institutions

There is then a wide spectrum of small groups organized for various purposes, with different cultures and each having some ethical and moral traditions. Every organization embodies some sort of ethical content; but our particular interest here is with groups concerned with the teaching, examination, and researching of ethical theories rather than simply using such. Until the coming of civilization, the only organizations that made ethics central to their business were the world's various religions. These have continued to flourish and to evolve to varying extents. Some of them are nowadays worldwide operations with millions of adherents and with great wealth and influence. They have wide responsibility for the education of children and the welfare of adults. They have immense real estate and financial assets. They embrace a spectrum of doctrinal belief, nearly all of them being founded on supernaturalist claims of one sort or another, although we should note that Buddhism and Taoism are less encumbered in this regard than the three monotheistic faiths that originated in the Middle East. Among the three (Judaism, Christianity, and Islam), there has been considerable evolution over time so that many of their sects are now considerably less brutal and occult than they were in the past. With the arrival of civilization, other institutions arose to challenge the religious hegemony on ethics: firstly, various secular schools and educational foundations and, secondly, the legal systems of different countries. Schools and universities provided homes for philosophers, historians, and scientists, all of whom could be categorized as truth seekers. The lawyers and judges might be described as in pursuit of justice. Educational and legal institutions have grown to sponsor great armies of acolytes with huge resources at their disposal. They also exert wide influence in modern society.

8.4 Planning and the Future: From Religion to Humanism

Let us now narrow our focus onto the groups in which ethical reformers have had to face their most onerous tasks. There have been some clerics who have dared to break away from their religions. One of the first to do so was Felix Adler who led his Jewish congregation to start the ethical culture movement in the USA. This quite wealthy community has several congregations with salaried leaders. In Britain, one rebellion started with a Baptist Church, which became the South Place Ethical Society, which dates from 1793. Book publishing in Britain was started by the Rationalist Press Association, and the British Humanist Association was begun in 1896. In the USA, the American Humanist Association was founded in 1941. Membership in the AHA is increasing rapidly at this time (2015), and it has recently grown to nearly thirty thousand members and supporters and over four hundred thousand followers on Facebook. There are some 185 local chapters and affiliates of the AHA. The Council for Secular Humanism was started by Dr. Paul Kurtz in 1980 and has grown to a membership of several thousand. Dr. Kurtz founded Prometheus Press in 1969, and this publishing house now supplies much of the free-thought literature produced in the USA. The Humanists of Houston is a chapter of the AHA, which was started in 1978. The North Texas Church of Freethought and the Houston Church of Freethought are independent organizations founded to provide churchlike environments for nonbelievers in Texas. There are several other organizations that serve the atheist and free-thought communities in the USA, including American Atheists, the Freedom from Religion Foundation, and Americans United for the Separation of Church and State. The number of people who regard themselves as having no church affiliation in the USA has now grown to 14 percent of the population, or about forty-two million, a number that is growing. Both Catholicism and fundamentalism have lost members to the unaffiliated category according to Duncan (2004).

Strategic Decisions

Planners for these reforming groups face a number of strategic decisions. Conscious search for the best way to live began with the coming of civilization; and the humanist heritage grew to glory in classical Greece, the Renaissance, and the Enlightenment. The highlights of our heritage are summarized in documents such as the American Humanist Association's 2003 Humanist Manifesto III and in appendix 1 to this book. But the highlights are only a small part of a vast corpus of knowledge we hope to pass along to future generations. There are two main threads to this heritage: firstly, lessons learned for the lives of individuals and, secondly, the conduct of societies. We usually begin with the first of these, but I would like to put some emphasis on the latter: the Humanist Society. Some of the thinking presented here would also apply to other organizations to the extent that they are humanist and some of the ideas might be relevant to a wider community.

Aims for Humanist Groups

What is the purpose of humanists getting together in an organization? There are several aims that we might have:

- education
- advancement of the sciences of humanity
- broadening of fellowship and community
- organization building
- outreach beyond the humanist community
- celebration and commitment

We might say that our purpose is to promote and advance humanism and to extend its benefits to ourselves and others. We might talk about the theory of our humanist organization. Some fundamentalist sects grow principally through the education of their own children, but we have to rely mainly on the recruitment of new adult members and educating them into the ways and knowledge of humanism. If the internal structure of the association is successful and if it helps members to live more fulfilling lives, then they will stay with it. Members need to feel pride in and commitment to their organization and feel like celebrating its strengths and accomplishments. We need outreach to contact potential new members and make our political influence felt. This is clearly not going to be successful unless our members are committed and enthusiastic. In short, our purpose should be the preservation, improvement, and promotion of humanism. It might be argued that it clearly benefits us if all organizations with similar beliefs do the same, i.e., if the whole humanist movement or the whole community of reason has the same aims.

The subject of scientific management of business and corporate planning really began in the early twentieth century and has been the subject of many books since Peter Drucker produced his monumental work on management in 1973. Two of the best popular volumes, which would be useful to humanist groups, are *The Board Members Guide to Strategic Planning* by Fisher Howe (1997) and *Doing Good Better* by Edgar Stoesz and Chester Raber (1994). There have been a number of attempts to follow the prescriptions these authors offer. It is of some interest to recount some of these efforts.

Humanism in Florida

Perhaps the earliest group to try a planning process was the Humanists of Florida, as described in a most informative PhD dissertation by Gin Kohl Lieberman (2002). Her area of study was communication theory, and much of what the dissertation contains shows how this subject bears on our present topic. However, the other half of the interest comes from reading her very articulate story of the change that occurred in Florida humanism over a period of several years. It might be thought that the large number of AHA chapters in Florida must be due to the retirement of wealthy liberals from the East Coast for golden years in the sun. But Kohl Lieberman points out that another factor could have been the influence of Dr. Edwin H. Wilson, a signer of the original Humanist Manifesto, first editor of the *Humanist* magazine, and first executive director (from 1949 to 1970) and later a board member and president of the AHA. After retiring as executive director Wilson moved to Cocoa

Beach, Florida, where he lived until 1990 and was instrumental in establishing several AHA chapters and influencing a whole generation of humanist leaders in the state. Wilson finally moved to Salt Lake City where he started the Humanists of Utah before he died at the grand age of ninety-eight. Everyone he came in contact with mentioned Dr. Wilson as inspirational in their involvement. Kohl Lieberman saw the elements of charisma in Dr. Wilson's leadership. He was described as a wonderful talker with great ability to speak with everybody and anybody with a gift of being open, welcoming, and kind.

The dissertation opens with a chapter describing HOF around 1990. The problems that Kohl Lieberman detailed involved the group arguing over being too philosophical and insufficiently activist or vice versa, a lack of vision or strategic planning, and an absence of young people. President Sol Klotz lined up an advocate for change and an eventual successor: Jerry Lieberman joined the board in 1998 and became president in 2002. The key to Jerry's success was to inject some vision, planning, and new resolution into chapter affairs. He pursued funding by identifying progressive-oriented foundations and philanthropists in Florida.

Kohl Lieberman takes us through the formulation of the first of HoF's strategic plans. The process started under the presidency of Nan Owen, who had come from Chicago where she had at one time been a member of a far right group. She had progressed from this through atheism to humanism. After arriving in Florida, Jerry's initial goals included increasing membership, preparing a three-year budget and fund-raising, providing paid professional management, strengthening and adding chapters, increasing visibility, and building partnerships with other progressive groups. The process continued with drafting, debating, and eventual approval of a Progressive Social Action Plan. In parallel to this, there was a Strategic Planning Committee (chaired by Jerry himself) and a Program Committee. These deliberations are what eventually led HoF to start a charter school program. Implementation of the plans continued with the hiring of Jennifer Hancock as executive director in 2001.

The Five-Year Plan of the American Humanist Association

Another example to relate is the experience of the American Humanist Association itself. In 2004 the AHA board began the process of formulating a long range plan. Jerry Lieberman was a consultant to the group for its duration. The work eventually came to fruition with a document completed in 2007 under the chairmanship of Carleton Coon. The opening sections of this document read as follows:

> The purpose of the American Humanist Association (AHA) is to advance and disseminate knowledge of Humanism and promote Humanism as an important and helpful influence in people's personal and civic lives. The AHA's vision is for a global community of peace and progress governed by reason, compassion, and tolerance.

> The AHA seeks to increase public awareness and acceptance of Humanism, to demonstrate the validity and relevance of Humanist ideas, and advance original scholarship. The AHA also works to unite the millions of Humanists in America, many of whom do not currently identify as Humanists, and to encourage cooperation with other organizations supporting common causes.

> Individually and united, Humanists in the AHA are staunch advocates for secular government, civil liberties, social justice, a robust public education system, a compassionate approach to the use of science and technology, and a foreign policy centered on universal human rights, democratic values, and the goal of a world at peace.

> The Programs and Priorities of the AHA are to provide organization, staffing, services, publications, and infrastructure to support its programs and activities. Its priorities for the next five years are to:

- Improve the standing and awareness of Humanism through a vigorous advertising and public awareness campaign, and public advocacy and lobbying for Humanist positions on topical issues.
- Strengthen the AHA by improving the ways AHA chapters are supported; expanding the AHA membership base; and cooperating with like-minded organizations.
- Develop Scholarship and Research through increased ties with the wider academic community, while developing original papers on topical issues, such that the AHA becomes a recognized resource on policy.

The strategic goal of the AHA for the five year period is to grow its membership and raise the awareness and capital needed to accelerate its larger vision and purpose. The AHA's current membership is 7,800 and its annual operating budget is one million dollars. Doubling both these figures during the five-year period of 2007 through 2011 will verify that the AHA is on the correct course. Although a significant portion of the AHA's income is generated from annual dues and subscriptions to publications, growth must be financed through increased support from major donors and foundations.

In other words, the effect of the five-year plan of the AHA should be to change the habits of the organization from just talk to a well-rounded and rational program for an ethical community offering education, development, outreach, and social action as a viable alternative to religion.

Humanists of Houston Five-Year Plan

The population of Houston has grown substantially in recent years; and the proportion of that number who might be described as nonbelievers (atheists, freethinkers, and humanists) has grown along with it, probably as an ever-enlarging proportion of the whole. There are about four hundred contacts on various lists who are divided among the groups mentioned above. HOH formulated its five-year plan in

2007. A focal point of the plan was to institute central and regional gatherings. We quote:

> The main gathering will continue to be on the third Saturday of each month. The space we have been using for this in the Religious Education room of the Wirt Road Unitarian Fellowship is becoming overcrowded with our growing attendance and we see a priority in the immediate future to find a better accommodation.
>
> We will expand the HOH "Brunch" forum concept and begin having local or regional gatherings on the first Saturday of each month. There will be perhaps 3-4 of these happening simultaneously at first, depending on volunteer response for organizers, but with eventual plans to expand to seven regions in and around the Houston area (Spring Branch, Inner Loop, Clear Lake, Sugar Land, West Houston, Jersey Village, and Pasadena). These areas have been placed strategically after considering population densities, projected growth, potential interest distribution, and more. They have also been selected so as not to conflict or overlap with the current meetings of other Alliance organizations.

HOH has lived with this plan until the present. There are currently three main groups of nonbelievers in the Houston area: (1) HOH, which includes a women's group, a lunch group, and two "clubs"; (2) Houston Church of Freethought (HCOF); and (3) an American Atheist chapter. There is also a development fund that is growing despite a difficult investing environment. Another objective of the plan was the institution of a "patron program" of members contributing $20 per month, which was anticipated to grow to about fifty patrons in five years. The chapter planned to cooperate fully with the AHA in its objectives. As its contribution to the effort, the Sugar Land Forum has sponsored courses with monthly meetings leading to two texts on beginning humanism, this book being one of them.

Humanist Purpose and the Future

Most humanist organizations are poverty stricken and consequently spend much time trying to raise funds and resources. We have to look beyond immediate difficulties and remember that the world faces a large number of problems for which political solutions are required. We feel that these problems could all be solved if the world's population and its politicians could be educated sufficiently. Paul Kurtz has written extensively about the Promethean possibilities of the future. Jeffrey Sachs (2005) has explained how relatively small expenditures could essentially eliminate poverty throughout the world. It should be relatively simple to provide enough food and minimal financial aid to everyone. Ray Kurzweil, in his remarkable work the *Singularity* (2005), has predicted that the increasingly rapid speed of technological advance in computer science and biology will bring the benefits of instant encyclopedic knowledge to everyone. We may eventually be able to provide everyone with the wealth enjoyed only by the privileged few today. We feel that it is the task of the humanist movement to bring the good news of the possibilities of knowledge to the world. We have to work to overcome the scourge of war and the hatred fomented by religious and political ideology and replace these pernicious influences by humanistic societies, ethics, and morals. We will, of course, need to preserve the environment on Earth and protect ourselves from meteors from space. If research continues, we should be able to eliminate disease, cancer, and hereditary defects. It should be possible to extend the lifespan as far as each person desires. We might be able to redesign humans to eliminate the design defects which nature has encumbered us with. It seems that physics may be close to a theory of everything, perhaps based on string theory, which may answer ancient questions about the origin of the universe and indeed why there is something rather than nothing. We may discover life, even intelligent life, elsewhere in the universe. Each generation has to test the limits of human achievement. It is said that the ticket collectors on the trains in India ask passengers three questions: Who are you? Where do you come from? Where are you going? Written large these are the questions we all face, and answering them is what provides humanist purpose.

9. Ethical and Moral Problems

9.1 The State of the Art in Ethics

Summary of Humanist Ethics
Happiness, Liberty and Moderation
Impediments to Humanist Ethics

9.2 Theistic Ethics

Issues of Life and Death
Harris on Good and Evil
Religious Extremism

9.3 The Subjection of Women

Jimmy Carter: The Greatest Moral Challenge
Violence against Women
Possible Remedies
Carter's Humanism

9.4 The Golden Rule and Other Ethical Puzzles

Gensler
Free Will

9.5 The Ethical Project

Kitcher, Shermer
Tentative Nature of Ethics
Relativism
Happiness and Moderation

9.6 Animal Rights

Singer
Biophilia

9.7 Ethical Science

The Rachels
Grand Unifying Pessimism
Optimism Must Return

9. Ethical and Moral Problems

9.1 The State of the Art in Ethics

We recognize that we have instinctive morals that date from our evolutionary past as lizards, mammals, and apes. In addition, there are evolutionary layers that date from the early human period of our history. As humanists, we aim to recognize these instinctive feelings for what they are and if necessary control what would pass for excesses in the modern era. With the coming of speech and thinking, we began to formulate values to guide our behavior. There are a number of ancient values to which humanists still subscribe. The first of these is a suite of teleological (goal oriented) values, based on such emotions as benevolence, sympathy, and empathy together with logic, linguistic skills, and reciprocal understanding as well as other cognitive abilities. These values include altruism and freedom, health, wealth, and happiness and excellence in many combinations and variations, in planning for ourselves and others in families, groups, corporations, schools and associations, and governance. We may formulate our interests in certain values as great objectives and express our aims as wanting to become certain types of people such as soldiers, priests, teachers, politicians, bankers, farmers, etc. The second of our assemblies of values are those of a deontological nature, i.e., our duties that include using all the principles we have learned over the millennia, as in the use of reason, naturalism, science, knowledge, art, and technology, and in acting in moderation. We subscribe to the goals of fairness and equality for all people, and we value the laws of the societies in which we live. We have learned from the study of psychology that our mental goal is to attain happiness and that the way this is accomplished is by striving to achieve one or more of the objectives we have just mentioned. Different humanists will have different goals so that in general we should not expect to find the humanist community to be in solidarity over objectives. Humanists, however, are closer to unanimity on the methodology they will use, even though different people will be at different stages of development at any one time.

Why are there different ways for people to work out ethical goals and plans? Human beings have been arguing and discussing how to behave for at least two or three thousand years. We might suppose that the methodological issues would be settled by now, but quite to the contrary, the debates are still intense. There are several reasons for this. Partly, the disagreements come from ancient and not-so-ancient religious traditions. Prophets and priests who set out proscriptions and rules during their lifetimes are still venerated today, often by followers who cannot conceive that there may be any deficiencies in their beliefs. Then there are the aristocrats, plutocrats, and politicians who have left us with systems, laws, and traditions in the public arena. The philosophers who have been working on the issues all these millennia are also divided among themselves. Even the scientists who came on the scene from Charles Darwin to E. O. Wilson while certainly bringing us some new insights, especially through evolutionary psychology, have also, in fact, generated new controversies. And it is out of this often-contradictory tangle, which is contemporary ethics, that the average person has to take advice on his or her individual life-stance. And society has to try to resolve the public dilemmas of business and politics.

There are hundreds of texts on ethics, and recently, new titles are being added with great frequency. From this wide bibliography, there are just a few that define the main issues most clearly. Perhaps the book that set off the modern era was E. O. Wilson's *Sociobiology* (1980) in which he described the social behavior of animals from ants to monkeys but raised alarm bells by including humans in the final chapter. Wilson brought academic ire down on his head by suggesting that biology might explain human morality better than philosophy. This claim was countered in another now-famous work by Peter Singer,

The Expanding Circle, first published in 1981, in which he accused Wilson of staging a takeover attempt on ethics, in behalf of science, by ignoring the two millennia of work by philosophers. He went on to argue that the historical growth in size of the human group was a result of better understanding between its members. This then is the expanding circle, and Singer claims it might eventually encompass all humanity as well as apes and other intelligent and sentient animals. Singer's book *Animal Liberation* was the basis for the movement for humane treatment in animal husbandry, which has caused so much controversy in recent years. There are many other books on ethics including recent contributions from Simon Blackburn (2001, 2013), Sam Harris (2010), and Philip Kitcher (2014).

The focus of this chapter is on certain particular impediments that have prevented the full benefits of the ethical project from being realized by everyone in all areas of the world. Blackburn and Kitcher are especially lucid on these topics. A major impediment at this time, as it has been for millennia, is the prevalence of theism and illogical thinking. There are issues with life and death that come about because of ancient theistic teachings. Even when theism is put behind us, there are still overly simplified and erroneous moral concepts, such as the golden rule and free will, which prevent people from grasping more up-to-date viewpoints. But perhaps our greatest handicaps at the level of family ethics are the subjection of women and the remnants of racism. The main cause is the predisposition to violence on the part of the male of the species. And in this regard, we may trace the causal chain back to our fear of other dissimilar groups. We have made some evolutionary progress through improved hierarchical social governance, but still, the institution of the nation state remains as the last link in the containment of the worst violence of all: open warfare. Hopefully in the future, we will learn how to deal with even this threat, but the discussion of it will take us beyond the scope of this chapter.

9.2 Theistic Ethics

We have already discussed how the fear of death was used by primitive shamans and priests as a device to attach people to incipient religion. People were led to believe in the concept of life being vested in an immortal soul that departed the body at death. These beliefs are the source of the opposition to suicide and euthanasia as well as abortion. The traditions and practices that have grown up around death for theists have become so entrenched that they have crowded out the understanding of death as the cessation of life and the naturalistic morals and ethics that accompany it. There are also many beliefs spelled out in the Bible and the Koran that depend on the traditions of the priesthoods of past millennia. In some cases, the traditions could be of tribal origin, predating their accommodation into religion. Many of the prejudices about women, sex, and childbirth are probably of such provenance. We are familiar with the work of Islamist terrorists who read the Koran literally and feel obliged to follow its orders to kill people who do not honor its prophet. But many people do not realize that there are similar instructions in the Bible for Christians. One interpretation of this situation is that the Christian religion has moved on since the wars between the Catholics and Protestants whereas the Shia and Sunni denominations of Islam are still involved in conflict.

Harris presents a general discourse on *Good and Evil*. He starts with a claim that there is nothing more important than human cooperation. He reviews the discussion of altruism and evolution but recognizes that we do not have proportionate feelings for the emotions of people in large numbers. Harris stresses that there are right and wrong answers to moral questions, and we learn that he is committed to moral realism and consequentialism. The philosopher and neuroscientist Joshua Greene has used neuroimaging to study morality. Greene finds that we are well adapted to making moral judgments and argues that this must mean that we have a uniformity in our underlying moral outlooks.

Harris maintains that morals rest on human well-being and continues by making the point that it should be possible to answer moral questions with answers that are plainly right or wrong. He has many graphic illustrations of such questions, one example being the issue of whether the Taliban are justified in their subjection of women and girls and denying them education. Afghan women have a 12 percent literacy rate and a life expectancy of forty-four years. Afghanistan has close-to-the-highest maternal and infant mortality rates in the world. Harris states that the most moral response to this is not to throw battery acid in the faces of young girls for the "crime" of learning to read. The Taliban think they themselves are being very moral. Unfortunately, many social scientists believe that it is taboo to answer moral questions in the face of moral disagreement. How would we confront the Taliban in the above instance? Harris believes that the answer is we should point to the many societies that do not subjugate women and the clearly superior results of equal treatment. Those policies are the morally correct answer to the question of how to treat women. It goes without saying that Harris thinks we should confront the people who have been persuaded by bad philosophy and political correctness into positions of silence.

Harris is well-known for his antireligious views, and he devotes a chapter in his book to the problem of how religion leads people to seek well-being not in this life but in one beyond the grave. He cites the Catholic Church for excommunicating women who want to become priests but does not excommunicate priests who rape children. The church is more concerned about stopping contraception than stopping genocide. Some of the most atheistic societies in the world, e.g., Denmark and Sweden are, in fact, the most ethical in the sense of promoting human well-being. There have been many publications recently stressing how it is possible to be good without God, of which works by Greg Epstein (2009), Ronald Aronson (2008), and Richard Carrier (2005) are representative.

Life and death at one time was seen as the infusion into or departure from the body of a mysterious thing called a spirit or a soul. Science now explains the life process in physicochemical terms. The issue of abortion involves morality, politics, and science. Pro-choicers believe the personal moral choices of the mother take precedence over the rights of the fetus. Pro-lifers often speak of abortion as murder as if pro-choicers are in favor of murder. But murder is the killing of a person. Shermer argues that moral and political decisions are grounded in binary logic whereas science is grounded in fuzzy logic. Pro-lifers believe life begins at conception. With fuzzy logic, Shermer assigns probabilities to human life: before conception (0), at the moment of conception (0.1), multicellular blastocyst (0.2), one-month embryo (0.3), two month-old fetus (0.4), and so on until birth when the fetus becomes a human life form at 1. Eggs and sperm are not human individuals. The eight-week-old fetus has recognizable human features but lacks the neuronal synaptic connections for thinking. After eight weeks, embryos begin to show primitive response movements, but the embryo could only exist on its own after six months (twenty-four weeks) when the lungs and kidneys mature. Not until twenty-eight weeks does the fetus acquire sufficient neocortical complexity to exhibit some of the cognitive capacities of newborns. There is no evidence that the fetus is a thinking human individual before the end of the second trimester, after which time virtually no abortions are performed. Shermer concludes that there is no scientific justification to shift the abortion issue from a personal and moral one to a social and political one. Abortion remains a personal moral choice.

Should cloning be allowed as a means of producing stem cells or as a reproductive strategy? Shermer cites some of the idiocies that have been proclaimed about cloning. Seventy-four percent of Americans believe that cloning is against God's will. President Clinton spoke against cloning and tried to get a ban on the practice passed by the Congress. It is frequently overlooked that identical twins are clones. It is also overlooked that about half the variance between us is accounted for by genetics and the rest by the environment. Hence, cloning is no threat to unique personhood.

Harris (2010) is incensed about the way in which morality is tied to religion and especially to fundamentalist religion of the Christian and Islamic varieties. Theistic moral systems are based on the idea that without God there is no ultimate basis for determining right and wrong. Unfortunately, many of the problems that bedevil contemporary society are due to the holdover of religious influences. We have already shown the limitations of theistic ethics, but now Shermer asks two additional questions: (1) What if the moral issue is not discussed in the sacred text of the individual's religion? Cloning, stem cell research, and genetic engineering are not discussed in the Bible. What should Christians and Jews think about these issues? (2) What if the issue is discussed but is clearly wrong? Thus, in Deuteronomy 22:5: "A woman shall not wear anything that pertains to a man, nor shall a man put on a woman's garment; for whoever does these things is an abomination to the Lord your God." An even worse abomination apparently is a rebellious child for whom the appropriate punishment, according to Deuteronomy 21:18–21, is stoning to death. The Bible's recommendation for dealing with a woman who may have had sex before marriage is stoning to death at the door of her father's house (Deut. 22:13–21). Finally, if a man is found lying with the wife of another man, both of them shall die (Deut. 22:22). Shermer wonders if Jews and Christians really want to legislate biblical morality and post the Ten Commandments in public schools and courthouses, especially in view of the moral character displayed by some prominent religious leaders in recent years. Shermer wants to be fair and points out that not all biblical ethics are so extreme. The problem is one of consistency how do believers justify the abolition of slavery in view of passages in Exodus 21, giving the rules for the proper handling of slaves or biblical pronouncements on the sinfulness of homosexuality?

9.3 The Subjection of Women

9.3.1 Jimmy Carter and our Greatest Moral Challenge

Quite recently, former president Jimmy Carter published a book *A Call to Action: Women, Religion, Violence and Power* (2014). The book is a recital of injustices done to women and girls and an indictment of the failures of society to end iniquitous practices of individual men, religions, armed services, universities and other institutions in the USA and other countries. He points out the similarity between the racial prejudice as it existed in the Deep Southern USA where he grew up, and the worldwide prejudice, discrimination, war, violence, religious teaching, physical and mental abuse, poverty, and disease, which fall disproportionately on women and girls. Men and boys are presumed to be superior to women and girls. He tells of the work that he and his wife, Rosalynn, have performed for their nonprofit organization, the Carter Center. Carter has become convinced that the most serious and unaddressed worldwide challenge is the deprivation and abuse of women and girls. In addition to the unconscionable human suffering, there is a devastating effect on economic prosperity caused by a loss of contributions of at least half the human beings on earth. He decries the use of some selected scriptures by powerful male leaders within the Christian, Jewish, Muslim, Hindu, Buddhist, and other faiths to proclaim the lower status of women and girls. This claim spreads to the secular world to justify sustained acts of discrimination and violence against them. Carter does not mention the pioneering work of John Stuart Mill, and he writes from his Christian perspective, but it is surely significant that this former U.S. president should take up this subject so vehemently.

Carter is a deacon in his church, and he explains that there are usually several hundred people who come to hear him preach Bible lessons when he is at his church in Plains. He mentions a number of contentious issues and in particular an emphasis on Bible verses calling for wives to be "submissive" to their husbands. There are some Old Testament passages that trouble Carter, but he claims that Jesus Christ was the greatest liberator of women in a society where they had been considered throughout biblical history to be inferior. Christ treated women as equals. On the other hand, there are a number of selections that indicate that Saint Paul had a bias against women. Apparently, Carter does not take seriously the arguments on male superiority from Genesis (God creating male and female in his own image, the female from a male rib). There is a passage in the Bible (Deut. 22:13–14) that states that if a man finds no proof of a new wife's virginity, "she shall be brought to the door of her father's house and there the men of her town shall stone her to death." "Honor" killings are still a prevailing custom in many communities when a woman has been raped, refuses to accept an assigned husband, has an extramarital affair, or even wears inappropriate clothing. It is done in order to salvage the honor of the besmirched family.

When Carter moved into the governor's mansion in Georgia, he discovered that it was staffed with black women from the *women's prison*—all trusted inmates. He relates several stories of injustices done to these women. When he visited state prisons, he found terrible discrimination against the poor, black, and mentally handicapped. He initiated an overhaul of the state's prison policies. When Carter was a governor in the 1970s, only one in a thousand Americans was incarcerated, but there are now more than five times as many in prison and the number of black women has increased 800 percent. This is primarily due to drug laws. The United States has 4.5 percent of the world's population but 22 percent of the world's prison population. Since Carter's time as president, the emphasis has been placed on punishment and not rehabilitation. There has also been a substantial increase in the proportion of women being incarcerated globally. These are frequently for "moral" crimes such as drug trafficking and sex outside of marriage. Women face increased risk of sexual assault inside prison. There are devastating effects on the children of women in prison.

Another extraordinary response to crime has been the *death penalty*, and here, the Carter Center has been taking a firm stand against capital punishment. Carter argues that there are overwhelming ethical, financial, and religious reasons to abolish this brutal and irrevocable punishment. He points out that 90 percent of all executions are carried out in China, Iran, Saudi Arabia, and the United States. The Carter Center has worked on sexual discrimination and abuse of women in more than seventy developing nations. They have found that liberated women can play a vital role in correcting the most serious problems that plague their relatives and neighbors. Almost everywhere, women are relegated to secondary positions but almost always do most of the work. The center tries not to duplicate the efforts of other organizations but has found to its own surprise that it is being most called upon to help with tropical diseases. One of the most publicized of these is the Guinea worm.

Another serious and pervasive example of gender abuse is the *marriage of young girls*, often without their consent and contrary to their best interests. There are an estimated fourteen million girls married every year before they reach the age of eighteen, and one in nine of these is younger than fifteen. This includes 48 percent of young brides in South Asia, 42 percent in sub-Saharan Africa; 29 percent in Latin America and the Caribbean, and 18 percent in the Middle East and North Africa. Girls from poor families are nearly twice as likely to be married at an early age as girls from wealthier families. When poverty is a factor, marrying off a daughter is seen as a convenient way to eliminate the need to feed her. Girls are not considered as equal in value to boys and thus has evolved the payment of financial incentives to or from the bride's family. There has been an increased killing of brides by greedy husbands who don't receive enough money or jewelry from the bride's parents or in lieu of returning unsatisfactory brides (along with their dowries) to their parents. Young brides and their babies are more vulnerable than older brides and children. The young girls are inarticulate, their families have selfish financial interests, and political leaders consider the prohibition of forced child marriage a taboo issue because it is supported by traditional and religious culture.

9.3.2 Violence against Women

Sexual assault and rape is a subject of great antiquity with very recent interest. Carter describes an incident that occurred while he was governor of Georgia when he and Rosalynn accommodated a girl for a few days in the governor's mansion while she was awaiting dormitory housing. This young woman went on a date but returned in tears to the mansion, reporting she had been raped. It is rare for the victim to be willing to report an incident, and consequently, an increasing number of cases are undocumented and their perpetrators unpunished and uncorrected. Carter learned more about the situation as a distinguished professor at Emory University. The most startling aspect is the fact that the majority of rapes are the work of a few serial rapists. One in three college assaults is committed by student athletes. There is a similar near-epidemic crisis of sexual assault and rape in the military occurring partly as a result of the inclusion of women in combat roles.

The genocide of girls is a major world problem largely due to India and China trying to limit their population growth. In India, nurses, including Carter's mother, were asked to teach sex education and assist with mandatory vasectomies on fathers after their second child. The sterilization of fathers was abandoned after two years, but coercion of mothers' sterilization continues. On a global basis, slightly more males than females are born for unknown reasons. But the World Health Organization reports that in India the ratio of girls to boys is 100 to 112, and in China in 2010, the ratio was 100 to 118. The reason for this discrepancy is infanticide. Inexpensive sonograms have aided parents in ascertaining the sex of a developing fetus as early as twelve weeks after conception. The Indian Nobel Laureate Amartya Sen estimated that in 1990, there were 50 million "missing" females in China and more than 105 million worldwide. The terminations of these girls' pregnancies were decided privately, within families, and not ordained by governments. Sexual discrimination also occurs among children who survive birth. India's under-five child mortality rate in 2012 was fifty-six deaths per one thousand, the highest in the world.

There have been several horrible *gang rapes* in India, including one in Delhi in December 2012. Death sentences were assessed for the Delhi incident, but many human rights advocates raised alarms that these sentences might actually harm the cause of women's rights. Vinita Bharadwaj, a journalist writing in the *New York Times*, described her life in India as being subject to "stares, glares, whistles, hoots, shout-outs, songs, 'accidental' brushing-past, intentional grabbing, groping and pinching" by men. Carter follows this with a description of rampant rape and abuse of women in a refugee camp for Hutus after the Hutu-Tutsi genocide. The ramifications of this have included a terrible civil war in Zaire and the worst epidemics of rape in history as militia men surge back and forth in control of disputed territory. The Congo has become known as the world capital of rape.

Although *legal slavery* is ended in the world, the Global Slavery Index estimates that there are 12.5 million people enslaved today, including those living in bondage as laborers, those in marriages against their will, and prostitutes engaged in sexual trade. The International Labor Organization reports there are 20.9 million people engaged in forced labor. Experts on the slave trade in young women and girls agree that the best way to combat it is to concentrate on the male customers who provide the enormous financial profits that keep the slave masters and brothel owners in business. The US State Department estimates that about eight hundred thousand people are traded across international borders each year and that 80 percent of these victims are women and girls. The World Health Organization reported in 2013 that more than a third of all women are victims of physical or sexual violence. About a third of countries do not have any laws against domestic violence, and many wives consider it mandatory and proper to submit themselves to their husbands for punishment. At some time in their lives, one-fourth of all American women are victims of domestic violence. The FBI reports that between 2000 and 2006 there were 10,600 domestic homicides in the United States, 85 percent of the victims being women. Female genital cutting (FGC) is one of the most serious examples of abuse of girls involving the removal of all or part of the genitalia. It is sometimes referred to as female circumcision. The operation is usually performed without anesthesia by means of a knife or razor blade by women known as cutters. Some cutters use sutures to close the wound, leaving a small hole for the girl to pass urine or menstrual blood. At the time of marriage or childbirth, the hole has to be enlarged to accommodate the husband's penis or the infant. FGC can result in lifelong health consequences including chronic infection and severe pain during urination, menstruation, sexual intercourse, and childbirth. The girl may have psychological trauma. Some girls die from the cutting, usually as a result of bleeding or infection. The World Health Organization estimates that about 125 million women and girls have undergone FGC. The reason given for the procedure is to "purify" the girls by reducing their enjoyment or desire for sex. The World Conference on Human Rights in Vienna in 1993 declared FGC a serious abuse of small girls, and the UN General Assembly passed a resolution banning the practice in 2012.

9.3.3 Possible Remedies

Women are denied full participation in political affairs on a global basis despite the UN's Universal Declaration of Human Rights. In the United States, black women did not get the vote until the Voting Rights Act of 1965. Women did not serve in the US Cabinet until Franklin D. Roosevelt chose one in 1935. There has been a steady increase in the number of women serving in legislative positions worldwide, but they are still much below equality in all countries. There are very few women judges, and a factor in this is the small number of women entering and graduating from law schools. Another widespread example of sexual discrimination is the pay disparity in compensation for work. There has been much progress in health care for women, but it also lags behind in most countries. Carter gives an extensive review of the status of women in various countries followed by lists of specific actions that might be taken to move matters forward. Carter cites a major international conference on women in 1980 when he was president, which closed with a call to

- involve more men in improving women's roles in society;
- let women exert more political will;
- recognize crucial contributions women were already making to society;
- permit women to participate in planning for the future in all aspects of life;
- assess societal damage caused by a shortage of women in decision-making positions;
- publicize the benefits of women's leadership in cooperatives, day care centers, and credit facilities;
- acknowledge the value of making even small financial resources available to women; and
- give women more access to information about their government and untapped opportunities available to them.

9.3.4 Carter's Humanism

I have always admired Jimmy Carter, the peanut farmer who went into the US Navy and became a nuclear engineer, persevering on to become governor of Georgia and then president of the United States. Of course, as a humanist, I have to take note of his stance as a born-again Christian. However, to gain equality for women and girls would surely be an accomplishment similar to the abolition of slavery. As I read his book, it began to dawn on me that he must have a deeper character and vision than most politicians. He must have had courage to put forward the views expressed. It is one thing to think some of these thoughts, but it calls for great experience and human sympathy to carry them into the political arena with prospects of getting them enacted into law. Carter does not mention pornography, at least some of which is clearly harmful. Another query would be why he makes no mention of people who have raised the issue of women's subjection before now. The obvious candidate is John Stuart Mill who published the influential essay *The Subjection of Women* in 1869. Carter does not mention suttee, the practice whereby a man's widow is burned alive on his funeral pyre. Mill believed that his East India Company had succeeded in getting this stopped, and it has been banned several times, but isolated cases have still occurred even in the twenty-first century.

Another thought I had was that it is clear that many men do not respect women. Why should this be so? Even more perplexing thoughts concern those feminists who gave Mill his reputation. Why does Carter not mention Hypatia, Wollstonecraft, Friedan, de Beauvoir, Gilligan, Held, Noddings, Ruddick, Rand, and many women writers? There is an excellent review of feminist ethics on the Internet in the *Stanford Encyclopedia of Philosophy*. The ethics of caring features prominently in these works, and we know that women are greatly interested in the humanities and the psychology of relationships. If we were to explore these subjects with the same zeal we males give to justice, rationality, and hard science, we might begin to realize that women do, in fact, have abilities equal to those of the male. Surely, we should welcome women's contributions to their own salvation. We have only just started to investigate the psychology, neuroscience, and biology of reproduction, within which the roles of men and women were shaped.

9.4 The Golden Rule and Other Ethical Puzzles

The subjection of women is not only one of the most challenging impediments to morality, but it is probably the oldest, having begun way back in prehuman evolution. There are some other remnants of old thinking on ethics that have persisted from prehistoric times until the present. Some of these are quite plausible and can still be helpful to the aspiring ethicist (or hindrances if they are not investigated carefully). One of them is the so-called golden rule. This is often presented as the injunction "Do unto others as you would have them do unto you." It has recently been the subject of a book-lengthy dissertation by Harry J. Gensler (2013) who includes an intriguing "GR" chronology. This starts with an entry for 1 million BC in which the fictional Fred Flintstone helps a stranger who was robbed and left to die. He says "I'd want him to help me." GR thinking is born! But this is followed by some quite serious references to ancient times including one from 700 BC: In Homer's *Odyssey*, goddess Calypso tells Odysseus, "I'll be as careful for you as I'd be for myself in like need. I know what is fair and right." We are told that the Roman emperor Alexander Severus adopted the rule as his motto sometime between 222 and 235 and displayed it in gold on his wall. This is why it is called the golden rule. The point is that the rule is very old and is probably based on the hunter-gatherers having acquired the ability to formulate reciprocal understanding of others. In one sense, this is a remarkable advance over the abilities of our apelike ancestors, and the persistence of the rule is an amazing example of fossilized thinking. And it is all the more surprising that it is still useful, as a first approximation, in ethical deliberation.

The only regret I have to share with the readers is that the golden rule is of limited utility. We can see this in the first place from the defining statement quoted above. The implication is that the ethical reference is in the mind of the user. It does not follow that the other person is, in fact, best served by being treated as a clone of the user. The two people concerned may differ in age, sex, intelligence, social position, nationality, career choice, philosophy, or many other ways. A large part of Gensler's book comprises prescriptions for how to correct for these differences. By the time we have corrected for the differences, we might just as well have reasoned a plan for interaction de novo.

Shermer (2004) points out a problem with the golden rule is that the moral doer and the moral recipient may not feel the same way about the action. Men and women do not feel the same way about adultery for instance. Thus, Shermer modifies the rule to what he calls the ask-first principle. Truth telling and lying are relatively easy moral issues, and Shermer chooses to start his discussion with these. White lies, where we exaggerate our accomplishments, are ranked 0.1 or 0.2 on a fuzzy logic scale where the criterion for immorality lies at 1. Lies of omission rate 0.3 or 0.4. Lies of commission, where false information is supplied deliberately, rank 0.5 or 0.6. Big lies rank 0.7 to 0.9 and are much more immoral than white lies. How would the receiver feel if the liar were found out? Shermer's proposal is that we should never tell a lie if it leads to someone else's unhappiness or loss of liberty. There are circumstances where telling the truth would be immoral. If an abusive husband asks if you are harboring his fearful wife, it would be immoral to tell the truth because it might lead to the abuse or even death of the wife.

There are a number of other puzzling aspects of ethics that can act as impediments. An example is the question of free will. Here the problem is often posed by pointing out that every action we take is the result of some prior set of circumstances. This is often represented as the law of cause and effect. So the argument proceeds that every action is, in fact, predetermined and thus there is no room for any freedom of action on our part. This then contradicts our belief in personal responsibility, which is a foundational assumption in the operation of the law. The difficulty here is that we simply do not have a sufficient grasp of neuroscience to be able to describe the details of the processes within the brain to give a completely convincing account of the process of decision making. The best explanations to date, as, for example, by Daniel Dennett (1991, 2003), emphasize that processes involving choice are, in fact, not deterministic. Dennett points out that that the freedom to do certain things, to fly, for example, depends on scientific and engineering knowledge, both of which evolve as time goes by.

9.5 The Ethical Project

Sam Harris is one of the quartet of "new atheist" authors also including Richard Dawkins, Christopher Hitchens, and Daniel Dennett. One of the criticisms made of this group is that although they argue the case for the nonexistence of God, they offer nothing positive in return for the beliefs and social systems associated with the theistic religion that is undermined along with belief in God. Theistic morality needs to be replaced with some other ethical system. Harris came to the rescue here with his book *The Moral Landscape* (2010). He argues that we can derive an ethical system based on science. Actually, the book turns out to be largely an adaptation of Harris's PhD dissertation in neuroscience at UCLA. The book starts with Harris's definition of morality as that which contributes to human well-being or flourishing. Harris compares morality with physical health. It may be difficult to define either well-being or health, but both are clearly meaningful. The concept of a moral landscape is similar to what we are calling the state of the art in ethics and seems to mean some measure of morality as distributed in different places around the world or a representation of morality as found in different segments of society. Another excellent way of characterizing the distribution of ethics around the world is with the phrase the *ethical climate* found in Blackburn's book *Being Good* (2001). Perhaps the best description, which has the advantage of not using an analogy, is Kitcher's *The Ethical Project* (2011).

One thrust of Harris's thesis comes in his championing of "moral truth." He claims to have heard from thousands of educated men and women that morality is now a myth. In a footnote, he states that he did not arrive at his conclusions by engaging with the academic literature on the relationship between human values and knowledge but by considering the logical implications of progress in the sciences of mind. He argues that science can help us decide what our values should be. Many educated secular people believe there is no such thing as moral truth. But he then cites several examples where his readers will probably be outraged, including the case of someone who wants to torture all conscious beings to the point of madness. Harris asks, how can we can prove this devil isn't moral? He also cites numerous religious conceptions of moral law (does morality depend on worshiping the gods of the Aztecs, including human sacrifice?). He asks if we are justified in combating the Taliban. The God of Abraham said kill children who talk back to their parents—but even Christian fundamentalists ignore such "laws." Harris asks, how could anyone argue that a state of the worst possible misery for everyone is not bad? He condemns moral blindness in the name of tolerance, as in acquiescence to compulsory veiling, genital excision, bride burning, and forced marriage. He argues that moral relativism has to be answered by the facts about human flourishing.

Harris does not refer to the outstanding work by Blackburn (2005, 2001) on truth, be it scientific, moral, or otherwise. Blackburn points out that truth does not have to be absolute and unchanging, and the fact that morality is indeed relative does not mean that anything goes. Our understanding of nature, of morality, and of numerous other human systems evolves; and this is the reason that they are all relative. Engineered structures, for example, are designed with adjustments relative to the situation in which their use is intended. Kitcher's phrase *ethical project* captures this meaning very well. The tentative or provisional nature of ethics and morality has been emphasized by a number of authors.

The Science of Good and Evil by Michael Shermer (2004) has most of the features that we have maintained are crucial to a modern humanistic treatment. In the first place, Shermer understands that our morality started with biological evolution, as detailed in our earlier chapters, and that it continues to evolve through the medium of culture. This sets him generally in the company of Hume, Bentham, and Mill, Darwin, and the Huxleys. And it sets him somewhat apart from Kant, Sidgwick, Moore, and Singer. Of course, all these authors understood that reason was a major factor in shaping ethical systems, but starting with Hume the first group realized that the consequences of ethical decisions had to be evaluated using emotions: "Reason is the slave of the passions," as Hume put it. The second group, however, thought that morals should be based on reason alone. Shermer has an ethical theory that is a variation of the evolutionary ethics propounded in our earlier chapters. He calls it provisional ethics and claims that its true test is in solving real-world problems. Another important feature of Shermer's ethics is that he sees it as a science, with a provisional character, so that it is subject to evolution in the way that Darwin, the Huxleys, and Popper have all propounded. Ethics has evolved over the years so that the problems that engage us now are different from those that concerned people in the past.

Shermer's book has a useful chapter bearing on contemporary moral problems. This chapter is entitled "How We Are Immoral: Right and Wrong and How to Tell the Difference." The chapter discusses a number of principles by which we can tell the difference between right and wrong. It goes on to apply the principles to some contemporary moral issues. Shermer's principles are as follows:

- Ask God.
- Use the golden rule.
- Use the happiness principle.
- Use the liberty principle.
- Act in moderation.

Shermer's five principles can serve as a framework to investigate contemporary ethics.

It is interesting to compare Shermer's principles with the listing we discuss in appendix 1. Shermer has chosen to start his list, after a nod to theism, with the golden rule. As we have already said, the golden rule can be seen as a lynchpin for an ethical system since it employs two human traits that are embedded in our neuroanatomy: exchange reciprocity and reciprocal altruism. According to Matt Ridley (2010), these are the traits enabled *Homo sapiens* to build the cultural and social systems that set us on the road to economic prosperity. Hume stressed the importance of our recognition of the various constancies in our lives and the use of habitual behavior. This has come to be known as systems science, which underlies pragmatism, in general, economics, law, politics, and natural sciences. We are well advised to be systematic as embodied in several of the principles in the listing of appendix 1. Finding the truth in science and its de-emphasis by the evangelical Christian movement in promoting the teaching of creationism and intelligent design in American schools are examples of impediments to moral thinking of supreme repugnance to humanists.

Another criterion used to judge right and wrong is what for millennia philosophers have observed: that we seek pleasure and avoid pain, as we discussed in chapter 4. Happiness is a good synonym for pleasure, and thus, we might seek the emotions that produce happiness and avoid those that are associated with unhappiness. Shermer notes that the happiness principle is to seek happiness with someone else's happiness in mind and never to seek happiness when it leads to someone else's unhappiness. Shermer defines liberty as the freedom to pursue happiness and the autonomy to make decisions and act on them in order to achieve that happiness. What he calls the liberty principle states that it is a higher moral principle to always seek liberty with someone else's liberty in mind and never to seek liberty when it leads to a loss of someone else's liberty. It is only in the last two or three hundred years that the concept of liberty as applying to everybody has begun to spread. There are still parts of the world, especially in the theocracies, where the idea has to be fought for against intolerance and dictatorship. Extremism too often leads to violence, terrorism, and even war. The moderation principle states that when innocent people die, extremism in the defense of anything is no virtue and moderation in the protection of everything is no vice. The point is that killing anybody else in the name of anything else means that someone is seeking happiness and liberty at the ultimate expense of somebody else's happiness and liberty. Happiness, liberty, and moderation are examples of values, as expounded in chapter 5, which have been invented by thinkers over the course of history and which we can use as behavioral guides to morality. There are, of course, other values we may draw upon in particular situations.

Carter makes no mention of pornography while Shermer depicts three types: mental, positive, and negative. They are mainly harmless although there is some evidence that negative pornography (depicting harm or violence against women, such as pleasure in being raped) is harmful to at least some people. Mental pornography, or autoeroticism, is simply fantasizing about sexual activity. The sexual images exist in our imaginations. This is the commonest form of pornography. It may have come about together with all imaginary activity as a result of our large cerebral cortex. Western religion has generally prohibited sexual fantasies, and the medieval church proscribed penances for church leaders so indulging. In fact, according to Shermer, fantasizing can have several useful functions, and provisional ethics should reflect that mental pornography is not an immoral activity. There are similar considerations for positive pornography, i.e., images depicting individuals or couples involved in masturbation or in nonharmful and nonexploitative sexual situations. Soft-porn films leave something to the imagination, and this genre seems to be the preference of women. The male of the species is more inclined to favor hard porn. Shermer does, however, argue that positive pornography can become negative if it comes to take the place of sex with one's partner. Negative pornography comprises images that enhance sexual arousal by depicting sex as violent, abusive, or exploitative, especially those that show women being seduced and raped against their will. Shermer investigates the contention that pornography leads men to rape women and concludes that there is no evidence for the proposition. Rape was a tragic part of human history for thousands of years before pornography first appeared. Some studies even show a cathartic effect of pornography.

9.6 Animal Rights

The issue of animal rights was the focus of Singer's work (1975). Shermer has proposed a biocultural evolutionary pyramid, which shows biophilia, the love of all life on Earth, at its apex. The pyramid is Shermer's amalgamation of Maslow's pyramid of values (1971) and Singer's expanding circle (2011). In moving up the pyramid, the liberty principle has been expanded to cover more members of our own species. It is only a century and a half since slavery was abolished and only in the last century that women have begun to approach anything like the rights enjoyed by men. Gays still only have the right to marry in a few countries. What hope can there be for nonhuman animals? No one is proposing that animals have the right to vote or the right to a public education. Animal rights are more basic. They already have the right to be treated humanely in some countries, and humans can be convicted for cruelty to animals. The trade in animals is so extensive that the economy would grind to a halt if it were banned. The blood and fat from cows is used in a huge variety of products, not even to mention the food industry. The Bible says that God bestowed on man the dominion over all other animals just as it used to justify the subjugation of women and slavery. Legally, animals are products and property for humans to buy and sell. Shermer advocates fuzzy animal rights and shows a scale propounded by animal rights activist Steven M. Wise. On this scheme, category A (0.9 to 1) includes species who clearly possess sufficient autonomy for basic liberty rights, which are primarily whales, dolphins, and the great apes. Category B (0.5 to 0.89) include honeybees, dogs, elephants, and some parrots. The mind of Koko the gorilla is on a par with that of a six-year-old human child. She has a sense of self and has learned hundreds of symbolic language signs. She has even tried to teach language signs to other gorillas. There are chimpanzees, bonobos, and orangutans that are functionally equivalent to Koko. Shermer says that giving such animals rights could be quite simple: don't kill them, don't eat them, don't wear them, and don't cage them. Just let them be.

9.7 Ethical Science

There is a collection of readings on contemporary moral issues in Rachels (2007). The authors of this book, a father-and-son team, are traditional philosophers, and they respectfully present readings from the works of many philosophers on various subjects and leave their readers to form their own conclusions. To quote from their preface: "The point of the book is not to provide a neat, unified account of 'the truth' about ethics. That would be a poor way to introduce the subject. Philosophy is not like physics." The Rachels offer a work that expands on and extends the treatments given by ethicists to other controversial topics such as suicide, euthanasia, and the death penalty as well as other contemporary issues that concern humanists, such as feminism, homosexuality, and racism. There are other issues that extend into the political arena, including violence and warfare, treatment of the environment, drug use, punishment, gun control, energy use, and poverty. In fact, many of the most controversial issues of our time are moral issues, and it is to be hoped that we humanists will be able to work through them all given the time. Our work is not physics. It is a work of systems science, in which many of the concepts are much fuzzier than those in physics. Nevertheless, there is a need for much more unification than in the Rachels' book. We should respect the philosophical approach, but this does not preclude our investigating modern moral problems with a scientific outlook. Singer and Habermas have also tackled the issue of poverty and the problem of extending human rights to everyone. These questions that are also among contemporary moral problems demand to be solved in the near future and present us with far-reaching political as well as ethical problems. But even when all the contemporary issues are solved, evolutionary ethical discussion will continue. In the meantime, there are technological developments that are proceeding at such a pace that we need to consider them urgently. These are the subjects of our next chapter. Beyond the near term lie such issues as the exploration of space including the recently discovered exoplanets. It is possible that extraterrestrial life-forms have been mounting intelligent and sentient exploration to find us for millennia.

This is a time when it is easy to feel pessimistic. The Western world faces the scourge of extremist Islamist terrorism. In Africa the birthrate has been increasing so as to threaten the planet's population with unsustainable growth. The climate seems to have gone beyond control. Simon Blackburn (2001) writes that part of the fear threatening ethics is a grand unifying pessimism coming from philosophical theories. So great is the apprehension in many quarters that we need to hear Franklin Roosevelt's admonition again: we have nothing to fear save fear itself. It is our task to remind the world of the need for tolerance. Altruism and good government have enabled us to survive in the past. Given our determination, optimism will return and ethical science will prevail.

10 Humanism and Technology

10.1 Review and Introduction
10.2 System Science

Constants and Intentionality

10.3 Lessons from Evolution

Basalla, Darwin

10.4 History of Technology

Stone Tools
Agriculture, Building, Transportation, Writing, Books
Power, Telephone, Radio
Weapons, Warfare
Language, Mathematics, Symbols, and Computers
Chips and Wireless
Internet and the Technium

10.5 The Modern Age

Engineering Education
Robots and Energy

10.6 Future Scenarios

Space and Exoplanets
Genetic Engineering
Kurzweil: Singularity
Life Extension
General Intelligence

10.7 Kevin Kelly: Generalist

What Technology Wants

10. Humanism and Technology

10.1 Review and Introduction

We have reviewed how both reason and emotion factor into the process whereby we arrive at a science of ethics. We have used our knowledge of biological evolution to explain how much of our ethology is instinctive and how altruistic behavior predated our becoming human. We have discussed how psychology can be used to uncover these ancient predispositions as well as more modern emotional inclinations. We examined the beginnings of ethical reasoning in the construction of values and virtues. We also looked at the search for happiness started by the Greeks. Then we reviewed the methods of ethics developed by philosophers in the past few millennia and considered how we might apply Socrates's injunction to examine our lives. This brought us to modern times, and we surveyed some contemporary moral problems. As individuals, we have to ask ourselves: what are our objectives? Are we aiming at being healthy, wealthy, or wise, or maybe we will opt for all three? Is our concern to be a good lover, husband, or wife? Or a good mother or father, a good citizen? We might be interested in choosing a career such as an engineer, a scientist, a lawyer, a politician, an artist, or even a humanist counselor. Most of the remaining chapters are intended to help with the answers to these questions.

I have chosen to start with a discussion of technology since it was one of the first activities in which early human beings became involved, and it also illustrates very well two of the capabilities added by evolution to the primate mind: the ability to recognize constancy and the characteristic of intentionality. David Hume pointed out that we rely greatly on finding constants in our lives, and these various constants have come to be called systems. We recognize constancy in repeated situations, objects, or occurrences, any of which we call systems. Intentionality is the purposeful pursuit of some action. While there is no doubt that both of these abilities were present in many prehuman mammals, it is also clear that humans did the most to exploit them. It was the working of stone artifacts that was the beginning of technology, as argued for instance by Nicholas Toth (1987). The earliest stone artifacts have been dated to over 2.5 million years ago, a date that is only about three hundred thousand years after the first appearance of humans. Chimpanzees use twigs to catch termites, and quite likely our ancestors did too, but twigs do not fossilize so that we have no evidence that technology predates the creation of stone artifacts. Humans may have used twigs or even have produced spoken words (which are artifacts also) before making stone tools, but technology will have to be dated to the start of stone artifact working.

10.2 System Science

The great increase in the human brain size started with *Homo habilis* about 2.5 million years ago. Now Hawkins (2004) has argued that the growth in size of the human brain resulted in our acquiring additional memory in the form of extra layers in the cerebral cortex. This, in turn, gave us the capacity to recognize patterns of higher order in the activity in the lower cortical layers or, in other words, the ability to recognize systems and constancies of greater sophistication than we would have sensed otherwise. It is the memory of these higher-order constancies and systems, which we call knowledge. Our behavior has evolved since we first started to acquire such knowledge, and it is appropriate to remind ourselves of how the history progressed. Advanced activity started with hunting, gathering, toolmaking, speech development, narrative, and, of course, religion. In all these activities, there are certain situations that recur; and indeed, it is this repetition of earlier circumstances we can recognize from constancies (and which actually enable us to name the activity). David Hume pointed out that we rely on constancies extensively in our thinking. And as Peter Singer has pointed out, it is totally rational, in responding to a recurring situation, to use our earlier response again, provided that the outcome was satisfactory in the first instance. This is what the lawyers would call following precedent. During the twentieth century, and notably during the Second World War, the science of constant situations and their treatments became known as *General System Theory.* It was Anatol Rapoport who first pointed out the importance of constancies in his work general system theory (1986), thereby establishing the link to Hume's thinking of two centuries earlier.

Most human thinking involves straightforward processes together with occasional decisions. We may prescribe the steps involved in the form of formal protocols or programs and even represent such systems in graphical form in the manner that has become familiar for computer programs. In the human case, there may be emotional overtones to the cognitive activities in our minds. Systems can be combined or expanded out, often following well-known rules. We have discussed systems earlier, and we remind the reader of figure 3, a system representing an individual human being. Murray Gellman (1994) has explained how every system can be represented by a quintessential idea called its schema. We may reduce a system of language to a single unit we call a *word*. Language itself is a system comprised by a grammar and a lexicon. Systems of words comprise sentences; and sentences combine into paragraphs, chapters, and books. In science, engineering, and other pragmatic disciplines, these combined systems are what practitioners learn to become conversant with the state of the art in particular fields. The human beings involved, the societies, groupings, and associations that practice the arts and sciences are themselves sometimes referred to as systems. There are also a number of very complex systems of which religion was one of the first examples, and for that reason, it would be useful to discuss it in more depth. Many of the other complex systems have evolved from religious beginnings as we see when we trace human history.

10.3 Lessons from Evolution

Evolution did not stop when men and women appeared on the earth but continued on in the development of the various artifacts and practices we humans have created. These nonbiological forms of evolution are much faster than the genetic mechanism. Basalla (1988) has pointed out that many artifacts can be arranged in the form of a family tree, similar to the tree of life. But the essence of an artifact is contained in its design encapsulated in the blueprints and specifications produced by engineers. Human technology encompasses much more than physical artifacts and extends to a wide assortment of systems we have invented, ranging from language to mathematics and science, business, finance and economics, medicine and surgery, laws and government, poetry and literature, art and music. Hickman (1990) has argued that this is the position of none other than the great John Dewey himself. In all these designed and activity systems, we find the equivalent of the design cycle. The future will be evolved in a pragmatic way. Responding to changing circumstances and anticipating the future is a discipline known as management. For an excellent exposition of the process, we may turn to the works of Peter Drucker and in particular to his magnum opus *Management* (1973). In other books, Drucker has shown how adaptations of the methods can be applied to civic, religious, and nonprofit organizations. The discipline of management is a part of the science of systems, specifically the control of intelligent adaptive systems.

The idea of evolution dovetails neatly into systems theory. We must first realize that real systems do not always remain strictly constant: they can vary. This is the way systems can adapt to changing circumstances. Slowly changing schema will result in changes of the expressed system. It is these changes whose progressions can be recognized from external appearances that we call evolution. Darwin did more than anyone else to make scientists realize the importance of evolution to biology. Mendel supplied the understanding of an underlying genetic mechanism as the schema of biological systems. Finally, Crick and Watson pointed to DNA as the molecular key to the genetic mechanism.

The book by Basalla (1988) discusses technological evolution and it shows much borrowing of ideas between branches of the tree. Kelly (2010) is particularly interested in convergence in both biological and technological evolution and illustrates this with a number of instances, of which the blowgun is a singular example. It seems to be a characteristic of both biological and technological evolution that complexity increases as lines advance. Kelly has an interesting section on the evolution of brains in animals and humans. He draws our attention to the increasing complexity of networks, both of nerves and blood vessels. In plants, there are networks of roots and chemical interactions that show increasing complexity in more advanced types. Darwin himself pointed this out.

Kelly argues that beauty and the appreciation of beauty also advance with evolution. In physics the increase of entropy (disorder) is often cited as an indicator that our civilization and indeed the universe itself is doomed to wind down to a state referred to as heat death. But Kelly features work that has been done to show that complexity, diversity, sophistication, ubiquity, freedom, sentience, "mutualism," and beauty all increase as evolution advances, a phenomenon he refers to as exotropy.

10.4 History of Technology

There are a number of works that recite the history of technology and systems within the human context, one of the best being Jared Diamond's *Guns, Germs and Steel* (1998). We do not need to repeat such material except to remind the reader of its broad scope and make a general point. Consider our history starting from hunting and gathering and how the development of agriculture and animal husbandry vastly increased the productivity of the land. After learning how to control fire, our campsites became more hospitable to our families and protected them from animal predators. Buildings in villages and towns have given us shelter and warmth in winter. Glassware, pottery, and cutlery have graced our tables and ovens have allowed us to cook. We learned how to harness the horse to increase our efficiency in plowing and transportation of goods and our own bodies. We discovered the power of symbols for writing and recording information and narratives. Books and libraries give us access to all history and science as well as literature, drama, and poetry. The study of medicine has yielded cures for most infectious diseases, and anesthetics and pharmacy have greatly relieved us of pain. We learned how to use steam power to drive machinery, locomotives, and ships; and finally, we developed the internal combustion engine to power automobiles and trucks. In the nineteenth century came the telephone, the telegraph, and the radio. In the twentieth century, we added television and, finally, the computer. The lesson to be drawn is that we are sometimes inclined to forget the almost miraculous progress that we have actually made since we left our jungle origins.

Weapons and Warfare

The first stone tools were probably knife edges used for cutting or scraping, but after a while, the idea of using a sharp point on a spear would have occurred to a hunter as a benefit of avoiding close contact with the prey. Kelly (2010) presents evidence that the blowgun was invented in two different parts of the world. This device is very old, having originated in both the Amazon and in Borneo. In both cases, the method of use is similar—a rotating motion for spotting the target and timing the blowing for a hit. The hunter's stance and method of transporting darts are also identical in both cases. In other parts of the world, stone provided the heads for arrows once the bowstring had been invented. Metal made an excellent substitute for arrowheads and cutting tools once it had been discovered, and once again, weaponry both for hunting and warfare advanced. The means of launching projectiles progressed in Roman times and in the Middle Ages in Europe. Elastic propulsion attained its zenith in the form of the trebuchet in the fourteenth century. Eventually, gunpowder, after its debut in China, found its way to Europe; and cannons appeared on Western battlefields to be followed by rifles and handguns. Bombs and mines powered by explosives proliferated, and by the time of World War II, atomic power was pressed into service. But the escalation of warfare brought more inhumane weapons and greater numbers of fatalities and injuries.

Language, Mathematics, Symbols, and Computers

We have already mentioned the invention of language and writing and how the use of mathematics made engineering and science more efficient processes. The invention of algebra and calculating machines sped these processes along. Charles Babbage realized that it should be possible to make a general purpose computing machine in the nineteenth century, and he and Countess Lovelace developed the first computer programs. The first working computers came about in the twentieth century, using vacuum tubes and transistors followed soon thereafter. Great increases in reliability and reductions in size were the result of the invention of the integrated chip. Personal computers (PCs) became common in the 1970s, with the invention of word processing and spreadsheet programs. Radio linkages permitted the transmission of data for processing of long-distance messages and interactions. This was the beginning of the Internet. There is an informative history of computers through 1980 by Stan Augarten (1984).

The Internet

Some of the most interesting of Kelly's (2010) observations concern the Internet. The snowballing success of search engines, such as Google, cause him to wonder if the coming artificial intelligence (AI) will be confined to a stand-alone supercomputer or instead be born in the superorganism of a billion CPUs known as the web. This global system encompasses the Internet, its services, all the peripheral chips, and affiliated devices, from scanners to satellites and the billions of human minds entangled in one vast network. This gargantuan machine already exists today. It incorporates a billion online PCs (about as many as there are transistors in an Intel chip in one computer). Kelly points out that the Internet acts like a very large computer that operates at about the clock speed of an early PC. It processes three million e-mails each second, which means that network e-mail runs at 3 megahertz. It also contains 2.7 billion cell phones, 1.6 billion land phones, 27 million data servers, and 80 million wireless personal digital assistants (PDAs). The web holds about a trillion pages. The human brain holds about 100 billion neurons. Each neuron has synapse links to thousands of other neurons. Each webpage averages links to 60 other pages, and thus, there are a trillion synapses among the static pages on the web. The human brain therefore has one hundred times that number of links, but brains are not doubling every few years whereas the global machine is. He chooses to call the global machine the Technium.

Kelly points out that numerous technologies have enabled virtuosos to excel in specific fields. He cites, for example, Bach who flourished on the newly invented harpsichord, Mozart with the piano, Alfred Hitchcock with the movie camera, and van Gogh with cheap oil paint. He takes us into game theory with a discourse on the difference between finite games (chess, football, etc.) and infinite games (his examples include evolution, life, mind, and the Technium). It seems to me that games are subcategories of systems. Finite games are played to win and then cease, but we try to never reach end points with infinite games. The name *game theory* is used because the subject started with the study of finite games but was later extended to infinite games. Wittgenstein did much to popularize the topic with his references to "language games."

10.5 The Modern Age

The early toolmakers presumably passed on their knowledge and skills by imitation, but by the Middle Ages, this situation had evolved into the system of guilds and apprenticeships. Eventually, some of the engineering disciplines required at least rudimentary mathematical abilities; and thus in the nineteenth century, academic programs were started for civil and mechanical engineering. Electrical engineering followed soon afterward, and chemical engineering appeared on university campuses around 1910. Such engineering specialties as railroad, automotive, marine, aeronautical, and others came to answer demand. After World War II, some of the academic engineers suffered from envy of science and mathematics departments, and this resulted in the neglect of the traditional engineering design and practice and their modern incarnation in systems and industrial engineering. Consequently, we now have many schools teaching "technology" with curricula weak in mathematics.

Robots

The first robots were entirely mechanical with clockwork workings and were more in the way of toys and amusements. The first robots with economic significance were used in automobile manufacture, where they incorporated programmable instructions and were used in highly repetitive operations. As time progressed, the complexity of the tasks undertaken has been increased. Until now, we have automated household vacuum cleaners as well as self-driving automobiles. A recent newspaper article (*Wall Street Journal*, February 25, 2015) reports that automation threatens all manner of workers, from drivers to waiters to nurses. There are now hundreds of thousands of industrial robot installations. Although there are certain tasks that are still beyond robotic capabilities, such as folding laundry, even these are rapidly yielding to research.

One of our most problematic situations at present is the energy supply. Until the millennium, we saw the best long-term solution to this as nuclear fusion and solar satellites. At present, the most popular remedies are seen in wind power and solar cells. The accumulation of carbon dioxide in the atmosphere has become widely recognized as a problem now. For a while, it was a moot point as to how much of the present global warming is due to human activity and how much is part of a natural cycle. But hopefully, when we are past the immediate crisis, we will be able to bring about some weather and climate control on a long-term basis. We may be able to make better use of the world's desert areas in the future. The situation seems to be in flux at the present due to the new technique of hydro fracturing of rock and its consequent release of both oil and natural gas.

10.6 Future Scenarios

There are a number of engineering advances that might be expected to impact the lives of individuals, such as advanced robotics, speech recognition, correction of genetic defects, control of the aging process, etc. We still have a hankering to travel into space, the putative goal at the present being the planet Mars. We are also still committed to listening for signals from extraterrestrial life or at least to locating possible sources for it such as the exoplanets, which we now believe to exist in profusion. One of the most remarkable pieces of literature to be published in this area of futurology is the book *Singularity* by Leonard Kurzweil (2005). Kurzweil had an academic career in electrical engineering at MIT. In the course of this, he developed the first reading machine for the blind and the first text-to-speech synthesizer. He started companies, marketing some of the best music synthesizers and voice recognition software. In the late 1980s, he wrote *The Age of Intelligent Machines*, which predicted that machine intelligence would become indistinguishable from human intelligence in the first half of the twenty-first century. In the 1990s, he realized that the power of ideas to transform the world is itself accelerating: this is the law of accelerating returns. In 1998 came *The Age of Spiritual Machines* in which he predicts that machines will eventually reveal spirituality. In *Singularity*, his predictions for computer technology go even further, and he also ventures into the world of genetics and biology. Some of Kurzweil's predictions are really startling, and the best way to convey an idea of them is to list some in ascending order of shock value. He starts by arguing that technological progress is accelerating along exponential paths, the best-known example being Moore's law. In the mid-1970s, Gordon Moore, a leading inventor of integrated circuits and later chairman of the board of Intel, observed that we can squeeze twice as many transistors onto an integrated circuit every twenty-four months. There are several other examples of such exponential acceleration in technology.

Kurzweil made the point that the law of accelerating returns also applies to biology and genetic engineering, e.g., DNA sequencing, communications, brain scanning, brain reverse engineering, and in the size and scope of human knowledge. He declared that the law of accelerating returns is fundamentally an economic one. When a machine is improved by some technological innovation, there is an economic incentive to replace that machine. The cumulative effect of many such advances is a steady gain in economic productivity. The values of the mathematical function $1/x$ approaches infinity as x approaches 0, and the point $x = 0$ is termed a *singularity*. In astronomy, if a massive star undergoes a supernova explosion, its remnant collapses to a point of zero volume and infinite density—a singularity. Light cannot escape from it, and so it is called a black hole. We believe that the universe began with such a singularity. Kurzweil defines an ultra-intelligent machine as one that can far surpass all the intellectual activities of the cleverest man. Therefore, an ultra-intelligent machine could design better machines than itself, and therefore, there will occur an intelligence explosion. As time goes on, evolution will be faster and faster, and there will be a singularity in intelligence.

Kurzweil has also investigated the computational capacity of the human brain. He estimates that we should be able to replace the computer capacity of the human brain with a PC by 2020 for an estimated cost of $1,000. By 2050, $1,000 worth of computing power will exceed the processing power of all human brains on earth. Finally, he sets the date of singularity at 2045. If everything turns out as he expects, this will indeed be a profound and disruptive transformation in human capability. After singularity, things will be as different from our human past as it was from that of lower animals. Can the pace continue to speed up indefinitely? Can we imagine what one thousand scientists, each one thousand times more intelligent than contemporary humans and operating one thousand times faster, could come up with? Kurzweil stresses that the postsingularity civilization will continue to be human, and indeed, what we have is already a human-machine civilization. Can we really live forever? Kurzweil seriously claims that baby boomers will make it to the "designer people" generation and will be able to live as long as they choose.

Such changes would not mean that people would opt to live forever just for as long as they want. How much longer would they want to live on the average? The earth's population is excessive already by some reckoning. Where are all these extra folk going to live? Would space habitation become the norm? The way we live now we rely on one generation succeeding the next. What happens when we start living forever and younger generations do not come into an inheritance from their long-lived parents? When everyone is as rich as Croesus, what will happen to economic incentive? Perhaps it is the next thirty years, before singularity arrives, that will be the hardest to endure. Who would want to be the last person to die? How many people will opt to be frozen to ensure making it through to singularity?

Another aspect of the prediction with far-reaching implications is the explosion in general intelligence. Computers and the Internet have already resulted in one of the greatest increases in intelligence since the invention of the book, but the prospect of everyone being superintelligent and superfast in intellectual processes seems to be profound. So much of our lives are spent defending or combating patently stupid traditions that it is hard to imagine a world of Einsteins living free of superstition. Kurzweil discusses not only the experience of virtual worlds but also the possibility that consciousness is a form of virtual reality. We may, in the future, be able to experience the consciousness of another person.

10.7 Kevin Kelly, Generalist

Kelly describes his career as it relates to technology, which is more important than might be supposed at first sight because it seems that his understanding of the subject has advanced with each phase of his career. Many people who write about technology have received a training in mathematics, physics, or engineering, starting in high school and progressing through college before entering employment in industry or academia. On the other hand, Kelly is a generalist. He was a college dropout who went to Asia and, following his muse, absorbed the lore of living in the East. When he returned to the United States, he began selling mail-order travel guides and later became involved with the Whole Earth Catalog. He was impressed by the way in which artifacts of old technology remain available years after becoming obsolete. His interest was then captured by the growth of the Internet as a supplier of merchandise and then of information. He was one of the founders of *Wired* magazine. He is obviously widely read and has acquired a broad knowledge of technology in general as well as an understanding of the physics and mathematics behind it. His career is interesting because he did not become a specialist as is so often the case with technological people, who, as they say, learn more and more about less and less. Kelly is interested in the general field of technology and is unafraid of getting out of one area as most specialists would be. It might be best to summarize the broad thesis of his book at this juncture.

10.8 What Technology Wants (2010)

An interesting issue is Kelly's provocative claim, as exhibited in his book's title that technology "wants" something. He acknowledges that almost all technologists deny that technology wants anything. We can doubt that technology acts as a coherent whole. I share these doubts myself, at least as regard the present state of technology, and wonder if Kelly did not choose the title to get his work off the bookshop shelves. We often speak of some system "needing" something or the other. For example, we might speak of a house "needing" an extra room or of a dish "needing" some seasoning. What we are doing then is inserting our own human evaluation of the system and what we ourselves "want" from it. It does not imply that the system itself has any emotions or instincts. We are projecting our own feelings onto the inanimate object. However, there is another sense in which *wanting* might seem to be an appropriate word, and that is in connection with robotic behavior. Kelly has sections on artificial intelligence and discusses how it might be included in autonomous robotic systems. Engineers have used software to help with the design of new robots. Thus, self-reproducing machines could be programmed to design improved versions of themselves. These new designs could include objectives that might then be said to be what the robots "want." In fact, Kelly has an account of a visit he made to a company called Willow Garage, a robot manufacturer that has made an automaton operating on battery power that can recharge itself when the battery runs down. When necessary, it goes in search of an outlet to plug into. It has been programmed not to interfere with any human so that if anyone does stand in its way to an outlet, then it has to edge around them. Kelly says that the machine's movements are then easily interpreted as its "wanting" to reach the outlet.

Pessimistic Scenarios: In contrast to Kurzweil's Promethean vision, a number of authors have offered us some quite nightmarish scenarios. One of the most authoritative of these comes from Sir Martin Rees, England's Astronomer Royal, who wrote *Our Final Hour* (2003), a warning of how terror, error, and environmental disaster threaten mankind's future. Since most of the problems Rees discusses have been well worked over in other places, I will not dwell on them further. They certainly all exist as threats, but many of them can be averted if we put our minds to the issues involved. Another set of nightmare scenarios are described by Virginia Postrel in *The Future and Its Enemies* (1998). Apparently, Postrel was targeting Al Gore and his propensity for control. Gore (2006, 2007) himself has written some interesting books.

Like the writer of a good who-done-it, Kelly keeps the suspense going into his final chapter before he reveals what it is that he believes the Technium ultimately wants. And Kelly's idea is that the Technium "wants" to continually increase the range of choices available to us. There is a review of the book by David E. Nye (2011) in the *Scientific American*, which is somewhat critical of the many pronouncements that Kelly has advanced. Kelly himself offers some comments on other writers on technology, which are of some interest. There is an extensive list of such works in his annotated reading list, many of which I was not previously aware. He describes Ray Kurzweil's (2005) concept of singularity as a myth, unlikely to be true but that which will never go away, to be reinterpreted forever. In contrast, Kelly's version of the future does not include discontinuities but is instead an accelerating march of progress. He does not predict an end to death as Kurzweil does, instead remaining silent on that subject. He calls Kurzweil an unabashed atheist while he himself waxes eloquent on all the choices the Technium is about to bring us, which will lead us to process theology, in which God learns as he goes along. Both Kelly and Kurzweil have presented us with books that border on the sensational. But there is a sense in which they are both correct: the assumption that it is technology that can make the greatest impact on our futures. But we will probably need much more conservative analyses to convince the world that progress is bound to continue.

Kelly's expositions of the philosophies of the Unabomber and of the Amish present some further negative scenarios. The Unabomber claims that the Technium is destroying our freedom and that we must destroy it. The Amish claim that technology is contrary to the will of God and that we should ignore it and continue to live in the old ways. Kelly has made a valuable contribution in challenging singularity and has given us a wealth of thought about technology. We can extend his thinking about the Technium wanting to continually increase the range of choices available to us to the whole of humanist ethics as an answer to the situation with which we started this chapter, at which point we were still left with the problem of finding our way forward. We must realize that humanist ethics is an infinite game and is a part of the Technium, which is not simply restricted to autonomous automatons but covers all manner of organizations. There are many movements operating under the banners of agnosticism, atheism, nonbelief, humanism, and free thought; and many organizations and subdivisions of organizations under all sorts of commercial and governmental banners, and they are all playing "games" according to numerous rules. Kelly's claim that we should play our infinite games with a perpetual objective of increasing choices seems to me to be a useful expression of our destiny.

10.9 Coda

Our theme in this chapter has been that it is technology that has, in fact, been the source of our growing freedom, although we will need to keep a watchful eye on the various impediments to our ethical progress. But we also learn that there are other great objectives we will also have to pursue if the promise of technology is to be realized. We emphasize again that the undertaking must be ethical. It will require planning both on individual and societal levels. We will need to maintain our commitment to knowledge through reading, learning, and research. We will need to continue economic investment to develop the capital and prosperity we will require as the future unfolds. We should find ways to bring health, wealth, and wisdom to everybody, everywhere. We have to be optimistic and find ways to counter the negative scenarios that will come along. We must help our fellow creatures, with art, technology, and science in loving, altruistic endeavors. We need to find a way around the heat death of the universe and determine a purpose for the continued transcendence of the human race and our living allies in this universe.

11 Humanist Individuals

Outline

11. Humanist Individuals

11.1 Self-Control:

We are now well along in our investigation into the evolution of ethics. Recollect Figure 2 that showed that there has been a series of evolutionary changes that have enabled us to control our lives and bodily movements with increasing complexity. We have reviewed how both reason and emotion factor into the process whereby we arrive at a science of ethics. We have used our knowledge of biological evolution to explain how much of our ethology is instinctive and how altruistic behavior predated our becoming human. Psychology teaches that in addition to the basic drives we share with most animal species, we humans have a number of instinctive morals such as empathy and a certain amount of altruism that are also felt as reciprocal emotions. Biological evolution worked on us when we were forced out of the forest and onto the savannah with its dangerous predators, favoring bipedal locomotion and dexterous hands. Evolution provided us with growing brains of increasingly advanced cognitive capabilities. We can recognize natural systems, invent new ones, and, simultaneously, be conscious of what we are doing. The capacity for speech has enabled us to model nature, to communicate, and to invent ways of dealing with repetitive situations. These inventions also provide us with social cohesion. Prominent among them are cultural systems of value, such as altruism, liberty, loyalty, and fairness. Evolution strengthened a number of other modules in our brains, including what we call common sense, and vastly increased the capacity of our memories.

We have discussed how psychology can be used to uncover our ancient predispositions as well as more modern emotional inclinations. We examined the beginnings of ethical reasoning in the construction of values and virtues. We also looked at the search for happiness started by Aristotle and Epicurus. One interesting point was made by Graffin and Provine (2007) who reported that a substantial majority of evolutionary scientists see religion as an adaptation, which was a part of evolution. Then we have reviewed the modern methods of ethics developed by philosophers in the past three centuries and have seen how we might apply Socrates's injunction to examine our lives. This brought us to modern times around the period of World War II. The preeminent humanist writers at that time were Corliss Lamont, John Dewey, Bertrand Russell, H. J. Blackham, and Jaap Van Praag. We surveyed some contemporary moral problems. The American Humanist Association and the *Humanist* magazine were established in the USA and similar organizations in several other countries. In the last chapter, we speculated on how humanism and, in particular, humanist ethics might proceed into the future including some speculations on the future of technology. There is an illuminating work by Daniel Dennett (2003) who pointed out that even freedom evolves. The point here being that it is our knowledge of natural science and engineering that has enabled us to do all manner of things that were impossible without it. Academic interest in humanism continued to grow in the postwar period with the establishment of the Humanist Institute and teaching programs at several localities. We may think of all these instincts and capabilities as tools or instruments as at our disposal to control ourselves and our behavior.

11.2 Seven Ages of Man

A key question is, of course, how are individuals doing actually living as humanists in this day and age? Do people flourish better as members of humanist organizations or, instead, by simply living by themselves or with their families and friends? Has all the academic questioning and training taken away the emotional commitment of the traditional religions? E. O. Wilson has recently put this rather well in his latest book *The Meaning of Human Existence* (2014) where he asks, "Are we built to pledge our lives to a group . . . or to place ourselves and our families above all else?" The answer has to be that there is, or should be, a benefit to the individual who adopts a humanist ethology that will accrue directly to that person, and also indirectly through the effects on society, there should be benefit to everyone. In other words, we have both legitimate egoistic as well as altruistic values. It is then the consequence of electing to follow a humanist ethology that is the subject of this chapter. The answer to our questions should become clearer as we further expound on the content of past chapters and then explore further in the remaining chapters. Humanist churches, forums, and congregations have been growing rapidly and encountering certain problems that might have been surprising to the WWII generation. The situation may be illustrated by the exercise immediately following.

We have seen how several authors from Shakespeare to modern psychologists witness Maslow, in particular, have described the various stages of development that we go through in our lives. It follows that a contemporary congregation of any size may contain members at every life stage, from infants to the senile. It also follows that the programs offered by the group must contain points of attraction for all the ages. Otherwise, we will see members dropping away from attendance. In the past, a country church would have offered one service per week to the entire congregation and simply ignored dissatisfaction in the ranks. But nowadays, in the urban environment, with well-educated members, it would be a recipe for failure to ignore sections of the congregation. So we might expect to see the following additions to the regular program:

- For the mothers and fathers of babies, workshops on child rearing and social gatherings for parents
- For children and their parents, Sunday schools, play periods, picnics, camps, and games
- For the youth contingent, schools, dances, and parties
- For young marrieds, workshops on budgeting, household management, and raising children
- For the middle aged, career counseling, discussion groups and social gatherings
- For retirees, classes and outings

The leader of such a congregation is probably expected to give informative talks on philosophical and psychological topics as well as counseling to individual members. He or she would also be expected to serve as a business and strategic coordinator for the group. All in all, we can see that the modern humanist group in actual practice could be a very busy affair with many overlapping activities.

11.3 Studying Humanist Ethics

Nearly forty years, ago a number of philosophers produced a symposium on the subject of humanist ethics edited by Storer (1980). The first observation to be made about this work is that there is in fact a very close correspondence between humanist and academic ethics. Storer made the point that university philosophy faculty members are predominantly humanist. The reason given for the symposium was that with all the trouble in the world at that time, there was a great need for the health and harmony that might be supplied by moral thinking. But Storer was concerned that humanists were at odds among themselves about morality. Many of the leading humanist ethicists of that time contributed to the proceedings with ideas on how a greater morality might improve the world. Prof. Konstantin Kolenda (of Rice University and Humanists of Houston) proposed that a start might be made by building a consensus on international affairs. Another prominent contributor was a young Dr. Paul Kurtz who argued that humanism has, or should have, an ethic of responsibility. He stressed that there are several humanist theories, all secular but differing on meta and normative issues: existentialism, emotivism, pragmatism and utilitarianism being the main examples. Existentialism, which is largely the product of philosophers of the European continent seems to be following a parallel path to Anglo-American humanism. Humanists differ over any number of concrete issues: capital punishment, euthanasia, abortion, sexual mores, etc. We may have liberal or radical approaches, be socialist or capitalist. Humanists may be libertarian, devoted to a cause, or be committed to "humanity as a whole." Kurtz stated that "the truth is that humanism has attracted many diverse tendencies in the world under its banner and it may be impossible to find agreement among all those who claim identity with the humanist banner." He also cautioned that if someone is identified as a humanist, there is no assurance that he or she will be moral.

11.4 Ethic of Responsibility

Dr. Paul Kurtz first proposed an ethic of responsibility in the symposium edited by Storer, under which the freedoms and rights of the individual are to be balanced with responsibilities. In a later work (Kurtz 1988), he expounded the proposition in greater detail, setting out responsibilities to the self and the family, including a warm accolade to his own extended family. He argued that our responsibilities extended all the way through our local and national humanist organizations to our membership in the world community. In effect, he carried us beyond the confines of personal value theory to a recognition that we must include others in our ethical thinking. Kurtz emphasized the need for moral education at some length. Other articles in the same volume included one by Markovic on *Historical Praxis as the Ground for Morality* and another by Radest on *Relativism and Responsibility*, both of which seem to hint at management approaches. The ironic thing is that despite his pessimism in the Storer volume, Kurtz himself went on to use management techniques to establish a very successful humanist organization. Thirty years later, Kurtz was recognized as one of the leading thinkers on humanism. Would the Storer symposium authors now, after the appearance of "evolutionary psychology," be more receptive of systems theory and adaptive change in ethics and in human behavior? Kurtz's presentation of responsibility is primarily normative. It does not explicitly state how we are to decide on the ends to be pursued to benefit everyone. Are we, the exercisers of the ethic, to be the deciders, or are the beneficiaries to have a say in the ends to be pursued? Additionally, there is little guidance in the simple statements of the ethics as to the methods that are appropriate to the decision-making process.

11.5 Evolutionary Ethics

Another aspect of humanist theory is that it recognizes the importance of evolution in ethics. This viewpoint was most emphatically expounded by Julian Huxley, a grandson of Thomas Henry Huxley and an early professor at Rice University. The theory was presented in his book *Evolutionary Humanism* first published in 1964 and reissued in 1992 with an introduction by H. James Birx. Ethics is only a portion of the subject matter of the work and is not even listed in the index. It is useful to start with an earlier summary of our essential humanist beliefs. There have been several earlier summary statements such as the Humanist Manifestos I and II, Corliss Lamont's *Central Propositions of Humanism* (1982), Paul Kurtz's *Secular Humanist Declaration* (1983), and Fred Edwords's *The Humanist Philosophy in Perspective* (1984). We will agree with most of the statements made in these articles but with a few changes of emphasis to reflect our changing times. One way to approach the problem of formulating our basic principles is to work backward from the various fields of knowledge, summarizing what we know and abstracting the methods that have led us to our present status. This seems to be the method used by Corliss Lamont. As our knowledge grows in different areas and the literature in humanist libraries accumulates we should expect to revise our basic statements, and they in turn will influence the future growth of our knowledge. A willingness to adapt and change should be a characteristic of humanism distinguishing it from dogmatic and inflexible religion. Similarly, we would not expect every adherent of the humanist movement to subscribe to every one of its principles.

Starting with Hume, there has been a growth in understanding of human psychology, as we have already discussed in chapter 4. There has been a growing appreciation of the differences between the sexes. This is such an important topic that we devote the whole of the next chapter to it. Another aspect of the psychological discoveries has been the growing understanding of habits. Again, it was Hume who pointed out that our recognition of constancies enables us to respond in prescribed ways and develop what we call habits. There have been a number of books published over the years since then that describe the action of habits and detail both good and bad habits. These are what provide the structure to our everyday behavior. The reader is referred to Mursell (1953) and Duhigg (2012) as representatives of the genre. Various strategies for behavioral modification have been advocated, and commercial companies have experimented with some of them. A person may develop habits quite privately but is much more likely to do so in interaction with others. We all incorporate specific values in what we do, and the aggregates of those values are what we recognize as our individual characters. Good character traits are said to be "virtues," and their study has been a facet of ethics since the earliest times. We understand now that well-established habits may actually be reinforced in the brain by the growth of new neurons and that there is a plethora of neurotransmitters that can strengthen the interneuronal synapses. Habits have recently become a subject for investigation in neuroscience and we refer to an article by Graybiel and Smith (2014), which recounts some of the recent findings in this area. They describe experiments with rats that reveal how the brain learns to treat a behavioral sequence as a single unit of behavior. They have been able to trace the paths followed by circuits through the brain during the learning process and their work explains how we are able to act without thinking. A concern has been to find the effects on behavior of rewards, behavioral interventions, and various drugs.

Since the introduction of sociobiology by Wilson and evolutionary psychology by Barkow, Cosmides, and Tooby, the linkage to Darwin has been thoroughly understood. Much of our morality and many of our pragmatic systems are rule based. Sociologists seem to use the word *norm* as an equivalent to *rule*. We learn many of these rules when we are children. They are typically of the "thou shalt" or "thou shalt not" variety. They apply in certain situations whose constancy we recognize. As we reach adulthood, we start making rules and habits for ourselves and begin to generalize the rules we already have into wider ranging categories. We discover that many rules can be subsumed under more general rules and conversely that some rules can be broken down to serve us in different categories. In appendix 1, we list a highly aggregated set of humanist principles, which are intended to contain the main lessons of our intellectual history. Discourse may result in rules that are followed by an entire family. Eventually, as families grow into tribes, we may find that these rules constitute important parts of a culture. The tribal rules and cultures were often shared by religious institutions and eventually by civic authorities, giving rise to the legal systems of the modern state. Kant was much concerned with the similarity between the exercise of rules and the law and the workings of logical rationality. He distinguished between categorical imperatives and hypothetical imperatives. In Habermas's terminology, perhaps these correspond to moral and ethical concepts. Hume recognized the importance of both rationality and emotion in the working of habits and culture. There are important emotions such as the feelings of obligation and loyalty that are generally attached to the operation of moral and rule-based systems. The role of discourse in the establishment of both moral norms and ethical values is an important part of Habermas's philosophy. He stresses, following Kant, that the rules of discourse should apply universally to women as well as men and to all social classes, ethnicities, and races. Following the rules of rational discourse is one of the great benefits of humanism. Belief in the supernatural is not rational, but many religions are burdened in this way. But surely, as it is overcome, the religions might be able to progress.

11.6 Breaking with Religion

Let us now narrow our focus onto the groups in which ethical reformers have had to face their task. There have been some clerics who have dared to break away from their religions. One of the first to do so was Felix Adler who led his Jewish congregation to start the Ethical Culture movement in the USA. This quite wealthy community has several congregations with salaried leaders. In Britain rebellion started with a Baptist Church which became the South Place Ethical Society and dates from 1793. Book publishing in Britain was started by the Rationalist Press Association and the British Humanist Association was begun in 1896. In the USA the American Humanist Association was founded in 1941. Membership in the AHA is increasing rapidly at this time and it has recently (2014) grown to over 24,000. There are over 100 local chapters of the AHA. The Council for Secular Humanism was started by Dr Paul Kurtz in 1980 and has grown to a membership of several thousand. Dr Kurtz founded Prometheus Press in 1969 and this publishing house now supplies much of the freethought literature produced in the USA. The Humanists of Houston is a representative chapter of the AHA which was started in 1978. The North Texas Church of Freethought and the Houston Church of Freethought are independent organizations founded to provide church-like environments for non-believers in Texas. There are several other organizations which serve the atheist and freethought communities in the USA, including American Atheists, the Freedom from Religion Foundation, and Americans United for the Separation of Church and State. The number of people who regard themselves as having no church affiliation in the USA has now grown to 14% of the population, or about 42 million, a number which is still growing, according to Duncan (2004). Both Catholicism and Fundamentalism have lost members to the unaffiliated category. A Gallup Poll published in 2014 found 29% of Americans were nonreligious.

This very rapid growth in disaffection with religion in the U.S. has resulted in the increase of groups of nonbelievers. The atheists have no belief in God and take their ideas from such exemplaries as Voltaire, Frederick Nietzsche, Thomas Hobbes, Ayn Rand, and Richard Dawkins. Freethinkers are not constrained by religious or political dogma and are exemplified by Jeremy Bentham, John Stuart Mill, and Gerald Larue. Agnostics do not think it is possible to know if God(s) exist and include Thomas Henry Huxley, Robert Ingersoll, and Bertrand Russell. Humanists believe that humans created our own beliefs and include philosophers from Confucius and Thales to Socrates, Aristotle, David Hume, and John Dewey. These categories are not mutually exclusive, and many of these icons of nonbelief could be described with several of the labels we have just listed. The same is true for most of the modern nonbelievers. Of course, very few of the millions of modern nonbelievers have the same depth of knowledge or understanding as the great philosophers we have listed above. It is for that very reason that we are producing so many new texts on humanist science and ethics at the present time.

The reasons for the great emigration from religion at this time are quite evident. The Western world is still reverberating from the violent attack of 9/11, which killed three thousand innocent civilians. The continuing horrors inflicted on inhabitants of the Middle East and

African countries in the name of Islam are being recounted daily on
newscasts. In the USA itself, the fundamentalist Christian sects continue
their efforts to impose creationist curricula in schools; and Christians,
in general, support theistic ethics, frequently opposing abortion and
women's rights. They often oppose homosexual freedom and same-
sex marriage as well as organizations for transsexuals. The Amish and
similar groups continue to limit the educational opportunities for their
children and still practice the barbarous act of shunning any of their
numbers who attempt to leave the faith. They are gradually taking over
much of the fertile farmland in the states where they live by their policy
of unlimited childbirth and restricting the education of their children
to an exclusively agricultural life. The Roman Catholics have revealed
that priests have carried out sexual abuse of children for years. As a
result of these and other offenses, it is not surprising that many people
are discovering nonbelieving organizations of atheists, freethinkers, and
humanists. The memberships of these are inclined to spend their time
reciting the latest horror stories and debating the current situations. Of
course, religion is not the only source of unethical news items: there is
always a steady stream of criminal and immoral activity in the business
world, which is generously reported on television and the Internet.
Humanists continue to dwell on greed in the capitalist class. And there
is still a world of immoral, unethical, cruel, and thoughtless behavior
to be contended with in everyday secular life.

Religious organizations do offer some beneficial services including
companionship and social stability, and for these reasons, many of their
adherents are given to apologetic behavior, claiming that they have
spirituality, whatever that might mean. It is possible that eventually
most churches will adopt humanist views and ethics.

11.7 Black Nonbelievers

The black churches served as a home for slaves and then freed men
and women for many years. It should not have been a surprise then
when groups of black citizens began showing up at humanist meetings
after the millennial year. In Houston there was further growth with the
appearance of the journal *Essays in the Philosophy of Humanism* edited by

Dr. Marian Hillar. Black humanists took an interest in this publication by producing an issue devoted entirely to *The Colors of Humanism* (2012) under the editorship of Anthony Pinn. One of the most dramatic pieces in this volume was an essay by Sikivu Hutchinson titled *The Forked Road Ahead: The "Look" of Black Community in Action.* This was our introduction to the Black Lives Matter movement. Sikivu was moved to action after a seven-year-old black girl named Aiyana Jones was murdered on May 16, 2010, in her sleep by the Detroit Police after a military-style raid on her home.

I remember when Donald Wright first came to a meeting of Humanists of Houston to speak on the subject of his book *The Only Prayer I'll Ever Pray: Let My People Go* (2009). Gradually, he was joined by others, and in 2013 the group decided to establish their own organization: Houston Black Nonbelievers. *The Colors of Humanism* is a collection of essays by several contemporary humanists, which we will examine in some depth in the remainder of this and later chapters. One of the most informative descriptions of humanism as it is actually functioning is Dr. Anthony B. Pinn's *What is Humanism and Why Does it Matter?* (2013). This book is also a collection of essays by various authors. We will refer again to several of the essays, but for the moment we focus on the first one in the volume: "Humanism as Experience" by Howard B. Radest. Now Radest served for many years as the founding dean of the Humanist Institute and clearly was a firm believer in the provision of a sound academic education for humanist leaders, modeled after that of religious seminaries. But it was difficult to provide this to part-time candidates for leadership of groups having minimal funding. Consequently, the education given by the institute has tended to be rather metaphysical, concentrating on arguments like the being or nonbeing of the deity. Many members of local humanist groups get minimal education, if any, and the world-shaking ideas that ought to emerge from humanism are little seen.

11.8 Human Rights and Preferences

There has been a women's caucus in the AHA for many years. A group of women in Humanists of Houston decided to organize their own group and have now been meeting for several years. The group of about ten members gets together for coffee and conversation once a month. Although they are happy to be able to talk without having to be told what to think, they are not simply opposed to the male of the species and are interested to discuss the broad scope of human rights and preferences. They are pleased that HOH is a prominent participant in the Houston Gay, Lesbian, Bisexual, and Transgender Parade, which takes place once per year. HOH "Ideas Club" as well as its Sugar Land Forum have discussed sexual preferences and have welcomed gay and lesbian couples to their meetings. Many members of HOH have been distressed with the poverty and homelessness found in the city and have organized and/or participated in donations and events intended to help the less fortunate.

11.9 Secular Alternatives to Religion

A central theme of this book is the assertion that religions evolve. Furthermore, we will argue that the direction of the evolution is toward various forms of humanism. We point out that humanism is itself evolving and that in this case the direction of the evolution can be consciously determined by humanists. This guided evolution may be thought of as a series of experiments whereby humanists adapt their systems to changes in the world in which they function and to improvements in human understanding of the natural world. From this viewpoint, we will argue that religions, and their humanist successors are part of the integrative systems vital to all individuals and societies and as such will continue to have an important role to play in the future.

If there were no benefits to religion, real or perceived, then it might be expected to fade away as indeed was predicted for many years. This viewpoint, however, seems to overlook several facets of religion, which adherents find to be of benefit. Paul Kurtz (2006) points out that "religious creeds have provided important support systems, and they have cultivated charitable efforts and the bonds of moral cohesion . . . Where mainline religious denominations have built what were in fact secular communities of friends, they have satisfied important psychological-sociological needs, often without imposing authoritarian overlays. Secular humanists can learn much from the denominations about the need to build communities." Many observers recognize that religion does not simply provide an explanation for the universe and man's place in it but also provides a social structure for the individual, an idea propounded by Michael Shermer (2005) who states that there is a "twofold purpose that religions serve . . . (1) explanation and (2) social cohesion." He continues on, "Never have so many—professed a belief in a deity. Although explanations for this remarkable trend are as varied as the theorists proffering them, a general causal vector can be found in the second purpose of religion, that is, its social mode."

Similar points can be derived from the philosophy of Jürgen Habermas, which has been summarized by Finlayson (2006). Habermas has advanced the thesis that what makes the coherence of human society possible is our extensive and continuous discourse. He has expounded this viewpoint in his magnum opus *The Theory of Communicative Action* (1984). Habermas sees ethical and moral discourse as a part of the theory of society, i.e., we cannot understand the one without the other.

Kurtz (2006) argued that looking to the future is the equivalent of religious prophecy and is closely related to the building of community. Habermas (1984) sees ethical and moral discourse as the basis of a general theory of society. Our primitive emotions are used to build values and social structures and culture and in Habermas's view discourse is a vital part of that process of building. In other words, through discourse, we should be establishing paradigms of nature, society, arts, and state. We should be looking to the future with Kurtz's Promethean vision. Kurtz (2006) lists the following conditions that need to be satisfied by our alternative to religion:

1. A direct confrontation of the basic existential questions on the meaning of life, from suffering to death
2. Development of ethical values and principles grounded in human experience
3. Appeal to the heart as well as the head
4. Use of the arts to create new narratives and to celebrate life and the march of reason and development of communities of people committed to science and reason

The part of the future over which we have some measure of control is in our own lives and, if we are humanists, in the lives of our humanist institutions. Beyond those areas, there are the wider governmental, commercial, and social worlds where we interact with people of many creeds and religions; and this is part of our focus in subsequent chapters.

11.10 Humanist Social Theory

Humanism and free thought have always been committed to the great progressive values of truth, freedom, and equality. In fact, humanism has always stood in the forefront of the social struggle for democracy, abolition of slavery, women's rights, and international brotherhood. We could attempt to reform religion by getting it to drop its bad features. Another approach was discussed by Paul Kurtz (2006) who proposed that, as humanists, we can create secular and humanist alternatives to religion as mentioned in the previous section. We see philosophy as the repository of all knowledge, so that humanism could be the science informed by all the other disciplines and used as the cognitive basis for our alternative to religion. When we look back over time, we realize that it was our ability to learn and the accumulation of knowledge that have contributed to a major part of our species' advance and that comprise the heritage we humanists wish to pass on. The invention of spoken language was followed by writing and then the development of books and libraries, the tools that made it all possible. There have been many institutional inventions: schools, universities and academic societies, and research laboratories that have enabled succeeding generations to absorb the stories to date and then to permit the growth of knowledge. Today we live longer, healthier, more interesting lives as a consequence of these advances. Education, the foundation of it all, is the process of learning and is not necessarily conducted in the style of the university lecture. We can learn in many different ways: reading books, browsing the Internet, viewing films or television, conducting experiments, visiting museums, and joining discussions or debates or discourses.

11.11 Humanity Today

We have concluded that humanity, meaning the human race, might be poised on the brink of great changes. But there is another sense of the word *humanity*: the quality of being human, as the dictionary states, or human nature, especially our desirable characteristics. So we should be able to answer the question of where we individual humans stand today in the evolutionary quest for desirable character. We would like to think, of course, that the person with such qualities would be exemplified as a quintessential humanist, but we should not be so ungenerous as to claim that only avowed humanists would make that exalted grade.

We discussed how people have attempted to codify the lessons of history into statements of principles. These statements can be regarded as the schema of a system whose expression is the ethical conduct of the person who follows those rules. Let us remark that the sum total of the principles defines our purpose for living. Alternatively, we might say that the direction in which this purpose carries us is our destiny. The single word *humanity* is then a name for our purpose. As humanists, we recognize that the rules as we understand them, and our purposes and destinies as we experience them will change as time goes on.

What, then, distinguishes the individual humanist from other people? In fact, there is no quintessential humanist, although there have been a few exemplary figures at some points in history. There are women and men, gays and lesbians, young and old, black, white, and members of every race. There are humanists with every variety of character and there are humanist converts from every religion and followers of many ideologies. Even if there are only a few humanists who adhere to every one of our principles, there are others who score only on a few or a fraction of the total. These may be "newbies" or people who are slow learners. There are some whose scores are so low that there is a serious question as to whether they are truly humanists. Different professions require different skills or commitments; and thus, we have members who are medical practitioners, lawyers, teachers, civil servants, laborers, farmers, builders, businesspeople, journalists, military personnel, and so forth. Members differ with respect to their moral and ethical understanding, knowledge of history, or financial, managerial, and organizational acumen. There is a growing humanist membership for what is known as the clergy project, consisting of former pastors and priests. These are people joining the ranks of humanist celebrants and chaplains. Unfortunately, some of this group think of themselves as exhibiting spirituality as opposed to humanity. Many humanists oppose the use of the term with its connotation of spirits and souls occupying the human body.

Since the proposal of evolutionary psychology as a working theory, there has been more emphasis on group governance by elected boards both at local and national levels. HOH is pleased to have Vic Wang as its president and his relationship with Roy Speckhardt, the executive director of the AHA, as well as Maggie Ardiente, the organization's development and communications director. HOH has a development fund for long-term investment. It tries to use modern technology for e-mail to its membership using a system known as Meet-Up.

11.12 Humanist Purpose and Meaning

There is no better way to conclude this chapter than to quote Bronowski's (1977) urging a "sense of the future" to set a balanced tone. We must be systematic and define our objectives and purpose: the search for humanity and the mutual education on our humanist principles of our members. We should be able to offer our members the benefits that religions accord to theirs. We need to understand the importance of philosophy in terms of being aware of our own history and heritage in science, literature, and the arts and in free-thought, rationalist, and ethical culture movements. The humanist movement could learn much from secular institutions such as the universities. Humanism has to present the latest paradigms in science, ethics, politics, arts, and practical living. We should learn from the business world the lessons of management, planning, and budgeting. There are both optimistic and pessimistic predictions of the future. But the evolutionary benefits clearly are on the side of an optimistic outlook. We should have faith in humanity as it struggles to find its way forward.

Consider our progress to date. Life for the individual has been steadily improving over the centuries. We live longer with less disease, better nutrition, more pleasant housing. We are continually learning how to alleviate pain and suffering. Psychology shows us how we can experience loving and secure relationships. It is not necessary to force people into drudgery to earn a living or to lead existences governed by fear. Our quest for humanity puts meaning into our lives as individuals and helps other people to improve the world and ourselves. We need to work toward the elimination of such ills as poverty, drug abuse and crime, overpopulation and pollution, to end war and guarantee human rights everywhere. We must reiterate the promise of the enlightenment.

Both Drucker (1973) and Checkland (1981) stress that the defining of purpose as the key to the design of an artificial system: before we attempt to design a future world, we have to ask ourselves what it is that we are trying to accomplish. For example, after the French Revolution, the purpose of the republic became *liberté, egalité, fraternité*. The French attempted to overturn everything in pursuit of these ideals but actually instituted a reign of terror. Karl Popper said that they would have been better off if they had pursued their goals by evolution rather than revolution. Nevertheless, they did succeed in bringing about change. The special point to emphasize is that change can be brought about with management techniques. Management science and planning are the most vital parts of the ethics of adaptive systems. We also need to relate our individual purposes and those of our personal relationships to the purposes that have been established for the social world. We can achieve happiness and, by accepting it as our duty, achieve a consonance of purpose between ourselves as individuals and of society as a whole. We can refine the analysis by asking the purpose of each one of the divisions of the social world, and if as individuals we each try to help in accomplishing those purposes, then we may venture to predict that that is the way the world will actually evolve. In other words we may predict that it is our best prophecies that will come to pass.

12 Sex, Selection, Culture, and the Family

12. Sex, Selection, Culture, and the Family

12.1 Sex and Human Nature

There was a period, about two to three million years ago, when the size of the hominid brain grew by a factor of nearly three times in volume. During this interval, there is evidence that the mental abilities characteristic of humans such as tool and weapon making, hunting, use of fire, cooking, artwork, and the use of musical instruments all grew rapidly. This we know from the fossil record, and we may surmise that speech and thought grew alongside the tangible evidence. There was likely a revolutionary change in the whole of human nature, which we discuss as the chapter progresses. The biology of modern *Homo sapiens* emerged during this period. Compelling theories argue that these revolutionary changes were based on the sex lives and sexual selection practices of our ancestors at this time. They are, in fact, nothing less than an explanation for what makes us human.

We have not said much about sex, reproduction, or the family in the treatment so far. But these systems have a huge influence on our behavior, and we must tackle them now. Our knowledge of human sexual behaviors has advanced immensely in the past few decades, as summarized by E. O. Wilson (1975, 1978, 2014) and Campbell (2005) in biology, Michael S. Gazzaniga (2008) in neuroscience, and Donald C. Johanson (2009) in paleoanthropology among others. These discoveries have given us a much better picture of the evolution of human behavior than we had erstwhile. The narrative can begin with the realization that there was a time before sex played a major role. Textbooks, such as *Zoology* by Miller and Harley (1999), describe how evolution in plants and animals became more efficient once the sexual method was initiated. This was because genes from two parents were mixed, thus allowing adaptive change in the offspring and descendants to take place much faster than in asexual reproduction. Ever since the start of sexual reproduction, there has existed the need to bring members of the opposite sex together and then to keep them together for as long as it might take to inseminate an egg, give birth, and start the process of child rearing (see again Miller and Harley [1999] and Campbell [2005], who give detailed descriptions of the great variety of means that nature has evolved to secure sexual attraction between mates of animal species). There are many and often exotic types of body shapes, plumages, and behaviors that have been evolved for this purpose. In fish and amphibians, the process of fertilization took place external to the parents' bodies in surrounding water. But with land-dwelling reptiles, fertilization took place internally. In oviparous reptiles, the fertilized eggs then are deposited outside the body. In ovoviviparous reptiles, the eggs hatch inside the female before the young are born outside. In mammals, the length of the gestation period was increased: the young were nurtured for some length of time internally before birth and then fed externally by lactation for a period after birth. As biological evolution in mammals progressed, the young started life in an immature state, requiring increasing periods of care from the mother. As time went on, the father was also involved in the process of rearing the young. This then was the start of family life. The Australopithecines, the apes immediately preceding the human line, were drawn into this process increasingly as the brain size increased, requiring longer and longer time for infants to mature.

12.2 Marriage and the Male-Female Bond

We come now to one of the most interesting topics of the family system, namely, the male-female bond, which in popular speech is known as love. The great ape species were, of course, among the lineages involved. It is interesting that there are differences as well as similarities among them. The gorillas and orangs sport considerable dimorphism between the sexes as do the chimpanzees, although to a lesser extent. The male and female bonobos, on the other hand, show much less size differentiation and have evolved life styles in which sex is used as an attractor for friendship without reproductive purposes (see Frans de Waal and Frans Lanting, 1997). Homosexual activity occurs among all the ape species. Thus, although we do not know for sure the evolutionary advantages of homosexual relationships in humans, it seems clear that they are naturally occurring and that there are no adverse effects of their existence except for social pressures. The differences between bodily and pair-bonding arrangements in the various species may be related to food supplies in the indigenous areas. Thus, the gorillas and chimpanzees that inhabit the same jungle terrain probably had to compete for resources while the bonobos were free of competition in their own area south of the Zaire River. On the other hand, the hominins were out on the open savanah and needed to be alert to predators.

Wilson (1978) argues that the male and female attitudes to mating must have been influenced by the difference in the "investment" of the two sexes in the reproduction process. "This difference in investment begins with the anatomical difference between the two kinds of sex cell. The human egg is 85,000 times larger than the human sperm. The consequences of this gametic dimorphism ramify throughout the biology and psychology of human sex. The most important immediate result is that the female places a greater investment in each of her sex cells. A woman can expect to produce only about 400 eggs in her lifetime. Of these a maximum of about twenty can be converted into healthy infants. The costs of bringing an infant to term and caring for it afterward are relatively enormous. In contrast, a man releases 100 million sperm with each ejaculation. Once he has achieved fertilization his purely physical commitment has ended." Raising a family was, and still is, a greater commitment of time and bodily discomfort for the female than for the male. These measures are probably what were reflected in the constitution of the bonding process and its later extension into the legal concepts of marriage.

"Males are characteristically aggressive, especially toward one another and most intensely during the breeding season. In most species, assertiveness is the most profitable male strategy. During the full period of time it takes to bring a fetus to term, from the fertilization of the egg to the birth of the infant, one male can fertilize many females but a female can be fertilized by only one male. Thus if males are able to court one female after another, some will be big winners and others will be absolute losers, while all healthy females will succeed in being fertilized. It pays males to be aggressive, hasty, fickle, and undiscriminating. In theory it is more profitable for females to be coy, to hold back until they can identify males with the best genes. In species that rear young, it is also important for the females to select males who are more likely to stay with them after insemination." Our societies vary in terms of culture (behavior, fashion, etc). We are moderately polygynous, with males initiating most changes in sexual partnerships.

"The evidence for genetic difference in behavior is varied and substantial. In general, girls are predisposed to be more intimately sociable and less physically venturesome. From the time of birth, for example, they smile more than boys." Boys are more physically venturesome in all cultures from the!Kung San to New York. Wilson argues that there is a universal sexual division of labor from birth, which is not entirely an accident of cultural evolution. In view of the struggle for women's rights spreading throughout the world, each society must now make one or the other of three choices:

1) Condition its members to exaggerate sexual differences in behavior, this being the existing pattern in most cultures.
2) Train its members so as to eliminate all sexual differences in behavior. Wilson states that this might be possible, using quotas and sex-biased education.
3) Provide equal opportunities and access but take no further action.

12.3 Structure of the Brain

When the hominins split away from the chimps and the bonobos, all three were quite similar in size with brains in proportion. But the hominin brain then began to grow, and this focuses our attention on what the differences between the brains of the different species might be. Gazzaniga (2008) begins his book on neuroscience by discussing brain regions, with particular attention to the cerebral cortex, which is about the size of a large dish towel pleated and laid over the rest of the brain. The cerebral cortex is perhaps the most complex entity known to science. It has six layers of nerve cells and connections. The neocortex is where sensory perception, generation of motor commands, spatial reasoning, conscious thought, and language take place. The neocortex in humans is more than 76 percent of the brain by weight. We have learned that there are many regions of the brain that are the locales for specific types of information and the human brain has been likened to a swiss army knife. Usually, when brain regions change shape, their internal structure also changes, just as a business organization adds specialists. There are billions of neurons—if stacked like a cake, they make up cortical regions; if bunched, they are called nuclei. It has been determined that the frontal lobe in humans is no larger than expected in a primate with our brain size. How then to explain the increased functioning, such as language? It seems we have greater interconnectivity within the brain than is the case with the apes. There is an evolutionarily new region attached to the prefrontal cortex, which is called the lateral prefrontal cortex and which handles the rational aspects of decision making. It is densely interconnected with other regions that are larger in human brains. It also includes the ability to inhibit automatic responses. Cortical areas in the frontal lobe are involved with impulse control, decision making and judgment, language, memory, problem solving, sexual behavior, socialization, and spontaneity. The frontal lobe is the location of the brain's executive that plans, controls, and coordinates behavior. Areas in the left temporal lobe are specialized for speech, language comprehension, naming things, and verbal memory. Prosody, the rhythm of speech, is processed in the right temporal lobe. The ventral part of the temporal lobes does processing for faces, scenes, and object recognition. The hippocampus is involved in the transfer of short-term memory to long-term and spatial memory.

We do not seem to have many more cortical areas than other primates, however. But our cortical areas may be wired differently. What has been found to be unique in humans is in the area called the planum temporale (a part of Wernicke's area).

Each of the six layers of the cerebral cortex can be thought of as a sheet of neurons stacked on top of one another. Each neuron within a sheet lines up with neighbors in the sheets above and below to form columns. Columnar cell numbers vary across mammalian species. The neurochemicals vary within columns. Gazzaniga tells us that the various layers connect to specific destinations, e.g., the most superficial layers, the so-called infragranular layers, project primarily to other layers within the cortex. Several scientists believe these participate heavily in higher cognitive functions. They receive sensory inputs from high-order sensory systems and interpret them in the light of similar past experiences. They function in reasoning, judgment, emotions, as well as verbalizing and storing ideas. Many of the uniquely human brain functions are processed in distinct modules, which appear to play the role of independent "computers," which have been added to the brain by evolution.

12.4 The Split Brain

The corpus callosum is a fiber tract that connects the two hemispheres of the split brain. It appears that the only cure for extreme forms of epilepsy which affect both hemispheres is to cut the corpus callosum right through. This operation was first performed in 1940 and was found to be successful in minimizing the epilepsy without producing side effects. Gazzaniga, whose original research specialized on split-brain patients, states: "It may turn out that the corpus callosum was the great enabler for establishing the human condition." Maybe natural selection began to modify one hemisphere but not the other because of shortage of space. One of the major findings of split-brain research is that the left hemisphere has marked limitations in perceptual functions and the right hemisphere has even more prominent limitations in its cognitive functions. The callosum integrates these developments.

But what are the costs of this to the right hemisphere? The two hemispheres are not identical. Many of the new capacities are not present in the right hemisphere of a split-brain subject. Such new capabilities as mirror neurons, in monkeys and in their much more advanced forms in humans, are examples of how the human mind became unique. The FOXP2 gene discovered in the mid-1990s is associated with language ability. FOXP2 is present in many other animals including the mouse. Some differences occurred after the human-chimp divergence. There are increased levels of expression in humans. The conclusion is that the difference between human and chimp is not purely due to size: there are many unique features in the human brain.

Human brains rocketed in size after the divergence from the ancestral line. A chimp's brain weighs about 400 grams whereas the human's is about 1300 grams. There is a theory that this is correlated with the decreased size of the human jaw muscles, which thus do not require the massive skull of the gorillas or chimpanzees as an anchor. Thus, the brain continued to expand. This may have coincided with the invention of cooking, in effect, a way of predigesting food. But Gazzaniga is not too convinced that brain size per se is the explanation for superior mental ability. There are many genes active in humans that do not function in other primates. There appear to have been periods of accelerated evolution in humans: one such occurring about thirty-seven thousand years ago coinciding with the emergence of culturally modern humans.

There are some similar speculations that can be advanced about the parent-child bond that we sometimes call mother love. There are some typical characteristics of very young children that make them attractive to parents and older people: wide eyes, round faces, and ready smiles guarantee that babies will not be neglected. The human child is probably one of the most helpless young animals and requires years of care and protection while acquiring the basic skills of living. Thus, learning to walk, language, and moral instruction are all part of the behavioral suite in which the human youngster has to receive instruction, largely from the parents, and over a matter of years before reaching adolescence. Rachel Caspari (2011) has presented evidence that there was a steady increase in the proportion of older people in the human population and that this ratio increased rapidly around thirty thousand years ago. In other words, grandparents became common in human societies at about that time. According to Caspari, the results of this increase in longevity were that the grandparents were able to contribute economic and social resources to their descendants. In addition, the grandparents also reinforced complex social connections by telling stories of ancestors that link them to relatives in other generations. Caspari states that this information is the foundation on which human social organization is built.

It is obvious that men and women think differently, and it seems that this must be a result of differences in their brains. But the neurological differences are not readily apparent which makes them hard to study. It was not until fMRI and PET scan techniques were introduced that differences in both structure and function were uncovered. There is an account of these results in an article on "Neuroscience of sex differences" in *Wikipedia*. Brain structures associated with learning ability, such as the hippocampus, are consequently prone to sexual selection over time. Females show enhanced information recall compared to men. The amygdala plays a large role in emotional memory formation and storage. Men have a larger amygdala than women. Estrogen can exhibit both feminizing and defeminizing effects on the human brain.

12.5 Sexual Selection

It was Charles Darwin who first drew the world's attention to the importance of this subject when he proposed two important evolutionary selection methods. The first was what he termed *natural selection* in which he proposed that the driver behind the appearance of new species of plants and animals was the action of natural events and circumstances favoring the survival of some organisms rather than others. This he described in the book *On the Origin of Species*, which appeared in 1859. Now although the implication was present, Darwin did not explicitly state that this was the way in which human beings had arisen. This conclusion was so revolutionary that he hesitated as long as possible before making the claim. He realized for example that it would greatly disturb his wife, Emma, who was deeply religious. He finally took that logical next step in 1871 with the publication of *The Descent of Man* and *Selection in Relation to Sex*. Darwin also realized that the book contained a second shocker with its references to sex. Sexual intercourse is a natural event, but it is not random. It is the result of choices by two partners. Darwin realized that sexual choice is a major determinant of the direction in which bodily structures and certain mental qualities will develop through the generations. In other words, Darwin also claimed that we humans are ourselves important guides to the direction of our own evolution. It might be helpful to recollect Darwin's background to see how he would have realized the importance of this mechanism.

Darwin had grown up in a house in Shrewsbury near the Welsh border with an extensive library of his father's natural history books, a greenhouse with many exotic plants, and an aviary where his mother kept fancy pigeons. He also had access to a bank of the River Severn. He was very well aware of the way in which pigeon fanciers were able to breed birds of many varieties. He was fascinated by the colorful plumage and melodies of birdsong, especially from the males. But all these experiences seemed tame compared to the astounding volume and diversity of nature's ornaments he encountered on his voyage with the *Beagle*. One particular example he found amazing was a species of golden bugs he found in the Brazilian forests a thousand miles from civilization and churches. Up until his time, theologians had claimed that God had created the great diversity of life and then ornamented it for the delight of humans. The thought occurred to Darwin that such ornaments might instead be for the benefit of the beetles themselves. In all the species he observed, the males did most of the displaying for the benefit of females. The peacock's tail became an icon for male display. He was greatly puzzled by this behavior, which seemed so pointless because natural selection should shape every trait to some purpose. But eventually, he began to understand sexual selection well enough to devote a few pages to it in *On the Origin of Species*. By the time of publication of *The Descent*, he was ready to devote five hundred pages to sexual selection in other animals and seventy pages to sexual selection in human evolution.

The study of sexual selection faded away after its initial publication, and there was a one-hundred-year hiatus before the idea came back into the mainstream of biological and philosophical attention, as recounted in *The Mating Mind* (2000) by Geoffrey Miller. Miller maintains that Darwin "intended to smuggle into popular consciousness his outrageous claim that mate choice guides evolution." The key idea here is that if animals of a given species came to prefer a certain trait when choosing sexual partners, that trait would tend to grow in size, complexity, and quality over evolutionary time. The more complex the animal's brain, the more intelligent its choice of mate could be.

Darwin started the second part of the *Descent* with a chapter on the principles of sexual selection in general terms but then proceeded with details of over one hundred instances in which it is overwhelmingly the male of a species who shows some unusual feature or ornament that does not have an obvious explanation in terms of natural selection. The best-known instance is the case of the peacock's tail. Another well-known example is the growth of antlers on deer. Darwin gave an extensive systematic cataloging of species throughout the animal kingdom from lower animals such as mollusks, through insects, including butterflies, beetles, ants and wasps, fishes, amphibians, and reptiles. Birds received an extensive treatment including bower birds, the birds of paradise, and the argus pheasant in addition to the peacocks already mentioned. Darwin dwells on the choice exerted by female birds and their taste for the beautiful both in the visual setting and in listening to the vocalizations of male songsters. We are then led through a review of sexual behavior in mammals, including seals, whales, and the great apes, finally getting to humans.

12.6 The Century of Hiatus

Miller tells the story of how sexual selection theory developed after 1871. The natural selection theory was widely accepted, but sexual selection was almost universally rejected by Victorian biologists. For instance, Alfred Russel Wallace, who independently discovered natural selection, was a leading critic of sexual selection and suggested that male ornamentation was a side effect of greater male energy. Wallace's objections led mate theory to be viewed for the next hundred years as Darwin's most embarrassing blunder. This viewpoint was adopted by many other leading biologists including Julian Huxley, J. B. S. Haldane, and Ernst Mayr. The modern machine aesthetic, which abhorred ornamentation as morally decadent, also contributed to the eclipse of the idea. Instead, Freud's Paleolithic fantasies dominated the view of prehistoric sexuality. But during the hiatus, paleontology advanced with the finding of fossils including many "missing links." The synthesis of genetics and evolutionary biology occurred around 1900, thus providing a mechanistic foundation for evolutionary theories culminating in the elucidation of the working of DNA by Watson and Crick in 1953 (see Watson, 1968). A serious problem, dubbed the runaway brain, was the estimation that, unchecked, sexual selection should have led to even faster evolution than was actually found. It was also unclear why there should not have been much greater sex differences in brain size and creative intelligence than is in fact the case. A crude form of the runaway-brain theory would suggest that the male brain grew into the human form while the female retained her ape brain. But in fact, male brains are only slightly larger than those of the female, and there is no apparent sex difference in IQ.

Another issue was that many of the unusual features or ornaments were actually impediments to survival and most of the rest did not appear to have any direct physical survival value. The peacock's tail is heavy and a drag to carry around. Why then should these traits be selected by females? The answer to this problem came with a 1915 paper by R. A. Fisher, who suggested that the problem traits all were indicators of fitness in the male. The brain itself is a particularly good fitness indicator because its growth depends on half the genes in the genome. The brain also consumes over 25 percent of the body's metabolic energy. Male gorillas and orangutans are considerably bigger than their females while chimpanzees and bonobos also show sexual size differentiation. The human species also shows a sexual size difference, but there are more important differences than just ornamentation between us and the other apes. Most outstanding is the growth of the brain, which occurred after the separation from the common ancestor. Eventually, we learned from the fossil record that the brain of the hominins grew from about 600 cc to 1400 cc in a comparatively short interval of about two million years. Darwin did not know about this because it was not discovered until after his death when, in fact, he was concerned with finding any traces of a missing link between us and our ancestors. However, he did comment in the *Descent of Man*, "No one, I presume, doubts that the large size of the brain in man, in comparison with that of the gorilla or orang, is closely connected with his higher mental powers." Archeological evidence from campsites indicates that our species began to make stone tools, became far more proficient at hunting, learned about cooking, and, it is deduced, acquired language all in the same time period. These skills are mental capabilities, and it is reasonable to presume that they are associated with the growth of the brain. But what drove the growth in brain power and its improved abilities? Again the suggestion arises that the two developments were both the result of sexual selection. The idea seems to have first occurred to Darwin whose final passage on sexual selection in the *Descent* reads: "He who admits the principle of sexual selection will be led to the remarkable conclusion that the cerebral system not only regulates most of the existing functions of the body, but has indirectly influenced the progressive development of various bodily structures and of certain mental qualities." In other words, Darwin saw psychology as a driving force in biological evolution.

The most convincing theory is that advanced by Geoffrey Miller (2000). He proposes that both male and female favor idealized prototypes for sexual selection and that it these complex models he calls the mating minds. Although they are by no means identical, they have both evolved to serve biological functions. We might call them a matching set. The implication is that the time for development of this complex system was somewhat slower than the estimate for the simple runaway brain theory.

12.7 The Red Queen:
Sex and the Evolution of Human Nature

The Red Queen is a book by Matt Ridley that gives an account of some of the remarkable discoveries about sex during the century after Darwin. Matt Ridley is a member of a titled British family. He is also known as the Fifth Viscount Ridley and has served in some prominent political roles. But it is interesting to note that he trained as a zoologist and has written a number of books to explain complex scientific issues to the layman including *Nature via Nurture, Genome, The Origins of Virtue,* and *The Rational Optimist.* In 1993 he turned his hand to educating us on an intimate subject in *The Red Queen: Sex and the Evolution of Nature.*

The book begins with an exposition on how remarkable it is that the preeminent feature of human nature, namely, our intelligence, has been considered without mention of sexual selection. He argues that sex is a central feature of human nature. Culture is a product of human nature as well as of our individual volitions and histories. Our sexual choices are an important factor in our development. The title comes from Lewis Carroll's *Through the Looking Glass* in which *The Red Queen* was supposed to keep running hard just to stay in the same place. The term was introduced into biology by Van Valen who realized that the human environment (or that of any large creature) is driven by rapid changes in the genetics of successive generations of small creatures such as bacteria or parasites.

Sex has a number of important but enigmatic aspects. Its primary function is the mixing of genes in meiosis. This is what permits the rapid operation of natural selection. The Vicar of Bray hypothesis explains how sex allows breeding to respond rapidly to environmental changes. (The Vicar of Bray was an English parson who was famous for his rapid compliance with changes in the religion of the king from Catholic to Protestant etc). Ridley recalls some other developments in evolutionary theory. For example, George Williams showed how collective effects could flow from the actions of self-interested individuals. He discussed the "cost of sex" and how some animals adopt different strategies varying from asexual to sexual and indeed the use of both with various periods in between.

Parasites became one of the main themes in evolutionary theory after Van Valen's discovery. Ridley starts his third chapter with a description of Bdelloid rotifers, which are asexual and can dry out completely and blow about as "tuns." Williams offered the "tangled bank" hypothesis, according to which, in a saturated economy, it pays to diversify. Longer-lived mammals exhibit chromosomal crossovers. Ridley champions the Red Queen hypothesis, according to which sex is all about combating an "enemy," which in turn fights back. Parasites are especially deadly. The immune system would not work without sex. William Hamilton produced a computer model of sex and disease. The parasites themselves employ sex.

There is a viewpoint that genes resemble cunning individual personalities. The gene has to find a balance between cooperation and competition and genes are posited to have evolved many tricks to achieve their aims. Ridley describes conjugation by which genes can be transferred between bacteria. Jumping genes can cut themselves out of one chromosome to join another. He writes of mutinies (half suppressed) and selfish chromosomes. There are "segregation distortion" genes in fruit flies that can kill all sperm containing a second copy of a chromosome. Ridley defines males as small, mobile gametes versus females which are larger, immobile gametes. Such variations may explain how certain human families have daughters only. He discusses how human gender can be preselected. This can arise from cultural preference for boys. Daughters are preferred in poor cultures because they are more likely to lead to grandchildren and can marry up.

Polygamy is favored among men, but women are against it. Many men practice polygamy when they can get away with it, for example, in harems and in homosexual relationships. Polygamy is infrequent among chimps and human hunter-gatherers. But women seek monogamy, and even lesbians are not promiscuous. Attractive males make inattentive fathers. Human females have concealed ovulation. Jealousy is deep seated in men. A women wants a husband who will provide care and food for her children and a lover who will give them first-class genes.

There is evidence of gender differences in the brain. Men evolved to fight. Girls are better at verbal tasks. Boys are better at math. Female phalatropes and jacanas (birds) play a dominant role over males in their species and have higher testosterone. Baby girls do more smiling. Boys play more with things. Feminism is not egalitarian. Homosexuality is more common in left-handed men. Sexual fantasies are more visual and active in men but more emotive in women.

There is a chapter on various observations about beauty such as hourglass figures in women and height in men. But it seems to miss the truly crucial understanding which came with Geoffrey Miller, who was interviewed by Ridley. Brain size reached 1400 cc in humans, according to Ridley because of Red Queen selection. Chomsky's theory of language claims that there are modules in the human brain designed by evolution. Man is not the only tool user or hunter. There is value in gossip. The primary uses of intelligence are for deceiving and detecting deception. Hominid males and females became satisfied with nothing less than psychologically brilliant, fascinating, articulate, entertaining companions. Women had to show the Scheherazade effect, and men, the Dionysius effect. Scheherazade had to tell a different story every night to amuse the sultan and thus save her own life. Dionysius was the Greek god of fertility and patron of the arts. Dance, music, humor, and sexual foreplay are unique to humans. There is a sexual fascination with music. The head (brain) is the human equivalent of the peacock's tail.

12.8 Evolutionary Psychology

It has taken a great deal of time and effort to fully appreciate the importance of natural and sexual selection in human evolution. Part of the reason for this was rampant speculation about the significance of the phenomena. This time, during the latter half of the nineteenth century, was described by Barry Werth in *Banquet at Delmonico's* (2009). One of the first attempts to elaborate the story of human evolution was Wilson's *Sociobiology* (1975). Sociologists and philosophers reacted sharply to this work because it was looked upon as a takeover bid for the stewardship of ethics. This viewpoint was expressed by Peter Singer in his book *The Expanding Circle* (1981). Eventually, however, it was realized that the linkage of human development to evolution was a legitimate undertaking and psychologists in particular began to explore the opportunity. But Singer's analysis is thorough in showing us that philosophy and its ethical subdivision contain assumptions that go beyond the facts of biology. The work that best expounds the new viewpoint is the encyclopedic volume edited by Jerome H. Barkow, Leda Cosmides, and John Tooby, which is titled *The Adapted Mind: Evolutionary Psychology and the Generation of Culture* (1992). Cosmides and Tooby have also prepared a helpful Primer on the subject. They begin by asserting that the brain is a physical system that functions as a computer whose circuits are designed to generate behavior. These circuits were designed to solve problems that our ancestors faced during evolutionary history. These were not just any kind of problem: they were adaptive problems.

Adaptive problems have two defining characteristics: firstly, they were ones that cropped up again and again during our evolutionary history; and secondly, they were ones whose solution improved the reproductive rate of those ancestors. The adaptations arising from the solutions to problems thus correspond to our definition of a system, or a situational constant, as in section 4.15. William James was one of the first to write about such a concept of the mind in his book *Principles of Psychology* (1890). James referred to these modules as instincts thus echoing Hume. The adaptations resulted in the formation of specialized functional modules in the brain, similar to the bodily organs such as heart, liver, lungs, etc. Similarly specialized modules have been found by neuroscientists as reported by Michael Gazzaniga (2008). Many specialized circuits in the brain have been located by neuroscientists in recent decades, which goes to show that the brain is not constructed as a general purpose computer, as many workers in the field had initially expected. The different neural circuits are specialized for solving different adaptive problems. Consciousness is just the tip of the iceberg of mental activity, most of which is hidden from us. It takes a long time to design or evolve a complex circuit to function as a module in the brain, which explains why our modern skulls house stone age minds. There is now evidence for the existence of circuits that are specialized for reasoning about objects, physical causality, number, biological world, beliefs and motivations of other individuals, and social interactions. It is now known that the learning mechanisms that govern the acquisition of language are different from those that govern the acquisition of food aversions, and both of these are different from the learning mechanisms that govern the acquisition of snake phobias.

12.9 The Mating Mind

Miller's book *The Mating Mind* (2000) overlaps Ridley's work to some extent, but Miller has delved into the question of sexual selection in the most penetrating way. Miller states that Irwin Tessman was the first to argue that sexual selection can explain morality. But this cannot be true because, as pointed out by Pennock (1995), Darwin himself in the *Descent of Man* argues that an incipient form of morality could be found in in lower animals. Nevertheless, Miller's thesis is of enormous scope. He is proposing that most of our culture can be explained by sexual selection, the central idea being that its various aspects (language, morality, music, art and literature) were fostered by our own delighted emotional responses and our choice of mates who personified those accomplishments. We now draw attention to one of these fields in particular: morality. Miller's book has an extensive chapter on this which he refers to as virtues of good breeding. The chapter contains a number of moral instances that cannot be explained without the circumstances of sexual selection or sexual choice. He opens the chapter with a list that includes murder, unkindness, rape, rudeness, failure to help the injured, fraud, racism, war crimes, driving on the wrong side of the road, failure to leave a tip in a restaurant, and cheating at sports. He asks what they have in common and cites the answer we might get from a moral philosopher, namely, that they are all examples of immoral behavior. But then he adds that they are also things we would not normally brag about on a first date and would not wish an established sexual partner to find out that we had done. Miller argues that the second assertion contains a clarification of the evolution of immoral behavior through sexual choice. On the other hand, sympathy, kindness, sexual fidelity, moral leadership, magnanimity, romantic gift giving, and sportsmanship are all highly moral and things that would flourish in courtship. He quotes David Buss's (1989) finding that kindness was the most desired trait across all thirty-seven cultures he studied.

Another important instance is moral leadership. De Waal reported on a chimpanzee named Yeroen who showed moral leadership that earned him respect from the rest of his group. There are humans who exhibit the same traits and a few who show moral vision. How could these characteristics be explained on the basis of natural selection? The chapter explains how innate depravity cannot be a viable moral objective on the obvious basis of its threat to survival. Many of our attitudes to charity, male generosity in general, and especially in courtship are hard to explain without sexual selection. Evolutionary theories of morality all show genetic benefits of altruistic acts. The theory of kin selection says we benefit relatives by helping them. Reciprocal altruism can show benefit to oneself across time through repeated interactions with trusted trading partners. The hidden benefits of altruism could have had reproduction advantages since moral behaviors were sexually attractive because they were good fitness indicators (like the peacock's tail). There is also a discussion of skill, leadership, stoicism, sacrifice, and good manners. Male hunting of big animals could have evolved to attract multiple female partners who appreciated hunting ability as a fitness indicator. The chapter also includes a discussion of game theory and of Nash equilibria as well as a broadening of the concept of morality to include what Nietzsche called the pagan virtues (bravery, beauty, skill, leadership, stoicism, sacrifice, and good manners).

12.10 Mutual Selection and Art

The key idea behind Geoffrey Miller's book is an extension of Darwin's thinking that the selection underlying the choice of a sexual partner by the female animal reflects on the mental abilities of her chosen mate. The bond was one of mutual adaptation. This then is what drove the growth of the human brain during its evolution in the Pleistocene period. Rather than the club-wielding thugs earlier surmised to be her beaus, the woman preferred creativity manifested in talking, thinking, and singing by musicians, artists, and poets. Together, sexual partners passed on their preferences through their genes to succeeding generations, and both men and women finally concurred on views of a desirable human nature. The female, already committed to nine months of pregnancy followed by years of child rearing, was the one who most wanted a stable partnership with a mate who could defend the home and provide for their offspring, and this was the basis for family life. Miller argues that morality was a manifestation of the mind-set desired by both sexes, and so family life would have been the cradle for continued ethical evolution. The narratives, artworks, recitals, and protocols used to pass their creations on to others became the culture of their families and societies. Now many of these creative activities became specialized careers and professions, each with vast libraries of books and artifacts. All these men and women—hunters, gatherers, artisans, farmers, technicians, soldiers, shopkeepers, lawyers, doctors and nurses, tinkers, tailors, teachers, preachers, philosophers, artists and scientists, to name just a few—became members of human society. And they all set themselves great objectives, often in several areas at the same time.

It is interesting that E. O. Wilson (2014), in a recently published work *The Meaning of Human Existence*, seems to have arrived at a similar conclusion to Miller. He opens this work by suggesting that it is time to unify science and the humanities as was the objective of the Enlightenment of the eighteenth century. He maintains that effort fell short when the humanities lost patience with the endeavor. But there has been much progress made since that time especially with the theory of evolution and in explaining its driving mechanism. He also rejects the kin selection theory and now favors what he terms *multilevel selection*. This seems to be similar to Miller's mutual selection with an emphasis on group selection. Wilson puts great credence on "eusociality" among humans. This is a sort of supersociality, which is much stronger than in most animal species. Our cultural accomplishments are a direct consequence of the multilevel selection and eusociality. This echoes Miller's thesis and that of the proponents of evolutionary psychology.

It is ironic that Wilson seems to have abandoned his earlier disdain for philosophical ethics, which, in *Sociobiology* (1981), he recommended should be removed temporarily from the hands of philosophers and biologicized. This was the threat of a takeover attempt that prompted Peter Singer in 2011 to issue a new edition of his wonderful work *The Expanding Circle*. Singer's rigorously argued case for philosophy leaves us in little doubt that although biology has much to contribute to our understanding of ethics, there have to be other inputs to the discussion of ethics coming from our human value systems. On the other hand, Wilson's defense of the humanities in *The Meaning of Human Existence* (2014) has become positively ecstatic, where he writes of *The All-Importance of the Humanities*. And lest we have any remaining doubts, he defines the humanities as having many branches, from philosophy to law to history and the creative arts. For his part, Singer finally concedes that evolutionary psychology, although it may not be capable of taking over ethics, can certainly contribute understanding of how the subject might have started in the Pleistocene period.

The brain is a particularly good fitness indicator because its growth depends on half the genes in the genome. The brain also consumes over 25 percent of the body's metabolic energy. The production of art and the emergence of the aesthetic sense are linked to sexual selection, initially as forms of attraction. Evolutionary psychology has led to extensive theories of art by Ellen Dissanayake (1988), John Tooby and Leda Cosmides (2001), and Denis Dutton (2000). Gazzaniga (2008) has emphasized that these theories also feature prominently in the development of neuroscience and its explanations of the human brain. Males account for a large proportion of public cultural displays such as the invention and dissemination of art, music, ideologies, religions, philosophies, and science. It is these systems that exhibit the most profound aspects of humanity and which are our most meaningful contributions. The various unusual male features and ornaments, both the bodily and the mental, are what females recognize as fitness indicators. But it was realized that many of the indicators would be passed on to both male and female offspring and could then become preferences for both sexes, or desirable for *mutual* mate choice. Many of these desirable traits will be displayed in courtship behavior. By a similar logic, we may argue that there will be undesirable traits due to copying errors or mutations but that these will then be eliminated from the lineage as a result of sexual rejection. An interesting qualification was added in a paper by Amotz Zahavi (1975) who asked, what keeps low-fitness individuals from cheating by displaying high quality ornamentation? Zahavi answered that the signal sent should be of such high cost that no low-fitness pretender could afford to send it. This has become known as the handicap principle. And it is with these refinements that we have a mind fit for mating. Miller explains that there are analogies between courtship and marketing.

Based on modern studies of primates and hunter-gatherers, Miller asserts that courtship among hominins in the Pleistocene was not like the interactions between club-wielding cavemen and helpless cave women depicted in popular presentations. *Australopithecus* was probably monogamous or serially monogamous with a few polygynists. Rapists would have been ostracized or killed. The women would have favored self-confident, high-status men rather than those seeking long-term paternal involvement. In searching for replacement mates, even the children might be involved in the selection process. The beards, penises, and upper body muscles of the men and the female breasts and buttocks all show evidence of sexual selection. Art, morality, language, and creativity flourished under mate choice. The use of ochre pigments, cave paintings, and Venus figurines came about at this time as well as flint hand axes. Miller seems to side with Veblen who insisted that virtuosity in manufacture was the major criterion of beauty. He argues that language and the arts of seduction would have been the starting point for aesthetics but that there would have been a premium on protean behavior and neophilia.

From the point of view of the present book, Miller's section on the virtues of good breeding is particularly important. He stresses the sexual abhorrence of selfishness, lying, and cheating. Mate choices are made for sympathy, kindness, sexual fidelity, moral leadership, magnanimity, romantic gift giving, and sportsmanship. All evolutionary moral theories have to explain altruism. Kin selection does it by pointing out that genetic benefits can be spread across relatives by helping them, and reciprocal altruism theory points out that benefits to oneself can be spread across time through repeated interactions with trusted trading partners. But these theories leave most of human morality unexplained. Sexual selection provides an explanation of how selfish genes can give rise to altruistic individuals at all times and places because only the fit can be generous under the handicap principle.

12.11 Becoming Human

We share 98.6 percent of our genes with the chimp, but that figure is misleading. Humans have thirty thousand to thirty-one thousand genes; but only 1.5 percent of the DNA codes for crucial human genes, such as highly developed cognitive functions, bipedalism, or use of complex language. Five to seven million years ago, we shared a common ancestor with chimps. Then the line split between those who stayed in the forest and those who stepped out onto the open woodland. Among these were the *Australopithecus afarensis* including Lucy, the fossil found by Donald Johansen in 1974. We are the only survivors of the open woodland line, although there were several other hominid species along the way. The oldest hominid fossils found were *Ardipithecus ramidus*, first found by Tim White, and believed to date to about 4.4–7.0 million years ago. The Ardipithecines were bipedal. But they also had unique thumbs that could arch across to the little fingers in what is known as ulnar opposition, which chimps are lacking. We also have more sensitive finger tips. It seems that our hands were functioning by the time of *Homo habilis* about two million years ago. The latter's discovery was a shock because he showed toolmaking abilities, but his brain was only about half the size of the modern human. Toolmaking is not unique to humans—chimps, crows, and dolphins all use tools—but as Gazzaniga says, only humans have made Maseratis. Chimps cannot talk; never gained control over fire; don't cook; have no culture of art, music, or literature; are not particularly generous; are not monogamous; and don't grow food.

Other changes permit us to exercise a theory of mind (TOM), which lets us understand that others have thoughts, beliefs and desires. Monkeys seem to have an elementary theory-of-mind module, but in humans, it is much more advanced. Our ability with language is also much advanced. Our unique larynx enables us to speak. Mirror neurons, only discovered in 1996 by Giacomo Rizzolatti, fired when a monkey performed an action in which his hand or mouth interacted with an object. The mirror neurons also fired when the monkey merely saw another monkey or human perform the same type of action. Our mirror neuron system is far more extensive than found in other species and this has far more ramifications than just for language. One adaptation that rests heavily on the mirror neurons and seems very pronounced in humans is the use of the golden rule. This is the use of the reciprocity permitted by mirror neurons to understand others and then act toward them in ways that we would like them to act toward us. It is often quoted as being a fundamental tool of ethical or moral behavior. The golden rule and its variations have recently been described in considerable detail by Harry Gensler (2013). The golden rule is often cited as remarkable because of its prominence in most of the world's religions. Perhaps this can be understood because it may be a comparatively recent addition to our neurological repertoire. However, we should caution that although it is clearly a very useful tool, it should not be our only moral equipment.

These neurological changes are what enable us to navigate the social world. The shift to becoming highly social is what the human is all about. Many animals have some degree of social arrangement but none revel in it the way we do. As our empathy grew, so too did our social group size. Something triggered our interest in the "other guy" in living and cooperating in groups. Other incentives included the need to fight off predators and to find food. Whatever the reason, many authors now argue that our higher intellectual skills arose as an adaptation to our newly evolved social needs. Understanding the need to be social is fundamental to understanding the human condition.

Gazzaniga argues that in respect of ethics both David Hume (who emphasized emotions) and Immanuel Kant (who emphasized rationality) were right in a way. As the neurobiology of moral behavior becomes active, we shall see that some of our repugnance for killing, incest, and dozens of other actions is as much a result of our natural biology as are our sexual organs. At the same time, we will also realize that the customs that people generate to live in cooperation with one another are rules resulting from the thousands of social interactions we have every day, week, month, and year of our lives. And all this comes from the human mind and brain. Most of our life is spent battling the conscious rational mind and the unconscious emotional system of our brain. In politics, a good outcome happens when the rational choice is consonant with the emotions of the moment. A poor personal decision can be the product of a powerful emotion overriding a simple rational directive. In terms of evolution, it is as if we are not yet comfortable with our rational, analytical mind. We have other uniquely human traits: the emotion of disgust and a sensitivity to contamination, the moral emotions of guilt, shame, and embarrassment, blushing, and crying. We also have a know-it-all interpreter, which comes up with explanations for our unconscious moral intuitions and behaviors. People are capable of voluntarily, deliberately switching from one abstract perspective to another with easy flexibility. We can also manipulate what emotions we are simulating by imagination alone without any physical stimulus. We can transfer emotional knowledge with abstract tools, such as language or music, through books, songs, e-mails, and conversations. These abilities to simulate emotions from language and imagination, to alter our simulations by using perspective, and to project ourselves into the future and past enrich our social world and make our simulations more powerful and complex than those of other species.

12.12 The Family as a System

The family is a system—a constancy into which we are born. More than that, it is a system that has been around nearly as long as sex. And as we shall see later, it is the social system from which all other social systems have been derived. In view of this preeminence, it is surprising that it did not receive a detailed examination until after World War II when it became the focus of attention by Murray Bowen, a psychiatrist at the Menninger Clinic. Bowen had to treat a number of patients with such disorders as schizophrenia, alcoholism, and depression. He observed that the schizophrenics often showed behaviors that seemed linked to their families and he surmised that these traits might arise from the family acting as a system. Bowen went on to propose that there were certain interactions that occurred in all families and that when one or more of these interactions became excessively prominent the system would become dysfunctional. Bowen established a program for family systems therapy at Georgetown University Medical Center, and while he was there, he was joined by Michael Kerr, a gifted internist. Kerr became very enthusiastic about family systems theory and therapy and later wrote a book on the subject as a coauthor with Bowen (see Kerr and Bowen, 1988).

Kerr was concerned to strengthen the scientific basis of family system theory and studied E. O. Wilson's work on *Sociobiology* (1975). Wilson proposed that many sociological phenomena could be reduced to biology. Here, Kerr found expositions of mechanisms that could serve as communications in emotional, intellectual, and feeling systems within the body including hormones from endocrine glands, neuronal electrical currents, and neurotransmitters at synapses. Kerr and Bowen claim that although immunologists, endocrinologists, virologists, and geneticists can all describe the activity in pathological systems, they cannot account for what drives such processes. After explaining the nature of the emotional system within an individual, they go on to discuss how systems can be maintained between individuals when the transmissions are mainly auditory and visual cues. Kerr and Bowen then explain that the complex pathways followed by the chemical, neuronal, auditory, and visual signals define the systems governing the behavior of individuals and societies. The family is one of the oldest social groups, and Kerr and Bowen explain how people can get involved in pairs and triangles and then in more complex arrangements.

There is another issue of interest here, pertaining to the extended family. When the parents of a nuclear family die, the children will generally retain relationships that then add to the bonds of the extended family. The larger group will share memories, habits, properties, and peculiarities of speech inherited from the deceased parents. After a generation or so this group may grow into a tribe with shared cultural connections. In some cases, there may be love, warmth, and trust among all the members of the tribe; and they may share preferences for working or trading together. In many cultures, there is an interest in narratives of the ancestors: the history of where the tribe originated and their migrations, marriages, births, and deaths. These interests may even stretch to ancestor worship or a desire to enroll the dead in membership of a modern religion. Humanists have an interest in their ancestors, but they may ask, what is the survival value of such genealogy? De Caspari (2011) has suggested an answer, namely, that such narratives, by recording the progress of successive generations, draw people together. Unfortunately, most families lose all track of detailed family information within a generation or so. This being the case then, we might argue the case for recording the details of daily life as part of an inheritance for future generations. Some families arrange reunions and prepare a book of narratives to record the events.

There has been a continuous evolution in the form of the family during the history of animal life, and the following is a somewhat simplified sketch of its progress. Exactly how sex and the family originated is the subject of conflicting hypotheses, but it is clear that from its origin 1,200 million years ago, from the simplest unicellular forms through multicellular varieties, from marine to land dwellers, all the while as skeletons, organs, and capabilities improved; so the family has adapted. If the young could live longer under parental protection, their chances of survival increased. The period of gestation increased and then the mammals developed lactation. Eventually, the female drew her male partner into the business of protection, and the role of father was established. In the period of the hunter-gatherers, the typical division of labor involved the male in hunting while the female saw to child rearing. With the coming of civilization, the male became the farmer and the female, the housekeeper. The family was recognized as the sacred unit of society, sanctified by religious custom. As villages grew into cities, the rulers became the center of legal systems, and the arrangements of family life came under the legal rubric of marriage. In some states, it was customary to provide some rights to women but there were others which gave no such protection. There was frequently no specified minimum age for marriage or provision for women's property. At this stage of history, polygamy or other arrangements were also quite common, and it took a long while for monogamy to become the predominant practice. Prostitution has been known as long as marriage, and any woman who celebrated sexual union too enthusiastically has been castigated as a slut or whore. The reputation of pornography also has a somewhat similar ambivalent reputation which has changed throughout history and in different social milieus. Much of what was acceptable as public art in Roman and early Hindu civilization would not have made the grade in Victorian times. (See also 12.15)

There is now an acceptance of divorce as a remedy for dysfunctional marriages. Although polygamy is now banned in the enlightened world, there is still a movement to permit multiple unions in what Deborah Anapol terms *polyamory* (2010). Home economics, which emerged as a discipline about a century ago, has morphed into family and consumer science and may become a true science of the family. Women's centers have been started throughout the world to assist victims of rape and sexual predation.

12.13 The Expanding Circle and the Cradle of Culture

Peter Singer (1981) has pointed out that the history of ethics may be seen as our human progress in expanding the family circle. Thus, as Ridley has explained, the interaction across tribal boundaries represented by barter and trade enabled us to vastly extend our technological evolution. We have worked to overcome class, sexual, and racial discrimination largely through the evolution of the system of governance. We are presently endeavoring to include the other apes, dolphins, and elephants as creatures deserving the love and respect of relatives. We are rapidly approaching the point of being able to manufacture robots and cyborgs who may eventually surpass totally biological humans in their capabilities. And we may even discover intelligent life on other planets.

The family was also the cradle of culture. Gazzaniga asks "What's up with the arts?" and explains that the creation of art is now being recognized as a uniquely human contribution firmly based in our biology. But he asks, what is its evolutionary advantage? There is something that goes on in the human brain that has allowed us to engage in pretense, some connectivity change that has allowed us to decouple the true from the imaginary. Tooby and Cosmides (2001) have theorized that this enables us to be very flexible and break out of the of the rigid behavioral patterns that other animals are subject to. Thus, we can look at a cave wall and imagine it spruced up with a little fresco or to tell the story of the odyssey of Ulysses or see David trapped inside a chunk of marble or look at a strip of bay front property and see the Sydney Opera House. Human creativity is found in a wide variety of systems we have invented, including language, religion, law, governance, and science. Each of these is populated with a family circle of acolytes who maintain and develop the system and its ramifications. Some people belong to several such circles.

Matt Ridley (2010) has advanced an important idea, namely, that the key to rising prosperity over the course of human history has been the exchange of goods. By about 160,000 years ago, a new slender-faced *Homo sapiens* appeared in Ethiopia and around Pinnacle Point in S. Africa. Then came hints of trade in shells and obsidian. But in Europe at about the same time the ancestors of the Neanderthals, also with big brains, showed no signs of long-distance trade. About eighty thousand years ago, one quite small group of people began to spread over most of Africa, as shown by L3 mitochondrial-type genetic markers. They spilled out of Africa and exploded into global dominion. The essence of Ridley's thesis is based on what he calls the manufacture of virtue, i.e., the development of barter, trust, and rules some fifty thousand years ago. Ridley's thoughts are echoed by Geoffrey Miller (2000).

Anthropologists had a theory to explain the appearance of *Homo sapiens* as due to the volatility of African weather. But this could apply to lots of other species as well. A second theory was that human brains became configured differently to permit imagination, planning or some other higher function. A candidate was the FOXP2 gene, which permits speech and language, but the Neanderthals had this too. Ridley argues that the change was due to economics. Humans began to build a collective intelligence by bartering and exchange. Technology and habits changed faster than anatomy. There is little use of barter in other animals. It is more than the swapping of favors, but in Adam Smith's words: "Give me that which I want, and you shall have this which you want." Barter does not have to be equal. Although this theory is not original, Ridley takes the concept much further than previous writers. He argues that the social systems humans developed at this time permitted the growth of a "collective" brain. *Homo sapiens* had started a cultural evolution whereby ideas and systems could "replicate, mutate, compete, select and accumulate—somewhat as genes had been doing for billions of years." Bartering required humans who have a theory of mind and who could use their mirror neurons so that they could interact without wanting to kill their trading partners. They would be able to exchange goods originating at great distances and in the territories of other tribes. Ridley's comment is that "exchange is to technology as sex is to [biological] evolution." In subsequent chapters, we will be exploring how the ramifications spawned from altruistic social systems have been used to build our humanistic world.

12.14 The Agricultural Family

There are a number of books on the sociology of the family, of which the work by Ernest W. Burgess, Harvey J. Locke, and Mary Margaret Thomes (1963) is a good example. In the USA, the situation up until about one hundred years ago was that the predominant family was rural. Farms spread out to occupy the colonies with families consisting of husbands, wives, and typically a dozen children. The father usually served as the farm manager while the wife ran the household. The children were all expected to contribute to the farm economy starting with lighter tasks and gradually progressing to harder work as they grew up into apprentice roles for their parents. Marriage involving dowry payments and customs to cover inheritance came primarily from Britain, although other parts of Europe were also represented as time went on. The import of African slaves also affected the mix and, after the emancipation, resulted in significant numbers of black families whose customs were different from those of white families in varying degrees.

Wilson (1978) also discusses recent developments in family life: its general decline due to divorce and migration due to economic pressures. As the population grew, the cities became more important, and migration from the country into urban centers and manufacturing occupations grew steadily. This resulted in the diminution of rural farm families and separation of rural offspring from their parents. This trend was exacerbated by increased mobility and migration over great distances. People tended to become isolated from the homes of their youth, and marriage partners were increasingly disparate in culture and customs. After the Second World War, marriage breakdowns became more frequent and divorce rates rocketed. Along with this came the demand for family counseling through churches and government agencies. Such problems are, of course, important for nonbelievers as well as the religious and literature is needed to serve our community in greater detail than is possible in the scope of this essay. In most countries, a complete system of education has been put in place to assist the educational process, starting with reading and writing. And together with this, there is usually a raft of legal arrangements to protect the child's interests.

12.15 Sex at the Millennium

Attitudes toward sex have changed considerably during the course of civilization, with alternating periods of openness and reticence over sexual expression. The Victorian period, for example, is generally considered one of the most repressed; but one hundred years later, matters had opened up to a large extent. It had become common to find literature, films, and art with explicit sexual themes. By the time of the millennium, it had become common to find articles such as Jacobs and Speckhardt's (2004) asking "What Do We Do Now that the Sexual Revolution is Over?" Prostitution is another common topic as in the pages of the *Humanist* (2003) and in the piece by Alice Leuchtag in 2010. Out of hundreds of book titles and in addition to those already mentioned I refer to a representative selection by Alex Comfort (1972); by James Geer, Julia Heiman, and Harold Leitenberg (1984); and by Vern and Bonnie Bullough (1995), all of which were well-known toward the end of the century. Comfort's book, *The Joy of Sex* (1972), contains numerous line drawings and paintings as well as instructions on various positions for coitus and all manner of topics related to lovemaking. The volume by Geer et al., *Human Sexuality* (1984), is an academic textbook intended for university-level students that covers biology and development, sexual expression, homosexuality, sexual problems, sexual offenses, pornography and prostitution, and a history of sex education. The work by the Bulloughs is titled *Sexual Attitudes: Myths and Realities* (1995) and was written to free research on sex from the prudish burdens placed on it in the Victorian era. It examines hostility to sex, various views of sexual activity, "unnatural" sex, masturbation, gender, menstruation, contraception, abortion, infertility, impotence, artificial insemination, pornography and obscenity, prostitution, homosexuality, and stigmatized behavior.

The twentieth century also featured the first serious scientific sociological studies of sexual behavior. The primary examples of such works were the two Kinsey reports: *Sexual Behavior in the Human Male* (1948) and *Sexual Behavior in the Human Female* (1953). The latter of these was based on personal interviews with six thousand women. Data was analyzed for the frequency with which women participate in various kinds of sexual activity and looked at such factors as age, socioeconomic status, and religious adherence. Comparisons between females and males suggested women were less sexually active than men. The findings caused shock and outrage because they challenged conventional beliefs and because they discussed subjects that had previously been taboo.

Kinsey's methodology was criticized because it must have included collaboration with child molesters. Another criticism was that 25 percent of the sample had been prison inmates and 5 percent were male prostitutes. Parts of the Kinsey reports are frequently used to support the common estimate of 10 percent for homosexuality in the general population. Kinsey himself avoided and disapproved of using terms like homosexual and heterosexual to describe individuals, asserting that sexuality is prone to change with time and that sexual behavior can be understood both as physical contact as well as psychological phenomena (desire, sexual attraction, fantasy). Instead of the three categories—hetero, bisexual, and homosexual—the seven-point Kinsey scale system was used.

Between them, these books cover most of the basics of the topics that a reader concerned with sex might wish to learn about at a level of detail beyond the scope of the present volume. Such a reader should therefore consult the references given if she or he wishes to investigate in greater depth. There are, however, some subjects which demand further discussion. Foremost among these "advanced" topics is the role played by religion in past suppression in the Western world and in contemporary atrocities both in the West and especially in the Middle and Far East. We will take this matter up again in chapter 18.

12.16 Legacy

Another major issue appears in some more recent books, such as *The Moral Animal* by Robert Wright (1995) and *Sex at Dawn* by Christopher Ryan and Cacilda Jethá (2010). The latter book contains some interesting but earthy speculations on human sex life starting with the ancient evolutionary pair-bonding arrangements of the apes who constituted the last common ancestors of the gorillas, chimps, bonobos, and humans. Ryan and Cacilda maintain that the family changed from a gorilla-like alpha-male-dominated harem to one in which most males had sexual access to mates. They contend that the life of the newly agricultural human group changed from one of equality between the sexes to one in which women were suppressed. They provide copious details of the miserable sex lives that have followed, finishing with a scenario in which they present the options seen by many men as

1) to cheat, lie, and try not to get caught;
2) to give up sex with anyone but the wife for the rest of life; and
3) to be a serial monogamist, divorcing and starting over with a sequence of wives.

One has to have pity on the poor male in Ryan and Jethá's book. His lifetime obsession with sex has apparently left him tired and jaded. One wonders if his problem is that sex has become the sole object of his existence. One might have thought that all this activity would have resulted in some children whose progress in life would have provided some interest for poor old dad. Or perhaps the life of the family would have led to other diversions such as a career, in a profession or a business. He might even have joined some clubs or associations or have taken part in politics. But of course, the poor old fellow might simply be a literary device and a figment of the imaginations of Ryan and Jethá.

We have already pinpointed Darwin's work (1871) on sexual selection. Robert Pennock (1995) argues that Darwin believed that ethical behavior could itself be regarded as evidence for evolution. Unfortunately, Darwin's theory was misinterpreted for many years as supporting the "survival of the fittest," implying that might give rights to capitalistic exploitation or even Nazi ideology. This period is examined in Barry Werth's book *Banquet at Delmonico's: Great Minds, the Gilded Age, and the Triumph of Evolution in America* (2009). Eventually, this departure was corrected, and the scientific discipline of biology was reestablished.

Evolutionary psychology started with E. O. Wilson's book on *Sociobiology* (1975) and his follow-up volume *On Human Nature* (1978). Cosmides and Tooby produced a primer for the subject circa 1990 in which they explained that evolutionary psychology (EP) is a school of psychology that takes evolutionary laws into account. Wilson's (1978) book on *Human Nature* has the chapter on sex to which we have already referred, as well as a chapter on altruism by human and other animals (especially Wilson's favorite ants and bees). Wilson proposes a biological explanation for the phenomenon of altruism involving kin selection. This then links altruism, and sex to EP. (It was also the start of a long debate on kin selection as the driving force of evolution. In later work, Wilson [2014] has come around to replacing kin selection with multilevel and individual selection). Recent accounts of ethics have been increasingly committed to altruism as the foundation of ethics, as in Kitcher's *The Ethical Project* (2010).

The role of sexual conduct has been an important feature of the discussion of ethics, starting with Charles Darwin (1871), who favored monogamy, as was reemphasized by Robert Wright in his book *The Moral Animal* (1995). This book has an instructive chapter on evolutionary psychology. Darwin's stance was equated to a *Standard Model* by Ryan and Jethá (2010) who then proceeded to criticize it. But it is interesting to note that in their chapter 22, they finally tell us that sex is not as important as the rest of their book implies. They then hint that moral approaches are called for. Monogamy is clearly one variety of ethical pairing and it is favored by most societies. Another approach, which can be managed ethically, is known as polyamory, as described by Deborah Anapol (2010). This arrangement seems to be the objective of the polygamous marriages entered into by Mormons and some others. Even John Stuart Mill was prepared to accept polygamy as ethical, when its female participants themselves freely and genuinely concurred. The problem is that women have been frequently coerced under such circumstances.

We have to conclude that the arrangements for the male-female bond are often the source of conflict. There is no simple rule (or rules) for the operation of each and every coupling. Each set of choices has to be decided by the individual participants. It seems that if there is one overall principle it should be that the system must be ethical, i.e., that matters should be beneficial to everyone concerned. In other words, we should be mindful of everyone concerned: wife, husband, children, and relatives. We should not enter into something as serious as marriage without careful consideration. Sex is a part of the total picture, but it is not the only element. After all, coitus only lasts for a short time, whereas the male-female bond may last for a lifetime, and its aftereffects may endure for much longer still. It is this legacy that is so important to us.

In the remaining chapters of this book, we will be exploring the wider scope of our cultural legacy. We will consider the growth of languages, arts, and sciences. Philosophers ask what we know and how we know it while ethicists ask how we should live and how these lives might be just and honorable. We will review how human accomplishments have enabled us to venture throughout the earth, its land, sea, and sky. We have succeeded in traveling beyond our planet and in exploring the depths of the universe in space and time. In our minds, we ask if there is life elsewhere and what are the limits, if any, for future intelligence.

13 Humanist Culture and Institutions

Outline

13. Humanist Culture and Institutions

13.1 Introduction

We have reviewed how both reason and emotion factor into the process whereby we arrive at a science of ethics. We have used our knowledge of biological evolution to explain how much of our ethology is instinctive and how altruistic behavior predated our becoming human. We have discussed how psychology can be used to uncover these ancient predispositions as well as more modern emotional inclinations. We examined the beginnings of ethical reasoning in the construction of values and virtues. We also looked at the search for happiness started by the Epicureans. Then we reviewed the methods of ethics developed by philosophers in the past two centuries and how we might apply Socrates's injunction to examine our lives. This brought us to modern times, and we surveyed some contemporary moral problems. We speculated on how humanism and in particular humanist ethics might proceed into the future including some speculations on the future of the human race. We have also asked, what are the characteristics of the individual humanist? In this chapter, our subject is humanist institutions; and we are asking such questions as What is the purpose of a humanist institution? Is it a church or a school? Should it be regarded as an alternative to religion? How should it be managed? As a democracy or a hierarchy? Who are our allies? Our enemies? Should we raise money? Invest in stocks or buildings? Run charities? Discuss politics? Run businesses? Sponsor art and music? Do we have too many satellite meetings? Why are we not more popular with young people?

Before we start on a description of humanist institutions, it might be advisable to remind ourselves of what we mean by *humanism* and a *humanist*. Throughout this series, we have advanced a number of concepts that go along with a general theme that humanism is, de facto, applied philosophy. In a sense, it encompasses all knowledge but focuses on wisdom, i.e., on how to use knowledge to good purposes. The humanist might live and work as an individual or as a member of a family or in a group. Some people may accept all the principles except the need to belong to a group. So in what follows we should assume the statements apply to most of our members. We are naturalists, i.e., we believe that the natural world is the sum total of reality: we are nontheists who do not hold beliefs in God, gods, angels, goblins, fairies, or spirits. We are rationalists who use truth, justice and benevolence as measures to evaluate our theories. Over the years, we have come up with various maxims to guide our behavior and various manifestos and statements of our beliefs. In this book, we have been at pains to define a set of humanist principles as set out in previous chapters and repeated in appendix 1. Our topics have followed an approximately historical, order and the same thing could be said of our list of humanist principles. These general maxims are intended as broad guides to our behavior.

13.2 Science and Truth

We humans owe our general success in life to our big brains with their enhanced memory capabilities. We remember things and recognize when occurrences repeat, whether these are natural phenomena or human-made systems. Truth is basic to our trust of other people and our keeping of promises. We need to be honest about the rules for our groups and the qualifications for membership. Humanism includes all the knowledge we have accumulated, starting with the telling of narratives and then the gradual growth of science, followed by the writing of books and finally through the Internet, adding up to the total erudition used in the lives we lead. The scientific method is a refinement of the everyday processes of telling and verifying the truth. We have put this as our first principle because unfortunately there are many people, including most of the followers of religion who still believe in the supernatural. Many things that were formerly mysteries have now been explained scientifically and we neglect these advances at peril to our lives and prosperity. Philosophers, such as Simon Blackburn (2005), tell us that there is no absolute truth, just a best approximation and that this is what we seek in logic, mathematics, science, and everyday life. A prime example is neuroscience, the knowledge of the brain itself, and our modern understanding that it is the residence of ethics and conscience. Neuroscience was started by Locke, Hume, and Kant and progressed into the development of psychology and cognitive science. The recognition that animal behavior was governed by instinctive emotions before the human development of reasoning provides a foundation for the study of ethics.

13.3 Emotions, Arts, and Psychology

The life-stance of the individual is an important factor in ethics. There are some feelings which are distinctly moral and which arise from instincts, determined by evolution. There is a distinct ethical vocabulary which has been invented to describe the various emotions and rationalizations found in ethical discussion. A number of psychologists (including Freud, Fromm, Maslow, Piaget, Kohlberg, and Ellis) have studied how individuals develop in their ethical outlooks and how such changes can be described in terms of *happiness*, an overall measure of one's emotional state. Psychology, being the study of how people actually behave, is a part of natural science and can be related to ethics and morality, the studies of how people *should* behave, based on theoretical considerations. Psychologists refer to conscience, i.e., the emotional expression of the rules and policies which may be acquired throughout our lives partly from nature and partly from nurture.

Michael S. Gazzaniga (2008) includes a chapter in his book entitled "What's Up with the Arts?" He advocates a theory proposed by Tooby and Cosmides (2001) to the effect that the arts, including storytelling, visual arts, and music, all serve to convey emotions and values from the artist to the public. Tooby and Cosmides explained that there is an evolutionary advantage in this as a way of educating the public about new scenarios. There are predispositions to dichotomies between the sexes as readers of the arts and sciences and we need to be aware of this in designing humanist meeting programs. These manifestations in men and women extend to child caring, nurture, and sexual interactions.

One realizes the importance of optimism when contemplating the emotional content of business and investment decision making. The stock market is driven up and down by emotional waves. However, there has been a trend toward economic progress, evident for hundreds of years. The bias toward increasing activity is clearly the result of optimism and in itself is a manifestation of Thomas Sargent's dictum: "What is going to happen, is going to depend, at least partly, on what you think is going to happen." So we see that the future ability of the humanist movement to support professional staffers will depend on our maintaining an optimistic outlook.

13.4 Values, Theories, Communities, and Systems

A value is an idea that rests on emotions recognized by the members of a group. For example, the well-known golden rule rests on the assumption that different people experience similar emotions and have equal rights for consideration. One simple ideological approach is to base a theory on a single value. Thus we may have a libertarian theory, such as that proposed by John Stuart Mill, who advocated the maximum freedom for each individual. An alternative theory could be based on benevolence, as proposed by Hume, and according to which an individual devotes his or her life to the benefit of others. It is quite easy to see that such theories will conflict with one another and indeed Henry Sidgwick devoted much of his book *The Methods of Ethics* to exactly this problem. The solution Sidgwick and others proposed was to devise theories that were said to be utilitarian and that attempted to produce the greatest good for the greatest number. Recently attention has focused on virtue theories in which the aim is to find ways to develop the traits of individuals to the best advantage. Other modern humanist ethical theories have been proposed by Paul Kurtz (1988) and by Peter Singer (1981).

We stress the importance of groups of people acting as ethical communities. Such a group might consist of a family, a school, a humanist assembly, or an institution. The group might exist in a political or an economic context. By proposing and reviewing moral rules and ethical policies among themselves, such a group, in effect, "legislates" the long- and short-range behavior of the community. A scientific society, for example, might propose the accumulation and testing of facts and data as part of the process of advancing science in some sphere. Similarly, there is a communitarian approach to the development of law. We use the jury system to decide individual cases while the so-called "democratic" political system follows similar procedures in establishing law in the first place. Medicine also relies on ethical communities.

It is worth noting that in these situations there are certain common features among the established procedures. There is a cyclic aspect to the monitoring of any system. We begin by assessing the present situation and bringing to bear on our reasoning all the various morals, habits, and promises, which we have accumulated. This then results in decisions being made and actions being taken that impact the external world. The consequences are evaluated based on our human emotions and such ethics, plans, and pragmatics as we already have in place. These evaluations are remembered and create the knowledge and information to produce our future motivation. The process is adaptive and evolutionary. The same flowchart (see figure 3) can be used to describe the process used by individuals or communities.

13.5 Culture and Institutions

We have recapitulated some of the main principles and beliefs associated with humanism. Now is the time to discuss what happens when a group of people get together to help one another to live according to such ideas. In other words, we are now concerned with the arrangements these people might come up with to live as a group. Such arrangements could be termed the culture and institutions of the group. We might think of ourselves as adopting the viewpoint of a sociologist or anthropologist. Our group might have come together in the very early days of civilization or at any time up to the present in a modern city or country. There might be considerable differences in the membership of the group: in age, sex, or socioeconomic status. Even among groups with similar backgrounds in the categories just mentioned, there might be considerable variation in the educational attainments of members. Humanism employs a certain distinct vocabulary, some of which is listed in the glossary of appendix 3. There are a certain number of stories, allegories, and narratives known to the humanist community. There are numerous beliefs in various sciences, in history and social sciences, that are part and parcel of humanism and that are outlined in later chapters of this book. We also support a number of traditions and procedures in our meetings and gatherings. Humanism respects academic learning. Although it is not associated with many poetic, fictional, musical, or other artworks, there are some; and there is a growing interest within the movement in increasing our contributions in these areas. The same is not usually said about athletics although we do have an interest in keeping fit and living healthy lives.

13.6 Socrates, Plato, and Aristotle

What do we mean by humanist culture and institutions? The answer has to be the ethical values, theories, systems, and communities that humanists have produced in practice over the years. The greatest changes in the distinctive character of humanist institutions hark back to the fifth and fourth centuries BCE in Greece when Socrates, Plato, Aristotle, and Alexander the Great were living. These men were surely brilliant, and their ways of thinking and acting established the basic methods of ethics and politics we humanists still employ today. First, consider Socrates who traveled around Athens, asking apparently simple questions. When his audience supplied an answer, he would begin to challenge it, revealing its inadequacy until a better response had been formulated. He might repeat the performance as often as necessary to arrive at the best formulation. This process of repeated statements and rebuttals is known as a dialectic, and the gatherings were called symposia. In the work *The Republic*, there are many examples of such dialogues, resulting in the formulation of a complete ethical system. Socrates himself did not wish to write these exchanges down as he felt that this tended to make the participants forget what they had said. We are indebted to Plato for recording the discussions on scrolls for posterity.

It is generally agreed that the earliest "books" in the *Republic* are the thoughts of Socrates while the later ones are mainly Plato's own viewpoints. These contain the famous allegory of the cave and the prisoners who can see only the shadows of real objects. Figure 4 is a sketch by Fernando Casas that illustrates the situation in Plato's allegory of the cave, which evokes our imprisonment by the rules of society. The figure also teaches us about Plato's idea of reality as comprising an unchanging eternal order together with a visible order which is in a never ending flux. Plato felt that the eternal order was illuminated by a source, analogous to the sun, which also defined the world's morality. Aristotle was a student in Plato's Academy for some twenty years, according to Louise Ropes Loomis in her book *Aristotle: On Man in the Universe* (1943). Plato called him the mind of the school, but when Plato died, another man was appointed head.

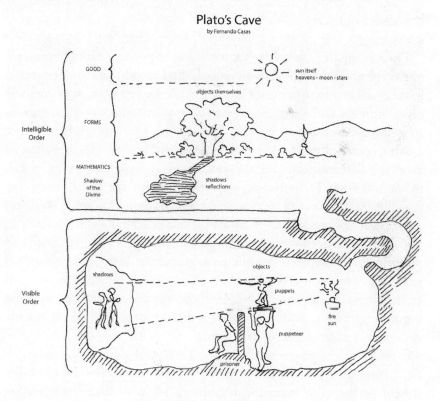

Fig. 4 Allegory of the Cave

Fig. 4. The Allegory of the Cave

Plato presented a cosmology (a theory of reality) in the allegorical description of prisoners in a cave. The divine objects of nature (sun, moon, and stars) are forms existing in the heavens. These divine objects cast shadows of earthly objects on the wall. The divine objects are the good. The visible order are the shadows of puppets carried by puppeteers walking on a parapet behind the prisoners who are sitting behind a wall.

Aristotle departed for Macedonia where King Philip engaged him as tutor to his son Alexander. Philip subdued all of Greece and prepared to launch a campaign against Persia but was murdered on the eve of its starting. Alexander succeeded him and went on to conquer Persia as well as a vast empire including Egypt, Assyria, and Turkestan as far as the border of India.

Not long after Alexander's assumption of power, Aristotle returned to Athens and founded his own school, the Lyceum, where he collected a library of manuscript books and collections of scientific specimens of birds, animals, and plants. At the school, Aristotle directed investigations in well-nigh every known field of knowledge. The Lyceum became the leading center of study in science, philosophy, and politics as well as in more familiar subjects. He may well be said to have "done over" much of Plato's work. He authored numerous books, the most famous of which is the *Organon*, a treatise on logic; *Metaphysics*; *Parts of Animals*; *Nichomachean Ethics*; *Politics*; and *Poetics*. Much other work was known to have been written but was lost. He was a great scientist and philosopher whose work was treated as gospel until about three hundred years ago. He disagreed with Plato about the existence of a world of eternal forms. He rejected Plato's ideal communistic aristocracy as being totally impractical and wrote that political arrangements should be those that a state can actually attain.

Aristotle's ethics rested on the belief that the aim of a human life should be the achievement of happiness. He maintained that we are most happy when living a life of moral and intellectual virtue. Moral virtue makes a man good and do his work well. We should choose a golden mean of conduct between an excess and a deficiency. Courage, for example, would be a mean between the excess of foolhardiness and the defect of cowardice. Temperance would be a mean between self-indulgence and unfeeling austerity. Liberality would be a mean between wasteful extravagance and crabbed miserliness. Justice is a fair balancing of claims between contending parties. We need to exercise our free will and do our duty. We should not become slaves of habit. Children need training in doing and choosing good. Our intellect should aim at seeking the truth of science, art and wisdom. "We can do noble acts without ruling earth and sea," he said. "We should, as far as we can make ourselves, strain every nerve to live in accordance with the best things in us . . . The life of reason is the best and pleasantest, and in this way man reaches his potentialities to the full."

Socrates, Plato, and Aristotle were a remarkable trio whose teachings and writings provided the world with the first comprehensive ethical systems. None of them would pass as completely modern humanists, but their arguments were rational and detailed; and although they themselves did not agree on all matters—and, in fact, were quite different characters—they were all humanists in that they provided examples of how to proceed with methodical deliberation based on experience. They did not rely on intuition or revelation or the traditional teachings of religion. Humanism has always involved discussion and debate and the careful evaluation of consequences.

13.7 Ethics and Pragmatism

Socrates, Plato, and Aristotle did not have the benefit of studying evolution with Darwin or pragmatism with Dewey or James. None of them were burdened with the later triumph of monotheism in the form of the Christian or Muslim god. Ever since Darwin's book *On the Origin of Species* was published in 1859 nonbelievers have been in the forefront of the battle to bring the subject of evolution into the mainstream of the advance of modernity. In one sense, it is the use of evolution that is the major contribution that humanism has to make to ethical theory. Darwin later ventured into moral theory with *The Expression of the Emotions in Man and Animals* (1872), and beyond that, he applied his theories on natural selection and sexual selection to the same subject (1877). These ideas have recently been revised by Matt Ridley (1993) and Geoffrey Miller (2000). Herbert Spencer propounded "an all-embracing conception of evolution as the progressive development of the physical world, biological organisms, the human mind, and human culture and societies," as *Wikipedia* has put it. Spencer's tireless advocacy of evolution eventually led to its triumphal acceptance among the business community in the USA. We should point out that when businesses are run well, with systematic and long-range planning, they provide outstanding examples of evolution by forethought and planning.

Julian Huxley (1957) presented a sophisticated analysis of individual and social "evolutionary humanism." He saw man as at only the beginning of a period of evolutionary dominance with vast and still-undreamt-of possibilities still lying ahead. Although Huxley could see the future importance of evolution in general terms, his exposition remained somewhat vague as to details. And as Lawrence Rifkin (2008) has recently pointed out, Huxley's ideas had no sooner been published than they came under attack from all sides. Some of the greatest advances in the application of social evolutionary ideas have actually come from law, engineering, medicine, and the business world; and one of the leaders here has to be Peter Drucker with his theories of management (1973).

13.8 Humanist Organizations

Suppose that a group of people become convinced that it would be mutually beneficial to follow humanist principles. The group might consist of a man and his wife, or it might involve several members. Then the situation could be represented by the illustration of figure 5. The more of the principles they follow, then presumably, the greater benefits would accrue to the group and the greater incentive they would have to persevere. But at the same time, we realize that individuals will vary in terms of the number of principles they apprehend and accept. There are many humanists who only accept some of the principles, and there are many nonhumanists who accept at least some and maybe all the principles. In that case, they are humanists in all but name. Once such a humanist group gets started, it acquires a history, and this may vary considerably

Fig. 5. Humanist Organization

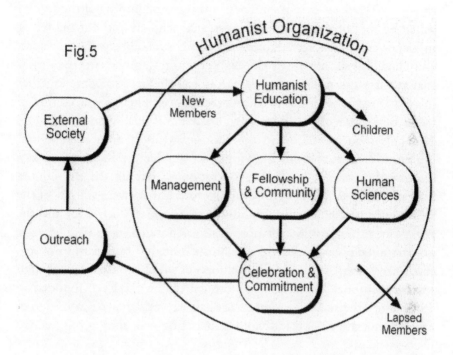

depending on its membership and its circumstances. A small group might operate purely by word of mouth while a larger number might agree on a formal constitution with by-laws. We might surmise that the larger organization would support six main functions: (i) the education of new and existing members and their children into the ways of the group, (ii) fellowship (and love) within the community, (iii) discovery of natural and human sciences, (iv) management of the group's activities and business, (v) celebration of and commitment to life, and (vi) outreach to the external society. I have written a paper around these themes (Finch, 2006). That presentation is what convinced me that humanist ethics needs to incorporate systems concepts and that our institutions have to be set up to facilitate the process. We need to revise our long-range plans every five years or so.

Although there were schools of thought in classical times in Greece and Rome that might have been termed *humanist*, such as those of the stoics and Epicureans, they were effectively obliterated by the coming of Christianity after Constantine. Glimmerings of humanist thought started again in the universities at the beginning of the second millennium, but these came from isolated scholars without money or influence and not powerful organizations comparable to the Christian churches. It was not until the eighteenth and nineteenth centuries that atheists and philosophers began to feel the need to come together in humanist institutions of any consequence. There are accounts of those developments in books by Epstein (2009), Grayling (2003, 2013), Lamont (1982), and the Morains (1998). Some of the first organizations apart from individual writers were publishing houses such as the Rationalist Press Association in Britain. In the United States, the *Humanist* magazine and its forerunners were started in the 1920s. The first Humanist Manifesto was published in 1933, and the American Humanist Association was incorporated in 1941. There are now national organizations of humanists in many countries in Europe, the Americas, Africa and India, over forty of which are affiliated through the International Humanist and Ethical Union (IHEU), founded in 1953. The Atheist Alliance International is a worldwide organization of atheist associations and individuals including over sixty groups across five continents.

13.9 American Institutions:

There are a number of nontheist organizations in the United States besides the AHA, including the Council for Secular Humanism (CSH), American Atheists, Society for Humanistic Judaism, Freedom from Religion Foundation, and the American Ethical Union. The CSH publishes the magazine Free Inquiry and is associated with a number of Centers of Inquiry around the country. The Unitarian Universalist Association (UUA) has a large membership some of whom describe themselves as humanists, and some are atheists but there are also many professed Christians included and a wide variety of other religious faiths. The humanists in the UUA have their own organization: the HUUmanists Association. The Humanist Institute offers university-level education to potential humanist ministers. There are also some smaller congregations of nonbelievers, such as the Houston Church of Freethought and the Dallas-based North Texas Church of Freethought. The Houston area is also served by a secular community known as the Oasis, which includes many former theists in its membership. This group was started around 2011 under the directorship of Mike Aus, a former Lutheran pastor and graduate of the Clergy Project. There are some publishing houses that specialize in nontheistic works including notably the Prometheus Press, founded by Dr. Paul Kurtz. The Secular Coalition for America is a political lobby for nontheists in America. The Secular Student Alliance organizes and serves student groups throughout the USA.

The AHA is the leading membership organization of nontheists in the USA. According to its by-laws, it is governed by an elected board of directors. It is comprised of ten thousand members who are served by a paid staff of some fifteen people including an executive director and the editor of the *Humanist* magazine. There are some seventy chapters and some sixty affiliates. Included under the AHA aegis are the Humanist Society, the members of which are the humanist celebrants and ministers. There are several specialized centers including the Appignani Humanist Legal Center, the Appignani Bioethics Center, the LGBT Humanist Council, the Feminist Caucus, the International Darwin Day Foundation, Humanist Charities, and the Kochhar Humanist Education Center. The AHA arranges an annual conference and sponsors publication of the essays in the philosophy of humanism.

The American Humanist Association is operating under a five-year plan adopted in 2007 of which the main objectives were the following:

- Increasing public awareness and acceptance of humanism
- Building robust humanist communities
- Increasing political influence
- Developing original scholarship and research
- Forging productive collaborations

The year 2012 should have been the time to assess this plan. Have its main goals been reached? Will the association continue with the same aims? Or should they be modified? Should the objectives be expanded by considering public policy in government, economics, health, defense, and world government? What should be the association's objectives in charitable endeavors? Humanists might argue that there should be no need for people to die on the streets or for women to die in childbirth. This should apply anywhere in the World but particularly in the USA. Starvation and poverty could be ended and education provided for all. Many of the same issues might be addressed by local groups or even by individuals since they serve as foundations for public policy.

13.10 Houston Area Nontheism

The Houston area is a large modern metropolis that provides a case study for the growth of regional humanism and other varieties of nontheism, which should be of interest in other parts of the world. The early history of atheism and free thought in Houston, going back to the nineteenth century, has been described by Arnold (2005). Humanism did not enter on the scene until Julian Huxley, received an appointment in 1910 as the founding faculty member of the Biology Department at Rice Institute. Julian was the grandson of Thomas Henry Huxley, an early associate of Charles Darwin. A symposium to mark the centennial of Julian's birth was held by Rice University in 1987 at which papers on various aspects of his career were given. These papers formed the basis of a book edited by Waters and Van Helden, which was published in 1992. It appears that Julian developed his views on science and religion while in Houston and gave a series of lectures *Biology and Man* after he left. These lectures later developed into what he called scientific humanism and later evolutionary humanism.

An informal group of humanists began meeting together on an occasional basis in the early 1970s in Houston. During this time, a leading light of the group was Dr. Ray Karchmer Daily, an ophthalmologist who was also a member of the Houston School Board for many years and its president twice. Dr. Daily convened a meeting to hear Bette Chambers, at that time executive director of the AHA, and there were 130 people present. Dr. Daily died at the age of eighty-three in 1975. Her son, Dr. Louis Daily, is a member of HOH to this day. The Houston Chapter of the American Humanist Association was chartered as the Humanists of Houston (HOH) in 1978. A set of by-laws was prepared by Ben Levy, a prominent area lawyer. An inaugural meeting was addressed by Beth Fennell who later married Dr. Corliss Lamont. Regular meetings were attended by as many as sixty participants. A newsletter was published continuously after 1985, during most of the first ten years under the editorship of Frank Prahl. Other people who have served in this editorial capacity include Daniel Strain, Ron Titus, Jim Knierien, and lately Noelle George. The Internet has more recently replaced print media for outreach purposes. Other members of note during the early years included Barbara Bullock, Charles Fisher, Moie Hamburger, Bob Helken, Douglas Hook, Professor Konstantin Kolenda, Frank Prahl, Joyce Terry, Ben Levy, and Abby and Ariel Thomann. Professor Kolenda continued his association with Rice University and wrote a column on philosophy in the *Humanist* magazine for several years. Professor Kolenda was also the author of several books including *Cosmic Religion: The Autobiography of the Universe* (1987). There have been humanist/nontheist groups at both Rice University and the University of Houston from time to time, but they have depended on individual students who leave when they graduate. HOH was the subject of two articles in the religion section of the *Houston Chronicle* (1978, 1981). Some early meetings of HOH were held in the Women's Center of Houston, followed by a move to the Montrose Library.

In 1985 a second chapter was started known as Humanists Involved in Greater Houston (HIGH). This group was led by Dr. Stephen Shafersman and Frank Prahl and was successful for some years. The two groups were reunited in 1992 when it was decided to call the chapter by the second name but to institute a development fund to be known as Humanists of Houston Development Fund using the $300 remaining in the treasury of the first group. The first volume of essays in the philosophy of humanism was published in 1992 under the editorship of Dr. Marian Hillar. The reunited chapter started meeting in the then-new Unitarian Fellowship building on Wirt Road in 1993 and moved to the Bayland Community Center in 2008. In 1994 the chapter voted to return to the name Humanists of Houston. The Humanist Association of Montgomery County was started in 1995. A conference was held at the University of Houston in October 1996 entitled ETHICS-96, partly funded by a grant from the AHA Chapter Assembly. Another group known as the Houstonians for Secular Humanism (HSH), affiliated with the Council for Secular Humanism, was started in 1998. This group was led by Daniel and Julie Strain and flourished for a while before Daniel and Julie moved to California. The Ideas Club was started as a book club and discussion group for HSH in 1998 and began meeting at a Borders Bookshop, and shortly thereafter, it later moved to Dr. Daily's family home on North Boulevard. Robert Finch was elected chairman of the AHA Chapter Assembly in 2000 and to the AHA board of directors in 2002. The national meeting of the AHA was held in Houston in 2002.

The Houston Church of Freethought (HCOF) was started by Art and Nancy Fay, Jim Ashmore, and others in 2001; and it continues very successfully with some joint participation by HOH members. One notable success of HCOF is the Sunday school run by Nancy Fay. Jim Ashmore serves as the "pastor" for the group, and he has provided sermons for the group's services for nearly ten years now. These services are known for outstanding audiovisual aids administered by Ed Uthman. HCOF hosts an annual picnic enjoyed by all nontheists in the area.

HOH undertook a self-study that culminated in the production of a five-year plan in 2007. This plan was an elegant construction, but the resources necessary for its implementation have been spotty. The Central Gathering has been moved away from the Wirt Road Unitarian Church and set up in new and more commodious quarters at Bayland Park in 2008. There has, in fact, been a considerable growth in nontheist activity around the Houston area. The establishment of regional gatherings for West Houston and Sugar Land has been implemented, and there are several other groups in operation including the Humanist Contemplatives and the Meyer Land Social Group. There is now a successful women's group and a lunchtime gathering called the Hungry Heathens. Several of these share membership with HCOF and the Houston Atheists. There is a Freethought Alliance that arranges cooperation among HOH, HCOF, and the atheist meetup groups for an annual picnic and celebration Darwin Day. If we were to regard all this activity as humanist in a broad sense, then it could be argued that we are very much on the targets set for the 2007 plan. All these groups have been greatly assisted by the meetup organization, which is a network social medium group.

There is an interesting aspect of these developments that has impacted the Houston area community, and that is the relationship between the national organization and its local affiliates. There is a lack of understanding between these, which continues to be a problem. This may even have its roots in the ancient division between Christian theism and Greek philosophy. The fear of death was repressed by the priests who also became servants of the state by rendering their congregations into compliant subjects. The state, in turn, supplied the clergy with their daily bread. After the US Constitution established a separation of church and state, the larger denominations eventually took over the role of financial support. Although the AHA has grown, it still cannot support full-time staff for local chapters although there are many volunteers from disenchanted clergy.

13.11 Commitment and Destiny

I am very hopeful on the present (2015) situation with HOH. Firstly, we see a younger generation taking over the management of the chapter. Vic Wang has taken over as president and is doing an excellent job of finding speakers for the monthly gatherings. The number of younger members and their participation in meetings has grown markedly. Some of them are very keen on volunteering to help charitable causes and on donating contributions. These two things help to give our chapter a positive image. One interesting development I did not anticipate is that the nontheist community has been very well served by the meetup organization in the need to disseminate information about our meetings. Meetup has grown and become a part of the social media including Facebook, Twitter, and LinkedIn. Vic Wang claims that the membership of the HOH Meetup Group, at over 1,500, is the second largest in the USA.

Another development that has been very positive is that the nonbelievers of the Houston area were singled out by Amanda Schutz, a PhD candidate in sociology at the University of Arizona, for her research project on (non) religion. Amanda has been very interested in studying "atheist churches" around the country such as Greg Epstein's chaplaincy at Harvard, Jerry De Witt's congregation in rural Louisiana, and the Sunday Assembly franchises in England and various places in Canada and the USA. She finds that these groups are more diverse than one might imagine. In selecting an area for her study, she chose Houston because it is a large cosmopolitan area but still has close contacts with the rural Southern religion. The greater Houston area has a rapidly growing population of five million; and it supports a large number of nontheist groups including atheists, humanists, free thought, former Christians, women, and blacks. Amanda is interested in the fact that HOH has numerous groups supporting all types of activities that can be listed as social, educational, political, charitable, spiritual, and communal. She ventured that HOH probably does the best job on education. She suggested that the toughest question to answer is so what? She sees an important role for the nontheists is to explain their nature to the religious community. In musing over this, it occurs to me that Amanda has not yet recognized that HOH started its many subgroups as a result of the 2007 self-study, reported in section 13.10. Furthermore, in my own opinion, it is important for the humanist movement, its institutions, and individual members all to continually reassess progress from time to time. Religious groups do not do this, which is the cause of their rigidity.

The greatest contribution that contemporary humanism has to make is in the future. For the individual, it is the examination of life that is the ethical requirement, and for society, the examined future is the equivalent imperative. Lifetime, five-year, and annual plans should be de rigueur for humanist organizations. In the future, ethics as a discipline might be expected to evolve and advance: it is definitely not a fundamentalist undertaking. It is clear that human civilization faces considerable challenges. We might be able to extend human life indefinitely; we might be able to design robots of all sizes from the ultrasmall to the size of cities, and these creatures may themselves participate in future engineering. We may encounter extraterrestrial intelligence. We may be able to initiate self-sustaining environments on Earth and build habitable satellites and terraform other planets. Some of these possibilities may seem bizarre and frightening, which is one reason that we should proceed with deliberate speed to assess them. On the other hand, if we advance into the future with vision, we may be on the verge of the most glorious chapters of life's history yet.

It is when we become committed to humanism and join with others in institutional arrangements that we encounter the need for tolerance. There is no one person who precisely embodies the qualities of a quintessential humanist because humanism is a moving target and each generation learns more that is relevant to the task. Even among committed humanists, there are wide differences in education and individual progress. Some of these differences are due to academic and general learning abilities. There are numerous humanistic organizations throughout the USA and the world, and each of these sets different curricula and/or exemplars of conduct. We have to be able to get along with the members of these organizations. Then, of course, there are wide varieties of religious organizations whose congruence with humanist beliefs can be very close in certain respects but counterproductive in others. In some cases, there are religious organizations that actually advocate killing their opponents. We obviously cannot tolerate such conduct or beliefs and will have to uphold the US legal system.

We conclude that humanity, meaning the human race, might be poised on the brink of great changes. But there is another sense of the word *humanity*: the quality of being human, as the dictionary states, or human nature, especially our desirable characteristics. So we should be able to answer the question of where we humans stand today in the evolutionary quest for desirable character. We would like to think, of course, that the person with such qualities would be exemplified in the individual humanist, but we should not be so ungenerous as to claim that only avowed humanists would make that exalted grade. We must be systematic and define our objectives and purpose: the search for humanity and the education of our own members as to our humanist principles. Humanism has to represent the latest paradigms in science, ethics, politics, the arts and practical living. We should learn from the business world the lessons of management, planning and budgeting. There are both optimists and pessimists in predictions of the future. But the evolutionary benefits clearly are on the side of an optimistic outlook. We should have faith in humanity as it struggles to find its way forward. Consider our progress. Life for the individual has been steadily improving over the centuries. We live longer, with less disease, better nutrition, in pleasanter housing. Violence is declining according to Steven Pinker (2011). We are continually learning how to alleviate pain and suffering. Psychology shows us how we can experience loving and secure relationships. It is not necessary to force people into drudgery to earn a living or to lead existences governed by fear. Our quest for humanity is to put meaning into our lives as individuals, and to help other people; to improve the world and ourselves.

14 Humanism and Knowledge

Outline

14.1 Introduction

Socrates, Plato, and Aristotle
2003: Humanism and the Unity of Knowledge
Unifications in Physics
Reduction of Chemistry
Evolution
DNA
Sociobiology

14.2 Recent Advances

Paleoanthropology
Increasing Brain Size
Memory
Human Nature
Computers

14.3 Reasoning and System Science

Neuroscience
Human Nature and Emotion
Artificial Neural Nets
Systems, Constants, and Precedents
Habits
Narratives and History
Syllogisms and Philosophy
Constants and the Laws of Science
The Arts

14.4 Anti-Intellectualism or Respect for Learning

 Universities and Religion
 Hofstadter and Susan Jacoby
 The Role of Teaching in Humanism

14.5 Theories of Everything

 The Standard Model
 Higgs Boson
 Smolin's Theory of Multiverses

14.6 Humanism and Its Moral Imperative

 Success of the Universities
 Specialized and Generalized Knowledge
 Multidisciplinary Research

14.7 Infinite Ignorance

 Popper on Ignorance and Gaps
 The Gap at the Beginning
 Life beyond Earth
 Wheeler's Four Mysteries

14.8 Conclusions

 Humanism as Cosmology
 Humanism as Collegiality

14. Humanism and Knowledge

14.1 Introduction

There are many varieties of knowledge, from the very formal mathematical and scientific rationality, to the poetic, emotional, historical, and trivial. The increased human brain size is what has been crucial to our ability to retain knowledge in memory; and it is to the ancient Mesopotamian, Chinese, Indian, Greek, and Egyptian philosophers that we owe our interest in it. In the previous chapter, we introduced the works of Socrates, Plato, and Aristotle. These people were the first to emphasize the importance of knowledge as the basis for philosophy. Thus, it was Socrates who said, "There is only one good: knowledge. There is only one evil: ignorance."

This saying was quoted by Diogenes Laertius in his book *Lives of Eminent Philosophers* and was quoted again by Arthur Jackson at the beginning of his own book on ethics (2010). Plato founded a school in his garden outside Athens, which he called the Academia, and was himself said to be the first professor. Plato's interest was general while Aristotle developed the specialized disciplines with which we are familiar today. Aristotle founded his own school, the Lyceum, and his philosophy for two thousand years was held to be the basic truth and wisdom of the civilized world. Unfortunately, the curiosity that propelled the growth of science and rationality was curtailed when religion came to dominance at the end of the Roman empire. But fortunately, the search for wisdom was renewed after the 1000 CE millennium when the first modern universities were founded. What is it that has made the universities so successful for the past thousand years? We will concentrate on this question in the present chapter.

In 2003 I wrote a paper "Humanism and the Unity of Knowledge," which told the story of the great unifications of science, starting with physics. Galileo had established the mathematical theory of gravity as it acts on masses close to the earth's surface: bodies fall down with an acceleration toward the center of the earth. Newton showed that the same force of gravity could explain why the planets orbit the sun on an elliptical path. There was another unification in physics when Maxwell showed that electricity and magnetism were just two aspects of the same phenomenon (electromagnetism) and that light was, in fact, an electromagnetic radiation. Many other forms of electromagnetic radiation were found after that (radio, X-rays, gamma rays, etc). Very small objects (atoms, molecules, etc.) were shown to obey quantum mechanics, and then the basic rules of chemistry were discovered to fit in with quantum mechanics, thus unifying chemistry with physics under one theory. These unifications of physical theories are rather like the fitting together of chunks of a jigsaw puzzle. Wilson has termed the process *consilience*. The first fundamental particles were formed in collisions before the big bang. The chemical elements evolved from thermonuclear interactions in the interior of stars according to a theory proposed by Fred Hoyle in 1946. Darwin proposed the theory of biological evolution of species in 1859. Mendel elucidated the laws of genetics. By the middle of the twentieth century, it was clear that natural and sexual selection together with genetics provided the mechanisms to explain biological evolution. Julian Huxley expounded views on evolution as an influence on the growth of the universe before the start of biology and then its continued role after the appearance of humans in language, culture, and technology. Finally, Watson and Crick showed in 1953 how the DNA molecule was the carrier of the genetic information. In effect, this provided a link between biology and chemistry-physics. The paper went on to discuss E. O. Wilson's theories of sociobiology, namely, how human behavior (including morality) might be derived from a knowledge of biology. We pointed out the importance of emotion in morality and religion. Finally, we stressed the importance of education and of creativity for humanism and humanity.

14.2 Recent Advances

It is over ten years since the 2003 paper was written, and there have been many advances in science and thinking that bear on the narrative we have just discussed. First of all, we should mention the impressive work that has been done in paleoanthropology. Donald Johanson became famous in 1974 for his discovery of the fossil now known as Lucy, an Australopithecine, some 3.2 million years old, which was uncovered at Hadar in Ethiopia. Johanson wrote a book with Kate Wong titled *Lucy's Legacy*, which was published in 2009 detailing all the finds up to that date. In that same year, there was a special issue of *Science*, the magazine of the AAAS, devoted to studies of fossils of *Ardipithecus ramidus*, some of which dated back to 4.4 million years ago, thus predating Lucy and coming closer to the time of the last common ancestor of men and chimpanzees. We now know a great deal about these fossils that are presumed to be ancestral humans from careful studies of the habitats, bone measurements, especially of skull and limbs. The hominids seem to have been most closely similar to bonobos among the apes still living. Carbon dating and other chemical methods have shown that the Australopithecines were followed by a succession of hominins including *habilis, ergaster, erectus, heidelbergensis, neanderthalensis*, and *sapiens*. It was as recently as 2001 that diminutive fossils now known as *H. floresiensis* were discovered in Indonesia. One of the interesting aspects of these discoveries, as reported by Dean Falk (2012), is that the size of the brain had increased since the time of the Australopithecines (343–515 cubic centimeters) to the time of *erectus* (909–1,149 cubic centimeters). For comparison, we cite Neanderthals (mean 1,487 cubic centimeters) and (mean 1,330 cubic centimeters) It seems clear that intellectual activity (toolmaking) started with *erectus* and thus correlates with increased brain size.

14.3 Reasoning and Systems Science

The next advance to be mentioned seems to be signaled from the previous section, and that is the continued advance in neuroscience. There are many people working in this area, and it is necessary to search for an authoritative review that pulls all the disparate lines together. One of the best is *Unity of Knowledge: The Convergence of Natural and Human Science* edited by Damasio, Harrington, Kagan, McKewen, Moss, and Shaikh (2001). Another comprehensive review is *Human* by Gazzaniga. One important point made by Gazzaniga is that the uniqueness of the human animal is to be found in our brains. As we have just pointed out, our brains are bigger than those of most other animals and have grown compared with those of our immediate ancestors. Gazzaniga describes how most of the extra tissue is to be found in the anterior cerebral hemispheres and in a number of additional modules with specialized functions. I want to focus on a few sections of Gazzaniga's book with special relevance to the immediate topic. Gazzaniga is best known for his work with split-brain patients. Extreme epileptic seizures could travel from one hemisphere to the other and were almost impossible to control. As a last resort, it was proposed to sever the corpus callosum, which joins the right and left hemispheres. William van Wagenen performed the first procedure to do this. The two hemispheres have different functions, and it was first feared that the result would be a split personality, with two brains in one head. In fact, the treatment was a success: the seizures were greatly abated, and the patients felt fine. In his book, Gazzaniga emphasizes the emotional behavior of chimps and then points out how we humans are also basically driven by emotion. However, we are also capable of switching from one emotional state to another by imagination alone. This is an ability that allows us to learn about the world without having to experience it all firsthand ourselves. This leads him into a discussion of the role of the arts. These abilities depend on our superior human memory power.

Toward the end of the book, he informs us of some theories on memory put forward by Jeff Hawkins. Hawkins's book *On Intelligence* is based on the connectionist ideas developed by the electrical engineers studying artificial neural nets. As Gazzaniga himself points out, the idea here is that the brain is built on hierarchical layers of neurons capable of observing the actions of lower layers. From these observations, we should be able to recognize constants in signals and develop reasoning by using precedents and evaluating syllogisms. This could be the basis of habit formation, the following of rules and laws, their incorporation into systems, and the building up of various sciences, both of natural and the artificial. It is also clear that neuroscience has much to teach us about the notions of culpability on which much of our legal system is based as David Eagleman (2011) has recently recounted.

14.4 Anti-Intellectualism and Education

In the period just after World War II, there was a movement in the USA focused on anti-Communism. The person with whom this was chiefly associated was Senator Joseph McCarthy. The paranoia was so great that Richard Hofstadter (1962) decided to write a book on the subject: *Anti-Intellectualism in American Life*. He pointed out that, in fact, anti-intellectualism was nothing new and that it had waxed and waned during the life of the country and even preceded the revolution. When President Eisenhower expressed his displeasure with the witch hunt, McCarthy and his movement quickly faded away. Hofstadter went on to explain that the phenomenon arose from American Protestantism. A similar message has been delivered recently by Susan Jacoby in her work *The Age of American Unreason* (2008). It is still the Jewish, Christian, and Islamic fundamentalists who believe that traditional religious cosmology and morality should prevail over rational and scientific findings. Respect for learning, science, and academic values continue to be at risk in America and other parts of the world. Since it was memory, language, and knowledge that first set *Homo erectus* on the evolutionary road to progress, and since these very traits are still in jeopardy, I would propose that we treat knowledge as the primary value and first principle of our humanist system. These values have been sufficiently undermined in recent years that we need to teach a humanist curriculum to whoever is willing to listen. A major part of the humanist curriculum should be a course or two on general knowledge. There have been some outstanding contributions in this respect recently, among which we might mention Bill Bryson's *A Short History of Nearly Everything* (2003) and Charles van Doren's *A History of Knowledge* (1991). Another source of knowledge that has become available in recent years is the Internet including *Wikipedia* and the search engines such as Google.

14.5 Theories of Everything

The last thing we should mention is that the reductionist agenda of physics is still very much on the cards. Several more of the forces of nature were incorporated into the scheme after Maxwell's triumph with electromagnetism. At present, all the forces are taken into account except for gravity. What is known as the standard model predicts the existence of all the elementary particles and, in fact, predicts the existence of one more, the so-called Higgs boson, which has now been created by the new supercollider at CERN in Europe. The Higgs field is believed to be the means for the evolution of the protons, neutrons, and electrons that are the building blocks for atoms. Thus, another step in evolution has been confirmed. There is also a theory proposed by Smolin that universes evolve and that reality might encompass "multiverses," perhaps containing the dark matter believed to be responsible for the accelerating expansion that has been found. Another exciting development in the area of astronomy is the discovery of planets orbiting other stars, which may even house life, which may even be intelligent. But it seems to me that it is the ability to recognize and invent new systems with emergent properties that is the single most important human ability and the one we humanists need to study the most closely.

14.6 Humanism and Its Moral Imperative

We return now to discussing the task of unifying science, which Wilson saw as the moral imperative of humanism. I argued in a previous essay (see Finch, 2002) that the local humanist group should be compared with a university in its function. But what we are seeking is a variety of university that has largely departed the scene. The opening piece in the Columbia centenary volume was written by Felice Battaglia (1955), professor of Moral Philosophy and the Philosophy of Law and rector of the University of Bologna. His assignment was to describe what accounted for the success of the university at its outset around the year 1000. His conclusion was that success came from the fact that it stressed universality in corporate structure, with masters and students working and living together, and in the universality of the knowledge pursued. At that time, as we have already mentioned, the unity of knowledge derived from theological concepts and natural law. Nowadays, the curriculum for our humanistic universities should cover a wide range of the history of ideas, ethics, comparative religion, psychology, management, sociology, economics, and politics. But we should also be striving for a sense of community similar in many ways to the college of those bygone days. Humanism also has to serve as an alternative to religion. The cognitive aspects of knowledge do not, however, fully substitute for the emotional role of religion. Huxley has stressed that religion grew around the feelings of the sacred. I would claim that humanism itself has to be regarded as sacred in the sense of being entitled to the highest respect. We need to define and emphasize the values that humanism implies. If religion is a vehicle for values, then humanism is a religion. The time that we spend in community meetings and work, writing manifestos and summaries and elucidating our principles, help in laying down long-term memories, thereby strengthening our confidence in humanist values and unifying our knowledge.

Jeffery's book (1950) contains an eloquent defense of the old Cambridge college system. He regretted that the founders of London University had passed over the old college model in their drive for economy, specialized knowledge being so much cheaper to impart. Here we see the source of C. P. Snow's two cultures (or even more cultures). Is it possible (or even desirable) to bring the cultures together? The first thing to observe is that there are many circumstances when different branches of knowledge become relevant to a particular problem. It has become fashionable to refer to such as interdisciplinary fields. So we have such areas as computerized acquisition of medical data or radio-carbon dating of archeological artifacts. But this overlooks the fact that the most important interdisciplinary field of all is the life of the individual human being. Every one of us has the prospect of a lifetime full of momentous decisions. How well we do this is a measure of the wisdom and maturity of our education and of the communities with which we associate. This is the challenge that Wilson sees for the humanist movement. Humanism is a search for the best ways for humans to live. Individual humanists are all researchers exploring different lifestances and social arrangements. Our chapters are analogous to universities where we come together to compare notes and record our findings.

The movement as a whole is analogous to an academic society. When we spend time defining the principles of humanism, we are, in fact, elucidating the main lessons we have learned on the search for the best ways of living. It is not a coincidence that the attributes of God are often found to coincide with the highest moral qualities of human beings. One of the major roles for humanism is to offer an alternative to religion in offering life-stance choices for the individual.

14.7 Infinite Ignorance

Karl Popper once commented that we are all equal in the infinite extent of our ignorance. The body of organized knowledge has grown enormously throughout history, but there are still many gaps and puzzles in what we know. Many of the gaps and puzzles involve extensions of science, which seem feasible in the near future. Their resolution may simply be of academic interest, but more likely, they will bring revolutionary changes to our conception of the world and the way we live. Furthermore, we remain ignorant of most of the space in the universe, of its history and its future. Much of the work of closing gaps and solving puzzles will be done by specialists in the various disciplines, but the humanist and generalist will become increasingly involved in reconnoitering and monitoring the whole field. Popper himself was one of the great philosophers of science, and he described its growth in terms of conjectures and refutations. This work will be an important part of the "graduate program" for humanism. We cannot even comment on all the aspects of a program with such a wide scope, but in what follows, we may perhaps point to its main subdivisions.

Mathematics and physics are the central disciplines in the body of science. There have been many unifications of parts of physics that have gradually extended the range of phenomena explained, and now chemistry and biology are being drawn into the picture. But there are gaps and puzzles that remain. We still have not produced the theory of everything, which will bring gravity into a unified physical theory. There are many mysteries surrounding the big bang and how the universe got started. We still cannot be sure of the fate of the universe. Perhaps other universes exist and can evolve. We still do not know for sure how life got its start. We still cannot predict the shape and configuration of any but the smallest molecules. We do not understand the mechanisms of the epigenetic rules postulated by E. O. Wilson. We may elucidate the mechanisms of death and find ways to circumvent them. We do not know if life has originated in other parts of the universe. We do not know if intelligent life and civilization has started elsewhere. We have never received a signal from another civilization. Here on Earth, there are still many mysteries surrounding the functioning of the brain. But this too is becoming a part of the body of natural science, leaving behind the old mind/body dualism. Even the most difficult issues of memory, consciousness, and emotions are beginning to yield. As we learn more of brain physiology, so some of the ancient puzzles in epistemology will be answered. Perhaps we will resolve the issue of whether knowledge is representational or a form of action and how cognition, emotion, and volition are tied together at a fundamental level. We may achieve a better understanding of the connection between knowledge as stored in the human brain and information theory. As brain science develops, psychology and psychiatry are also being revolutionized. Mental illnesses are increasingly being treated with pharmaceuticals.

Some of the most basic questions in the unification literature concerns physical cosmology. John Wheeler was invited to give the closing address at the Hermann Weyl Centenary Congress in 1985. Between them, these two men have made enormous contributions to modern cosmology. Wheeler's address was published as an article in *American Scientist* (1986), showing the width of Weyl's vision and accomplishments, and was also an exposition of some of the contributions that Wheeler and his students have made to the field. One very important issue is information theory. It has been shown by Wheeler's student Bekenstein that information has a physical correlate, entropy, and Wheeler points out that thermodynamics or statistical mechanics is a part of information theory. Weyl related information theory to the genetic code and was intrigued by the fact that only a limited number of molecular possibilities actually function as genes. Wheeler sees four great mysteries to be explained. The first is existence itself: why is there something rather than nothing? He feels that this may have a connection to the anthropic principle. The second mystery is the quantum. That quantum theory works is beyond dispute. The arguments concern the significance of the wave function. One interpretation of it is as a probability that a given particle will be found in a given place. This was the viewpoint that Einstein found so unacceptable. He worked to find a causal interpretation instead, and others have followed in his footsteps. Another viewpoint has it that the particle being described can occupy any of multiple universes. But no description has so far been completely successful. Wheeler believes that eventually we will have an explanation of utter simplicity that will be completely obvious when we see it. The third mystery that Wheeler sees is the continuum of the natural numbers. He argues that it does not physically exist, but yet we use the concept of its existence in our exposition of physics. Why is mathematics so unreasonably effective? We assume, for example, that time comprises an infinite continuum. Why time exists is the fourth of Wheeler's mysteries. There is, says Wheeler, a deep and hidden connection between time and existence: to explain the one we will need to explain the other. A recent book by Max Tegmark (2014) suggests that ultimately everything is mathematics.

14.8 Conclusions

We have seen that the phrase *the unity of knowledge* covers a variety of phenomena, which, on the face of it, do not have much connection. In the first place, it can refer to a process in which knowledge of different types is brought together with the intention of finding relationships between the ideas presented. Thus, there have been a series of conferences and proceedings on the theme. The point has been made that the university, as it was originally constituted, helped to bring about the unification of knowledge in the minds of the collegians who attended. The specialization of the academic disciplines that has occurred over the past century or so, with whatever benefits may have accrued, has been the enemy of unification. In the second place, we have seen that knowledge, in that it refers to mental activity, covers many phenomena: sense data, emotions and feelings, memories, intuitions, rational deductions, theories, and stories. Some of these lie in the private subjective worlds of the individual mind, but some of them are also cultural artifacts developed in the social interactions of several or many individuals. In the third place, the phrase could refer to highly formal accretions of knowledge such as the unified theories of physics, information theory, systems theory, and evolution. The humanities and human sciences also fall under this heading although the degree to which they are unified remains contentious. Finally, the phrase may refer to the religions or cosmologies in which we postulate the human position in the universe.

Returning to the question with which we started this essay, we can see that the unity of knowledge is relevant to humanism in all these senses. At the highest level, humanism is a cosmology. Its relation to religion is an ongoing subject of investigation. The persistence of religions of all varieties is similarly a topic for humanist research. We humanists continue to be fascinated by the unifications of physics and systems theory especially as they bear on the human condition. The unification community has not organized into any permanent society. This presents a great opportunity for organized humanism. Our annual conferences have always honored those scientists, literati, and luminaries of the world of affairs who have brought new light to bear on our general condition. Such conferences could consciously become platforms for progress in the unification of knowledge. Humanism itself is a noetic integrator. Unification can be a part of the research program of humanism. Summarizing the state of the art and the best of practices is a crucial part of the humanist agenda. There is a need for people with general knowledge and wisdom in its application to monitor the body of knowledge, which has been built up over the years. We could probably learn from religious organizations the importance of emotions and the value of community. But there is a problem with religious organizations we need to avoid at all costs, namely, the preservation of ancient superstitions and the failure to learn from experience and the intolerance, which is especially the hallmark of fundamentalism. We humanists might be better served by learning lessons from the universities by structuring our communities like colleges and making our organizational objective the systematic exploration of the unifications of knowledge.

15 Economics, Capitalism, and Prosperity

15. Economics, Capitalism, and Prosperity

15.1 Introduction

Now we are investigating the great objective system concepts in humanism, as John Stuart Mill called them. We discussed systems previously and how we humans have used systems to build our culture. The family was one of the first of the social systems we inherited, and this was the subject of a previous chapter. As human families expanded into tribal groups and defined territories for themselves, they at first were inclined to react with hostility when encountering their neighbors. Matt Ridley, in *The Rational Optimist* (2010), surmised that it was evolution of the impulse to sociality that allowed *Homo sapiens* to understand that they were encountering others with similar emotions to their own. In this way, our ancestors were able to realize the benefits of bartering and the exchange of goods. This ability distinguished *Homo sapiens* from the Neanderthals and all previous humans and allowed a vast expansion in the ideas and resources available to our species. Ridley contended that this was the start of the economic prosperity that marks our provenance. On the other hand, Peter Singer (1995) presents some research he has done showing how some of our contemporary economic problems also arose from the same historical background.

If we ask how the economy ought to be run, then we are making economics a part of ethics. But this is an issue that has given rise to schools of thought that are poles apart and are still strongly in contention. On the one hand, Ayn Rand and Alan Greenspan still have many followers for the views they expressed in their 1967 book *Capitalism: the Unknown Ideal.* Ethicists have also been very critical of aspects of capitalism as evidenced in works such as Peter Singer's *How Are We to Live?* (1993). That book challenges the pervasiveness of the commercial mind-set and its money-seeking values. Does the economic system bring fundamental benefits to humanity?

The first chapter of Ridley's book is devoted to describing the unprecedented prosperity we live in. He relates the fantastic success of the human species. He cites numerous facts and statistics to make his case overwhelming. Why has this happened? Because of cultural evolution, he explains.

15.2 Progress

Our collective brain has grown because of exchange and specialization in the two million year interval since humans first emerged. Nowadays, the world GDP is growing explosively. By 2050 the human race will have grown from ten million to ten billion in ten thousand years; and the vast majority are better fed, better housed, healthier, and are more likely to live longer than any of their ancestors. This generation has more calories, watts, lumen-hours, square feet, gigabytes, megahertz, light-years, nanometers, bushels per acre, miles per gallon, air miles, dollars, etc. Life expectancy in England in 1800 was less than forty years. Pollution is down. Life expectancy increases at a quarter of a year per year in the longest-lived countries. Nor is it true that that the quality of life in old age is decreasing. IQ is increasing especially among those with lower scores. Forensic use of DNA is improving identification of suspects and exonerating many innocent people. Light is getting cheaper. The true measure of something's worth is the number of hours it takes to acquire it. There has been a general increase in happiness. Unfortunately, there is a "crunch": life today is not good because of war, disease, corruption, and hate. There is a credit crunch. But these things will not in the long run "prevent the relentless upward march of human living standards." It is the cumulative accretion of knowledge by specialists that allows us each to consume more and more different things by each producing fewer and fewer, and this is the central story of humanity. How did this habit begin?

15.3 Trust and Barter

Ridley shows an illustration of a stereotypical bifaced axe of the Stone Age. Hominids made this same tool for about a million years in Europe, the Middle East, Near East, and Northwest Europe; and it did not change. The bodies and brains of the men who made these axes changed faster than the design. But by about 160,000 years ago, a new slender faced *Homo sapiens* was living in Ethiopia and around Pinnacle Point in S. Africa. Then came hints of trade in shells and obsidian. In Europe at about the same time, the ancestors of the Neanderthals, also with big brains, showed no signs of long-distance trade. About eighty thousand years ago, one quite small group of people began to spread over most of Africa, as shown by L3 mitochondrial-type genetic markers. About fifty thousand years ago, they spilled out of Africa and exploded into global dominion.

Ridley argues that the change was due to an improvement in ethics, the manufacture of virtue: trust and rules. It was on this basis that the new economics was founded. Technology and habits changed faster than anatomy. Humans began to build a collective intelligence by bartering. There is little use of barter by other animals. Barter is more than the swapping of favors, but in Adam Smith's words: "Give me that which I want, and you shall have this which you want."

15.4 Farming

Agriculture began about ten thousand years ago. In the conventional account, stored surpluses were made possible by agriculture, but Ridley says this is the wrong way around and that agriculture came about because of trade. Trade provided the incentive to specialize in farmed goods. Around 11,500 years ago, the temperature of the Greenland ice cap shot up by ten degrees; and the Natufian culture started to farm chickpeas, rye, and einkorn wheat. Exchange of grain for meat subsidized housing. Was agriculture invented to feed the first cities? The Greeks were among the first traders, and they were the ones who established agricultural colonies. Flooding of the Black Sea around 7,600 years ago sent refugees to northern Europe with wheat crops. Burning down forest yields soft, friable soil with high wheat yields. Thus, farming spread rapidly, and smoke from fires produced carbon dioxide and may have helped raise the temperature to its maximum six thousand years ago. Life in primitive agricultural communities was not idyllic as Ridley shows in detail. It may have worsened sexual inequality and promoted patriarchy. There was constant violence. The Industrial Revolution caused population to explode. But canals, steamships, railways, refrigeration, and the reaper-binder kept famine at bay. Then in 1830 came the discovery of fertilizer on islands off the South American and African coasts. This was followed by the invention of the Haber process of fixing atmospheric nitrogen. Still, by the 1960s, in Asia it seemed populations were on the verge of mass starvation. But then between 1952 and 1962, this situation had been reversed by Norman Borlaug's work on genetic engineering.

15.5 Cities

According to Ridley, cities exist for trade. They appeared roughly simultaneously in river valleys in several parts of the world about seven thousand years ago. The first were found in the Euphrates Valley where Ubaid-style pottery, clay sickles, and houses appeared. A class of middlemen and traders came into existence. Kings and priests arose. Uruck was the largest city with fifty thousand inhabitants under the kingship of Gilgamesh. Taxation and slavery soon followed. Late in the Uruck period, we find clay tablets used for accounting and writing. Specialists appeared among the working class. The first instance of mass production of pots is evidenced. The flag follows trade according to Ridley; and Uruck was followed by a succession of empires: Sumerian, Akkadian, Assyrian, Babylonian, Persian, Hellenistic, Roman, Parthian, Abbasid, Mongol, Timurid, Ottoman, British, Saddamite, and Bushite. There were similar patterns along the Nile, the Indus, and the Yellow Rivers. Akkadia had silver-based prices but no coinage. But it did have businesses with head offices, branch offices (including some in foreign territory), corporate hierarchies, extraterritorial business law, foreign investment, value-added activity, profit sharing, and investor partners.

The Philistines invented iron; the Canaanites, the alphabet; and the Phoenicians, glass. The Mediterranean Sea was a natural location for trade, and the Greeks established ports, starting with Tyre, all around its shores. The merchants realized that it would be of great benefit if they had some common items of permanent value to use as a medium of exchange for seasonable or perishable goods. Thus, it was that pieces of metal and later gold and silver coins were introduced into commerce. The upshot of this was that some merchants became extremely rich by hoarding the coins. Eventually, the government was drawn into the new technology that needed to be standardized and regulated. Plato's reaction was that the new government class should not themselves be compensated so that they would not be corrupted. In contrast, Aristotle recognized that it is part of human nature to want to acquire goods to meet one's needs, although if the acquisition ran to greed, it would provoke resentment. It was for this reason that the practice of charging interest encountered opposition right up till modern times.

In India, Asoka's government was very efficient and supported private firms. The invention of zero was accomplished there. Rome ruled from the Ganges to the Tiber and to Hadrian's Wall. But the Romans "discovered" India, and so the collective brain of humanity was extended across the entire Indian Ocean. Glass blowing was a Roman invention, and shipments of Roman glass made it to China while silk traveled to Europe. But the empire was corrupt, and even Cicero is said to have pocketed a fortune while he was governor of Cilicia. Learning barely survived the dark times and the invasions by Huns and Visigoths. After the Dark Ages, when the West recovered in the Renaissance, the city of Florence was a leader in reestablishing humanistic civilization.

15.6 Economic Evolution

How then can we decide if economic theory is consistent with ethics or otherwise? It seems to me that this can be done, and that it is worth doing so, by considering each of the major developments in economic history. Human economics started with our hunting and gathering ancestors and grew, as we evolved, to include varieties of agriculture and bartering for goods and services. The invention of money permitted a vast extension of the variety of goods available, and eventually, there came coinage employing precious metals and standardization by the proto-state. Prices were most efficiently set in the marketplace where participants could exercise free choice. The use of money also permitted the convenient accumulation of wealth (or "capital"). This, in turn, permitted the growth of banking. The banks devised various ways to lend money to individuals and groups, including the use of "bonds," which later became the main vehicles for companies as well as governmental organizations needing to raise large capital sums. During the Middle Ages, the joint stock company was invented. Merchant ships were sent to distant parts of the world, and the financing of these voyages were among the first incentives to capital formation as described by Fulcher (2004). The concept of insurance was developed at about this time to help mitigate possible losses to company capital. Stock exchanges came soon after this. Each of these innovations could be considered an ethical improvement because they benefited some people without harming anyone. The laws of property that had been developed empirically were finally provided with a philosophical basis by John Locke (1666). It was finally understood that money is a form of promise, and if the promise giver is true to his word, there is no need for any physical embodiment in terms of gold coins. Of course, each innovation also presented opportunities for dishonesty; and thus, each one had to be followed by legal refinements.

15.7 The Growth of Capitalism

Malthus predicted that population would grow to such a point that starvation would result. What Malthus did not anticipate was that with the introduction of birth control, and as women became better educated and the survival rate of children improved with better health care, so the birth rate would begin to diminish. Thus, in Europe, North America, and Japan, there has been a decrease in population growth. Similarly, the same trend is showing up in India and China. Thus, UN demographic projections are showing the world population as peaking out within the next century.

Ridley has an excellent chapter on energy whose theme is that the development of steam power and electricity has released millions of people from lives of drudgery and enabled them to live in freedom. Ridley is characteristically optimistic about the prospects for future energy sources.

Another concept in the evolution of capitalism is the "invention of invention," which is very similar to the thoughts of Ray Kurzweil on singularity and those of Kevin Kelly on technology. The process of invention is getting faster and faster. Eventually, we will rely on machines increasingly to speed the process, including the use of machines to design new machines.

15.8 Pessimism

As humanists, we should be striving for optimism. But among the population at large, pessimism abounds. Julian Simon was roundly condemned for his optimism in the 1990s, but no significant error was found in his book. Ridley says he has "listened to implacable predictions of growing poverty, coming famines, expanding deserts, imminent plagues, impending water wars, inevitable oil exhaustion, mineral shortages, falling sperm counts, thinning ozone, acidifying rain, nuclear winters, mad-cow epidemics, Y2K computer bugs, killer bees, sex-change fish, global warming, ocean acidification, and even asteroid impacts that would presently bring this happy interlude to a terrible end . . . he cannot recall a time when he was not being urged by somebody that the world could only survive if it abandoned the foolish goal of economic growth."

Ridley agrees that if the world continues as it is, it will end in disaster. But draws attention to the conditional *if*. The world will *not* continue as it is. His point is that the human race has become a collective problem-solving machine. The pessimists' mistake is to assume the future is just a bigger version of the past. Thomas Watson said in 1943 that there was a world market for five computers. We could cite many more gloomy and even ludicrous prophecies, but the overall trend in our history has been progressive. Ridley counters this outpouring of pessimism by taking the arguments one by one.

15.9 Capitalism and Ethics

Economics is an academic discipline, and it is interesting to inquire how economists define their subject. Samuelson avers that a general definition would be economics is the study of how people and society end up choosing, with or without the use of money, to employ scarce productive resources that could have alternative uses, to produce various commodities and distribute them for consumption, now or in the future, among various persons and groups in society. It analyzes the costs and benefits of improving patterns of resource allocation.

The ethical system is measured by how well our behavior agrees with our moral estimation and the benefits to people or, if the behavior is unethical, then how well do we recognize the problems and plan to correct them. Value in the economic system is, of course, conveyed by the actual goods and services purveyed. The boundaries of economics have been determined historically by these other systems through the limits of knowledge and the rules of government and law.

There have been times when capitalist systems have clearly resulted in unethical behavior. Cheating by using deficient weights and measures was endemic for centuries but was finally controlled by tough laws and rigorous standards. It was necessary to introduce laws to prohibit child labor and to permit workers to join unions among other examples of the control of unethical practices. Peter Singer has been one of the principal advocates of animal rights, and his work has led to considerable reductions in the cruelties of animal husbandry. We are also beginning to moderate the adverse effects of commerce on the environment as another result of ethical thinking. Singer's book starts by reciting the case of Ivan Boesky who demonstrated how to make a fortune by insider trading. There have always been fraudulent financiers who have lured investors into Ponzi schemes such as the recent instances with Bernard Madoff.

15.10 Manias and Crises

Manias and financial crises have had a long history. Some of the earliest, including the Mississippi Scheme and the South Sea Bubble were recounted by MacKay in his book of 1841. Kindleberger (1989) updated the account with details of many more financial crises and an analysis of what had been learned from them. Of course, the most severe was the Great Depression of 1929 and its aftermath. The central banks of the World, including the US Federal Reserve, and those countries' governments were all involved in the effort to correct the problem. But by the end of millennium, the lessons learned had been forgotten and our new century started with the "dot com" collapse and then came the financial crisis of 2008. The latter has been the most severe since 1929 and has raised several questions.

We might ask, what were the causes of the recent financial crisis? Was it the result of a defect in the capitalist system itself, or was it due to some unethical or even criminal behavior on the part of certain individuals? If so, who was to get the blame? The proximate causes clearly lay in such practices as the issuing of mortgages to people who could not afford to keep up their payments. These "subprime" instruments were encouraged by mortgage companies in the United States and Britain and then financed by many banks. After the event, it became clear to everyone, including the buyers and sellers, that new mortgage holders should be able to maintain their payments and that the abandonment of regulation on this was the next element in the causal chain leading to the 2008 crisis. In this case, it seems that some part of the blame attaches to those who purchased such mortgages and some to those who knowingly promoted the mortgages but also some part belonged to those who were responsible for, or who connived at the abandonment of regulation. Soros (2008) traces the problem back to the deregulation policies of the Reagan and Thatcher administrations and their successors. Johnson and Kwak (2010) place blame on the banks who pleaded for and obtained bailouts and painted them as being lured by greed, having taken over Wall Street, if not the government in Washington.

15.11 Regulation

Communist Russia as well as the social democracies of western Europe provided us with lessons on the failure of complete government takeover of the economy or nationalization of individual firms. But the failure of the opposite extreme, of unregulated capitalism, has only been shown by the policies of governments in the United States and Britain since the time of the Reagan and Thatcher administrations. Fortunately, we now have laws against insider trading, but we also need to enforce the laws because the temptation to engage in the practice can be very great. According to Soros (2008) and Posner (2009), the recent excesses came to fruition in the financial crisis of 2008. Soros and Posner have both attested to the unethical conduct resulting from deregulation and the need for renewed government supervision. Posner, an appeals court judge, draws the conclusion that the majority of the activity was simply the normal practice of economic operations within the framework of guidelines set by legislation and government regulation. But it is clear to everyone, including the buyers and sellers, that the abandonment of regulation on mortgage borrowing was the next element in the causal chain leading to the 2008 crisis. In this case, it seems that at least some blame attaches to those who were responsible for or connived at the abandonment of regulation.

15.12 Government Intervention in Capitalism

Economic theories have been developed to explain the occurrence of financial crises notably in the work of von Mises (1912), who actually drew on earlier ideas of Hume and Ricardo. Unfortunately, von Mises's book did not attract much attention in the Anglophone world until the events of 1929 when Keynes (1932) presented an analysis that actually influenced the course of events in Britain and the United States. World War II finally brought the Depression to an end, and this was followed by a period in which Samuelson and a newly quantitative economics held sway. Milton Friedman helped to spread the ideas of von Mises and the Austrian school. The 2008 crisis resulted in a number of companies facing bankruptcy with a threat of widespread economic hardship. The government reactions to this problem in the United States and other countries have been to step in to help the troubled companies with large loans, even at the cost of rising budget deficits. This, in turn, has prompted companies that had avoided unethical conduct and remained in good economic condition to complain that the government measures were unfairly favoring their competition. If capitalism is indeed to be regarded as a part of the ethical system, then it seems only correct that the government should put restrictions on its loans in the form of required repayments with interest and limiting salaries and other behavior in the assisted companies. The government is nothing other than an arrangement to serve the people, and we have now found numerous ways to benefit from such collective activities ranging from policing and defense to health services and education and research in science and astronomical exploration. All these are beneficial and ethical activities. The conclusion is that judicious government intervention can stimulate the economy and keep it on a steady course.

15.13 Management and Investment

Modern capitalism and entrepreneurial humanism were twin products of the Italian Renaissance, led by the de Medici family who rose to prominence through their expertise and innovations in banking. Management is the province of the business schools and practicing corporations and is a major contribution to the modern world quite on a par with the ethics taught by philosophy departments. Let us look to the positive side of capitalist management. Merchants, traders, and workers have gradually come to realize that ethical behavior builds trust and that the situation is then better than close legal supervision. The whole subject of management was developed at the behest of industry by such luminaries as Peter Drucker (1973). The key to the literature on the subject is the process of planning. From its very start, a well-managed company has to have a concept of its purpose and direction. The company has to decide which goods and services it is to produce and then raise the capital necessary to start production. Most companies need to plan over several years and anticipate the markets in which sales will be made in order to provide the staff and infrastructure necessary. Innovations and inventions are being made continuously, and as time goes on, there will be a need for research on changes in the world that might impact the company's way of business.

There is a section in Samuelson's *Economics* that describes the role of the investor in the capitalist system. Samuelson distinguishes four main classes of investor. The first are those who buy and hold. Because the national economy has a long-term upward trend, these people fare reasonably well over the long run. Conversely, it must not be forgotten that it is investment that fuels the growth of the economy and the companies that comprise it. The same point is made in Siegel's book *Stocks for the Long Run*. The second are traders, i.e., people who watch the market and buy and sell hour by hour. Samuelson's comment is that these people usually only make money for their brokers. The traders may not do themselves much good, but they do perform a valuable service in that they enable anyone to liquidate holdings at any time. The third are speculators who play intermediate swings of many months or years. Such people may do quite well if they discern underlying company, industry, and GNP conditions. The fourth are individuals who study special situations (bankruptcies, stock dividends, split-ups, and mergers). In each of these cases, it seems that there is a beneficial role to be played by the investors, and it seems reasonable to assert that they are all acting ethically.

There is a need for instruction on the details of investment. The humanist needs to be versed in the use of stocks and bonds as well as portfolios of mutual funds and the newer instruments such as exchange traded funds (ETFs) and hedge funds. We have great exemplars such as Warren Buffett and numerous others to follow.

15.14 Progress and Economic Growth

It is interesting that John Maynard Keynes is seen as an exemplar of ethical thinking in economics by his biographer, Robert Skidelsky (2009). Skidelsky points out that Keynes was a student of G. E. Moore, a leading ethicist of his day, and that Keynes was committed to Moore's point of view throughout his life. The strength of Keynes's legacy was not so much his economic theories as his practical political influence on the course of the Great Depression. Another great economist of the twentieth century was Ludwig von Mises, the prophet of monetarism who drew on the thinking of David Ricardo and David Hume, one of the greatest of humanist philosophers. We might argue that both of these men, Keynes and von Mises, are beacons of humanist economics. Von Mises showed how the poor might hope to grow wealthy by following economic principles while Keynes, a wealthy and successful investor, championed the obligation of the wealthy to intervene in the economy when the climate was filled with fear.

There is an excellent book that covers the philosophical aspects of economics by Robert L. Heilbroner (1986). The work reviews the lives, times, and ideas of the great economic thinkers from Adam Smith to Joseph Schumpeter. One of the topics discussed is the prognostication for the capitalist system itself. Adam Smith was very optimistic on the outlook whereas Thomas Malthus, as we have already mentioned, was exceedingly pessimistic. He believed that resources grew arithmetically, whereas the population grew geometrically so that eventually there would Not be Enough to Go Around the communal table. Marx believed that the demise of capitalism was inevitable and that it would be replaced by Communism. John Maynard Keynes was much more sanguine; and even in 1930, during the Great Depression, he forecast that the economy would grow until by 2030 the problem of Not Enough to Go Around would be solved. Everybody could then easily be given a generous helping at the communal table. Joseph Schumpeter in his book *Capitalism, Socialism and Democracy* propounded a new economic model in which profits accrued to capitalists who employed the work of entrepreneurs on inventions and innovations to lower the costs of production. He also coined the phrase *creative destruction* to highlight the process whereby unprofitable businesses could be eliminated under the capitalist system. He maintained there would be a gradual evolution toward some form of socialism.

Heilbroner explains that Schumpeter's view was that the final fate of capitalism would be in the hands of an elite class of neo-aristocrats. The conclusion is that visionary entrepreneurs will provide the profits to allow capitalists to grow and share wealth with everybody. The wealth could be held in endowment funds for families, schools, universities,

and all sorts of public associations, including humanist groups. The
majority of people could look forward to lives of independent means.
As humanists, we can believe that the steady evolutionary advances of
knowledge and incremental improvements of the economic systems are
what will permit everyone to become wealthy. We have ample support
for this case by simply looking at the stock market whose rise for
two hundred years in the USA has been documented by Siegel's book
(1998). All manner of problems have been encountered during this time
but overcome by scientific and technological ingenuity and political and
business acumen. Investors who have been convinced of the viability
of businesses and who have bought and held on to their positions have
been well rewarded. We have only to think of such pioneers as Cornelius
Vanderbilt, Dale Carnegie, John Rockefeller, Henry Ford, Charles Hall
(at Alcoa), Juan Trippe (at Pan Am) Graham Alexander Bell, Bernard
Baruch, John Templeton, Steve Jobs, Bill Gates, and Warren Buffett, to
name a few, and realize that such advances are indeed possible.

16: Humanism, Politics, and Law

Outline

16. Humanism, Politics, and Law

16.1 Introduction

Thus far, we have covered philosophy, history, religion, ethics, social issues, and economics as they relate to humanist ethics. In this chapter, our subject is humanism, politics and the law; and we are asking such questions as What is justice? Is the law ethical? What is right, and what is wrong? What is virtuous, and what is illicit? Is there a difference between public and private morality? What role should society play in regulating the conduct of the individual? What is the proper balance between the good of society and individual freedom? Is there a humanist ethics, humanist politics, or humanist law? We may think of ethics as the largely informal network of relationships and arrangements that enable people to live together in various communities. The law, however, is the more formal set of systems that codifies actual societal agreements on behavior, including penalties for infringements. There is thus a relationship between ethics and law. Systems of law or of ethics may, however, pertain to groups much smaller in size than a nation state. Thus, most religions and political jurisdictions have their own systems of law and/or ethics. The humanist movement has numerous such systems in place (or under development) as well as opinions on desirable systems for the larger social communities.

16.2 Evolution of the Law

There is an excellent summary on law in *Wikipedia* from which we may draw a few salient points. Every community has had to deal with conflicts and problems of ordinary people. We may surmise that law began with the establishment by custom of rules for the primitive regulation of society in respect of marriage, property, and social status. Eventually, it was realized that there were advantages in writing these laws down; and we see the codes of Hammurabi in Mesopotamia and similar records in ancient China, India, and Egypt. The same solon who pioneered democracy in Athens was also credited with advising a deputation of Roman citizens on law at half a millennium BC according to historians. The scribes who took down the proceedings were the start of the legal profession, and their product constituted the start of legal libraries and legal education. Roman law was in force for a thousand years and eventually covered contracts, property, wills, torts, domestic relations, and crime. Roman law became the basis for the systems in most countries in Europe (including Scotland) and in Ethiopia. In England, however, what was called the common law grew independently and was notable for developing the jury system among other innovations. Some lectures on English law were started by Blackstone in 1753 at Oxford for the benefit of country gentlemen and clergymen. According to Blackstone (1765–69), the common law contained the common sense of the community as crystallized and formulated by the country's forefathers. The distinction between case law and statutory law probably also arises from this same Anglo-Saxon origin and the transportation of British customs across the Atlantic. All these systems had to be connected with means for enacting legislation, at first religious, then monarchial, but later incorporating democratic institutions. It is interesting from our point of view that the concept of rights such as equality before the law, to a fair trial, to freedom of speech and religion were all developed first within the legal system. Clearly, such rights have to be financed and protected by society at large, and this was recognized by the British in their Declaration of Rights in 1689, as described by Michael Barone (2007) and later incorporated as amendments to the US Constitution.

Politics behind the creation of law can probably be traced all the way back to prehistory, but we credit the Mesopotamians and Chinese with the earliest legal codification and the Greeks and Romans with the first articulations of political and social theory. They were the first to express such concepts as rights, justice, and law. The philosophy of law has a long history that goes back to ancient Rome when the name of *jurisprudence* was attached to the body of judgments of the College of Pontiffs according to *Wikipedia*. Aristotle posited the existence of natural justice, rights, and laws. His views were accepted and developed in later millennia by Thomas Aquinas, thereby surviving till modern times.

16.3 Hume and Utilitarianism

In a previous chapter, we spelled out the development of humanist ethical theory. Hobbes (1651), as an atheist, proposed the first social theory to replace God with a human king but posited a preexisting state of nature. One of the most incisive thinkers on the matters of both ethics and the law was David Hume (1777 b) who realized that government began in the "woods and deserts." Adair (1976) pointed out that James Madison was a reader of Hume's work and introduced some of Hume's ideas into the US Constitution. Hume saw that our ethology rests on our natural desires and motivations (our "passions" as he put it) and was the first to propose that legal systems should be based on utilitarian principles, i.e., on the same desires for what humans wish to achieve. After Hume died, utilitarianism continued to be influential on English law through the work of Bentham (1789) and John Stuart Mill (1879). Marx was the first to set out a complete social theory as an explanation of the working of our morality, laws, and institutions. Popper (1957) argued that no social prediction based on historical observation can be exactly "true," and it has become clear that Marx was wrong in his idea that it was the economy that determined everything else. But it is still recognized that the economy is a part of the total social system within which we live, and it thus plays an important part in the scheme of things.

16.4 Justice

Statutory law advances through the actions of legislators, and case law comes from the arguments of lawyers in court. These people may or may not have philosophical or ethical considerations in mind. There have been attempts to develop philosophical systems independent of the actual law. One such system is the utilitarian paradigm, which we have already mentioned. But it became clear that this approach overlooked certain well-established ideas. Foremost among these were the requirements of justice as brought into the picture by among others, Immanuel Kant (1785), John Stuart Mill (1861), and Henry Sidgwick (1874). How can we organize a society, which is *just* in the distribution of goods, rights, and liberties? How can power be justly distributed? And how should retributive justice be administered? Kant and Sidgwick pioneered the concepts of universality and equality within the field of ethics, although, of course, both had been initially conceived in the practice of law. Kant arrived at the idea of world government from his thoughts on universality.

John Stuart Mill was the principal exponent of utilitarianism in Britain during the nineteenth century. His essay on utilitarianism was a somewhat modified version of Bentham's ideas. He was also celebrated as the author of the essay *On Liberty* (1849), which many people regard as the foremost exposition of libertarianism. He applied his ideas to the question of the subjection of women (1869) and came to the conclusion that the primary objective of feminist politics had to be the granting of voting rights to women. He actually proposed this in a bill to parliament in 1867. Although the bill was narrowly defeated and he lost his parliamentary seat in the next year, he was thought of as the father of feminism in Britain for many years thereafter. Women were finally granted complete suffrage in Britain in 1928.

16.5 Ethics and the Law

There was an earlier exposition on law as it relates to ethics and humanism in Robert Grant's *American Ethics and the Virtuous Citizen: Basic Principles* (1999), which was published by the Humanist Press.

This is really an informative presentation of the history of American law that brings out its underlying basic principles. One thing of interest was Grant's introductory musings on the nature of ethics, which he stressed is a search for pragmatic principles of social interaction that work to produce a peaceful and just society. Ethics is not "a study of religious values or theological mandates," Grant maintains. "It is on the contrary, a part of the *science* of sociology."

Grant aimed to establish those rules and principles that underlie the American constitution, laws, and court decisions. He recognizes that only those duties that society needs will be *imposed* upon the individual as the rules of ethics. Altruistic or virtuous conduct that enhances the commonweal is encouraged. In other words, Grant equates American ethics with enforceable American law together with an additional component of altruistic or virtuous conduct, which is not imposed. He cited five fundamental ethical principles that underlie and uniquely express American law and ethics:

1) All people are created equal and free, i.e., they are all equal in the eyes of the law with respect to human, political, and civil rights and are all to be treated fairly with respect to economic rights.
2) American ethics is based on consent and a social contract, not on authority.
3) Human rights are a quid pro quo for our ethical obligations.
4) Our values are secular.
5) Our public morality is limited by the right of privacy.

Grant examines each of these principles and their history in the various chapters of his book together with extensive quotations from landmark cases and documents influential in the evolution of the law.

Grant impresses us not only with the erudition of the authors of the US Constitution and their familiarity with the philosophy of the Enlightenment but also their practical involvement with politics and law. David Hume, John Locke, Tom Paine, and James Madison appear frequently in his pages; and we see the British Declaration of Rights of 1688 as a harbinger of things to come. As a general summary of ethics, it is difficult to do better than Sidgwick's conclusion that ethical conduct is that which is the most utilitarian (i.e., benefiting everyone) and the most just. Grant's book approaches ethics from a standpoint of his knowing the law. One can contemplate the design of a system of statutory law based on a foundation of theoretical ethics. From that point of view, there are some curious omissions from Grant's list of principles such as the importance of truth telling and of keeping promises. These two interrelated values underlie the laws of contracts and torts. They are basic to English common law and were taken over into American practice. Perhaps Grant simply felt that their inclusion should be taken as understood.

16.6 Twentieth-Century Developments

The twentieth century also saw some influential thinking on legal philosophy. John Rawls (2001), working at Harvard, introduced several new concepts including a division of ethics along the lines of "the right" and "the good." He further proposed that "the right" is associated with morality and "the good" with ethics. Rawls's theory uses a device that he calls the "veil of ignorance" so that we may arrive at decisions uninfluenced by race, sex, wealth, class, or any other distinguishing feature. Another Harvard luminary was Robert Nozick whose *Anarchy, State and Utopia* (1974) advanced a very articulate libertarian approach. From across the Atlantic came treatises closely consonant with the real world of the law from Adorno, Popper, and Habermas. Popper (1963), through his ideas on falsification, in effect advocated an ethic of trial and error, which closely resembles the evolutionary way in which the law has actually developed. Input from the community is crucial in the philosophies of all these three, calling to mind the jury system as it actually operates in the Anglo-American system. Habermas has studied on both sides of the Atlantic, and his mature philosophy includes thinking influenced by both Europeans and Americans.

16.7 Theistic Influence

Nevertheless, for the humanist, there are many problems with American law as it stands. Let us start by considering the influence of theistic religion on US law. A number of essays about these issues have been collected by the Rachels (2007). Another work along similar lines is Shuwoth's *Rough Country* (2014). This covers the history of Christianity in Texas, although it is clear that Shuwoth thinks of Texas as a model for the whole USA since he has devoted a lifetime to studying the influence of Christian religion on Texas's society and politics. Fundamentalist Christianity has always been second only to Islam in its desire for the subjugation of women and its interest in the bedroom. Its proscriptions on sexual conduct and the violence of its punishments for infringements are still being contested at the present time. Homosexuality, adultery, pornography, and prostitution have all been, and still are, matters where ancient religious taboos have had to be overcome. It is likely an instinctive urge that makes abortion a procedure that no woman undertakes lightly and often only under extreme circumstances of danger to her life or when the life of a child would be one of unending misery. The humanist position has to be that no woman should be forced to bear a child against her will and that she must be the judge of what may happen to her body. But yet there has had to be a continuing battle with religious extremists to secure the mother's right to abortion. Theistic religion has opposed suicide and euthanasia, and here the battle is yet to be fought. Drug laws in the United States are close to insane, and largely as a consequence, our prisons are among the most highly populated of any country in the world as detailed by Lawrence Jablecki (2009). These proscriptions also are inspired by medieval religious mentality. Finally we might mention that the punitive approach to retributive justice comes from the same source. In all of these instances the basic problem is the denial of the findings of naturalistic science.

16.8 Ethical Discourse

Traditional societies, according to Habermas, are held together by a shared ethos through the use of words, writing, and legislation. People are brought up to acquire the identities and motivations required to function smoothly in the society's institutions. People think of themselves as conducting their own lives by general principles and the particular reasons that apply to them. Habermas proposed that the central function of holding society together is played by moral and ethical discourse. Modern social arrangements also require political institutions and laws. Political and legal theory require moral theory as well. Habermas sees a two-track structure of politics: the formal and the informal. The informal is a chaotic collection of voluntary organizations, political associations, and the media. On the other hand, the formal includes parliaments, cabinets, elected assemblies, and political parties. The state is a separate administrative system. A political system functions well when the decision-making institutions are open to the input of the civil society. Modern people will tend to abide by policies and laws whose rationale they accept. Political discourse is like a workshop where a whole range of experiments can be made. Habermas combines in his proposal two political conceptions that are usually taken to be alternatives: liberal democracy with the idea of civil rights and civic republicanism with the idea of popular sovereignty. The former protects the interests of individuals while the latter permits self-realization of the community as a whole. Such an arrangement seems to evoke a two-party system. We have to value the immense work that has been put into constructing our state and respect our constitutional law as the means of protecting pluralism in values, religions, and cosmologies. We are fortunate to be living in a country where the future course of the law is determined by ethical discourse and where we still have the opportunity to have humanist principles prevail.

16.9 Good Citizens

Protagoras and Socrates argued that we should aim to be good people in a good society. Good behavior on the part of individuals is primarily the subject matter of ethics. In this chapter, we consider how the good society should conduct itself, a society being any group of individuals including families, businesses, schools, churches, and local or countrywide communities. Aristotle used the term *politics* for the subject of the correct conduct of societies. The word derives from the Greek *polis*, which meant *city*. But the Greek cities were unique in their style of government, which generally involved all the male residents except for slaves. Athens was perhaps the most advanced with a system celebrated for its institution by Solon, which, by the time of Pericles, had become a prototype for modern democracy, where democracy means government by the people. There is an account of the Athenian system of government in what is referred to as Pericles's funeral oration, as recorded by Thucydides (431–400 BCE). Unfortunately, after Pericles's time, Athens got involved in the Peloponnesian wars and democracy fell into the hands of uneducated men. It was during this time that Socrates was questioning established institutions and finally forced to commit suicide. This was probably why his pupil Plato became so disenchanted with democracy and wrote *The Republic* (380–350 BCE) a blueprint for a rather high-minded version of aristocracy. Plato's most famous pupil was Aristotle whose book *Politics* restores our confidence in Greek wisdom. Aristotle, in turn, served as tutor to Alexander the Great whose extraordinary conquests established an empire that was sometimes cited as a proof that the concepts of the city-state could be extended to a much larger realm.

16.10 Political Science and Systems

Some of the most important concepts in social theory arose from the development of law. It was the Greeks who provided us with the vocabulary for political discussion: autocracy, government by a single individual (dictatorship); oligarchy, government by a small group (such as the wealthy); and aristocracy, government by the best. The Roman law, during its heyday, nurtured the ideal of learning from its proceedings and developing a literature to support the endeavor. With the Renaissance, interest in the philosophy of government was rekindled, and we usually regard Machiavelli's *The Prince* (1532) as the start of modern political science. Since Machiavelli's time, we have learned a great deal about social systems under the various rubrics of political science, law, economics, sociology, business, and management. There are many books and specialized disciplines about the conduct of different types of society. There are some general principles we have learned. These principles reflect the values of the ethical systems we have studied such as justice, equality, liberty, etc., as listed in our humanist principles. Those who will be subjected to or affected by decisions should be consulted or represented during the decision-making process. Evolutionary change is both necessary and to be preferred to revolutionary change. Sweeping and simplistic ideological theories are suspect in comparison with "piecemeal social engineering." The good society is an open society in which good ideas can always get a hearing, wherever they are invented.

In one sense, theism is an old social theory, namely, that there is a god who created the world and everything in it and maintained order by setting out the laws for mankind to obey. Hobbes wanted God replaced by a human sovereign. We advanced further as the structure of the state was made more sophisticated by the institution of parliamentary democracy. In effect, we introduced systems theory to provide for minorities and branches of government such as armies, a civil service with multiple departments, and a legal system with lawyers and police. In the earliest states (Mesopotamia and Egypt), the government included both religious and economic institutions as well as the civil service and the army. But fairly early on, it was discovered that it was more efficient to leave economic matters largely to the merchants and the marketplace, and this led to the development of capitalism. One of the problems we still have not completely solved is management of the economy to provide for the poor and disadvantaged. Most advanced countries in the world have arrived at health care systems that can handle the whole population while fairly compensating the health care providers. Welfare systems for the homeless, the mentally impaired, and the incompetent are also a problem tackled in different ways in different countries. Methods of taxation test our conceptions of justice. Another problem arises with the policing of the state against criminal activities. There is still much debate over the use of guns in America, as discussed by Lee Nisbet (1990). Where every citizen is permitted to carry guns, there should be a program to train citizens in the use of the weapons.

16.11 Social Contracts

It was at the time of the Renaissance that the works of the classical thinkers of antiquity came to light again, and philosophers began to consider the question of how we should behave in the absence of the Christian assumptions of divine commandments. One of the first of these new philosophers was Thomas Hobbes who lived through the tumultuous time of the religious and civil war in England in the seventeenth century, which culminated in the beheading of King Charles I. This occurred at the start of a period when Britain was, in effect, a republic under the leadership of Oliver Cromwell. Hobbes had served as a tutor to the son of the unfortunate Charles I, and on the restoration of the monarchy, the son became the first "constitutional monarch" as Charles II. Hobbes was a materialist and an atheist and wanted to find a theory on which to base our ethical and political behavior. He started by considering "the state of nature." By this, he meant a time before the institution of law and government by man. According to Hobbes, the lives of men at that time were "nasty, short and brutish." He supposed that men got together and made a "social contract" whereby they agreed to follow certain rules that were to be enforced by the state, with the king as its representative. Hobbes was followed by John Locke who also presupposed a state of nature but reintroduced the Almighty into the scheme of things to provide the ultimate basis for the king's authority. In some ways, Locke improved on Hobbes's ideas by being the first in the English-speaking world to introduce the concepts of the "separation of church and state" and "separation of powers," which, according to Hillar and Allen, (2002) had originated with the Socinians. The French philosopher Jean-Jacques Rousseau also took up the idea of a state of nature, but in his system, it was supposed to be an idyllic state of affairs, a golden age.

16.12 The Origin and Growth of Government

Hume realized that these concepts of the state of nature and the golden age were both, in fact, "philosophical fictions." He observed that men are necessarily born in a family society (see Hume, 1777a, para. 151), and in his essay (1777b) "On the Origin of Government," he explains that we maintain society from natural inclination and from habit to support the legal system and to ensure the peace. In "Of the Original Contract" (1777b), he traces government to its beginning "in the woods and deserts," probably beginning with the ascendancy of one man over multitudes during a state of war. His view was that if there was such a thing as a social contract, "it was not written on parchment, nor yet on leaves or barks of trees. It preceded the use of writing and all the other civilized arts of life . . . and is traced to the *nature of man.*" Hume's opinion has been borne out by the work of many sociologists and anthropologists from Auguste Comte to Talcott Parsons. Although they may not use the same words to describe it, in effect, they see the process of the start and growth of government as the recognition and growth of systems. Madison read Hume and Douglas Adair (see Livingston and King, 1976) credits Hume's essays "That Politics May Be Reduced to a Science" (1777b) and "Idea of a Perfect Commonwealth" through their influence on Madison, with having had an effect on the US Constitution. The founding fathers especially Franklin, Washington, Jefferson, Adams, Madison, and Hamilton were all influenced by the thinking of the Enlightenment as well as being practical men and experienced in government, the military, and commerce. The United States and its constitution has been a remarkable success story in the two centuries of its existence and is a good example of evolutionary progress. The union has grown from the original thirteen colonies to the current fifty states, which comprise the most powerful country in the world at present. The abolition of slavery nearly tore the country apart, but the leadership of Abraham Lincoln eventually prevailed and preserved the union. A number of amendments to the constitution have been made in a peaceful and democratic way including the extension of voting rights to women. One of the most important features of the constitution is the separation of church and state whereby religion is prevented from becoming a divisive factor in the life of the country.

16.13 Social Theories

Karl Marx (1867) argued that it is possible for a social system to get established based on the economy or the means of production as he put it. He pointed out that throughout history different economic systems had succeeded one another (hunter gathering, agriculture, manufacturing, etc.) and that the social order in each case was a necessary consequence of the economy. He believed that the capitalist system, which existed in his own time, would inevitably be overthrown in a revolution to be succeeded by Communism. His followers, while convinced of the inevitability of the revolution, thought it would be beneficial to assist matters by means of armed struggle. We now know that Marxism in practice, when it came, turned out to be totalitarian, brutal, and inefficient. The people of the Soviet Union threw it out. Friedrich Hayek (1944) explained in his writings why Communism was doomed to fail. Karl Popper (1957) emphasized the scientific shortcomings of Marx's predictions. In Popper's view, theories can only claim to be scientific if they contain falsifiable predictions. Thus, Marx's theory was scientific in that it was falsifiable but wrong because it was, in fact, shown to be false. For example, according to Marx, revolutions were supposed to start in the most advanced countries whereas, in fact, they occurred in backward ones. Popper favored development by the solution of problems one by one. In the political sphere, he called this piecemeal social engineering. Popper (1945) is also regarded as the champion of openness in political and social dealings.

Habermas criticized Marxism, particularly for using labor as the main category of human realization and economic emancipation as the main measure of freedom. Instead, Habermas studied the American pragmatism of William James, John Dewey, George Herbert Mead, and C. S. Pierce, as well as the hermeneutic tradition (i.e., the study of extracting meaning from writing and speech). As we have already stated, Habermas advanced a theory that human actions are coordinated by speech and language. When agents use speech in this way, they enter into commitments to justify actions for good reasons.

16.14 Enlightenment and Modernity

The social theory propounded by Habermas, as also by Paul Kurtz, is for our society to return to the values and goals of the Enlightenment. Habermas argues that modernity arose in the Middle Ages. When his *The Theory of Communicative Action* was published in 1981 there was an argument going on as to whether the modern period had ended and we were in the postmodern era. He pointed out that modernization comprises several related developments:

1) a massive growth in knowledge, especially in the natural sciences
2) a decline of the Aristotelian tradition and waning of church authority
3) a separation of technically useful knowledge that led to the separating out of three distinct spheres of value: scientific/technical, moral/legal, and aesthetic/expressive

These correspond to the three kinds of validity: truth; rightness and truthfulness, which in turn correspond to three spheres of discourse: theoretical, moral and aesthetic, which correspond to three domains of knowledge: natural sciences, moral and law, and the arts. Modernity brought an increase in the amount and depth of specialized knowledge, which tends to get detached from the moorings of everyday life.

In 1980 Habermas made a speech in which he opposed postmodernism, which was then very strong. He claimed that modernity is a project rather than a historical period and that the project is not finished but should be. The chief problem as he saw it is to reconnect specialized knowledge with common sense and the lifeworld to harness its potential for good. Habermas argued that post-metaphysical philosophy has to be a stand-in and interpreter for the specialized sciences at the center of modern life. He thinks these problems have not yet been solved. But he views the proposed antimodernistic alternatives as worse, including Alasdair MacIntyre's communitarianism (a reversion to the Thomist tradition of moral virtues) and Heidegger's proposed return to a medieval rural and traditional way of life. Habermas argued that we should not sacrifice the gains modernity has brought: an increase in knowledge, economic gains, and expansion of individual freedom. We must critically accept the possibilities in the light of humanitarian ideals. He says we must preserve ourselves from the corrosive effects of the instrumental system. He points to the emergence of secular morality and argues that modernity must create its normativity out of itself. It has to be self-created because it must come from communication and discourse. One subplot is the program of discourse ethics, an objectively good and just way of life enabling each individual to answer the question: what should I do? He claims that the more a society is in step with the ideals of communication and discourse, the better off it is. But he defends the idea of social progress and likens social development to a learning process. Modernization on the negative side causes social pathologies; but on the positive side, there are cognitive, economic, and practical gains. Habermas contends that the trick is to work with the dynamic of modernity, not against it.

16.15 Federalism and World Government

Union Now was the title of a book published just before the Second World War. The author was Clarence Streit, an American correspondent who sought to avoid the looming conflict by promoting a federation among the United States, Britain, and other democratic countries. The concept of federalism was well-known in North America because of its success in bringing unity to the thirteen formerly British colonies. The idea was to build agreement out of the factors where there was a clear consensus and gloss over the controversial issues. Thus, the structure of the government could be agreed upon, but an issue such as slavery could not be resolved, and so it was omitted in the hopes that it might be resolved at a later date as the union strengthened. Unfortunately, it took a dreadful civil war to finally settle the question of slavery, but by the time that happened, it was clear that there was a determination to preserve the union. Streit's effort to avoid the catastrophe in Europe was unfortunately too late, but by the end of the conflict, militant nationalism in Europe had been dealt a death blow and the idea of a federal union had gained wide support. Gradually, supranational institutions were built up starting with a treaty to coordinate the production of coal and steel, followed by a customs union and then several other treaties culminating in a European parliament and an executive for the growing bureaucracy. The European Union for a while was seen as a major player on the world stage with a major influence in its future.

Habermas has strong opinions on the events in Europe since World War II. He has a startling view of the German revival, maintaining that one of his country's greatest achievements has been the adoption of democratic institutions. He was, however, highly critical of the way in which the reunification with East Germany took place. He felt that the East was pressured into becoming a part of West Germany without its citizens having the opportunity to participate in the structuring of a new Germany. But he wholeheartedly supported the growth of the European Union and Germany's role in it.

There has been another venture in unification since World War II and that is the growth of the United Nations and other global institutions. For this, we need to thank the Roosevelts, Franklin and Eleanor, and their humanistic and enlightened outlook. One of the first major acts of the United Nations was the passage of the Universal Declaration of Human Rights in 1948 (see *Essays in the Philosophy of Humanism*, vol. 6, 1998, pp. 1–6). The thirty statements in that document should guarantee the quality of life for all the world's citizens if it were really observed. The trouble is that the UN is an organization of nation states whose sovereignty is still guaranteed by the 1648 Treaty of Westphalia. This arrangement enables national governments to manage their internal affairs without external intervention. But for all its failures and limitations, the UN and its agencies have many credits in making international law, securing cooperation in health and medical matters, care of children, meteorology, transportation, etc. It has also had some successes in limited security operations where it has been permitted to do so by the United States and other large nations. But our problems are increasingly global at this time—population, energy supply, pollution, terrorism, etc.—and it behooves us to find solutions all the world's citizens can truly endorse.

16.16 Progress and the Future

The subject of law and its intersection with ethics is a difficult issue due to the fact that real law contains a number of accommodations among the different values esteemed by various people and groups. One good example would be in the clash of values between Christian fundamentalists and humanists. And there are all sorts of other moral and ethical divergences. Philosophers have tried to find principles that could be used to resolve these divisions, but there remain numerous issues that have not been resolved to the satisfaction of all parties, and in fact, the number of contentious arguments seems to be increasing as time goes on. But the law has to accommodate these differences as best it can. It is clear that the humanist community does not have the numbers to influence any legislative body directly. Furthermore, we may not agree on what measures should be taken. We need to study alternatives and publicize the options to the larger community. We could work together with like-minded organizations and get involved in the political process. Doubtless, our work as humanists will have to prioritize the correction of the religious legacy: of Judeo-Christianity in America and of Islam and Hinduism in other parts of the world. The American Humanist Association recently became the home of the Appignani Bioethics Center, which is a think-tank providing thoughtful, timely research, and analysis of bioethical challenges facing the national and international community, including the following:

- organ and human trafficking
- end-of-life care and decision making
- reproductive and sexual rights
- stem cell research and therapeutic applications
- neuroscience, in assessing culpability for crime
- infectious diseases and human epidemics
- genetically engineered food

Beyond these bioethical problems, there are a number of other issues calling for reform. We might quote from the website of the New South Wales Law Reform Commission, which is required to consider the laws of New South Wales with a view to

- eliminating defects and anachronisms in the law;
- repealing obsolete or unnecessary enactments;
- consolidating, codifying, or revising the law;
- simplifying or modernizing the law;
- adopting new or more effective methods for the administration of the law; and
- systematically developing and reforming the law.

But even beyond these modifications to the existing law, there are concerns about the advance of technology as suggested in chapter 10 and in a recent article by Clay Farris Naff (2014). Here the fear has begun to spread that large corporations have so outstripped the capabilities of individual humans that they will be able to control the world. In fact, it is envisaged that individual robots will have such capabilities. The political and legal communities will need to be equipped with comparable abilities in order to counterbalance any dystopian tendencies that might arise. On the other hand, we have to realize that forthcoming developments have enormous potential to enhance life, whether it be human, nonhuman, or transhuman; and we should not allow backward members of our species to try to stop them.

So we see that there will be a need for law reform as far as the eye can see. In the USA, the links between humanism and politics remain weak even in the twenty-first century. In a speech to the IHEU World Humanist Congress in 2014 at Oxford, Maggie Ardiente related how she had boasted to the British conference organizers that there was a member of the United States Congress who was an atheist, only to be told that there were 115 such members of the British parliament! Although nonbelievers are the largest minority in the USA, they are largely ignored. There is a strong antiatheist prejudice, as exemplified by the fact that 53 percent of Americans would not vote for atheists. We must get involved with such means as funding of congressional candidates. The collection of papers by Seidman and Murphy (2004) is a start on the process of building a political humanism. Another useful development has been the introduction of comparative government, in parallel with comparative religion, as in the excellent text by Blondel (1995). Mortimer Adler (1991) published a study by the Aspen Institute in which he investigated what it would take to establish a society of "haves without have-nots." Perhaps this is a question that the humanist movement could take up over the next few years. One of the most illuminating comparisons is between the United States and Scandinavia. These Nordic countries are among the least religious in the world whereas the United States is among the most religious.

This is the subject matter of a report by Phil Zuckerman (2008). The Nordic countries are also among the most generous to the poor and disadvantaged. But by some measure, it is the Scandinavians who are the wealthiest, and it seems that we should be investigating exactly what the differences are between them and the United States and whether the United States should be following their various leads.

17 Humanism and Art

17. Humanism and Art

17.1 Introduction

Evidence of the production of art began to develop in prehistoric times with paintings such as those on the walls of the caves of Lascaux. We also have the ancient steatopygous female cult objects sometimes thought to be fertility figures. Archeologists have also discovered pipes similar to flutes in prehistoric excavations, and so it is presumed that music also originated very early. Activities such as painting and music do not have direct and obvious survival value, and we wonder what motivated their creators. Once mankind had a spoken language, it could be used not simply for communication but also for storytelling, poetry, song, and drama. And in those activities, we recognize the beginnings of literature or the art of words. The *Gilgamesh* and the *Odyssey* tell strange and wonderful tales of a world still being explored. Primitive art can still be found in various parts of the world, and even to the jaded tastes of those of us who consider ourselves civilized, it still casts a wild and startling spell. Consider, for example, the wonderful collection illustrated in Judith Miller's *Tribal Art* (2006). An interesting point here is that early art was not accurately representational. Even the animals at Lascaux, while certainly recognizable, were in no way photographic images. Historians originally conjectured that they may have had the purpose of instructing their viewers about hunting. The ancient Egyptians used art in stylized forms in pursuit of their religion. It was not until the time of the Greeks that artists began to produce statues that were anatomically accurate, and it was the Greek philosophers who first began to think about art and gave us a vocabulary for the subject.

My wife and I took an interesting course on aesthetics and the philosophy of art given by Fernando Casas. It strengthened my conviction that art is very relevant to ethics, the subject of our present investigation. In one sense, I believe that the philosophy of art comes closer to the heart of the matter than many other topics we have covered thus far. As we went through the course following a historical approach, I fancied that I saw how the philosophers of art had uncovered the various elements of a modern viewpoint on the subject. We started by posing the ancient questions such as "What is beauty?" and "What is art?" which lie at the center of aesthetics and the philosophy of art and art criticism. As we progressed, we received the original references to the major sources in the subject, and I will cite some of these again as we get to them. But to start with, I should mention the book edited by Stephen David Ross *Art and Its Significance* (1994), which provides an overview of the complete journey. One of the interesting observations that can be made about the early periods of art history is the way in which artworks retain similar forms for hundreds if not thousands of years. Thus, the art of Mesopotamia has recognizable characteristics that change only slowly with time. Then there are many similarities between that ilk and the art of Egypt and again between that of Egypt and early Greek work. There is an evolution in works of art.

17.2 Plato and Aristotle

It was Plato and Aristotle who offered the first theories of art. They saw the production of beauty as the objective in any work of art. Beauty is a most extreme form of pleasure; and it might be revealed in various ways: line, color, form, texture, proportion, rhythmic motion, tone, behavior, attitude, etc. They described the ways of accomplishing beauty as technique or "techne." They saw art as "mimesis" or representation and explained its production as due to the human urge to imitate nature. In his book *Poetica* (c. 336), Aristotle wrote: "Just as color and form are used as means by some . . . and the voice is used by others . . . so also . . . the means with them as a whole are rhythm, language and harmony . . . either singly or in certain combinations." Plato and Aristotle both believed that the living human possessed a soul that left the body at death and that these souls belonged to a realm of the divine presided over by the gods. Their views were given their ultimate embellishment by Plotinus, a transcendentalist and mystic who lived in the third century CE and is often referred to as the last classical mind. In Plotinus's scheme, God is the highest level of the transcendental and is referred to as the One. It was only a hundred years or so later that that these ideas entered the Christian world through the teaching of Saint Augustine in his two books *De Ordini* and *De Musica*. The coming of Christianity saw a radical shift in the foundation of art, its evaluation, and in what was perceived as beauty.

17.3 The Renaissance

For a thousand years, the philosophy of art remained under this Christian domination while sculptors and painters poured out the stylized versions of the Virgin with Child and Christ with his Apostles, which filled the churches of Europe. In the Middle Ages, prosperity returned to Italy, and under the Medicis, Florence became a center of trade and civilized learning. The Medicis were themselves innovators in finance who used to the fullest extent the new coinage of Florence and the invention of double-entry accounting with meticulous bookkeeping. After Ficino translated Plotinus in 1492 and wrote *De Amore*, matters began to change in the art world. The focus shifted from God and religion back to the human. The Medicis sponsored architects (Brunelleschi), sculptors (Donatello, Michelangelo), painters (Botticelli, Fra Filippo Lippi, and Leonardo da Vinci), and scientists (Galileo Galilei). Perhaps the greatest artist of this time was Michelangelo who was accomplished in painting as well as sculpture. According to Vasari (1568), Michelangelo, when still a boy of fourteen, was taken to the garden of Lorenzo the Magnificent where he sculpted the head of a fawn, never having held a chisel in his hand before; and it was so good that Lorenzo took him into his own household. Michelangelo was an innovator and actually dissected bodies to understand the disposition of blood vessels and muscles under the skin. But he was not a "scientific" artist in the mold of da Vinci. In other words, he was not a realist:

he wanted to represent "ideal" beauty. His figures—for example, his David—were frequently out of proportion.

17.4 Hume's Theory of Art

We have already discussed Hume's version of the acquisition of knowledge in earlier chapters. He pointed out that we make sense of the world by recognizing constancies in our observations. It was much later that Rapoport (1986) suggested that these constancies be called systems, and there is a case for supposing that there are systems that exist over and above our basic neural circuits. Very complex systems, such as the human mind, may seem to be "free," and so it is convenient to ascribe to them "wills" of their own. Hume supposed that our knowledge of the world comes from experience and is registered in the form of "outer" impressions or sensations. But we also have "inner" sensations he termed emotions or passions. The mind is then the total collection of impressions. He saw a fundamental distinction between facts and values. Plotinus had not made such a distinction. Hume's theory of art follows similar lines to his theory of ethics and was set out in his essay "On the Standard of Taste" (1757). He argues that we all support a variety of values such as elegance, simplicity, etc., but that there may be a thousand different sentiments all of which may be excited by the same object. We would have to say that they are all right because no one sentiment represents what is really in the object. This seems to support relativism, *but* then Hume's story takes a different turn. He argues that there is another species of common sense that modifies the conclusion. "Who," he asks, "would assert an equality of genius between Ogilby and Milton?" That would be as absurd as saying that a pond is equal to an ocean. The true rules of composition do not exist a priori like rules of mathematics but are found by experience, as with all practical sciences. The rules of art have their foundation on what has been found to please in all countries and in all ages. Homer pleased in his own time and still pleases. Hume argues that the requirements of a high standard for taste are (1) a healthy mind, (2) normal circumstances, (3) delicacy of imagination, (4) perception of exactness, (5) practice, and (6) freedom from prejudice. If these requirements are met, then the principles of art are the same for all men of all ages. However, Hume concludes that there are few people who meet the qualifications. Hume and his successors saw that morality is not purely relative because it is actually arrived at, as Habermas would say, by a discourse among the ethical community.

17.5 Kant's Philosophy and Theory of Art

Immanuel Kant (1724–1804) was one of the two great philosophers of the Enlightenment at the end of the eighteenth century, along with Hume. In fact, he helped the latter get established by declaring that Hume's work had served to awaken him from his dogmatic slumbers. After that, Hume was taken much more seriously. Kant was also one of the first to propose a world government. He was also a physicist of some repute. He put forward a theory of planetary formation that was widely accepted for a while and helped to explain how the solar system could have come into existence without the need to invoke divine agency. So he had a number of claims to fame, and he is definitely someone we should respect. He was the author of three great works:

- *The Critique of Pure Reason*
- *The Critique of Practical Reason*
- *The Critique of Judgment*

A fourth book, *Prolegomena*, was written as a preliminary introduction for future teachers.

In the *Critique of Pure Reason*, Kant proposed a theory of neuroscience, which has been very influential. Kant's theory of neurophysiology starts out like that of Locke and Hume with the arrival of sensations from the external world, which comprises "things in themselves," which exist in space and time. We access information on these objects through our senses. The sensations of physical objects he called phenomena, and he regarded these as the province of science. He referred to our ability to detect these physical signals as our sensibility, and he regarded the entire process up to that point as fully deterministic. He diverges from the British philosophers in his discussion of how we achieve understanding. Kant suggests that the human brain sorts the phenomena into various categories, much as in Aristotle's scheme. And beyond that, there are *noumena* (ideas, we might say), which are nondetermined, i.e., free systems. The self, the soul, and God are all noumena. And according to Kant, our morality operates at the level of the noumena. The teleological explanation of the action of noumena is as free moral agents that can have intentionality. Thus, we might explain a clock in deterministic mechanics or alternatively as a device designed to tell the time.

Kant's book on ethics is titled the *Metaphysics of Morals*. He claims that we have a number of ends, which are rather like Plato's eternal forms. In his book, he claimed that we experience moral influences called imperatives, which can be either absolute or undeniable, in which case they were called categorical imperatives, or optional, in which case they were "hypothetical imperatives." If we skeptics do not believe in the existence of objective morals, then categorical imperatives have to be rejected. Mackie (1977) makes this plain when he states that "my thesis that there are no objective values is specifically the denial that any such categorically imperative element is objectively valid." Unfortunately, Kant was so much attached to his categorical imperatives that he maintained that they must be of divine origin. So it is sometimes said that Kant showed God out of the front door, only to let him back in again through the back door.

About one-half of the *Critique of Judgment* is devoted to art, and Kant's influence in the world of art endures to this day despite his declining influence on moral philosophy. He offered some important observations on aesthetics, the pleasure evoked by beauty. Kant believed that we have a faculty of judgment that provides the link between nature and the noumena. Beauty is associated with quality and form.

Kant's *Critique of Judgment* influenced numerous philosophers and artists. Some people spend their lives interpreting Kant. This being the case, we are justified in reciting some of Kant's thoughts. For instance, there is the statement that "judgment grasps nature as teleological," i.e., judgment regards nature as the purposive embodiment of an intelligence. Kant thought that external sensations have to conform to the structures of the mind starting with space and time. We impose patterns of logic on our observations. There are various kinds of judgments such as of quantity (universal, particular, or singular), of quality (affirmative, negative, or infinite), of relation (categorical, hypothetical, or disjunctive), and of modality (problematic, assertoric, or apodictic). Kant distinguished three kinds of liking: the pleasant (satisfying desire), the good (measuring objective worth), and the beautiful (that which simply pleases without inclination or desire). He analyzed aesthetics in terms of the feeling of pleasure but saw beauty as not being purely a feeling in the mind. Analysis of the beautiful has four similar moments from the standpoint of quality, quantity, relation, and modality. Kant also compared the beautiful and the sublime: they have common features but are different in that beauty is associated with quality and form whereas the sublime is associated with quantity and formlessness and is represented as a totality. Kant gave as an example of the sublime a storm over the ocean. Such a sight is terrible and, according to Kant, causes the mind to think of higher "purposiveness" and that we have within us a supersensible power. Another example of the mathematically sublime is St. Peter's in Rome. He discusses fine art and genius, the difference between art and the beauty of nature, and the difference between fine art and craft. He writes about fine art being an end in itself, and he also talks of human beings as ends in themselves. He maintains that the beautiful is the symbol of the morally good.

There are a number of expositions of Kant's philosophy, including that by Carl J. Friedrich (1949) and by Patricia Kitcher (2011). Kant was the first of a series of continental philosophers including Hegel, Schopenhauer, Nietzsche, Kierkegaard, Marx, Husserl, Heidegger, Sartre, Camus, and Habermas. Many of them are included in the existentialist movement. In a way, these men have followed a path that seems to parallel that of the Anglo-American English-speaking writers. Nietzsche built on Schopenhauer's legacy and famously declared "God is dead," which set the European tradition on an atheistic path. Kierkegaard explored the importance of decision making in ethics, and Marx was one of the first to realize the importance of social and especially economic influences on ethical thinking. Husserl was the originator of the theory of phenomenology, which was built on the idea that reality consists of the impressions that physical stimuli evoke in our minds.

17.6 Darwin's Theories on Animal Aesthetics and Sexual Selection

It was not long after Kant and Hume that Darwin's thinking arrived on the scene. His first contribution came in *On the Origin of Species* (1859) where he presented his theory that animals have evolved through a process of natural selection whereby those who are the best adapted to their environments tend to survive and leave the most offspring. What is not so well-known is that he gave much thought to animal aesthetics, as is clear from several of his works, including *The Descent of Man, and Selection in Relation to Sex* (1871) and *The Expression of the Emotions in Man and Animals* (1872). He pointed out that there are many preaesthetic elements in primitive animals, such as brilliant tints in corals, sea anemones, and jellyfish as well as elegant stripes and shading. Many flowers and fruit show colors and shading to attract insects, birds, and beasts. He famously remarked that birds are the most aesthetic of all animals. The sphere of animal aesthetics begins with charming the female. He first recognized the full aesthetic workings of selection in butterflies and realized that this was the result of female choice. Sexual selection is a strategy complementary to natural selection. He thought that deer's antlers were used in sexual selection but saw that they compete with natural selection when the animal tries to run through the woods. There are a number of devices for sexual attraction: odors, songs, love dances, antics, and ornaments. Females are not passive but exercise choice. One of the most spectacular examples of this is the peacock's tail, but there are many others. There have been transfers of aesthetic sense from the female to the male as in the case of the bowerbird where the male prepares a beautiful reception hall for the delight of the female. There is a paper by Jared Diamond (1982) on the evolution of these bowers. Darwin gives a long account of musical tones and rhythm, originating in insects, reaching a summit in birds, and extending to the half-human progenitors of humans. He pointed out that there was a coevolution of beauty and a sense of beauty.

Darwin saw animal and human aesthetics as a continuum, but he did not know why the female should be attracted by beauty. As he remarks in *On the Origin of Species,* "How the sense of beauty in its simplest form—that is, the reception of a peculiar kind of pleasure from certain colours, forms, and sounds—was first developed in the mind of man and of the lower animals, is very obscure. The same sort of difficulty is presented, if we enquire how it is that certain flavors and odours give pleasure, and others displeasure." However, these observations did not receive much attention from the biological or philosophical communities because it was not evident how an aesthetic sense restricted to sight and sound and used only in the service of reproduction could have evolved into a sense evident in as many aspects of life as it is among humans.

17.7 Collingwood Asks: What Is Art?

Even though these musings by philosophers through the time of Kant give us an inkling of the issues involved in aesthetics, there still remains the question: what *exactly* is art? Tolstoy famously asked this question and answered that art is an *expression* of emotion. Tolstoy gave us the example of a boy who, having experienced an encounter with a wolf, describes the scene vividly, wishing to evoke his own feelings in others. Art must therefore call forth the artist's feelings in the spectator. The argument is that to evoke a feeling, one must first have experienced it. The artist must be sincere. Some similar ideas were expressed by Collingwood in his *The Principles of Art* (1938), which opens by stating, "The business of this book is to answer the question: What is art?" Collingwood then takes us through four chapters in which he argues that art does not reside in craft, in representation, in magic, or in amusement. Then he gets to discuss the characteristics that art proper really entails: (1) emotional expression and (2) creativity and imagination. He concludes that the work of art is actually an imaginary object. He argues that both thinking and feeling are involved in the act of imagination. He goes through the history of the philosophy of art that we have covered showing how it leads up to the conclusion he has reached. Conscious experience is the necessary correlate of art. Finally, he argues that art is language.

17.8 John Dewey: Art as Experience

Now while Collingwood argues that art is language, Dewey (1934), on the face of things, appears to take a contradictory tack by claiming that art is experience. But when we begin to think about it, we realize that matters are not so much at variance as they first appear. It is clear that both Collingwood and Dewey are denying that art is the physical manifestation of the artist's effort: the painting, sculpture, or sounds of the symphony. They are both arguing that art is something within the artist's mind. Dewey was famous for his philosophy of instrumentalism, and he claimed that thought was an instrument in the relation between a living organism and its environment. The process of doing and undergoing an interaction with the environment is what Dewey defines as an experience. He differs with Collingwood in that his experiences cover the realm of the everyday although he does allow that such experience comes to its fullest fruition in the aesthetic. He states that it is meaningfulness that provides the aesthetic experience. He makes the point that it is not the physical object itself that is the art but its functioning with the artist and spectator. For that reason, he objected to the isolation of artwork in museums. Similarly, he argued that to understand a building such as the Parthenon, we need to understand the cultural context of Athens. Nowadays, art can reside in movies, jazz, comics, and newspapers. He wondered why people regard the attempt to link everyday things with high art as betrayal. And he answers his own question by speculating that it is because of dualism. But he says that many things are experienced but do not amount to *an experience*. An experience only occurs when an interaction runs its course to completion. Dewey sees life as a collection of histories, each with its own plot and movement toward closure. In an experience, all the elements are integrated by a pervasive emotion he calls the aesthetic quality. The enemies of the experience are the humdrum, but there is no clear separation between the aesthetic and the intellectual.

17.9 Music, Aesthetics, and Creativity

Writers on music recognize that there is a transmission of emotion by music and that the aesthetic experience is itself a variety of emotion.

Susan Langer, a musicologist and philosopher of art, in her book *Philosophy in a New Key* expounded the view that music bears a close similarity to the forms of human feeling. In her opinion, music is a tonal analogue of emotional life, but she disagrees with Collingwood and denies it is a language. She argues that sounds are easier to produce than feelings. She pointed out that music is an articulated form, i.e., its parts fuse together to yield greater unities.

We have not remarked very much on the institutions of the world of art: the museums and other housings for paintings and sculptures, the books, libraries, and the schools often with substantial numbers of people in routine employment. We may probably ascribe the persistence of art styles to the conservatism of systems where initiates learn their techniques through apprenticeships to established masters. And there are the concert halls and infrastructure created for the enjoyment of music. Nor have we said very much about the role of society in art. For all this, perhaps we should pay heed to Theodor Adorno whose magnum opus *Aesthetic Theory* was first published posthumously in German in 1970 but not until 1984 in English. Adorno studied philosophy and music composition as a student in Germany but was expelled by the Nazis in 1934. He went to England and then the USA where he worked with Max Horkheimer as part of the Institute for Social Research on what became known as critical theory. Adorno and Horkheimer were horrified by the commercialization of art and indeed all of life in the USA when they arrived from Germany. Critical theory appears to be very similar in its concept to the evolutionary epistemology outlined by Karl Popper in connection with science. Adorno wrote several books and became the mentor for Jürgen Habermas. Adorno wrote in an interdisciplinary style, which, in fact, together with his intricate German, made his work difficult to read and translate, which probably accounts for why he is still relatively unknown in the English-speaking world. But many of his devotees see him as the preeminent philosopher of aesthetics to the present time.

Another line of investigation concerns the question of creativity. Creativity refers to the invention of any new thing (product, artwork, literary work, or even a joke). Creativity is found in all disciplines: psychology, cognitive science, philosophy, technology, art, and science in general. There is a review of creativity in *Wikipedia*, and we find it can be can be traced back to Plato, who actually denied its existence claiming that art was something that could only be discovered. We now believe that creativity is a result of human activity and that art is the product of this activity. In the present instance, our interest in creativity rests in the proposition that new ethical systems can be invented by humans.

17.10 Neuroscience

There is another way in which the twentieth and twenty-first centuries are influencing our thinking on art, and that is through the advances of neuroscience. As a result of investigations on the brain, we now realize that there are trillions of neuronal connections in the brain, many of which are contained in a five-layer thick blanket overlaying the primitive brain. The study of the way in which these layers work is a part of the subject of connectionism and from this has evolved a new theory of how the brain works. A leader in this work is Jeff Hawkins who has published an exposition of his work in *On Intelligence* (2004). The central idea seems to be that intelligence is due to the extra layers of neurons present in the cerebral cortex. The "new" outer layers then monitor what is going on in the inner layers and hence provide information on the systems and patterns of activity to be found in our own thinking. Hawkins's theory offers a possible explanation of the way in which the brain recognizes systems and their schema. Beyond that, it might account for the ease with which humans can follow language and narratives together with the information embedded in them. Ray Kurzweil has taken up this theme in a book *How to Create a Mind: The Secret of Human Thought Revealed* (2012).

Gazzaniga, in his book *Human* (2008), argues that we can all benefit from living in an aesthetically pleasing environment. Thus, it is now recognized that this uniquely human art is firmly based in our biology. But what is its evolutionary advantage? Is there something that goes on in the human brain that has allowed us to engage in pretense, some connectivity change that has allowed us to decouple the true from the imaginary? Tooby and Cosmides (2001) have theorized that this enables us to be very flexible and break out of the rigid behavioral patterns that other animals are subject to. Thus, we can look at a cave wall and imagine it spruced up with a little fresco or to tell the story of the odyssey of Ulysses or see David trapped inside a chunk of marble or look at a strip of bay front property and see the Sydney Opera House. It is still not clear if this ability was a change in the prefrontal cortex as a result of some small genetic mutation or if it was a more gradual process.

There has been an effect on the philosophy of art as a result of the evolutionary psychology movement. This effect is displayed in the career of Ellen Dissanayake and her book *Art and Intimacy: How the Arts Began* (2000). The work focuses on questions of origins: When did art begin its evolution? And when does art start in our lives? Ellen feels the answer is that art began with the primates, all of whom show close mother-infant bonds, and it continues in the human case with babies who learned to smile and with their adult caregivers who have learned to respond to smiles with love and affection. Dissanayake traces the development after that through the exchange of facial expressions, kisses, ornamentation, necklaces, ceremonial actions and gestures, body painting, dancing, drumming, toolmaking, fishing and hunting, weapon making, various skills, and competencies, culminating in building. The whole book is a celebration of the family's contribution to the beginning of civilization. Geoffrey Miller, in his book *The Mating Mind* (2000), as we have mentioned previously, revived Darwin's thinking on the importance of sexual selection in evolution. Another participant in the revival of interest in the Darwinian theory of animal aesthetics is Wolfgang Welsch (2004) who argues that the perception of beauty is a necessary precursor in the sexual selection process. He maintains that evolution could have arranged for other transfers and extensions in the human case to account for our cultural development. We use poetry to improve our writing and speech, as well as pictures and patterns to improve our painting and forms in architecture. But we go even further when we refer to theories in science as being beautiful. And beyond that, we may envisage beautiful constructions in ethics and morality. Welsch even proposes there may be forms of aesthetics appropriate to the transhuman range. He suggests that evolutionary advances in aesthetics are due to emergence and argues that the energy for aesthetic pleasure comes from sexual desire. Darwin himself linked a sense of beauty with high emotional and intellectual capacities. He opined that animals with appreciation of the beautiful in sound, color, or form must also be capable of love, jealousy, and exertion of choice. He believed the explanation of the diverse sensations of pleasure, as for the emotional and intellectual capacities required by the aesthetic sense, "there must be some fundamental cause in the constitution of the nervous system."

17.11 The Supremacy of Art and the Humanities

How may we summarize this excursion through the philosophy of art? Ever since thinking about art began, there has been a discussion on the meaning of form, how representation should be done, and on the role of beauty. We have seen how Hume described "impressions" as being the first results of sensations arriving at our brains. Hume also emphasized the importance of emotion in art. How the artist tries to capture a certain emotion and how we may regard his work as successful if that same emotion is engendered in the mind of the spectator. But then Hume himself points out that there is more to the story than that. There is an important cognitive function at work as well when we exercise our taste. We recognize constancies or systems (which could include Kant's phenomena and noumena). We judge artwork in various ways: in terms of the technical skill of the artist as well as the impression it leaves in our minds. We perform this judgment each according to his own standards (tastes). We have also been through a discussion of where the "art" itself resides, coming to the conclusion along with Collingwood that the vital contribution of the artist is his acts of creativity and imagination. And we have seen how Dewey extends the idea to the proposition that art resides in the minds of both artist and spectators who have to have meaningful experiences as a result of viewing art.

If art consists of creativity and imagination, then it must reside in other activities. As Dewey says, "when we say that tennis-playing, singing, acting, and a multitude of other activities are arts, we engage . . . in saying that there is art in the conduct of these activities." There must be art in mathematics, science, technology, and numerous other disciplines. All these human activities are systems and show the characteristics of adaptive systems: they evolve. There are several parallels between the ways science and art grow, but perhaps the most important is that the formulation or modification of theories in science is as much a creative and imaginative process as the germination of a work of art in aesthetics. We may eventually understand the analogy between music and emotion that Langer has proposed as a parallel between similar systems. Finally, we return again to ethics, the topic of this book. Here again, there is a call for the invention of new theories; and thus, we conclude that ethics must include art. Adorno saw art as a significant factor in the economic and hence the social world and believed that to understand the human world we have to discourse on history, social theory, ethics, and aesthetics as interacting systems. Such a system may provide us with a basis of a theory of the financial value of art. We also see the advisability of having an ethic whereby we conduct our lives using the best practices in each of our human systems. Adorno seems to have supported the idea of one unified and critical theory for all of human science and art, as its critical element is then the key to understanding all civilization. Thus, we reach our final conclusion: that art and ethics must both be partners to social theory and humanism is that social theory whose goodness must depend on art and ethics. In his latest book *The Meaning of Human Existence* (2014), E. O. Wilson also claims that it is "the humanities, including philosophy, law, history and the creative arts that are all important."

18 Religion and the Evolution of Humanism

18. Religion and the Evolution
of Humanism

18.1 Introduction

The central thrust of this chapter is the assertion that religions evolve. We will argue that the direction of the evolution is toward various forms of humanism. We will point out that humanism is itself evolving and that in this case the direction of the evolution can be consciously determined by humanists. This guided evolution may be thought of as a series of experiments whereby humanists adapt their systems to changes in the world in which they function and to improvements in human understanding of the natural world. We will argue that religions and their humanist successors are part of the integrative systems vital to all individuals and societies and as such will continue to have an important role to play in the future. Our purpose here is not to present a survey of religions in all their profusion of beliefs and practices, a subject covered in an extensive literature and with which it is assumed the reader has some familiarity. Monroe's (1995) work on comparative religion would provide a useful reference in this regard. Our first point of focus is the very fact of the diversity of religion. Sources on comparative religion (see, for example, *www.adherents.com*) commonly list a dozen major religions (Babi and Baha'i faiths, Buddhism, Confucianism, Christianity, Hinduism, Islam, Jainism, Judaism, Shinto, Sikhism,

Taoism, and Zoroastrianism). Virtually all these religions have several branches. For example, in the case of Christianity, the same source lists the following eighteen major denominational families in order of numbers of adherents: Catholic, Eastern Orthodox, African indigenous sects, Pentecostal, reformed (Presbyterian, Congregational, etc.), Baptist, Anglican, Lutheran, Methodist, Jehovah's Witnesses, Latter-Day Saints, Adventist, Apostolic and New Apostolic, Stone-Campbell (Restoration Movement), New Thought (Unity, Christian Science, etc.), Brethren (including Plymouth Brethren), and Mennonite and Friends (Quakers). This classification omits the many "primitive" religions of Africa, North and South America, Polynesia, and Australia. We might also mention the many new age religions. There are also a number of quasi-religions and loosely organized cults. The anthropologist Anthony Wallace (1966) has estimated that mankind has produced on the order of one hundred thousand religions. In addition, there are the many varieties of "unbelief": atheism, agnosticism, free thought, and humanism. We also have historical evidence for the existence of religions that have passed out of existence: those of Babylon and Egypt and of ancient Greece and Rome and the paganism of Europe. We know from comparative studies that many of these religions and their branches share doctrines, beliefs, and practices. We know from the historical record that many of them have emerged as a result of schisms and divisions of others.

Fig. 6 TreeofReligion

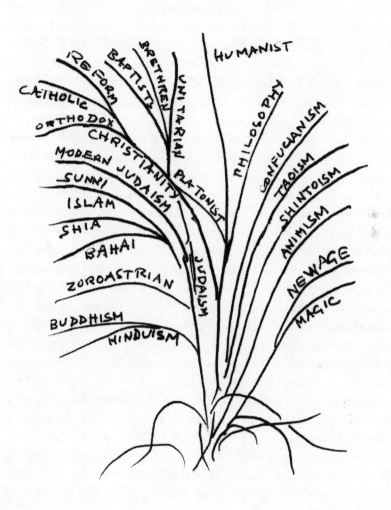

Fig. 6. Tree of Religion

Many of the world's religions have had interconnections. We cannot represent them all accurately, but we do offer this whimsical illustration to show some genealogical relationships between them.

The figure is intended to indicate that organized religious movements arose from primitive systems of polytheistic and magical beliefs. The monotheistic religions (Judaism, Christianity, and Islam) dominate the Western world while Buddhism and polytheistic Hinduism, Taoism, Shintoism, etc., are more prevalent in the East. Animism still flourishes in Africa. Philosophy has ancient roots in many parts of the world, especially in Greece. Philosophy has influenced religion as in the effect of Platonism on Christianity. And philosophy is a direct progenitor of organized humanism.

We may also apply the word *religion* to the state of mind or way of life of an individual follower of a particular religion. The derivation of the word from the Latin *religare, to bind back*, probably arises from this meaning, in the sense that the beliefs are that which binds the individual to his way of life. But the dictionary tells us that the word can also be used to designate any set of principles or practices that govern an individual's life, as in cleanliness was a religion to him. The word in this usage is no longer connected with the supernatural or the superhuman. This use of the word could be extended to cover cosmology, a theory of the existence of the universe and our place in it. In this sense, we might argue that humanism could be classified as a religion. There is some other useful vocabulary that we might clarify at this point. A *cult* is a loosely organized religion, and a *church* refers to an independent religious organization, particularly a Christian Church. The word *cult* has a somewhat pejorative connotation. A *denomination* refers to a subdivision of a religion, which can be distinguished by doctrine or in some other way from its peers, as in a *Protestant denomination*. A *sect* refers to a small denomination, usually one that has broken away from an established church. Sects, religions, churches, cults, and denominations are all examples of what may be called complex adaptive human activity systems.

18.2 Religious Systems

David Hume (1748) pointed out that we are able to recognize entities that have some constant character, and Anatol Rapaport (1986), much later, made the connection between such entities and what we now call systems. The constancy can be associated with some underlying schema or governing law that can often be stated in mathematically precise terms. A system might be as simple as a mass vibrating on a spring in which case the underlying schema is stated by Newton's law of motion. A human being is a system whose constancy is governed by the genome. We can recognize that a human being is made up of many subsystems, the bodily organs, each of which is determined by the action of the genes in building up particular proteins. We can also recognize constancies in the ways a person behaves, which are termed *human activity systems*; and there are constancies in the behavior of groups of humans, which we term *social systems*. We can still recognize the continuity of a system with a slowly changing, or even an adaptive, schema. An adaptive system has the ability to change its "output" in response to changes in its environment. Evolution is nothing other than the slowly changing expression of an adaptive system. This viewpoint has been championed by Pascal Boyer in his book *Religion Explained* (2001). The present purpose is to point out that there is evidence that evolution has occurred in the case of a particular complex system, namely, religion. The irony is that religion has been the very home of the most intransigent opposition to evolutionary theory. But since Darwin's time the evidence has been steadily mounting that such an evolutionary process has indeed been going on in the area of biology with its great variety of forms, living and dead. We now have a variety of methods, ranging from studying the fossil record to noting the changes in DNA, that enable us to construct "trees" of life tracing the lineage of these evolutionary changes. There are similar trees to be found in connection with the development of other types of complex system notably including languages and artifacts.

One religious system can be distinguished from others through its characteristic beliefs, practices, and forms; and these same essentials (with perhaps slight changes) allow us to recognize a religion's persistence from one generation to the next. But in any system analysis, a key question is, why does the system persist? As an example, we might ask, how it is that the Catholic Church is able to live on through the centuries as its individual members pass away? Sets of beliefs are held by individual people. Obviously, the mechanism of persistence involves the addition of new adherents to the membership. Many of these may have been born into and educated in the ways of the religion while others came by way of conversion in later life. The experiences of these children and adult converts that cause them to adhere to the religious society must be, in some sense, satisfactory, or they would not stay. Comfort may be derived from the familiarity of rituals especially in extreme and life-changing situations. Religions may offer "glad tidings," extending hope to those whose lives are otherwise poor and dreary. Religion may be an important part of providing a sense of identity, which is of enormous importance where a country has ethnic divisions. Religion may offer a world view not only of the physical universe but also of human society and a justification of the individual's place within it. Although there is a cognitive element in religion (a theory of everything), it is clear that the ties that bind most individuals to their faiths are emotional and are the subject of psychology, a study famously associated with William James and his work *The Varieties of Religious Experience* (1902).

It was E. O. Wilson (1975, 1978) who pointed out that there is a strong biological influence on the psychology and behavior of individuals, including the behavior of individuals in groups, and an argument that many cultural, moral, and religious behaviors could have developed under the tutelage of Darwinian evolution. The subject is termed *sociobiology* or *evolutionary psychology*. Wilson argues that we have an underlying human nature developed over hundreds of thousands of years, encoded in our genes, and regulated by hormones and neural transmitters, which predispose our behavior in certain directions. All religions are associated with morality, a basic set of rules for human behavior we carry with us in the form of powerful emotional reactions, which we call values. Taking care of our children, refraining from murder and mayhem, and even telling the truth are all policies which have obvious benefits for the survival of our species. Various forms of altruistic behavior, which are difficult to explain on the basis of the evolutionary benefit to an individual alone, can be understood much more readily if we consider the survival of the genes of the group or the species as a whole. Thus, after hundreds of thousands of years, we find these behaviors "hard-wired" into our human natures. Wilson asserts that "the predisposition to religious belief is the most complex and powerful force in the human mind and is in all probability an ineradicable part of human nature." He looks to scientific naturalism to explain traditional religion, its chief competitor, as a wholly material phenomenon. He did not profess to have all the details of such an explanation marshaled at the time of writing but believes that the outlines of an explanation lie in the ability of the human genes to "program the functioning of the nervous, sensory, and hormonal systems of the body, and thereby almost certainly influence the learning process. They constrain the maturation of some behaviors and the learning rules of other behaviors. Incest taboos, taboos in general, xenophobia, the dichotomization of objects into the sacred and profane, nosism, hierarchical dominance systems, intense attention towards leaders, charisma, trophyism, and trance induction are among the elements of religious behavior most likely to be shaped by developmental programs and learning rules. All of these processes act to circumscribe a social group and bind its members together in unquestioning allegiance."

There is a very straightforward explanation of the importance of religion to the individual, in the sense of its being a cosmology and regulator of the way of life. Once animals evolved to a level of conscious awareness, then it would be only a small incremental step to wonder how the individual might fit into the overall scheme of things. If the "theory" of one's place in the universe led to a realistic model of the world and an optimistic assessment of one's chances of success, then the incipient "religion" would have survival value. There is no evidence that prehuman animals had religion, but it seems to have first appeared with the Neanderthals. This explanation of the importance of religion in our lives also explains why it is so closely tied in with our sense of identity. If the lesson of the value of a theory of our place in the universe were genetically encoded, as Wilson suggests, then religion might indeed have a biological basis. These "theories" could also be easily encoded in the form of myths and thus be reinforced by society into the bargain. Gods and magic would certainly provide ready explanations for the vagaries of the natural world and would engender confidence in the votaries of the religions which portrayed the gods as on our side. Even though today many of us have ceased to invoke magic and the supernatural in explaining the universe, there remains a legitimate yearning for an understanding of who we are and where we are going.

One of the primary characteristics of religions is their component cultural systems, i.e., their creeds, tenets, and literature—the beliefs which are more or less shared by the membership. In primitive religions, the culture is populated by spirits, demons, and gods. Childbirth, puberty, growing old, and death are all the subject of legends and magical practices. The weather and other natural phenomena; and warfare are all springboards of emotion and belief expressed in invocations, incantations, and myths. This culture permeates the whole of daily life including the practices of hunting and fishing. For an account of the myths and legends, which grew up based on these beliefs, one can refer to *The Golden Bough* by Frazer (1922). One important development was the emergence of monotheism in Judaism, Christianity, and Islam. So important is the Almighty to these religions that the entire culture is termed *theology*. This can be argued to be an improvement in religious theory in that it replaced the arbitrary caprice of a pantheon of petty gods with the wishes and demands of a single theistic authority. Over the passage of time theologians have refined the accounts of how this omnipotent God acts and the nature of the morality he calls for. It is the variations in these beliefs and the practices of his followers that show up as the branches of the trees in figure 1. God, however, remains supernatural, over and above the forces of nature and, as such, as much beyond nature as his magical predecessors. For an account of how religious adherents have seen change take place, one might refer to Karen Armstrong's *A History of God* (1993).

Religion has a sociological aspect. The religions that are usually of the greatest interest and concern are those that are shared by large communities, sometimes numbering in the millions. We quickly recognize that such sharing does not come about fortuitously: there is teaching, reading, meetings, and other communal activities that are the instrumentalities whereby the beliefs get shared. Furthermore, these actions of belief transmission are not mere transient events but rather the result of more or less permanent organization with specialist agents devoted to the ongoing process of socialization of the religious culture. These are the priests, preachers, missionaries, and bishops who dedicate their lives to the purpose and whose livelihoods frequently depend upon it. There may be substantial economic resources devoted to the service of a religion: buildings, land, monetary, and financial investments. Religion in the past has at times permeated the economic sphere and the polity. There are still countries where interest payments are forbidden.

Kings have risen or fallen depending on the wishes of the churches. Class divisions and civil wars have paralleled religious distinctions.

Graffin and Provine (2007) presented the results of a recent survey of *evolutionary* scientists. They started out with a concern over the distinction between theism (personal God who intervenes in human life) and deism (impersonal God who starts the universe but does not intervene). They discovered that the evolutionary scientists really do not believe in either. But what they did find surprising was that the substantial majority of their respondents (72 percent) see religion as an adaptation and a part of evolution. They stated that "the tenets of religion should be seen as an unstable social adaptation subject to change and reinterpretation." In other words, religion has evolved. Only 8% of the respondents agreed with Stephen Jay Gould's position that religion and our biological heritage should be regarded as non-overlapping magisteria (NOMA). Graffin and Provine found another surprise in the very small support for a third choice, that evolution and religion are mutually exclusive and separated by a gulf that cannot be bridged. This was the answer chosen by Richard Dawkins who has a strong reputation for declaring that science has much better answers for human society than does religion. The position taken by Dawkins and the other new atheists is that they see no benefits whatsoever in religion. Graffin and Provine continued the discussion of the implications of their poll by stating that eminent evolutionists currently see religion as subsumed under sociological evolution or what is now known as sociobiology.

Social evolution was first proposed in the nineteenth century by Herbert Spencer (1852) as a part of his wide-ranging theory, predating Darwin, that the whole universe evolves. There has been a revival of the thesis by Matt Ridley in his book *The Evolution of Everything* (2015). Many theologians claim that the study of evolutionary change in religion is of little interest and brush the topic aside. The pioneers in the sociology of religion were Spencer, Durkheim, and Weber. The aim of their inquiries was to understand the nature of change in the chosen field. One way to understand change in religion is by tracing the necessary adaptations to the emotional and cognitive supports it offers to the individual. Weber was particularly motivated to explain the rise of capitalism in Europe. His theory was that a major change came about as a consequence of the Protestant ethic or the idea that every individual is responsible for his own conduct. This contrasted with the medieval attitude that the church and its priests would intercede with God on the individual's behalf. Another sociologist of some influence in the field was Talcott Parsons (1975) who propounded a general theory of sociological evolution, which can be applied to the case of religious development. Parsons maintained that our human actions can be thought of as being driven by four main systems: the cultural, the personal, the social, and the behavioral organism. These correspond to the influences we have outlined in the preceding paragraphs. Parsons explained evolution as a growth of adaptive capacity arising from the differentiation of these subsystems. Parsons also proposed a similar theory for the evolution of society as a whole, to which we shall return in a later section. Martin (1978) was one of the first sociologists to categorize these and certain other changes as a trend to secularization, but the theory has been most extensively developed by Bruce (1996) and by Boyer (2001). Let us now examine some of the major tendencies in religious evolution proposed by these authors.

18.3 Decline of Theories of Magic and the Supernatural (The Secularization Thesis)

It appears that the family trees of religion arose from various magical beliefs invented by our ancient forbears in contemplating the innumerable strange and often frightening phenomena of their lives, from wild beasts to meteorological and geophysical events, which they explained in terms of spirits and anthropomorphic gods. These beliefs are represented by the bramble patch in figure 6, from which the modern religions have grown. As science and philosophy have provided an increasingly successful naturalistic account of the world, so has the role of magic and superstition receded in religion. Bruce (1996) has presented an extended summary of the decline of the supernatural in the period since the time of the reformation. The trend is most clearly seen in Europe, and Bruce cites evidence gathered in Britain on which to base the case. Before the Reformation, nine out of ten of the rural population were members of the Church of England. Everyone wanted protection against evil, with blessing for their houses, fields, food, and weapons. During the Middle Ages, belief in the devil and hellfire was widespread but is no longer a tenet of mainstream Christianity. The ritual churching of women after childbirth has completely disappeared. Membership of the Church of England had declined to about 18 percent of the total British population in 1800, and although it rose somewhat during the nineteenth century to about 26 percent in 1900, it had declined again to 14 percent by 1990. Bruce cites figures for the town of Cheltenham in 1882, when some 47 percent of the population was found to attend some kind of Christian church on a wet Sunday, increasing to 61 percent in fine weather. The figure nowadays is 12 percent. In 1947 6 percent of the population were found not to believe in any sort of spirit/God or life force. By 1968 this number was 11 percent. By 1981, 4 percent were reported to be atheist; and by 1991, 10 and 13 percent respectively claimed to be atheist and agnostic. Nowadays, 25 percent claim "no religion." Although 72 percent claimed to believe in some sort of supernatural power, in the same survey, only 50 percent said they believed in God. Only 24 percent said they believed in the devil or in hell.

There are other evidences of decline in religious belief in Britain. In 1900, 65 percent of births were baptized in the Church of England while this had declined to 27 percent by 1993. In 1900, 70 percent of weddings were white, i.e., carried out in church, a number that had fallen to 53 percent by 1990. Religious radio broadcasts have been losing their audiences and sales of religious books are down. In the Middle Ages, there was wide acceptance of the doctrine of trans-substantiation, i.e., that the bread and wine of the mass actually became Christ's sacrificed flesh and blood. Many of the famous Thirty-nine Articles of the Church of England would embarrass most contemporary Anglican clergymen. Major elements of the Christian faith have been quietly dropped: e.g., the miracles, the virgin birth, the bodily resurrection of Christ, the expectation of his return, and the reality of eternal damnation. The faith has been relativized: a tenet is judged by how useful its effects are on adherents. Now competing convictions are seen as equally valid. No longer is the world divided into the saved and the damned: we are all God's children now. Bruce notes that this pattern is common to most industrial countries, except the USA.

18.4 Religion and the Growth of Social Complexity

What then is the explanation of this decline in belief in the supernatural as detailed in the preceding section? Bruce first attempts to eliminate what he believes to be a misleading explanation, namely, that religion has declined because people have become better educated and less credulous. He continues, "Committed atheists—the sort of people who join rationalist and humanist associations—and some very liberal Christians believe that religion has lost its medieval dominance because modern people are too clever to believe in old superstitions." Bruce dismisses this by pointing to the dreadful nonsense that people do believe. Whether something is true and whether it becomes widely accepted are two very different questions. Now despite the fact that this author is one of those who join rationalist and humanist associations and finds the arguments for atheism unassailable, as presented by George Smith (1989), Sam Harris (2004), and Richard Dawkins (2006), I am inclined to agree with Bruce that such direct cognitive appeals probably do not completely explain the decline of the supernatural in the religion of the majority of people. It seems to me that Bruce's contention that such evolution is driven by "social forces" is quite persuasive.

What are these "social forces"? Bruce reasons that the whole process of modernization, of which the religious changes are a part, is an economic one. One obvious feature of modernization is the division of social institutions into smaller more specialized units, a process Bruce terms *fragmentation*. The family was once the sole locus of economic production, of education, and of socialization. Now we have factories and schools. Religious institutions have been pushed out of many spheres: firstly from the economy, then from education, and then from social welfare. The pre-Reformation Church was often the government bureaucracy and keeper of national records. The church was frequently an arbiter of legal disputes, including claims to thrones. The church was also involved in health care, many of the first hospitals being religious foundations. In education both religious schools and universities are now indistinguishable from their secular counterparts. People increasingly move out of their "class" or "station" in life. Serfdom has collapsed and has been gradually replaced by democracy.

Different churches have become attached to different religious world views, which made sense of the lives of their adherents in different ways. The Church of England is Episcopalian: God at the top talks to the archbishop who talks to the bishop, who talks to the dean, who talks to the clergy, who talk to the laypeople in regard of what to believe and to do. The upper classes stayed with it after the reformation. James I understood the situation well when he said, "No bishop, no king." In England, the Church of England is strongest among the gentry and their farm servants. Independent farmers and the middle classes became Presbyterians, Methodists, and Congregationalists. The churches, with the strongest belief in the responsibilities of the individual in finding religious salvation, adopted democratic procedures in their governance with policy and doctrine being subject to majority voting in local congregations and national assemblies. These same "liberal" denominations were the first to open the ministry to women. The polity in many churches has become so complex as to justify the establishment of institutions of church law.

Another important trend to influence religion was the emergence of the nation state and the reorganization of life away from the local community toward the larger society of industrial and commercial enterprise, a process Bruce calls *societalization*. We quote from Bruce: "When every birth, marriage and death in generation after generation was celebrated and marked with the same rituals in the same building, then the religion that legitimated those rituals was powerful and persuasive because it was woven into the life of the village. When the total, all-embracing community, working and playing together, gives way to the dormitory town or suburb, there is less held in common to celebrate. Anything approaching the innocence of the tribe by the lagoon with its shared single world-view is no longer possible." Diversity has been created by migration of people. In other settings, it has resulted from the creation of new nation states by mergers of smaller political units. A third source of cultural pluralism has been the internal fragmentation of the dominant culture. In Bruce's opinion, the latter presents the greatest psychological threat. "The nineteenth century Scot, as well as knowing that, somewhere out there, were African pagans and Arab muslims, and, closer to home, Irish Catholics and English Episcopalians, had to come to terms with the presence among his own people of divisions into Kirk, free Church, Free Presbyterian Kirk, Old Seceders, United Seceders, Brethren and Baptists". In rural France, modern Catholicism has been pushed towards a transcendent humanism, according to Bruce. While dominant religious traditions have tried to enforce conformity the social costs of coercion have usually become too high and the state has had to give up.

The final major trend Bruce maintains as an explanation for secularization is "rationalization," by which he means a concern with routines and procedures, predictability and order, improvement, and ever-increasing efficiency. We live in a world of timetables and calendars. We do not expect invasions of the supernatural. Science showed the earth to be round and not flat. It proved that the earth moves around the sun and not vice versa. The earth and life are much older than the Bible suggests. And Darwin's theory of evolution is a better explanation of the origin of species than the account of divine creation. Nevertheless, Bruce argues that the overthrow of some of the early Christian beliefs was not the primary reason for the loss of plausibility of the supernatural. There are many ways in which people can get around unpalatable specifics as indeed the fundamentalists manage to avoid the evidence for evolution. But it is far less easy to avoid being influenced by the general climate of the scientific and technological world. We believe, for example, that complex entities can be broken down into components. We believe that complex actions can be broken down into simple acts that are reproducible—that a given cause has a given unvarying effect. We look for natural causal explanations, and there is little space for the eruption of the divine or supernatural. There are fewer disagreements among scientists than among the clergy. The secular professions enjoy the sort of respect that the church commanded in the Middle Ages. Technology has been very successful in delivering the goods, and we no longer need the supernatural in ever wider spheres of public life. Another way in which science and technology reduce the place for traditional religion is through the social power of their institutions. For example, life and death are now mostly administered for us by doctors and medical technicians in hospitals.

The shamans' use of magic in prehistoric religion was the beginning of the praxis of the various engineering professions and the priests deserve much credit for starting the systematic acquisition of knowledge, which has since grown into science. The universities by the time of the Middle Ages were, for the most part, organs of the church. It was not until the nineteenth century that the universities finally overthrew the authority of the church on the academic campus. The academic disciplines are now fiercely independent and feel no obligation to contribute to, or to fit into, any overarching cosmology. It takes an outstanding figure such as E. O. Wilson in his book *Consilience* (1998) to remind the academic world of the importance of the unification of knowledge in various disciplines to build up a single coherent picture of everything.

18.5 Religion and Ethnicity

There are a number of examples where religion has become inextricably entwined with the ethnicity of some group. Bruce (1996) gives an interesting account of this phenomenon. Perhaps the leading example of such a situation is that of the Jews and Judaism. Judaism has long been the religion of the "chosen race" who are the descendants of the ancient Hebrews. They do not believe in universal salvation. But of course there are other examples. The Scots who were settled in Northern Ireland by William of Orange retained their Protestant faiths and thus made religion into an identifying factor to differentiate themselves from the indigenous Catholics. There have been periods in the history of Northern Ireland when recriminations and counter-recriminations became the order of the day leading eventually to endless provocation and civil strife, which was the situation when the first draft of this chapter was being written. Similarly in the Balkans, the contending parties were Catholics and Orthodox with the admixture of followers of Islam since the time of Turkish occupation. In the Indian subcontinent, we have the apparently unresolvable conflict between the Hindus and Muslims. The conflict between the Jews and Arabs in the Middle East is assuming religious dimensions. During times of oppression such as experienced by the Irish before the creation of the Irish Free State, the Catholic Church was the only organization able to oppose the oppressors; and thus, the church grew in strength as the defender of Irish ethnicity. The situation was similar in Poland under Communist rule where again it was the Catholic Church that provided the only shelter for Polish nationalism. In the case of the Afrikaners and the Ulster Protestants, we have examples of Protestantism serving as a legitimator and guarantor of ethnic identity.

Another example is the case of religion in America. As waves of immigrants settled in the new world they brought their cultures with them and religious affiliations are primary among these. The pilgrims sought refuge from persecution in Britain and established the puritan tradition in New England. Martin (1996) traces the rise of the modern "religious right" all the way back to these early settlers. The Irish brought Catholicism to the USA. For the blacks, imported as slaves and living under conditions often calculated to destroy their culture, the Christian religion provided the only sociality permissible. Their identity grew from spirituals through jazz to black consciousness. Immigrants from Germany, Sweden, Norway, and Finland each brought their own native language varieties of Lutheranism. With the Russians came Orthodoxy. The separation of church and state under the US Constitution meant that all churches were equal and had to compete for membership. So it is small wonder that the situation in the USA was and is different from that in Britain and Europe. Church membership especially among fundamentalists flourishes in the USA.

Nevertheless, even in America, Bruce reports evidence that secularization is in process, a claim supported by the findings of the Pew Foundation. Although Americans claim a high degree of church involvement, the churches themselves find their denominations are shrinking. Evangelical churches are growing but not sufficiently to offset the observed overall membership declines. It was de Tocqueville who first suggested that the success of American Christianity was due to the need to appeal to the people directly in the absence of state financing. De Tocqueville's experience in France led him to believe that a close association of church and state alienates people from religion if they become disenchanted with the old social order. In the Catholic countries—Spain, Italy, and France—there is a polarization between the church and the secular block comprising the Communists and Socialists. However, as Bruce points out, in Protestant countries where the idea is well established that any individual can discern the will of God, and where bishops and priests are not necessary, then one can form one's own religious organization. The British did just that with the appearance of Methodists, Baptists, Presbyterians, Congregationalists, Quakers, and numerous other denominations. De Tocqueville believed that the American clergy worked hard from economic necessity, but others have suggested that pioneering clergy (especially the uneducated Methodists and Baptists) had such zeal that they could sustain congregations anywhere. Religious communities have tended to take root and grow in certain localities in the United States: Congregationalists and Episcopalians in New England, Baptists in the South, Mormons in Utah, Lutherans in the Midwest, etc. The churches tend to play the same role of legitimator and guarantor of ethnic identity as they do in some parts of the old world. Bruce maintains that this is the reason for the strength of religion in America. Bruce does not mention another striking piece of evidence for this thesis: the rapid growth of Islamic, Hindu, and Buddhist communities in many American cities in support of the many Asian immigrants of recent years. Finally, we must take note of the convulsions within Islam as the fundamentalist Islamist movement grows alongside the political revolutions of the Arab spring.

18.6 Countertrends

There are a number of reactionary countertrends to the processes of rationalization and growth of complexity in religion. In the first place, there are the fundamentalists who simply demand that the processes of modernization and secularization should be reversed and that the clock should be turned back to the olden times of the pure religion. In America, we have the puritanical moralizing religious right who have entered the political arena in an attempt to force their agenda on the whole country. This movement has been described by Martin in his book *With God on our Side* (1996). From crusading against the teaching of Darwin's theory of evolution, the effort has expanded to opposing birth control, sex education, and abortion. But the reaction in the West pales in comparison with that in the Islamic nations. There women are to be returned to subjugation, veiled and without education. Primitive barbaric concepts of justice with flogging and maiming for punishment are being brought back in Allah's name. Boys are sent to die in holy wars in the belief that they will earn eternal glory in exchange for martyrdom. In both East and West, the most egregious manifestations of fundamentalism are being contested by the secular world, and in addition, forces of moderation are growing within the religions themselves. Thus, in the West, the internal inconsistencies of the creationist movement may yet prove its undoing; and in the East, the moderate mullahs may wrest away the leadership of Islam. Some of the Christian fundamentalists, as we have noted already, are heavily committed politically whereas others completely eschew politics, seeking instead the "kingdom of God." Followers of the Socinian tradition, as recounted by Marian Hillar and Claire S. Allen (2002), believed in the importance of men using their individual reason and proceeded to strip the traditional Christian theology of its Greek appendages (the Trinity, for example) and returned to the beliefs of the early church. Perhaps eventually these denominations will ask themselves why they should wish to model their lives on two-thousand-year-old religious myths and prejudices.

A number of new religions arose in the 1970s. How do we understand these occurrences in terms of the secularization thesis? Bruce points out that that these new religions were of two principle varieties: world affirming or world rejecting. The world-rejecting new religions include the Reverend Moon's Unification Church (the Moonies), the Hare Krishna, Jim Jones's Peoples Temple in Guyana, and Charles Manson's "Family" in California. According to Bruce, the world-affirming new religions include Norman Vincent Peale's Power of Positive Thinking, Scientology, Transcendental Meditation (TM), and Rajneeshism, as it appeared in the Antelope, Oregon and Insight Weekends. The world rejectors renounce secular society and are typically puritan and totalitarian. On the other hand, the world affirmers, for the most part, are quite happy with the world, are mainly concerned with freeing the inner self (perhaps as a take-off from humanistic psychology), and are only vaguely theistic but may use drug induced experience to achieve their purposes. Bruce points out that typical adherents of the new religions are upper or middle class, with few members from the working class. Stark and Bainbridge (1985, 1987) have argued that the occurrence of these new religions is proof that the secularization thesis is incorrect and that religion is inevitable since, however much we have, we always need more. In support of this, we are reminded that

Durkheim explained the rise in suicide rates in times of prosperity in just such a way. To counter the argument, Bruce points out that it is the world-affirming new religions that have been successful and that the world-denying ones have either self-destructed or mutated into conventional forms.

Another countertrend is found in the new age. Bruce describes this as a term used loosely to describe a wide range of beliefs and practices, many with roots in the esoteric culture of the late-nineteenth century and others that are extensions of the new religions of the 1970s. Most elements of new age are cultic and organized around commercial enterprises and magazines. A typical advertisement is for tarot, crystals, oils, lava lamps, jewelry, incense, cards etc. A typical magazine could be *Wicca Brief*, a newsletter for Wiccans and pagans in German. The popularity of the new age cannot be measured from memberships. It is hard to estimate the popularity of UFO-ology, Ouija, astrology, tarot, hypnosis, crystals, reflexology, channeling, and I-Ching; but they are obviously attractive to many people. The volume of new age books sold is one gage of this. Magic lives on. Channelers hear voices, including that of the Almighty. New age practitioners believe they are developing new science, liberated from Newtonian thinking, i.e., rationality. Conventional scientists work in specialized disciplines, but new agers feel free to connect ideas from different fields on an ad hoc basis. New agers are greens who believe in Gaia and that small is beautiful. Human potential movements tend to become increasingly spiritual. New agers are typically quite tolerant except when they begin to approach medicine, when demands for standards arise, as in the case of the accreditation of aromatherapists. The Protestant notion that we can all discern God's will is amplified in the new age. But even some astrologers are trying to institute professional organization. One problem with the widespread tolerance in the new age movement is that there are no widely accepted grounds for disagreeing with any idea. Once again, it is to be observed that there are no working-class new agers. There are many more women involved than men, a phenomenon also discussed by Bruce at some length. There are some aspects of the new age that are progressive, the holism of new science, for example. However, the rejection of the technological as opposed to the natural does not seem to be humanistic. Finally, we note that the new agers are not very effective at the promotion of radical or specific change because they lack the cohesion and discipline of a sect.

The new age is closely akin to postmodernism. This is a movement within academic departments of philosophy and sociology that formally tries to reverse the preeminence given to rationality since the time of the Enlightenment. It almost appears as if some sociologists have fallen into the trap of accepting the new age beliefs of their subjects. This sorry state of affairs is described by Gross and Levitt in their volume *Higher Superstition: the Academic Left and its Quarrels with Science* (1994). In *The Golem*, Harry Collins and Trevor Pinch (1993) bring their sociological biases to bear on Einstein. They attempt to dismiss the theory of relativity as a product of purely social influences. This gross failure to comprehend the nature of the hard sciences and mathematics unfortunately detracts from some observations about the adequacy of science in the overall scheme of things. The first major point in this respect is that many scientists themselves fail to understand the distinction between the technological and the observational sciences. Sociologists themselves cannot decide if sociology is a science or a member of the humanities. Religion was thrown off the campus, and rightly so at the time, but has not been replaced by any other integrative discipline. Even if academics understand the work of their colleagues in other departments (which they rarely do), there is almost no attempt these days to offer any overview of the state of the total academic enterprise. The philosophers who in the past produced cosmologies and systems are no longer to be found and the discipline of philosophy is used only for the analysis of truths proposed by others. Religion, banished from the campus, struggles to satisfy many needs science overlooks. It continues to be the principle vehicle for instruction in ethics and morality. The academy has only just come to the realization through the writings of E. O. Wilson that much morality is instinctive. The campus offers no department of glad tidings, although futurology may help in the future. Economics ignores the integrative system. Emotions and the aesthetic are vital parts of the lives of ordinary people but are not properly integrated into the scientific world view.

18.7 Religion in the World

We may speculate that the family was the prototypical human social system. We can imagine that the polity, the economy, and the religious and educational institutions might have begun as parts of family life. As social evolution progresses, the tendency is for subsystems to become more specialized, as we have already mentioned, and for these units eventually to achieve greater and greater autonomy. Parsons presents us with a picture of the evolution of the social system, which is similar to his view of the systems encompassing the individual. He portrays the principal divisions of the social system as the maintenance of institutionalized cultural patterns, the societal community, the polity, and the economy. Parsons saw cultural evolution as the growth in complexity of these divisions. A similar but more detailed exposition again along systems-theoretical lines has been presented by Boulding (1978). Both Parsons and Boulding see religion as a part of the integrative system that is in turn a part of the cultural system. Over the years, the religious system has had extensive responsibility in education, health care, economics, and even political and civic administration. In Europe and America, these functions have been largely stripped away from the churches although in Islamic countries the fundamentalists have at least temporarily reversed the situation. What remains in Europe and America are those functions by which people take cognizance of their lives and determine the cultural basis of future trends. Bruce discusses the internal structures of certain churches whereby these functions are fulfilled. The Catholics have a hierarchical system with pope, cardinals, bishops, and parish priests. They also have a staff, the Curia, located in the Vatican, which includes not only the offices required to interact with the secular world in political (foreign) affairs and church investments, publications, and education but also an office for correct belief. Other denominations are much less structured but may include deliberative councils of lay members. Many Christian denominations have governance that is complex enough to require institutions of church law. I have not found a comparative study of the internal structure of various church institutions.

One problem for all religions and for their free-thinking successors is that educational levels vary considerably throughout the membership.

Christ said, "In my father's house are many mansions," a delightful mistranslation in the King James Version, which should have been rendered "in my father's house are many rooms," meaning that there must be tolerance for people at varying levels of understanding. One solution is to establish a priesthood well educated and respected by the laity who will then permit them to speak for the community. But where every member considers himself, a spokesman the religion will remain a cult. The problem is particularly acute among nonbelievers (e.g., freethinkers, atheists, agnostics, and humanists) where the difficulties of organization have been compared to trying to herd cats. As Bruce points out, the structure adopted by a particular religion will reflect its beliefs. If we believe in democracy, the laity must certainly have a voice in church affairs, but we need to be sufficiently disciplined to arrange matters that decisions can be made and adhered to long enough to assess their validity. Another problem, which can arise, is when the membership suspends its critical judgment, allowing itself to be swayed by emotional appeals and simplistic reasoning. Such ideological demagoguery was common in the Fascist and Communist movements, giving rise to fanaticism among the membership but can be found in religion as well, as described in Hoffer's *The True Believer* (1951).

18.8 The Future of Religion

The secularization thesis, as propounded by Martin (1975) and Bruce (1996), proposes that there are three major changes going on in religious evolution: (1) a decline in popular involvement in religion, (2) a decline in the scope and influence of religious institutions, and (3) a decline in the popularity and impact of religious beliefs. The evidence for these trends has been summarized in preceding sections. The measures of religiosity in which Bruce finds the greatest decline are those involving the supernatural. The decline in scope and influence of religious institutions involves the growing complexity of social life and the partition of various subsystems away from the religious. I would like to suggest that what is happening could equally well be described as humanization, i.e., a tendency for the various religions to evolve toward forms of humanism. In one instance, at least (the Catholic Church in France), Bruce actually states that this is so. We would find certain other groups, such as the unitarians, much further along the road than the French Catholics. In the USA the humanist movement was instigated by unitarians and continues to have a close association with them. On this basis, we would expect the future of religion to continue the ongoing trends. We would expect the various ramifications of the tree of religion to persist in the future but with all branches becoming increasingly humanistic.

The humanist movement fulfills a function in the lives of humanists, namely as an integrating system which provides a cosmological explanation of the universe and helps in the definition of desirable behavior. But this is much the same as the role that religions have settled upon or are at least approaching in this modern age. Every complex adaptive system needs a defining module in its structure: a theory for its existence. The humanist world view is naturalistic, explicitly repudiating the supernatural, whereas most religions still retain some traces of the supernatural, usually in the form of some vague belief in divinity. One ventures to predict therefore that the last remnants of the supernatural will eventually be dropped from religion. Perhaps the search for God or spirituality will be replaced by the search for humanity. The promise of humanism must surely be extended to everyone insofar as each individual can comprehend the attainment of a humane world.

A recent edition of *Free Inquiry* (2009, vol. 29, no. 1) contained two views on the future of religion. Both articles made some good points, and it seems appropriate to review them here. The first article, by Gregory S. Paul (2008/2009), starts by reminding us that the question "Why belief in God and Gods is so ubiquitous?" is frequently asked, for instance, by no less a personality than Alan Alda. The Templeton Foundation has embarked on a multimillion-dollar project to determine why people believe in God. Paul is then at some pains to show that it is a misconception that belief in religion is a universal part of human nature found in all cultures. This he establishes by reference to many sociological statistical surveys, by Gallup and Harris, among others, which show that theistic unbelief has been growing in recent years. The Pew Foundation has shown that the lowest measures of religiosity are found in Sweden, the Czech Republic, France, Britain, Bulgaria, Japan, and Russia. High levels are found in Senegal, Indonesia, Kuwait,

Nigeria, Pakistan, and Jordan. The United States, despite its high per capita GDP, occupies a middling position. He also reminds us that measures of social success—which are high for societies such as Norway, Denmark, and Sweden—correlate with high measures of secularism. The United States has low measures of secularism, which correlate with low measures of social success (high rates of homicide, incarceration, youth and adult mortality, suicide, STDs, teen pregnancy, abortion, marriage failure, alcohol consumption, corruption, life satisfaction, income disparity, poverty, work hours, and employment levels). Paul finds that religion has proved able to thrive only in populations whose living conditions are sufficiently defective to cause the majority to resort to petitioning speculative supernatural powers for aid. Paul's prognosis for religion is bleak.

The second article, by historian Alexander Saxton (2008/2009), traces the world's recent religious history as it relates to political and economic developments. Saxton starts by pointing out that the Enlightenment and the concomitant age of secularism was followed by two world wars with the Depression of the 1930s sandwiched in between. Science now stands at the apex of its achievements, having had recent breakthroughs in genetics and evolutionary biology that seem most alarming to fundamentalist believers. Best sellers by Sam Harris (2004) Richard Dawkins (2006), Christopher Hitchens (2007), Daniel Dennett (2006), and, most recently, E. O. Wilson (2012) in powerful polemical style all seem set to steam-roller the fundamentalist Christian position. The result has been that we have witnessed some strategic withdrawals from the fundamentalist theistic positions by the Templeton Fund, which has adopted the more moderate positions of Francis Collins, Freeman Dyson, and Charles Townes. The prestige of the fund, however, according to Saxton, has been growing despite its wealth and the fact that its awards exceed those of the Nobel prizes. Saxton contends that matters have entered some sort of neutral territory and that a reconstruction of religion may occur on the basis of the universal moral grammar posited by Marc Hauser (2006)

It seems to the present author that both of these papers are close to the position taken in this chapter, namely, that religions are ethical systems with moral precepts as well as practices and beliefs and that if these can be made consonant with natural laws and practices amenable to living humans, then religion will have entered the realm of humanism and be able to look forward to a future flourishing with benefit for everyone. Many Christian sects now recognize that theistic dogma is an impediment to modern members. In particular, the Unitarian Universalists include large numbers of atheists, agnostics, and humanists among their members. Members of the Ethical Union base their beliefs and liturgy on purely ethical considerations. It is possible that in the future there will be a movement in the direction of Lloyd Geering's *Christianity without God* (2002).

18.9 The Evolution of Humanism

Humanistic thinking has arisen in different parts of the world apparently quite independently. The Hindus, Buddhists, and Confucians first brought a philosophical approach to the human condition in the East. Humanism first appeared in the West through the thinking of the Greek philosophers; and we tend to look to Thales, Democritus, Protagoras, Socrates, Aristotle, and Epicurus as early humanists. Among the Romans, we had Lucretius, Cicero, and Marcus Aurelius. Classical thought was revived with the Renaissance and flourished with the growth of science and the universities. The period of the Enlightenment saw the growth of confidence in human reason and an expansion of the sphere of classical thought through the work of such thinkers as Erasmus, Moore, Descartes, Spinoza, Pascal, Bacon, Voltaire, Hobbes, Locke, Hume, Condorcet, and Kant. Although humanistic thought flourished within certain of the churches, philosophers who wished to completely discard the old beliefs in the supernatural worked largely as isolated individuals. It was not until the nineteenth century that substantial numbers of people began to declare themselves "freethinkers" or "nonbelievers" and began to associate together independent of the religious world. For the most part they listened to lectures, or held discussions. Comte's Religion of Humanity was an early attempt to reinvent traditional Christianity. In his early beliefs, Marx was quite humanistic, but the present-day humanist movement is strongly democratic following the leads of Russell and Dewey. In the nineteenth century, the important contributors included Darwin, Ingersoll, and Spencer. The knee-jerk left-wing ideology has been left behind in favor of an engineering approach based on a knowledge of political systems. The term *humanism* came to be widely adopted in the early years of the twentieth century. For more detailed accounts of the history and philosophy of humanism, the reader is referred to works by John Dewey (1934), Corliss Lamont (1949), Paul Kurtz (1983) Jaap van Praag (1982), Edward Erickson (1988), and Lloyd and Mary Morain (1998). Ayn Rand is close to the humanist position but not completely there.

There are humanist organizations now in over one hundred countries, and the International Humanist and Ethical Union (IHEU) represents over four million members worldwide. Humanism does not have organizational continuity with any religion or, for that matter, with any other institution. However, most of its members came from other organizations bringing ideas on structure with them. These ideas constitute the base from which humanism will evolve. Julian Huxley's book *Religion without Revelation* (1957) is a source for "religious" humanists. Some humanist organizations have put an emphasis on growing as secular institutions, and indeed, the humanist movement could learn much from the academic world and professional organizations. The humanist movement has similarities to, for instance, the ISSS (International Society for the System Sciences) or the AAAS (Association for the Advancement of American Science). One problem here is that these societies are elitist in their membership whereas humanism, like religion, has to accommodate members of all educational levels. Rather than be torn apart by the religious secular dichotomy, we should try to learn from Dewey (1934) who observed that there is a continuum from the religious to the secular. We should recognize that what we are building is neither religious nor secular in any traditional sense but something new that draws on the best of both worlds. Activities were limited at first by lack of resources, but now many humanist groups have buildings and full- or part-time employees. We aim to teach through conferences and publications, courses, discussion groups, book clubs, film clubs and, with whatever other media come to hand, how people can better themselves and the society in which they live. As other religions or social movements become more humanistic in their outlook and approaches, we should be able to find common causes for improvements in the social world, for charities and specific causes or political programs. The humanist life-stance (see Finch, 1998) rests heavily on the humanist psychology of Fromm and Maslow and should emphasize learning from experience.

Socrates's aphorism "Good people in a good society" is still an apt summary of humanism and its objectives. To express a similar thought in the language of Immanuel Kant, our search is for humanity both in ourselves and in society. But humanism, unlike many religions, regards change as inevitable and, if handled correctly, beneficial. The reason for this is that our understanding of what constitutes a good person or a good society changes with time. Evolution is, therefore, more than a matter of static doctrine for the humanist movement. Every so often, the humanist movement puts out a new manifesto to reflect our improving understanding. The major discovery that humanists have to show the world is evolution itself. We hope that humanism will evolve, taking the lessons of history to heart, so that it will adapt more readily than has been the case with religion. The evolution of humanism is, however, self-conscious and self-directed. Humanism will benefit from academic knowledge in all areas, starting with mathematics and the natural sciences but extending into the social sciences, medicine, engineering, law, and business. As already mentioned, some earlier humanists were beguiled into accepting Marxist theories. Surely, the failure of Communism should show us that capitalist economic systems are superior. This is not to say that the capitalist system cannot itself evolve and improve. But surely, the humanist movement will benefit from adopting businesslike methods and building endowment to finance its work. Similarly, it could learn from studying political systems. Some separation of powers among the institutions of the humanist movement seems to have evolved and to be of benefit to the health of the total system. However, there does seem to be a problem of resolving conflicts between these bodies; and for this, the author suggests the establishment of a judicial system, similar in function to the legal system in the body politic. Another problem that the humanist movement has in trying to operate a democratic governance is in adopting suitable procedures for operating the various boards it has set up at national and local levels. As various procedures are tried, we need to describe the results and pass the information on to other groups instead of repeating past mistakes. One of the problems of the past has been the difficulty of communication for a community widely scattered over vast areas such as the USA. Electronic "meetings" present unique challenges, and we need an electronic version of *Robert's Rules of Order* to keep matters under control.

The American Humanist Association was incorporated in 1941, and the IHEU was founded in 1952; and thus, we see that organized humanism in comparison with most religions is a recent development. What is the justification for starting a new movement as opposed to remaining within the existing religions to accelerate their evolution? The hope is that as a new venture without the old supernaturalistic and magical encumbrances, humanism can offer not only a rational life-stance for the present, as mentioned above, but also unclouded visions for the future (see *Humanist Futures* by Finch, 1999). As opposed to the "glad tidings" offered by Christianity, namely, the false promise of immortality in a mythical heaven, humanism projects attainable possibilities in this real world. There are many options with our evolutionary approach for the development of our destinies. In other words, there may be many different humanisms. But humanism suffers from some of the same problems as mainstream Christianity, as detailed in this essay, in its inability to compete with fundamentalism and the new age. How can we humanists be possessed of the most subtle truths the world has ever known or contemplate the most profound changes in technology and biology but be unable to persuade our fellow humans to give up superstition and the rituals of millennia long passed? The humanist message is not simple or calculated to appeal to the emotions that governed our Stone Age ancestors. We need substitutes for the myths of religion, the beauty of the church buildings, music, and liturgy. It is crucial that we humanists find ways to open the doors to deeper emotional artistry, feeling, and commitment to accompany our scientific knowledge and philosophical reserve.

19 Humanist Purpose

Outline

19. Meaning and Purpose

19.1 Milestones in Ethics

It is interesting that the literature of ethics, i.e., the academic writing that focuses on the theory of our behavior, has tended to progress on a path that is somewhat disengaged from, and behindhand, to what we actually do. Let us recollect some of the milestones in this literature, by which I mean to recall the major works of the philosophical discipline aimed at truly penetrating the theoretical bases of morality. Perhaps the first outstanding work of this kind was *The Republic*, which started with Plato's reprise of Socrates's thinking but then went on to present Plato's own developing philosophy. In a number of dialogues, there is laid out a complete cosmology including Plato's theory of physical reality (in the allegory of the cave) and his ideas on who should rule the city. This work was so startlingly original and impressive that it is still often used to introduce students to philosophy even today. Plato's student Aristotle was another giant of early ethical discourse. It was Aristotle who introduced us to the concept of eudaimonia (usually translated as happiness) as a goal for living. His work on logic and science stood for a thousand years as a touchstone of excellence. It was not until the time of the Renaissance that we find philosophers who could really challenge and improve upon the ideas of the Greek cosmologists with new renditions. This was the age of Hume and Kant who began again in the period of the Enlightenment to explore the structure of the human mind and offer pictures of how emotion and cognition operate in the working of our morality. Karl Marx gave us one of the first ethical theories based on sociology which he claimed was determined by economics. Charles Darwin gave us the concepts of natural selection and sexual selection as the two main engines of evolution. Many philosophers took up the work and by the time of the twentieth century we have such giants as Dewey and Habermas expounding pragmatism and the theory of communicative action. Most recently, we have Singer and the expanding circle, pointing out that our morality must extend to other sentient beings who can experience suffering. Paul Kurtz has shown us the relevance of ethics to our lives as humanists. Philip Kitcher has shown how ethics is a project that must incorporate the findings of archeology, primatology, anthropology, history, and psychology; but we need to see how to reconcile his views with those of Miller as regards sexual selection. It was Socrates who said that the unexamined life was not worth living and Nozick (1989) who called on us all to examine our lives.

19.2 Contemporary Humanism

But humanism is an academic project as well as being a lifestance, and we might best proceed by listing the characteristics we have elucidated for it in the preceding chapters

- It is evolutionary (inspired by Charles Darwin, Julian Huxley, Edward O. Wilson).
- It is atheistic (or Nietzschean vs Christian).
- It is part of sociology (inspired by Auguste Comte, Karl Marx, Talcott Parsons, and James Q. Wilson).
- It includes such topics as conscience, manners, honor, planning, and morals.
- It includes some instinctive behavior which has survival value today (fear, food, shelter, and sex).
- It includes humanistic behavior based on both emotion and reason (think both of David Hume and Immanuel Kant).
- It includes values and social systems that may be regarded as both measures and structures.
- It may include instincts, values, and principles to suit different situations.

- It may be include divisions into great objectives, with goods such as health, wealth, happiness, and wisdom, as mentioned by John Stuart Mill.
- It requires humanists to constitute ethical communities.
- It may include moral crusades such as listed by Singer and Kitcher,
- It should be forward looking, as we learn, evolve and find new visions for the future.

The nontheist's basis for ethical thinking does not include divine sanctions or supernatural revelations. The basis of our ethical knowledge is subjective emotion and meaning and our best understanding of the natural world, which we could call truth. Objective knowledge is what we can share with other people through language, reason, logic and mathematics. Hence, we need to build up natural science and cosmology, biology, psychology and social theory. We use the same cognitive tools in art and in inventing systems for business and economics. Finally, we see ethics as part of the practical panoply of politics and law and of the engineered world.

19.3 Social History

In the earlier part of this book, we set out some of the thinking that was developed by philosophers as they began to theorize about ethics. But several writers have pointed out that one of the most interesting aspects of our moral/ethical development has been the fact that some of the biggest changes have come about as a result of social situations rather than the influence of individual thinkers. Kitcher (2011) starts by citing some ancient examples of ethical change with the objective of clarifying the way(s) change came about so that we might anticipate how future changes might be effected. He refers to the change from the hunter-gatherer mode to small group living. There was the vanishing of the lex talionis or the concept of exact retribution or "an eye for an eye". Thus, if someone causes the death of the daughter of a senior, then the killer's daughter is to be put to death. A few centuries later, it is the actual perpetrator of the deed who must pay with his own life. The hunter-gatherer was par excellence a loner who answered to his own vision. If his group was to be involved in battle, he fought as an individual in the common project. But the Greeks devised a new form of warfare whereby a group of combatants locked their shields together and advanced on the enemy en masse in a phalanx. This put a premium on group solidarity so that it became necessary for there to be an agreed upon objective. The growth of civilized life then demanded an end to each man's striving to serve his own honor and the substitution of goals dictated by communal action.

In the ancient honor codes of the hunter-gatherers men and women had to live up to expectations of behavior. Men were expected to show bravery and courage when hunting game or when confronting human enemies. There were other demands on sexual behavior, such as avoidance of incest or unions outside of marriage. But with the coming of civilization many of these honor codes were changed in favor of legal arrangements enforced by group or government rules. In disagreement with Nietzsche, Kitcher contends that ventures undertaken in solidarity, as opposed to a common project and dominated by the thirst for honor, is at least a step forward.

Another example Kitcher gives is the coming of Christianity. In that case, there was a slow transformation of the ethical framework of the Greco-Roman world toward increasing compassion, forgiving enemies, and loving one's fellows. There came an understanding that the slaughter of prisoners of war, gladiatorial shows, and polygamy were all wrong. There was even a trend toward the abolition of slavery and ending of the subjugation of women.

A watershed event in England was the signing of the Magna Carta, whereby the monarch agreed to live by rules approved by members of a parliament of the nobility. This came about after long years of discontent. A sequel to that event occurred with the American Revolution resulting in an advance in democratization in the colonies.

19.4 Purpose

There is an aspect of our psychology that seems to be unique to humans and that is our need for meaning and purpose. This is an important subject for our discussion of ethics, which we have not entered into yet, so it is crucial that we at least touch upon it before closing the book. There is an excellent article on the subject on the Internet by Steve Taylor titled *The Power of Purpose*. Taylor quotes Viktor Frankl's famous work *Man's Search for Meaning*, describing experiences in concentration camps during World War II. Frankl observed that the most likely to survive were those who felt that they had a goal or purpose. Frankl himself spent a lot of time reconstructing a manuscript he had lost on his journey to the camp. It was his life's work.

Meaning and purpose are not words used by every humanist writer in summarizing our philosophy. Socrates talks about the need to examine our lives without pinpointing any particular feature of the examination. Epicurus and then Aristotle laid some emphasis on happiness as the crux of the matter, and this idea has been elaborated by philosophers such as Paul Kurtz and several psychologists in the twentieth century, as described in chapter 4. Happiness is clearly a component of the good life for many people. But many others find that they cannot be happy if their lives are without purpose or are meaningless. For these folk, the words of Jaap van Praag, the Dutch humanist leader in his 1982 book *Foundations of Humanism*, are like a clarion call. He has a section on "Meaning and Mode of Life" in which he declares that "providing meaning is the most fundamental need of human existence." He continues, "The reports on this are very clear indeed. A human being has a place somewhere outside structures and circumstances. That is where he finds his responsibility, that is where he starts providing a meaning. If his life does not make sense, if he lives in an existential void, that is when he is really in distress . . . Providing meaning is the key to a life worth living, not free from structures or circumstances, but directed to an inner force that makes their humanization possible."

I am grateful to Peter Derkx and his article "Humanism as a Meaning Frame" in the volume edited by Anthony B. Pinn, *What is Humanism and Why Does it Matter?* (2013) for reminding the English-speaking world of this work by van Praag. In the same article, the humanist public is introduced to a monumental work by Roy Baumeister *Meanings of Life* (1991). We will return to this important reference in the next section.

There is a speculation I would like to advance in connection with the importance so many people attach to meaning and purpose. My thought arises from the idea that the human use of language had its start in the period just after the separation of humans and apes. Surely, this was when meaning in its usual connotation entered our evolutionary heritage. Language and meaning must have grown up together in our experience. They must have come along together with hunting, art, cooking, music, and all the other prominent manifestations of human life. We soon reached the point where we so depended on picking up meaning that we could no longer do without it. Now this is meaning in its usual and simple sense—that is, the realization of a connection between speech or writing or artwork and some aspect of reality. Unfortunately, the discussion has been clouded by the extrapolation of meaning to cover some higher-level connection to religion or mystical aspect of nature. I propose we set this higher-level interpretation of meaning aside for the moment.

Taylor suggests several reasons why purpose is good for our psychological health. In the first place, it helps us overcome the internal discord that results when our attention is not externally directed. Our minds are then diverted by the associational chatter of our thoughts that can then generate negative feelings. We need to feel a part of something bigger than ourselves, to feel focused on something outside ourselves. This enhances our self-esteem, and we feel a sense of competence and achievement. We are then likely to experience Csikszentmihalyi's sense of flow (1990). Purpose is also related to hope.

There are several facets of religion adherents find to be of benefit, one of which is this very sense of purpose. Paul Kurtz (2006) points out that "religious creeds have provided important support systems, and they have cultivated charitable efforts and the bonds of moral cohesion . . . Where mainline religious denominations have built what were in fact secular communities of friends, they have satisfied important psychological-sociological needs, often without imposing authoritarian overlays. Secular humanists can learn much from the denominations about the need to build communities." Many observers recognize that religion does not simply provide an explanation for the universe and man's place in it but also provides a social structure for the individual, an idea propounded by Michael Shermer (2005) who states that there is a "twofold purpose that religions serve . . . (1) explanation and (2) social cohesion." A similar point can be derived from the philosophy of Jürgen Habermas, which has been summarized by Finlayson (2006). Habermas has advanced the thesis that what makes the coherence of human society possible is our extensive and continuous discourse. He expounded this viewpoint in his magnum opus *The Theory of Communicative Action* (1984). Habermas sees ethical and moral discourse as a part of the theory of society, i.e., we cannot understand the one without the other. Habermas's moral discourse is equivalent to Baumeister's meaning.

We are now nearing the conclusion of our exploration into evolutionary ethics. We have reviewed the major themes in our subject. One of the principal characteristics of the undertaking is its unfinished nature. We see that there is a continuous unfolding of subject matter the prospect of which stretches out into the future. We are not able to prophesy exactly what lies ahead and our present position depends on past history so that different groups of people are to be seen as residing and traveling on different evolutionary paths. It follows that various authors will have different stories to relate and that even in the course of the narration any one author will discover new material to record. The earlier chapters of this book contain much detail on the theory of ethics we do not need to repeat, and there are new insights constantly coming to light. In particular, I have been impressed by Philip Kitcher's (2011) *The Ethical Project* whose presentation hinges largely around altruism.

19.5 Meaning Frames

Derkx (2013) proposes a new way of thinking about humanism, namely, that it is a "meaning frame." To explain this, we first have to understand *meaning*. Derkx reminds us of van Jaap's discussion of this subject, which he equates to Roy Baumeister's presentation of the subject. Baumeister restricts his inquiry to the simple usage of the terms *reality*, *life*, and *meaning*. Reality corresponds to nature and culture. Nature is the physical world, or "world one" in Popper's nomenclature. The second category of reality is the world of meaning, or what Popper called the man-made world. Baumeister demonstrates that meaning is real but not the same as physical matter by using some examples. For instance, a building may exist as an idea in the architect's mind before it becomes a physical object. Blueprints, contracts, zoning restrictions, building codes, and other meanings play a vital role in the creation of the building.

Baumeister then explains how the concept of meaning can be used in clarifying four specific needs, namely, for purpose, value, efficacy, and self-worth. He defines a purpose as that which connects our present activities to some chosen future state. Value, or justification, seems to be equivalent to what we have termed ethics or moral conduct. Efficacy seems to correspond to pragmatic or engineering knowledge, and self-worth refers to our psychological need to compare ourselves favorably to others. Derkx argues the case for adding three more needs to Baumeister's original four. These three new categories are comprehensibility, connectedness, and transcendence. Comprehensibility reflects our need to understand the world we live in. Connectedness may be superfluous in the listing since meaning is itself already defined as connection. Baumeister points out that love and family are probably our most important source of meaning and connectedness. Finally, transcendence speaks to our need to relate to a structure that is bigger than our own personal interests.

Derkx proposes then that humanists can avail themselves of the meaning frame of seven elements to provide a sense of direction, stability, identity, continuity, and with criteria to evaluate situations and one's life course. I was impressed with this presentation and its similarity to the list of humanist principles gathered together in appendix 1. In the next section, I have tried to map Derkx's meaning frame onto the list of principles.

19.6 Humanist Principles

The following set of principles is arrived at based on historical grounds. Let us start with a summary of our essential humanist beliefs. There have been several earlier summary statements such as the Humanist Manifestos I and II, Corliss Lamont's *Central Propositions of Humanism* (1982), Paul Kurtz's *Secular Humanist Declaration* (1983), and Fred Edwords *The Humanist Philosophy in Perspective* (1984). I agree with most of the statements made in these articles but with a few changes of emphasis to reflect our changing times. One way to approach the problem of formulating our basic principles is by working backward from the various fields of knowledge, summarizing what we know and abstracting the methods that have led us to our present status. This seems to be the method used by Corliss Lamont. As our knowledge grows in different areas and the literature in humanist libraries accumulates, we should expect to revise our basic statements; and they, in turn, will influence the future growth of our knowledge. A willingness to adapt and change should be a characteristic of humanism to distinguish it from dogmatic and inflexible religion. Similarly, we would not expect every adherent of the humanist movement to subscribe completely to every one of the principles. Some of our members are more knowledgeable than others and may be leaders in the process of expansion and improvement. One rendition is set out in table 19.1:

Table 19.1 Principles of Humanism

1. *Nature.* Humanism is built on systems all of which have their foundation in the natural world in which people and their minds have evolved.
2. The *systems of the human mind* are products of the natural world that enable us to be creative agents and are the source of individual freedom, dignity, and responsibility and allow us to make collective cultural constructions.

3. We exist in a world of our own *human-made systems*.
4. *Emotions*. We have to recognize that emotions are the driving force of our behavior. We need to provide the loving relationships of a family for the security of young and old.
5. *Values*. People are able to share emotions and build and refine their values through various arts.
6. *Reason*. We should base our conduct on the best knowledge available and evaluate it with sensitivity and logic. All people are equal for rational analysis.
7. *Ethics*. We should use our emotions, values, and rationality in building ethical theories and systems to live by.
8. *Pragmatism*. We should uphold the methods of social systems that have proven to be successful in the past, including the law, science, and good practice, while working for their improvement.
9. *Commitment*. We need to belong to the communities and organizations that foster our world view and enable it to be tested and improved.
10. *Meaning, Purpose, and Destiny*. We believe that humanism should offer visions of the future that will inspire the individual and guide the policies of society.

The first three principles are aspects of the search for truth in which we follow Popper (1966) in recognizing the three worlds of nature, the mind, and the artificial. The naturalist principle is the affirmation of our belief in the fundamental reality of the physical world. We believe in the power of the scientific method to lead us to an understanding of the origin and development of the universe. We envisage that eventually physics may achieve a unified theory of space-time and the existence of the fundamental particles. We see the emergence of atoms, molecules and life-forms as an evolutionary sequence leading to the appearance of humans on the earth. We appreciate the beauty of nature, and we realize that since we exist within the natural environment, we need to treat it responsibly. We believe that the human mind, residing in the brain, is a part of the natural universe although we still do not understand completely at this time how the mind-brain system works. We believe the brain and mind die together. We believe that our five senses are the source of our information on the physical world. These sensations and conscious awareness we believe are aspects of psychology that we share with many other animal species. But humans have much greater abilities to recognize natural systems and to invent artificial systems than any other animal. We believe that humans experience emotions that are not felt by animals. These superior abilities of the human mind make every person a unique universe of experiences worthy of the same respect we each accord our own lives. Human life should therefore be treated with the utmost respect. To the extent that we are able to envision the consequences of our actions, we are responsible for them.

We believe that past progress has resulted from the use of such systematic methodologies, that this is what has resulted in the great complexity and extent of human civilizations. The invention of language and writing; the use of tools; the development of agriculture; the building of structures for shelter and transport; the growth of medicine and surgery; the invention of money and commercial arrangements; the establishment of law and political institutions, schools, universities, and the natural sciences; telecommunications and computers; music and the arts. The same abilities are used in the arts to share emotional and aesthetic experiences. It is clear that we are ourselves products of the worlds we live in. The languages we learn to speak, the customs we adhere to, the theories and beliefs we hold, the technologies we learn to use all shape the minds we have. Mathematics is a part of the man-made world. People have developed certain sensitivities we term *values*, which we use to judge information coming to us: truth, beauty, goodness, and justice being examples. Our aesthetic sensibilities respond to the ugly and the beautiful. Our moral sense responds to good versus evil. We respond to people with emotions ranging from love to hate. Furthermore, we are able to share emotions with others through the media of the various arts. In this way, we are able to imagine the effects of putative actions and policies.

We recognize the equality of other people and certain rights that they should have. We should tolerate their beliefs and treat them with goodwill unless they are clearly hostile. We particularly deplore hateful attempts to divide humanity along racial, ethnic, sexual, religious, or cultural lines. *Nonviolence* is the expression of a modern concept that has proved to be of great value. The family should provide the loving relationships necessary for the security of spouses, children, and old people. The members of a family need to recognize that they will change with the passage of time. The purposes and objectives of a relationship should be discussed honestly and mutually agreed upon. We should always try to be honest, and lying and deceit are unacceptable modes of conduct. The pragmatic principle is similar to the rationality principle but has been added here to emphasize that no human construct is absolute or immutable. We should uphold the social customs and systems that have proven to be successful in the past while always recognizing the possibility that they may be improved upon. For the humanist movement, this task devolves into a piecemeal study of certain perennial topics: sexual conduct, birth control, marriage, the family, friendship, workplace, and professional conduct, and dealing with the old, infirm, and disadvantaged. While we recognize the necessity of dealing with the direct effects of evil and crime, we also advocate understanding their causes and trying to treat these problems at their source. We advocate psychological treatment of problems if possible. We place a priority on a balanced education both of the young and of people at all ages. We should uphold democratic political processes and free market economic systems while identifying the problems they cause and recommending changes to alleviate them. Humanists argue that we are best served by open societies in which ideas can be freely exchanged.

The principle of commitment states our dedication to the improvement of the lives of all humankind. We need to belong to organizations that will educate us and disseminate findings on the basic principles which are outlined here. These may be professional organizations, religious, political, or secular societies that are concomitant with our beliefs. We believe that a collection of summary statements such as are given here, which we may call a world view, should be useful as a guide to everyday thinking and decision making. As individuals and in organizations, we should be prepared to modify these summary statements as improvements become apparent. We believe that problems are caused when organizations become dogmatic and allow their world views to become immutable creeds. Humanism as an organized movement is a comparatively recent phenomenon, and we note its similarities to organized religions. We are pleased to see the established religions reform and evolve in the same directions as the humanist movement is itself progressing. We should seek common cause with other religious organizations in pursuit of desirable social changes. Communitarian organizations (churches, schools, civic groups, and charities) have always existed with the objective of helping others, and we humanists need to do our part of this work.

We believe that human beings are responsible for our own destinies and purposes as individuals and collectively. We believe that by thinking and education we can disseminate ideas that will enable people to live meaningful, fulfilling lives growing in wisdom. We are optimists who fear only that pessimistic prophecies of naysayers will bring self-fulfilling doom. We believe that we should offer hope where we can. Considering how quickly science and technology have developed in the recent past, we find that extrapolation to one hundred or one thousand or one million years hence becomes increasingly uncertain. However, if we behave rationally and wisely, we believe that it is possible that everyone will at some time be independently wealthy. We believe that it is possible that most diseases will be eradicated. We believe that the rapid development of genetic engineering enables us to take our future evolution into our own hands. We believe that evil, violence, crime, and war could be banished. We believe that it is possible that we might discover life, even intelligent life, perhaps more knowledgeable than ourselves elsewhere in the universe. We believe that it may be possible for conscious minds to comprehend the existence of the universe and to determine its fate.

19.7 Ancient Altruism

Kitcher and others argue that the determining factor in our ethics is an altruism that predates our emergence as humans. To understand and feel convinced of the truth of this assertion, we need do little else than accept Darwin's arguments for sexual selection, as we set out in section 12.5. Once we realize that sexual partners are motivated by mutual altruism (love), then we have the basis for seeing how altruism entered the human world way back. Darwin's case, as well as the reasons it has been delayed in gaining acceptance, have been ably reviewed by Geoffrey Miller in *The Mating Mind* (2000). We should add to this the point made by E. O. Wilson (2012) that humans are one of a small group of eusocial animals whose altruism extends to all members of their groups. Wilson, Kitcher, and Miller claim that this altruism is both the cause and the explanation for our success. Meaning and altruism took over human life together.

Dawkins, in his book *The Ancestor's Tale* (2004), traces the human evolutionary tree backward and concludes that our kind, the hominins, split off from the branch of the evolutionary tree that we shared with the other apes sometime between five and seven million years ago. Even by this time, humans lived in groups of about fifty individuals, and Kitcher points out that this meant that we were forced to be altruistic to some extent at least. Frans de Waal writes in his recent work *The Bonobo and the Atheist: In Search of Humanism among the Primates* (2013) an account of the state of morality among our ape progenitors. It is now quite clear that there was a moral foundation for our behavior before we began on our evolution as humans. De Waal illustrates the similarity between an early hominin, known as *Ardipithecus*, and a modern bonobo, by showing silhouettes of their feet and arm-to-leg ratios. He also shows a family tree of the apes based on DNA studies, which places *Homo* between gorillas and bonobos. The inference is that we humans are the descendents of those early hominins.

19.8 Treatment of Women

The arrangements for sexual partnerships and pair bonding evidently predated the separation of hominins from their apelike ancestors. The females were biologically obligated to bear the young and then to care for them after birth. Presumably, these circumstances were what resulted in the subjugation of women in the subsequent religious and tribal societies. The institutions of marriage were evolved to cement these arrangements. Thus was the stage set for thousands of years of struggle as women sought status closer to equality. But in none of the instances above do we have any sources revealing how and why people made the apparently progressive shifts. For such clues, we need to move closer to the present. We find out much more about the feelings of participants in the great moral changes involving "second-sex citizens": women are no longer regarded as the property of their fathers or husbands and are treated as equals enfranchised to vote. But the advance of women has been a slow step-by-step process. Kitcher begins the story with Mary Wollstonecraft whose book *A Vindication of the Rights of Women* (1792) advocated education for women. This partial step was the way Wollstonecraft saw to get the process started. Subsequently, other authors built upon the start, working up to voting rights. There was a further advance in the book *On the Subjection of Women* by John Stuart Mill and Harriet Taylor (1859, 1869) which called for full equality in liberty. The process bloomed fully with the works of Virginia Woolf, Simone de Beauvoir, Betty Friedan, Catherine MacKinnon, and their successors. Kitcher makes the point that the process was, in fact, quite complex: as it unfolded, we learned that women wanted things traditionally denied to them, and "they found satisfaction in attaining some of these things; and that fulfillment of the wishes did not thwart desires previously seen as central to female life—public life combined more or less satisfactorily with family life."

The Chinese upper classes developed a unique way of subjugating women by binding their feet from the age of about four and upward. This process involved bending the arches of the feet with cloth until the deformed member resembled a "golden lotus flower" ideally no greater than three inches in length. This painful process of foot binding has been described by Kwame Anthony Appiah (2010), and it is a further example of a wrong-headed morality that afflicted the Chinese for about a millennium. Appiah details how this custom died quite quickly once China became open to European scrutiny. Western society, of course, only countenances foot torture in the wearing of high-heeled shoes. Appiah also points to the Western practice of dueling in which one aristocrat found it acceptable to kill another for insulting behavior. Dueling developed into elaborate codes of honor, which were only abandoned in the nineteenth century when the practice became recognized as laughable. Unfortunately, honor killings persist in some parts of the world even today where they are still not recognized as the travesties that they are.

19.9 Repudiation of Slavery

The other great change that occurred comparatively recently was the abolition of slavery, which started in the Western world. Although the ownership of one human being by another had been accepted since the early days of civilization, in the eighteenth century, revulsion at the practice finally grew so strong that it was abandoned throughout much of the world. There used to be many different concepts to distinguish those who might be enslaved from those who might not be. Each of these ideas drew its own counter arguments. Harriet Beecher Stowe wrote the novel *Uncle Tom's Cabin* (1852), which, according to Phillip Bacon's (1991) history of the United States, "did more than anything else to turn people in the North against slavery."

Kitcher should be commended for associating the changes in the moral climate that occurred in Europe and America with the repudiation of slavery. But if anything he has underreported the enormity of the transition involved. There were many people who came to understand the immorality of the institution in the hundred years or so before its final rejection. After reading the arguments from Kitcher cited in section 7.3, it occurred to me that there were similarities between the American Civil War and the two world wars, which, to my knowledge, have not been fully explored from the viewpoint of the history of ethics and morality. Surely, the greatest lesson of the world wars was what Eleanor Roosevelt called the stupidity of war. The deaths of millions of people were due to unbelievably wicked morality on the part of the leadership of supposedly civilized countries. The Holocaust was a precursor to the birth of the modern European Union and the State of Israel.

19.10 J. S. Mill and the End of Colonialism

We should now also be able to appreciate the importance of John Stuart Mill to the development of humanism and feminism. Mill was a major figure in both the theory and the politics of ending colonialism. His treatment of Utilitarianism is pivotal and is augmented by his panegyric on liberty. Together, his writings and experience set the stage for our modern humanist ethics. Mill is celebrated by Reeves (2007) as being the most important British philosopher of the nineteenth century and has been credited with being both the founder of the libertarian movement and with being the father of feminism. Mill rose to become "chief examiner" of the East India Company, a position that was equivalent to being head of the Indian Civil Service. He was widely credited with being a humane administrator and was influential in banning the Hindu practice of suttee, the burning of widows on a husband's funeral pyre. He was well-known in his day, but his reputation faded after his death in 1873, although it seems to have experienced somewhat of a revival in recent decades.

Mill was born in London on May 20, 1806. He was educated by his father, James Mill as recounted in his autobiography. He was somewhat of a child prodigy, learning Greek at the age of three and Latin at eight, but there is no doubt that he was pushed along the educational path. He had read three of Plato's dialogs by the age of six. He started logic at twelve and political economy at thirteen. He was doing mathematics from eight including geometry, algebra, and differential calculus. However, he preferred history for his private reading.

His father, James Mill, had become a friend and disciple of Jeremy Bentham, author of a book on Utilitarianism. The Mills lived with Bentham for a while in his country house outside London, and John Stuart Mill was sent at the age of fourteen to live with Bentham's brother's family in France to learn French and experience a different culture. On returning to England in 1821, John was given Bentham's book to read and became very excited by it. He said that it gave him a creed that inspired him to become a reformer of the world.

James Mill worked in London as an examiner for the East India Company, and he procured a position for John at its office in Leadenhall Street. John used to walk to work through St. James's Park, and it was there, at the age of seventeen, that he was began a life-altering experience one morning. The story is told by Richard Reeves in opening his book *John Stuart Mill: Victorian Firebrand*. Mill noticed a bundle lying beneath a tree. He carefully unpeeled layers of dirty blankets. Within them lay a newborn, newly killed baby. The infant had been strangled before being discarded. Mill reported his find to a watchman, who would not have been surprised: London in 1823 was full of poor families who could not afford another child. Mill, however, was moved to action. (For an account of the horrors of living in the time of the Industrial Revolution, the reader is referred to Christopher Hibbert's *Social History of Britain* [1987]). With a friend, he toured a working-class district of London distributing a pamphlet that described and advocated contraception. The pamphleteers were arrested for the promotion of obscenity and duly appeared before the magistrate at Bow Street. Once he realized who was in the dock, the magistrate lost his nerve and referred the case to the lord mayor of London. Despite an eloquent self-defense, John Stuart Mill lost his liberty for a couple of days.

He started as a prolific publisher in the newspapers from 1822 onward. He continued serious study of economics and politics and participated in numerous debates and public meetings. In 1826 he suffered a mental breakdown after reading Marmontel's account of the death of his father. He said that it was then that he realized he had feelings after all. He concluded that happiness can only be attained if a person does not seek it directly but instead pursues something else as an end in itself.

In 1830 he started a friendship with a married woman, Harriet Taylor. After the husband, John Taylor, died, they waited two years before getting married in 1851. They collaborated on a plan to produce several works for the benefit of posterity. *On Liberty* was one of these, which was published in 1859, a year after Harriet died.

19.11 On Liberty

This essay was, according to Mill, the expression of a single truth, the importance of "giving full freedom to human nature to expand itself in innumerable and conflicting directions." He says his subject is "the nature and limits of the power which can be legitimately exercised by society over the individual." He defends the absolute freedom of individuals to engage in conduct not harmful to others and the near-absolute freedom of individuals to express opinions of all kinds. This results in the recognition of a variety of individual characters and views.

In modern parlance, we might say that the book is about freedom of speech.

Mill paints a dismal picture of a society in which the individual has been suppressed or kept down by the weight of unexamined customs. These people fail to exercise the human capacity of making a choice and developing qualities of "perception, judgment, discriminative feeling, mental activity, and even moral preference." They only have the faculty of "apelike imitation."

Mill believes there will be benefits for all when society allows people the freedom to develop themselves. New and enlightened forms of conduct will be discovered by the few original thinkers, "the salt of the earth." Mill saw social progress and individual well-being in terms of the "free development of individuality itself, and as one of the principal ingredients of human happiness." He maintained that, if a person possesses any tolerable amount of common sense and experience, his own mode of laying out his existence is the best. However, even those who spurn self-development have claims not to be subjected to the enlightened coercion of original thinkers.

Mill also stresses both the instrumental value of freedom of discussion, this being the best means to the discovery of true beliefs. This makes it the main tool of philosophy. The instrumental argument is only a part of Mill's case for freedom of discussion. A more important part stresses the value of freedom even when we are sure we have true beliefs. Errors are fruitful to understand true beliefs. Some who have a true belief hold it as a mere prejudice, independent of argument. But J. S. M. aims to know the truth. This involves having an open mind to whatever objections can be raised against one's opinions and conduct. "All silencing of discussion is an assumption of infallibility . . . Complete liberty of contradicting and disproving our opinion is the condition which justifies us in assuming its truth for the purposes of action." Even if a person knows the truth, they are not entitled to believe it. The importance of this in a changing world cannot be overestimated, i.e., consider persons, religious, or otherwise who believe they have shortcuts to the truth, bypassing free discussion. They typically claim to have access to general principles, but these need to be applied to various circumstances. Unless they understand the rationale and proper basis, they would be unable to apply them to new cases and situations. For example, what is the scope of the principle "thou shalt not kill"? Does this apply to killing the embryo or fetus? Or to capital punishment? Or euthanasia? Technical developments constantly lead to fresh applications. True beliefs may need revision, refinement, or reformulation.

We also need institutional arrangements for the expression of a diversity of views, including universities granting academic freedom to teachers and researchers. We must have constraints on the ownership of the media of communication. Concentration of such media in too few hands represents serious dangers.

Mill's instrumental arguments for freedom of discussion would cut no ice with those, especially religious people, who believe they have infallible sources of knowledge. They claim to have infallible holy books. The case for religious toleration must rest on the right of people to be guided by their own religious convictions. If only one man held an opinion contrary to all the rest of mankind, mankind would not be justified in silencing him. Ordinary people are the most vulnerable to the "despotism of custom" and the most likely not to develop individuality. But great thinkers can survive even in an oppressive environment. It is mainly to promote flourishing among "average human beings" that Mill pleads for freedom of discussion. To be truly free, we have to live in a free society with free institutions and tolerance of diversity and dissent. He does, however, set some limits to freedom of expression. He says you can't express the opinion that "corn-dealers are starvers of the poor" before an excited mob outside the corn dealer's house, i.e., where the expression is a positive instigation to some mischievous act.

There is a similar absoluteness in the freedom Mill extends to the conduct of individuals. He puts a distinction between self-regarding versus other-regarding conduct. The former has absolute freedom but not the latter. The reason, according to Mill, is that self-regarding conduct has no adverse effect on others. The only purpose for which power can be rightfully exercised over an individual is to prevent harm to others. This is sometimes known as the harm principle and is probably the most widely quoted of Mill's writings. Interference with a man for his own good is not a sufficient warrant. This could be described as antipaternalism.

Many take as an injury to themselves, conduct for which they have a distaste. But there is no parity between the feelings of a person for his own opinion and the feelings of another who is offended at his holding it. Persons should be free to develop their individualities without the paternalistic and moralistic interference of others. But when there is harm to others, then balancing the costs and benefits of intervention is appropriate.

Mill claims that his case for liberty does not rest on "the idea of abstract right, as a thing independent of utility." He sees utility as the ultimate appeal on all ethical questions. But he argues that it must be utility "in the largest sense."

He was appalled by the Mormon institution of polygamy, which he called "a retrograde step in civilization." But he tolerated it on the assumption that the women participated voluntarily. Parents should not have absolute power over children. Husbands should not have "almost despotic power" over their wives. He opposed all those who seek to control the lives of family in the name of religion, culture, or deep moral principles.

19.12 Votes for Women

In 1865 Mill ran for parliament. He refused to spend money on the election or to answer questions. But he was elected as Liberal member for Westminster. He supported Gladstone's Reform Bill of 1866, which was unsuccessful. He himself proposed a motion to give votes to women, and although this was defeated, it got more support than expected. He was defeated in the 1868 election.

For the remainder of his life, Mill devoted himself to justice for women, emerging as one of the first to do so, for which reason Richard Reeves (2008) called him the "father of feminism." His book *The*

Subjection of Women (1869) spelled out the argument for equality. Reeves called it one of the finest polemics in the English language. Mill summarized the argument in the first paragraph. It was "that the principle which regulates the existing social relations between the two sexes—the legal subordination of one sex to the other—is wrong in itself, and now one of the chief hindrances to human improvement; and that it ought to be replaced by a principle of perfect equality, admitting no power or privilege on the one side, nor disability on the other." Mill continued, "Marriage is the only actual bondage known to our law . . . The family is a school of despotism." He tackled head-on the view that women were not up to gender equality. He did not deny that women were less well equipped for public life than men but insisted this was the result of their subjection rather than its cause. "What is now called the nature of women is an eminently artificial thing—the result of forced repression in some directions, unnatural stimulation in others." Women might appear to be focused solely on getting a husband, but this was only to be expected given the state of affairs at the time. Similarly it was hardly surprising that only a few women were crying out for political rights.

It was also undeniable that women did not feature on the list of pioneering artists or scholars, but it was imminently deniable that this was due to inherent inferiority. Mill said, "Institutions, books, education and society all go on training human beings for the old, long after the new has come."

Mill's most dangerous opponents were not the open misogynists, but the men and women who romanticized women's delicate domestic nature, seeing them as 'Angels in the House', after the 1854 poem by Coventry Patmore. Seventy-five years later, Virginia Woolf declared that killing the Angel in the House was part of the occupation of a woman writer. Even Dickens earned Mill's opprobrium by pillorying women's rights in Bleak House. Mrs Beeton's feminine ideal was in stark contrast to the sort of women Mill spent time with. In 1892 William Gladstone based his opposition to women's suffrage on his 'fear . . . lest he should invite her unwittingly to trespass upon the delicacy, the purity, the refinement, the elevation of her own nature, which are the present sources of its power.' Such attitudes towards women were the real causes of their oppression, Mill believed. He compared women's second class status with the domestic slavery practiced by the Greeks. The existing traditions tend to feel normal. Thus foreigners were astonished that England had a queen, but felt it unnatural that women should be soldiers or members of parliament.

One of the ways women were kept in the cold was through their exclusion from higher education. Mill bequeathed about half of his estate to women in higher education. He pointed out the absurd traditional custom among the Turks of seeing it as the height of indecency for women to be seen in the streets unveiled. Mill worked for the East India Co. and was proud of the fact that the company had succeeded in stamping out various barbarous practices of the natives, such as suttee --- the voluntary burning of widows on a husband's funeral pyre, and female infanticide. Another great inroad into Hindu prejudices was the legalizing of remarriage for widows.

In "The Subjection of Women" Mill covered the whole history of women's oppression but he was convinced that the key to unlocking the door for women was getting them the vote. He based his argument on the fact that women paid taxes. Women's interests were not necessarily safe in the hands of fathers, husbands and brothers since these men were frequently the most brutal abusers. He argued that if female suffrage would be good for women, it would also be good for men. Men were short changing themselves by lowering the quality of their life companions. For Mill, being around a passive, meekly subservient creature was not good for the soul. For him, equality was a necessary condition for liberty, and the virtue of human beings is fitness to live together as equals, claiming nothing for themselves but what they freely concede to everyone else. Universal suffrage for women was introduced in Britain in 1928.

19.13 Utilitarianism

Utilitarianism is the central philosophical doctrine of humanism. Its antecedents go back to Epicurus and Aristotle in ancient Greece and its modern resurrection started with David Hume. The next great advocate of its concepts was Jeremy Bentham whose version of the philosophy was given in (1789) in *Introduction to Principles of Morals and Legislation*. James Mill became a utilitarian through his friendship with Bentham, and it was he who introduced his son, John Stuart Mill, to the work in 1821. John immediately became an enthusiast and felt that the philosophy gave him a creed for his own thinking. His own version of the theory was first published in three installments in *Fraser's Magazine* in 1861.

Mill explains that he will attempt to offer something toward the proof of the utilitarian theory by showing that it contributes to things admitted to be good without proof. Health and the art of music are examples of good things that can only be accepted or rejected as good.

He says that everyone from Epicurus to Bentham knows that in the theory *utility* stands for pleasure itself. It might also stand for *useful* or *agreeable* or *ornamental* or *beauty* or *amusement*. It does not necessarily imply superiority to frivolity or pleasures of the moment. The principle of utility or greatest happiness holds that actions are right in proportion as they tend to promote happiness, wrong as they tend to promote the reverse of happiness.

Now the theory excites inveterate dislike, even in fine minds. These people suppose that if life has no better object than pleasure, nothing nobler for desire and pursuit, then the theory is worthy only of swine. To which, in fact, followers of Epicurus were contemptuously likened. The Epicureans answered this by pointing out that their accusers were the ones who suppose that human beings are capable of no pleasures except those of which swine are capable. Epicurean theories assign much higher values to pleasures of the intellect, to feelings and imagination, and to moral sentiments than to those of mere sensation and the body. It is quite compatible with the theory to recognize that some kinds of pleasure are more valuable than others. Quality should be considered as well as quantity.

It is unquestionable that those who have had such experiences give a marked preference to the manner of existence, which employs their higher faculties. Few humans would consent to be changed into any lower animal, even for a promise of the fullest allowance of a beast's pleasures. No intelligent human would consent to be a fool. It is better to be a human dissatisfied than a pig satisfied; better to be Socrates dissatisfied than a fool satisfied.

The philosophers who originally proposed the theory did not mean by happiness, a life of rapture, but some brilliant flashes of such in an existence made up of few and transitory pains, many and various pleasures, with a decided predominance of the active over the passive. Such a life has always appeared worthy of the name of happiness. And such an existence is even now the lot of many during some considerable portion of their lives. Mill thought that the wretched educational and social arrangements at his time were the only real hindrance to its being attainable by almost all.

Mill seemed to think that utilitarianism is equivalent to the golden rule of Jesus of Nazareth. There should be a direct impulse to promote the general good in every individual. Some objectors to utilitarianism say its standard is too high for humanity. It is too much to require people always to act for the general good of society. But no system of ethics requires our sole motive to be a feeling of duty. Ninety-nine out of 100 of our actions are done from other motives and rightly so if the rule of duty does not condemn them.

There is a powerful natural sentiment, once general happiness is recognized, which will constitute the strength of the utilitarian morality. This firm foundation is the social feelings of mankind. It becomes stronger with advances of civilization. The social state is so natural to man we never conceive ourselves otherwise. Society is impossible on any other footing than equality.

We cannot see everyone else as rivals for the means of happiness who we must defeat. The deeply rooted conception every individual, even now, has of himself as a social being tends to make him feel it as one of his natural wants that there should be harmony between his feelings and those of his fellow creatures. He needs to feel he is promoting their good.

Questions about ends are questions about what is ultimately desirable. The principle of utility is desirable as a final end; all other things are desirable as means to that end. So what is required of the principle of utility to make good its claims?

"No reason can be given why the general happiness is desirable, except that each person desires his own happiness." Each person's happiness is a good to that person and the general happiness and therefore a good to the aggregate of all persons. Happiness is therefore one of the criteria of morality. But it is not the sole criterion of morality. People desire other things, e.g., virtue and the absence of vice.

But does utilitarianism deny that people desire virtue? Mill argues that people place virtue at the head of things, which are good as means to the ultimate end. He points out that there are various ingredients of happiness and that each of them is desirable in itself and not merely when considered as swelling an aggregate. The principle of utility does not preclude music or health as means to a collective something called happiness. Virtue was not originally part of the end but is capable of becoming so.

Virtue is not the only thing originally a means that comes to be desired for itself. How about the love of money? Its worth is solely that of the things it will buy. But it can become a part of the end. The same can be said of other great objects of human life: power, fame, etc.

There is a difference between virtue and love of money, power, or fame in that all these may render an individual noxious to others. But there is nothing that makes him such a blessing to others as the cultivation and disinterested love of virtue. According to Mill, love of virtue is above all things important to the general happiness.

Mill discusses the connection between justice and utility by remarking that the subject is one of the strongest obstacles to the principle of utility. Justice is a clear and powerful sentiment resembling an instinct. This seems to point to an existence in nature as something absolute. Is the feeling of (in)justice sui generis like sensations of color or taste or a derivative of a combination of others? Could it be a branch of utility or expediency?

To illuminate the question, Mill proposes to find the distinguishing character of all modes of injustice. To find their common attributes, he surveys the objects themselves. Some help is derived from the history of the word *just*. In most languages, *just* is connected with ordinances of law. The common element is the notion of justice in conformity with law. Among the Hebrews laws came from God. But the Greeks and Romans knew their laws were made by men. They knew that laws might be unjust.

What distinguishes the obligations of justice from moral obligation in general? Duty is a thing that may be exacted from a person as one exacts a debt. This seems to Mill to be the turning point between morality and simple expediency. These ideas of deserving or not-deserving punishment are at the bottom of the notions of right and wrong.

Mill argues that the desire to punish an individual who has done harm grows from two sentiments: the impulse of self-defense and a feeling of sympathy. It is natural to retaliate against harm done to ourselves or to those with whom we sympathize. This is common to all animals. Humans differ from animals in two ways: we sympathize with all human and even all sentient beings and secondly we have a more developed intelligence. This also allows us to apprehend a community of interest with the human society of which we form a part. Thus, threats to the security of society generally is threatening to us and calls forth instincts of self-defense. This allows us to attach ourselves to the tribe, our country, or mankind. Just persons resent a hurt to society.

There follows a recital of a number of maxims that can appear to be either just or unjust depending on the light in which they are regarded. They are examples of the haphazard way in which the maxims of justice have been collected. They seem to have arisen largely from courts of law.

There are also conflicting ideas on apportioning punishments for offenses. A very popular maxim is lex talionis—an eye for an eye, a tooth for a tooth. This Jewish or Muslim precept is now largely abandoned in Europe. But Mill suspects that many minds secretly hanker after it.

Does a worker of superior skill merit superior remuneration? Should he be allowed to work for less time? Social utility can resolve such issues. Taxation raises another set of issues. Should it be proportional to means, with the rich paying more? Or should everyone pay the same? (p. 59). Mill's exposition does make a distinction between those who dismiss consequences as an element of morality (Kantians) and those who do not (as he does).

The moral rules that forbid us hurting one another are the most vital to human well-being. These include rules against interference with freedom. A person may not positively need the benefits of others, but he always needs that they should do him no harm.

He who accepts benefits but denies a return of them when needed inflicts a real hurt. The disappointment of expectation ranks high among human wrongs. It is the principal criminality in breach of friendship and/or promise. A person is only responsible for what he has done voluntarily. It is unjust to condemn a person unheard.

Impartiality is the first of judicial virtues. We should treat all people equally well. This rests on the first principle of morals, the greatest happiness principle. It reminds us of Bentham's dictum: "Everybody to count for one, nobody for more than one." Everybody has an equal claim to happiness. (In a footnote [p. 63], Mill claims that this is an example of consilience, as seen in all branches of science.) All social inequalities that have ceased to be considered expedient assume the quality of injustice. The entire history of social improvement has been a series of transitions by which one custom after another has passed into the rank of universally stigmatized injustice and tyranny. So it has been with the distinctions between slaves and freemen, nobles and serfs, and patricians and plebeians, so it will be with the aristocracies of color, race, and sex.

Justice is a name for certain moral requirements, which, regarded collectively, stand higher in the scale of social utility and therefore are of paramount obligation.

19.14 Millian Morality

Reading Mill's essays transports us back to the Victorian era in Britain. We struggle through long sentences and almost compulsory repetition. Most editions of the essays are presented without the convenience of an index. It was not until John Troyer's *The Classical Utilitarians* (2003) that there was a remedy to this last mentioned deficiency. But even with these problems, there still emerges a commanding presence from Mill's prose.

This feeling is enhanced by Richard Reeves's *John Stuart Mill: Victorian Firebrand*. The epilogue of the book makes some important points about Reeves's subject. It starts by quoting Sidgwick, another prominent Victorian ethicist, on the news of Mill's demise: "I can't go on—Mill is dead."

This reaction conveys the stature Mill had in his own time. Reeves quotes from a number of others in obituaries, and it becomes plain that there was a very mixed reaction overall, with Mill being seen very much as a controversial but eminent public intellectual. It might have been expected that there would have been a reaction to all the animosity since Mill after all was well ahead of his time in many ways, and there would normally have been a major positive appraisal of his work after a few years. But as Reeves points out, such a contribution was very late in coming, and his reputation gradually faded. There was a subscription raised to put a statue in his honor on the Thames Embankment, and this site was visited by a delegation of women after the institution of equal voting rights in February 1928. But it was not until 1991 when the tide eventually began to turn for his reputation, with the publication of the collected edition of his works. Reeves has done us all a great service by his balanced presentation of Mill's great contributions in ethics and his courageous work as a public intellectual.

My feeling is that Mill's spirit hovers over our movement at this very time twenty years into the new millennium. His two great essays on utilitarianism and liberty embody the way ordinary humanists think now in terms of the need for altruistic ethics coupled with freedom for thought and expression. But most of these ordinary people are not aware of how they were anticipated a century beforehand. There is also a resonance between Mill's personal involvement as the champion of women's rights and as the last head of the examiners of the East India Company and the modern membership of the humanist movement, which is strongly representative of women and nonwhites. But there is even more to matters than that in respect to the purposes in Mill's life. We have only partly brought this out so far when we described his remarkable education. It had to have started with the little lad who began his instruction in ancient Greek at age three and scarcely let up until his early twenties. The whole incredible reading list is all set out in his autobiography of 1873. There is no doubt that it was his father, James Mill, who forced the pace or that it was the great legal scholar Jeremy Bentham and his work on utilitarianism that provided the inspiration. John's father introduced him to Bentham's writings in 1821; and from thereon, he felt that he had an object in life: a reformer of the world. But by 1826, John was experiencing a crisis in his mental history. The trouble was that Bentham's formulation was a dry calculus of jurisprudence, useful for determining the greatest good for the greatest number but without the poetry and feeling John Stuart Mill needed to pull his life out of the long period of depression into which it had sunk. He finally credited the poetry of William Wordsworth with bringing some happiness back into his existence.

The word *happiness* had a critical role in the events of this period. Bentham himself had finally yielded to the idea that the sum total of utility in life was what produced a person's happiness and that, as Aristotle had preached two thousand years before, happiness therefore had to be the goal of life. This was what gave Mill his problem. He found that one could not find happiness simply by pursuing it. This is what he wrote in the autobiography: "Ask yourself whether you are happy, and you cease to be so. The only chance is to treat, not happiness, but some end external to it, as the purpose of life. Let your self-consciousness, your scrutiny, your self-interrogation, exhaust themselves on that;"

Thus, Mill was arguing that aiming at something else, people "find happiness by the way." It seems that John Stuart Mill anticipated Jaap van Praag, Roy Baumeister, and E. O. Wilson by some years although he did not use the word 'meaning'.

19.15 Great Objectives

In his book *Utilitarianism*, Mill refers to the great objects of human life. We may assume that that what Mill calls an *object* is the same as an *objective* in modern parlance. The examples of great objectives, which Mill cites, include power, fame, and money. One wonders how seriously Mill was actually endorsing such aims to be the overarching objectives of living or whether he was simply expressing his finding that many people actually do take such aims as these for life. The contention is that Mill was indeed recognizing that people do choose such goals in life. After all, happiness has been recognized as an objective of life at least since the time of Aristotle, and virtue has a similarly ancient pedigree. It is quite common for ordinary people to adopt such mottos as "Healthy, wealthy, and wise" as aims for life. But we know that having more than one such value can lead to conflicts. This had been a concern to Sidgwick as well as other nineteenth century moralists. A resolution to the problem was found by the time of the twentieth century when it was realized that we should not try to achieve definite objectives but instead look to some other consequentialist procedure, such as a variety of evolution, to shape our objectives. In that case, we make plans and evaluate them as we proceed. We should use our values, as Dewey recommended, for guideposts.

In this book, we have taken sixteen areas of knowledge that are vital to our civilization. A person might choose one or a few of these to study and have the objective of becoming an expert. It would probably be very difficult to achieve expertise in all areas however. In point of fact, a given population will divide among the various objectives, and this seems to be a generally satisfactory situation. The only problem with it is that it results in increasingly narrow specializations for the outlooks of the individuals concerned. Someone with no academic knowledge would like to be healthy, wealthy and wise. Mill himself was very accomplished in several areas, partly, of course, due to his early education, followed by his wide experience in the East India Company. In addition to his philosophical writings, he wrote distinguished scholarly works on botany, economics, logic, and religion among other topics. Reeves notes that he was very wide in his reading and tolerant of other viewpoints. Nowadays, we might employ expertise outside our own specialties in the form of tradesmen, lawyers, accountants, or doctors. However, we tend to reject the attentions of clergy trained in religion by seminaries. We are replacing this religious help with leaders specializing in sociology, psychology, philosophy, and political science. But it is clear that we have a long way to go to rival the churches in their ability to train professional help and then to provide employment.

19.16 Systems, Paradigms, and Destinies

Two thousand years ago, Aristotle thought that it was the heart that was the seat of cognition, and it was not until the time of Leonardo da Vinci that the idea appeared that it was, in fact, the brain that played that role. Three hundred years ago, psychology, the study of the mind, was regarded as a branch of philosophy. John Locke and David Hume speculated on the way in which sensation and perception were our window onto the external world. We have an account of the work done by psychologists in chapter 4 as it relates to morality, which we will not repeat here, except for the following few words of summary.

Our human brains entail such functions as sensation, perception, memory, and instinct, which date to our remote evolutionary past and are consequently said to comprise our lizard brain. The mind is constantly bombarded with information from the senses (sight, hearing, taste, smell, and the tactile senses of pressure and heat together with the sense of muscular tension and movement). Work on the detailed understanding of the mechanisms whereby physical stimuli give rise to sensations and then perceptions is still proceeding.

Much of our behavior is essentially the same as in our animal cousins. When our survival is threatened, for instance, by deprivation of oxygen in suffocation or drowning, all thoughts are driven from the mind but the primitive urge to breathe. Other life-threatening situations provoke similar reactions. In terms of urgency, our next priorities seem to be procuring food and shelter. Then come the sexual drives and other emotions such as the love of mother and child. Animals, including humans, are driven to action by what is called motivation. We have already mentioned that the most primitive and basic motivations are those concerned with breathing, feeding, survival, shelter, sex, care of the young, sleep, etc. These motivations also serve to direct our behavior toward specific goals. We are able to sense our motivations, and the experience is then said to be an emotion. Can there be any doubt that many animals can experience suffering in the same way as we humans? We should be grateful that Peter Singer (1975) has made it his purpose to waken the human conscience to the suffering and misery inflicted on countless animals in our drive for food and economic gain.

In addition to the instinctive motivations already mentioned, which are felt by individual humans, there are other cultural motivations that we acquire by virtue of our being members of a social species. Emotions are states of mind that reflect our motivations. Munn (1956) proposes that there is a continuum of emotional states in the mind comprising a relatively low-level background associated with everything we do and a number of high-level peaks that constitute the recognized emotions, such as fear, disgust, anger, jealousy, sympathy, joy, elation, affection, and love. The emotions may be divided into the pleasant and the unpleasant, and human motivation consists of seeking pleasure and avoiding the unpleasant. The idea that the goal of human behavior is happiness goes all the way back to Aristotle but has been recalled as the basis of psychology by Albert Ellis(1962) and by Martin Seligman (2002). There is also an excellent summary of the position by Jonathan Haidt (2006) in *The Happiness Hypothesis*. Seligman (1990) is also the author of an important study on Optimism. Contemporary psychological research has featured the use of mobile telephones to enable reporting of psychological states on an almost real-time basis.

Aristotle summarized our human goal of eudaimonia as meaning the summation of all good things. But we are indebted to John Stuart Mill pointing out that we might divide all these good things into the great objectives of human life, such as health, wealth, happiness, and wisdom. We would wish to attain all those great aims. The concepts might be extended to include all the humanist principles as listed in appendix 1.

Humanism has always been committed to the great progressive values of truth, freedom, and equality. In fact, humanism has always stood in the forefront of the social struggle for democracy, abolition of slavery, women's rights, and international brotherhood. We could attempt to reform religion by getting it to drop its bad features. Another approach was discussed by Paul Kurtz (2006) who asked if as humanists we can create secular and humanist alternatives to religion. We see philosophy as the embodiment of all knowledge so that humanism could be a species of philosophy informed by all the other disciplines and used as the cognitive basis for our alternative to religion. When we look back over time, we realize that it was our ability to learn and the accumulation of knowledge that has contributed to a major part of our species' advance and that which comprises the heritage we humanists wish to pass on. The invention of spoken language was followed by writing and then the development of books and libraries, the tools that made it all possible. As a former professor, I am also proud of the institutional inventions: schools, universities and academic societies, and research laboratories, which have enabled succeeding generations to absorb the stories to date and then to permit the growth of knowledge. Today we live longer, healthier, more interesting lives as a consequence of these advances. Education is the foundation of it all. Education is the process of learning and is not necessarily conducted in the style of the university lecture. We can learn in many different ways: reading books, browsing the Internet, viewing films or television, conducting experiments, visiting museums, and having discussions or debates or discourse. Kurtz (2006) lists the following conditions that need to be satisfied by our alternative to religion:

1. A direct confrontation of the basic existential questions on the meaning of life, from suffering to death
2. Development of ethical values and principles grounded in human experience
3. Appeal to the heart as well as the head

4. Use of the arts to create new narratives and to celebrate life and the march of reason
5. Development of communities of people committed to science and reason

The fact that some of our values work at cross purposes was probably best appreciated by Henry Sidgwick (1874). Somehow we have to invent subroutines that enable us to circumvent the contradictions. We have to remain optimistic and always look on the bright side, as the Beatles sang. Even the *Investor's Business Daily* lists aphorisms to keep us thinking positively.

We have written extensively on systems throughout the book, and we realize that organizational systems (families, churches, schools, universities, governments, businesses, economies) are the tools we use to manage our lives. To ask what is the purpose of life required a sophisticated human being: a philosopher. It is interesting that such people appeared in several parts of the world where civilization had started to flourish at about the same time: Greece, India, and China. The philosophers challenged the established religious and tribal leaders whose concepts were frequently inaccurate or lacking in other ways. They were the questioners who probed the established understanding of nature, society, religion, and state. Frequently, as a result of their inquiries, they rewrote the books in various fields. In some cases, the accounts they gave became the established paradigms for hundreds or even thousands of years. Many of Aristotle's opinions were still accepted as truth until recent times. But as time went on, political powers improved their leadership through the development of democratic processes and philosophers had to specialize into science and mathematics to produce improved paradigms. At the same time, pragmatists of various ilk, from engineers to medical doctors, businessmen, and lawyers, came to the fore from time to time through evolution of their own disciplines. In each field, there was a paradigm the specialists in that area had to grasp in order to be competent with the state of the art. The human race developed as many paradigms as were necessary for all the specialists to be fully employed. It is clear that there is no one paradigm that will guarantee intellectual leadership to philosophy or any other discipline. Although philosophy may still offer useful general summaries of all knowledge, it is not clear that executives with general responsibilities would not be served quite well with educations starting in almost any field. It is not clear how the curriculum for philosophy is determined in the modern age. We should note that Habermas played an important part in standing up to the postmodernist juggernaut when in 1980 he was awarded the Adorno prize and delivered a speech "Modernity—an Unfinished Project." He made it clear that he thought that the Enlightenment was an unfinished project, which had already yielded great benefits, and should be finished. He may have saved philosophy from itself. Postmodernists are not the only enemies we have. Humanists and all modernists need to take the initiative in forging new intellectual paradigms for self-defense in the face of Islamo-fascists, Christian evangelicals, and other assorted anti-intellectuals, barbarians, and troglodytes. One important lesson to be understood here is the need to train humanist leaders and celebrants.

We face a large number of moral problems for which political solutions are required. One feels that these problems could all be solved if the world's population and its politicians could be educated sufficiently. Indeed, the major part of our humanist duties as individuals, in communities, and in the world as a whole consists of promoting the principles of humanism, its manifestos, and the whole Declaration of Human Rights, which are all reproduced in the appendices of this book. We may look forward to a time when the governments of the world act in agreement and when those agreements are administered with tolerance, justice, and fairness to all. Of course, as we look further ahead into the future, matters become increasingly uncertain; and for that reason, we have to reevaluate our positions from time to time. Paul Kurtz has written extensively about the Promethean possibilities of the future. Other future humanist visions have been presented by Singer (1981) and Kitcher (2013). Jeffrey Sachs (2005) has explained how relatively small expenditures could essentially eliminate poverty throughout the world. It should be relatively simple to provide clean air and water and basic financial aid to everyone. Ray Kurzweil (2005) in his remarkable work, *Singularity*, has predicted that the increasingly rapid speed of technological advance in computer science and biology will bring the benefits of instant encyclopedic knowledge to everyone. We imagine a world where every child is wanted and loved—a world where everyone has basic nutrition and health care and where education is free. We may eventually be able to provide everyone with the wealth enjoyed only by the privileged few today. It should be the task of the humanist movement to bring the good news of the possibilities of knowledge to the world. We have to work to overcome the scourge of war and the hatred fomented by religious and political ideology and to replace these pernicious influences by humanistic societies, ethics and morals. We will, of course, need to preserve the environment on Earth and protect ourselves from meteors from space. If research continues, we should be able to eliminate suffering, disease, cancer, and hereditary defects. It should be possible to extend the lifespan as far as each person desires. We might be able to redesign humans to eliminate the design defects nature has encumbered us with. It seems that physics may be close to a "theory of everything," perhaps based on string theory, which may answer ancient questions about the origin of the universe and indeed why there is something rather than nothing. We may discover life, even intelligent life, elsewhere in the universe. Each generation has to test the limits of human achievement. It is said that the ticket collectors on the trains in India ask passengers three questions: Who are you? Where do you come from? Where are you going? On the grand scale, these are the questions we all face, and it is answering them that provides humanist purpose.

Appendix 1

The Principles of Humanism

Truth and knowledge: We should base our conduct on the best available knowledge of the natural world, in which people and their minds have evolved, and on our human-made systems.

Rationality: The systems of the human mind, based in the natural world, enable us to think and be creative agents and are the source of personal freedom, dignity, and responsibility.

Emotions: We have to recognize that emotions are the driving force of our behavior. We need to provide the loving relationships of a family for the security of young and old.

Values: People are able to share emotions and refine their values through the various arts.

Ethics: We should use our emotions, values, and rationality in building ethical theories and systems to live by.

Pragmatism: We should uphold the methods of social systems that have proven to be successful in the past, including the law, science, and good practice, while working for their improvement.

Commitment: We need to belong to the organizations that foster our world view and enable it to be tested and improved.

Destiny: We believe that humanism should offer visions of the future that will inspire the individual and guide the policies of society.

Appendix 2

Affirmations of Humanism

Another statement is shown in table A2.1, a listing originally made by Paul Kurtz that is becoming accepted by several organizations.

Table A2.1 The Affirmations of Humanism

- We are committed to the application of reason and science to the understanding of the universe and to the solving of human problems.
- We deplore efforts to denigrate human intelligence, to seek to explain the world in supernatural terms, and to look outside nature for salvation.
- We believe that scientific discovery and technology can contribute to the betterment of human life.
- We believe in an open and pluralistic society and that democracy is the best guarantee of protecting human rights from authoritarian elites and repressive majorities.
- We are committed to the principle of the separation of church and state.
- We cultivate the arts of negotiation and compromise as a means of resolving differences and achieving mutual understanding.

- We are concerned with securing justice and fairness in society and with eliminating discrimination and intolerance.
- We believe in supporting the disadvantaged and the handicapped so that they will be able to help themselves.
- We attempt to transcend divisive parochial loyalties based on race, religion, gender, nationality, creed, class, sexual orientation, or ethnicity, and strive to work together for the common good of humanity.
- We want to protect and enhance the earth, to preserve it for future generations, and to avoid inflicting needless suffering on other species.
- We believe in enjoying life here and now and in developing our creative talents to their fullest.
- We believe in the cultivation of moral excellence.
- We respect the right to privacy. Mature adults should be allowed to fulfill their aspirations, to express their sexual preferences, to exercise reproductive freedom, to have access to comprehensive and informed health care, and to die with dignity.
- We believe in the common moral decencies: altruism, integrity, honesty, truthfulness, responsibility. Humanist ethics is amenable to critical, rational guidance. There are normative standards that we discover together. Moral principles are tested by their consequences.
- We are deeply concerned with the moral education of our children. We want to nourish reason and compassion.
- We are engaged by the arts no less than by the sciences.
- We are citizens of the universe and are excited by discoveries still to be made in the cosmos.
- We are skeptical of untested claims to knowledge, and we are open to novel ideas and seek new departures in our thinking.
- We affirm humanism as a realistic alternative to theologies of despair and ideologies of violence and as a source of rich personal significance and genuine satisfaction in the service to others.

- We believe in optimism rather than pessimism, hope rather than despair, learning in the place of dogma, truth instead of ignorance, joy rather than guilt or sin, tolerance in the place of fear, love instead of hatred, compassion over selfishness, beauty instead of ugliness, and reason rather than blind faith or irrationality.
- We believe in the fullest realization of the best and noblest that we are capable of as human beings.

From time to time, we need a very short explanation of humanism. In case a humanist is riding an elevator and another passenger notices his lapel pin and asks, "What is humanism?" this requires an answer in one sentence such as "Humanism is a search for the best way to live" or "Humanism is a search for the good life." These might serve as definitions of our life stance.

Appendix 3

Humanist Manifesto III
HUMANISM AND ITS ASPIRATIONS

Humanism is a progressive philosophy of life that, without supernaturalism, affirms our ability and responsibility to lead ethical lives of personal fulfillment that aspire to the greater good of humanity.

The lifestance of Humanism—guided by reason, inspired by compassion, and informed by experience—encourages us to live life well and fully. It evolved through the ages and continues to develop through the efforts of thoughtful people who recognize that values and ideals, however carefully wrought, are subject to change as our knowledge and understandings advance.

This document is part of an ongoing effort to manifest in clear and positive terms the conceptual boundaries of Humanism, not what we must believe but a consensus of what we do believe. It is in this sense that we affirm the following:

Knowledge of the world is derived by observation, experimentation, and rational analysis. Humanists find that science is the best method for determining this knowledge as well as for solving problems and developing beneficial technologies. We also recognize the value of new departures in thought, the arts, and inner experience— each subject to analysis by critical intelligence.

Humans are an integral part of nature, the result of unguided evolutionary change. Humanists recognize nature as self-existing. We accept our life as all and enough, distinguishing things as they are from things as we might wish or imagine them to be. We welcome the challenges of the future, and are drawn to and undaunted by the yet to be known.

Ethical values are derived from human need and interest as tested by experience. Humanists ground values in human welfare shaped by human circumstances, interests, and concerns and extended to the global ecosystem and beyond. We are committed to treating each person as having inherent worth and dignity, and to making informed choices in a context of freedom consonant with responsibility.

Life's fulfillment emerges from individual participation in the service of humane ideals. We aim for our fullest possible development and animate our lives with a deep sense of purpose, finding wonder and awe in the joys and beauties of human existence, its challenges and tragedies, and even in the inevitability and finality of death. Humanists rely on the rich heritage of human culture and the lifestance of Humanism to provide comfort in times of want and encouragement in times of plenty.

Humans are social by nature and find meaning in relationships. Humanists long for and strive toward a world of mutual care and concern, free of cruelty and its consequences, where differences are resolved cooperatively without resorting to violence. The joining of individuality with interdependence enriches our lives, encourages us to enrich the lives of others, and inspires hope of attaining peace, justice, and opportunity for all.

Working to benefit society maximizes individual happiness. Progressive cultures have worked to free humanity from the brutalities of mere survival and to reduce suffering, improve society, and develop global community. We seek to minimize the inequities of circumstance and ability, and we support a just distribution of nature's resources and the fruits of human effort so that as many as possible can enjoy a good life.

Humanists are concerned for the well being of all, are committed to diversity, and respect those of differing yet humane views. We work to uphold the equal enjoyment of human rights and civil liberties in an open, secular society and maintain it is a civic duty to participate in the democratic process and a planetary duty to protect nature's integrity, diversity, and beauty in a secure, sustainable manner.

Thus engaged in the flow of life, we aspire to this vision with the informed conviction that humanity has the ability to progress toward its highest ideals. The responsibility for our lives and the kind of world in which we live is ours and ours alone.

Appendix 4

The Universal Declaration of Human Rights

Preamble

Whereas recognition of the inherent dignity and of the inalienable rights of all members of the human family is the foundation of freedom, justice and peace in the world,

Whereas disregard and contempt for human rights have resulted in barbarous acts which have outraged the conscience of mankind, and the advent of a world in which human beings shall enjoy freedom of speech and belief and freedom from fear and want has been proclaimed as the highest aspiration of the common people,

Whereas it is essential, if man is not to be compelled to have recourse, as a last resort, to rebellion against tyranny and oppression, that human rights should be protected by the rule of law,

Whereas it is essential to promote the development of friendly relations between nations,

Whereas the peoples of the United Nations have in the Charter reaffirmed their faith in fundamental human rights, in the dignity and worth of the human person and in the equal rights of men and women and have determined to promote social progress and better standards of life in larger freedom,

Whereas Member States have pledged themselves to achieve, in cooperation with the United Nations, the promotion of universal respect for and observance of human rights and fundamental freedoms,

Whereas a common understanding of these rights and freedoms is of the greatest importance for the full realization of this pledge,

Now, therefore,

The General Assembly,

proclaims

This Universal Declaration of Human Rights

as a common standard of achievement for all peoples and all nations, to the end that every individual and every organ of society, keeping this Declaration constantly in mind, shall strive by teaching and education to promote respect for these rights and freedoms and by progressive measures, national and international, to secure their universal and effective recognition and observance, both among the peoples of Member States themselves and among the peoples of territories under their jurisdiction.

Article 1

All human beings are born free and equal in dignity and rights. They are endowed with reason and conscience and should act towards one another in a spirit of brotherhood.

Article 2

Everyone is entitled to all the rights and freedoms set forth in this Declaration, without distinction of any kind, such as race, colour, sex, language, religion, political or other opinion, national or social origin, property, birth or other status. Furthermore, no distinction shall be made on the basis of the political, jurisdictional or international status of the country or territory to which a person belongs, whether it be independent, trust, non-self -governing or under any other limitation of sovereignty.

Article 3

Everyone has the right to life, liberty and security of person.

Article 4

No one shall be held in slavery or servitude; slavery and the slave trade shall be prohibited in all their forms.

Article 5

No one shall be subjected to torture or to cruel, inhuman or degrading treatment or punishment.

Article 6

Everyone has the right to recognition everywhere as a person before the law.

Article 7

All are equal before the law and are entitled without any discrimination to equal protection of the law. All are entitled without any discrimination to equal protection of the law. All are entitled to equal protection against any discrimination in violation of this Declaration and against any incitement to such discrimination.

Article 8

Everyone has the right to an effective remedy by the competent national tribunals for acts violating the fundamental rights granted him by the constitution or by law.

Article 9

No one shall be subjected to arbitrary arrest, detention or exile.

Article 10

Everyone is entitled in full equality to a fair and public hearing by an independent and impartial tribunal, in the determination of his rights and obligations and of any criminal charge against him.

Article 11

1   Everyone charged with a penal offence has the right to be presumed innocent until proved guilty according to law in a public trial at which he has had all the guarantees necessary for his defence.

2   No one shall be held guilty of any penal offence on account of any act or omission which did not constitute a penal offence, under national or international law, at the time when it was committed. Nor shall a heavier penalty be imposed than the one that was applicable at the time the penal offence was committed.

Article 12

No one shall be subjected to arbitrary interference with his privacy, family, home or correspondence, nor to attacks upon his honour and reputation. Everyone has the right to the protection of the law against such interference or attacks.

Article 13

1 Everyone has the right to freedom of movement and residence within the borders of each state.
2 Everyone has the right to leave any country, including his own, and to return to his country.

Article 14

1 Everyone has the right to seek and to enjoy in other countries asylum from persecution.
2 This right may not be invoked in the case of prosecutions genuinely arising from non-political crimes or from acts contrary to the purposes and principles of the United Nations.

Article 15

1 Everyone has the right to a nationality.
2 No one shall be arbitrarily deprived of his nationality nor denied the right to change his nationality.

Article 16

1 Men and women of full age, without any limitation due to race, nationality or religion, have the right to marry and to found a family. They are entitled to equal rights as to marriage, during marriage and at its dissolution.
2 Marriage shall be entered into only with the free and full consent of the intending spouses.
3 The family is the natural and fundamental group unit of society and is entitled to protection by society and the State.

Article 17

1 Everyone has the right to own property alone as well as in association with others.
2 No one shall be arbitrarily deprived of his property.

Article 18

Everyone has the right to freedom of thought, conscience and religion; this right includes freedom to change his religion or belief, and freedom, either alone or in community with others and in public or private, to manifest his religion or belief in teaching, practice, worship and observance.

Article 19

Everyone has the right to freedom of opinion and expression; this right includes freedom to hold opinions without interference and to seek, receive and impart information and ideas through any media and regardless of frontiers.

Article 20

1   Everyone has the right to freedom of peaceful assembly and association.
2   No one may be compelled to belong to an association.

Article 21

1   Everyone has the right to take part in the government of his country, directly or through freely chosen representatives.
2   Everyone has the right to equal access to public service in his country.
3   The will of the people shall be the basis of the authority of government; this will shall be expressed in periodic and genuine elections which shall be by universal and equal suffrage and shall be held by secret vote or by equivalent free voting procedures.

Article 22

Everyone, as a member of society, has the right to social security and is entitled to realization, through national effort and international co-operation and in accordance with the organization and resources of each State, of the economic, social and cultural rights indispensable for his dignity and the free development of his personality.

Article 23

1 Everyone has the right to work, to free choice of employment, to just and favorable conditions of work and to protection against unemployment.
2 Everyone, without any discrimination, has the right to equal pay for equal work.
3 Everyone who works has the right to just and favourable remuneration ensuring for himself and his family an existence worthy of human dignity, and supplemented, if necessary, by other means of social protection.
4 Everyone has the right to form and join trade unions for the protection of his interests.

Article 24

Everyone has the right to rest and leisure, including reasonable limitation of working hours and periodic holidays with pay.

Article 25

1. Everyone has the right to a standard of living adequate for the health and well-being of himself and of his family, including food, clothing, housing and medical care and necessary social services, and the right to security in the event of unemployment, sickness, disability, widowhood, old age or other lack of livelihood in circumstances beyond his control.
2. Motherhood and childhood are entitled to special care and assistance. All children, whether born in or out of wedlock, shall enjoy the same social protection.

Article 26

1 Everyone has the right to education. Education shall be free, at least in the elementary and fundamental stages. Elementary education shall be compulsory. Technical and professional education shall be made generally available and higher education shall be equally accessible to all on the basis of merit.

2 Education shall be directed to the full development of the human personality and to the strengthening of respect for human rights and fundamental freedoms. It shall promote understanding, tolerance and friendship among all nations, racial or religious groups, and shall further the activities of the United Nations for the maintenance of peace.

3 Parents have a prior right to choose the kind of education that shall be given to their children.

Article 27

1 Everyone has the right freely to participate in the cultural life of the community, to enjoy the arts and to share in scientific advancement and its benefits.

2 Everyone has the right to the protection of the moral and material interests resulting from any scientific, literary or artistic production of which he is the author.

Article 28

Everyone is entitled to a social and international order in which the rights and freedoms set forth in this Declaration can be fully realized.

Article 29

1. Everyone has duties to the community in which alone the free and full development of his personality is possible.

2. In the exercise of his rights and freedoms, everyone shall be subject only to such limitations as are determined by law solely for the purpose of securing due recognition and respect for the rights and freedoms of others and of meeting the just

requirements of morality, public order and the general welfare in a democratic society.

3. These rights and freedoms may in no case be exercised contrary to the purposes and principles of the United Nations.

Article 30

Nothing in this Declaration may be interpreted as implying for any State, group or person any right to engage in any activity or to perform any act aimed at the destruction of any of the rights and freedoms set forth herein.

Appendix 5

GLOSSARY

The following is a list of words that have been used in this book. Most of them are uncommon, and their standard meanings are given to assist the reader where needed. Included are some arcane items found in the literature of the arts, engineering, philosophy, politics, and sciences. In addition, the listing includes some common words that may have multiple meanings but where the author has chosen the definitions given so as to most closely represent the sense of the text. Most of the words are modern English, but there are a few foreign and ancient contributions, as noted. Other useful glossaries may be found in Roy Speckhardt's *Creating Change through Humanism* (2015), Edward O. Wilson's *On Human Nature* (1978), and Gregory Pence's *A Dictionary of Common Philosophical Terms* (2000).

Academy. A garden outside Athens where Plato used to teach, hence a
    school or research establishment.
acolyte. An attendant or follower
agape. (Greek) love
agnostic. A person who does not believe there is a way to establish the
    existence of gods
allegory. A story in which people, things, and happenings have another
    meaning, as in a fable or parable.
allele. (Biology) a variant form of a gene

aphorism. A short concise statement of a principle

atheist. A person who does not believe in the existence of gods

church. An independent religious organization

compatabilism. (Philosophy) the belief that free will and determinism are compatible ideas and that it is possible to believe both without being logically inconsistent

consequentialism. (Philosophy) the belief that the morality of an action is to be judged solely by its consequences

conscience. The moral content of the mind

cult. A system of religious worship or ritual (somewhat pejorative)

denomination. Subdivision of a religion

deontology. Ethical theory concerned with duty or rights

dialectics. The science of asking and answering questions

dirempt. (Verb) to separate something forcefully

emotivism. Emotivism is a meta-ethical theory claiming that moral statements are simply expressions of emotions and, thus, meaningless.

ethics. The study of how to behave morally

ethology. The science of ethics or character

etiology. The cause or set of causes of a condition (or disease)

eudaimonia. (Greek) usually translated as *happiness* but closer to *flourishing*. Another source says it refers to a state of being healthy, happy, and prosperous.

eupraxophy. Good conduct and wisdom in living

freethinker. Someone who is skeptical about traditional belief, especially religion.

gamete. (Biology) a reproductive cell that can unite with another to form a new organism

Gene. (Genetics) an element by which hereditary characters are transmitted and determined

genome. The complete set of genes in every cell of an organism

genotype. The constitution of an organism in terms of its hereditary factors.

good. That which will be to the benefit of a person or individual.

hermeneutic interpretive, especially of Biblical text.

hermeneutics. The study of the extraction of meaning from writing and speech.

hominid. The group consisting of modern and extinct great apes (e.g., modern humans, chimpanzees, gorillas, and orangutans plus all their immediate ancestors). Definition has changed over time.

hominin. The group consisting of modern humans, extinct human species, and all our immediate ancestors (including members of the genera *Homo australopithecus*, *Paranthropus*, and *Ardipithecus*).

humanism. The accepted beliefs of humanists at a given place and time; the search for the best way to live.

induction. (Philosophy) arriving at a theory by inference as opposed to deduction; (physics) production of a voltage by an incident electromotive force.

ineffable. Too great to be expressed

intentionality. (Philosophy) the power of minds to be about or to stand for things, properties, and states of affairs.

Magi. Wise Men of the East

meiosis. The process of nuclear division in germ cells

moral. (Adjective) pertaining to the distinction between right and wrong

nature. The sum total of all things in time and space

naturalism. The belief that the natural world is the whole of reality

neotic. Of the intellect

neotony. The retention of juvenile features in the adult animal

neophilia. Love or enthusiasm for what is new

nosism. The practice of using the pronoun *we* to refer to oneself when expressing a personal opinion

oviparous. Producing eggs that hatch after leaving the female's body

ovoviviparous. Designating various animals that produce hard-shelled eggs that are hatched within the female's body

panoply. A complete covering or array

phenotype. An organism distinguished by visible characteristics rather than by genetic traits

polyandrous. Having more than one male mate at one time

polygamy. The practice of having two or more wives, husbands, or mates at the same time.

polygynous. Having more than one female mate at one time

protean. (Adjective) tending or able to change frequently

protocol. A record of the points of agreement between negotiating parties.

qualia. The internal and subjective components of sense perceptions

schema. An outline of a systematic arrangement

sect. A small religious denomination

secular. Belonging to the world or worldly things as distinguished from religious affairs

solidarity. Complete unity of purpose

spirituality. Appreciation of beauty in nature

steatopygous. Having enlarged hips and buttocks

system. A set or arrangement of things so related or connected as to form a unity or organic whole; a constant.

suborn. To induce a person to commit an unlawful act

theist. A person who believes in the existence of a god or gods.

tort. A wrongful act or an infringement of a right, leading to civil legal liability.

Ubaid. A prehistoric period of Mesopotamia

value. A system having equivalent emotional components in the minds of two or more people, evoked by an objective linkage between them (see figure 4.1); a term used in sociology; a fair or proper equivalent in money for something sold.

votary. A person bound by a vow or promise wisdom. The use of knowledge for good purposes

Appendix 6

Humanist Bibliography

02/01/2016
Compiled by Robert D. Finch

This Bibliography was compiled in the course of writing essays on various aspects of humanism and its history. With each new essay the references which seemed to be the most pertinent were listed at the end of the individual texts. Each such essay entailed adding several references which were new to the overall bibliography and they were inserted at that time, with the date of the latest revision being given in the title above.

It would be a good goal for the future to annotate each reference with a brief description, but this would likely take some time and it has not been attempted yet. However, there are some books with extensive bibliographies of humanist works which a serious student might like to examine. The paramount example of these is Howard B. Radest's (1987) "Toward Common Ground".

AAAS (2009), "Ardipithicus Ramidus", Special Issue, Science, vol 326, 60-106.
Anapol, Deborah (2010) "Polyamory in the 21st Century", Rowman & Littlefield.

Anscombe, G.E.M., (1981), "Modern Moral Philosophy" in her "Collected Philosophical Papers, vol. 3", University of Minnesota Press.

Appiah, Kwame Anthony (2010), "The Honor Code: How Moral Revolutions Happen", W.W. Norton and Co.

Arendt, Hannah (1951), "The Origins of Totalitarianism", Harcourt Brace.

Aristotle, (350 BCE), "Physics" and "Nichomachean Ethics"

Aristotle "The Nicomachean Ethics" in "Introduction to Aristotle" Modern Library Edition, (1992)

Aristotle (1992), "Introduction to Aristotle" Richard McKeon, Ed., The Modern Library.

Austin, J.L. (1962), "How to do Things with Words", Clarendon Press.

Bacon, Sir Francis, (1620), "The Great Instauration". See also Benjamin Farrington, (1949), "Francis Bacon" Collier Books, 1961.

Bacon, Phillip (1991), "The United States: Its History and Neighbors" Harcourt Brace Jovanovich, Inc.

Balsalla, George, (1988) "The Evolution of Technology", Cambridge University Press.

Barkow, Jerome H., Leda Cosmides and John Tooby (1992) "The Adapted Mind:

Evolutionary Psychology and the Generation of Culture", Oxford University Press.

Barnhart, Joe, (2005), "Common Ground: Ethics for Theists and Naturalists" Essays in the Philosophy of Humanism vol. 13, 51-57, Marian Hillar, editor.

Baumeister, Roy F., (1991), "Meanings of Life", Guilford Press.

Bennett, Jeffrey (2008) "Beyond UFOs", Princeton University Press.

Bentham, Jeremy (1789) "Introduction to Principles of Morals and Legislation."

Bird, Caroline, (1983) "The Good Years: Your Life in the Twenty-First Century", E.P.

Dutton, Inc.

Blackburn, Simon, (2001) "Being Good", Oxford University Press.

Blackburn, Simon, (2005) "Truth: A Guide for the Perplexed", Penguin Books.

Blackburn, Simon, (2010) "Ethics: A Very Short Introduction", Oxford University Press.

Blackham, H.J. (1950) "Living as a Humanist", Rationalist Press Association.

Blackham, H.J. (1952) "Six Existential Thinkers", Routledge.

Blackham, H.J. (1953) "The Human Tradition", Routledge.

Blackham, H.J. (1968) "Humanism", Penguin Books.

Blackstone, William, (1765-69) "Commentaries on the Laws of England."

Boyer, Pascal, (2001) "Religion Explained: The Evolutionary Origins of Religious Thought" Basic Books.

Briggs, Asa, (1983) "A Social History of England", Viking Press.

Brinkerhoff, David B. and Lynn K. White (1085) "Sociology, Second Edition" West Publishing Co.

Bronowski, J. (1977) "A Sense of the Future", Massachusetts Institute of Technology.

Bryson, Bill (2003), "A Short History of Nearly Everything", Broadway Books.

Bullough, Vern L., and Bonnie Bullough, (1995) "Sexual Attitudes: Myths and Realities", Prometheus Books.

Burgess, Ernest W., Harvey J. Locke and Mary Margaret Thomes (1963), "The Family:

From Institution to Companionship", 3rd Edition, American Book Company.

Buss, D. M., (1989), "Sex differences in human mate selection: Evolutionary hypotheses tested in 37 cultures. Behavioral and Brain Sciences, 12, 1-49.

Butler, Gillian and Tony Hope, (1995) "Managing Your Mind: The Mental Fitness Guide", Oxford University Press.

Caspari, Rachel, (2011) "The Evolution of Grandparents", Scientific Am. 305, 45-49

Comfort, Alex, (1972), "The Joy of Sex", Simon and Schuster.

Carnegie, Dale (1936), "How to Win Friends and Influence People", Pocket Book Edition, 1964

Carrier, Richard (2005), "Sense & Goodness Without God", Author House.

Carter, Jimmy (2014), "A Call to Action", Simon and Schuster.

Checkland, Peter (1981) "Systems Thinking, Systems Practice" John Wiley & Sons.

Chomsky, Noam, (1957) "Syntactic Structures", Mouton, The Hague.

Chomsky, Noam, (1965) "Aspects of the Theory of Syntax", MIT Press.

Churchland, Patricia Smith, (1986), "Neurophilosophy: Toward a Unified Science of the Mind/Brain" MIT Press.

Clark, Andy (2003) "Natural-Born Cyborgs", Oxford University Press.

Cockburn, David (1991) "Human Beings" Cambridge University Press.

Comte, Auguste, (1848), "A General View of Positivism"

Comte, Auguste, (1891), "The Catechism of Positive Religion". Reissued by Cambridge University Press, 2009.

Compte-Sponville, Andre (1996) "A Small Treatise on the Great Virtues", Metropolitan Books.

Coon, Carl, (2014), "A Short History of Evolution", Humanist Press.

Cosmides, Leda and John Tooby and Jerome H. Barkow, (1992), "Introduction" in "The Adapted Mind: Evolutionary Psychology and the Generation of Culture," Oxford University Press.

Cosmides, Leda and John Tooby, (1997) "Evolutionary Psychology: A Primer" Center for Evolutionary Psychology, University of California, Santa Barbara.

Cosmides, Leda and John Tooby and Jerome H. Barkow, (2000), "The cognitive neuroscience of social reasoning", in M. Gazzaniga (Ed.), The New Cognitive Neurosciences (pp. 1259-1270), MIT Press.

Covey, Stephen R., (1991) "Principle Centered Leadership", Summit Books.

Csikszentmihalyi, Mihaly, (1990) "Flow: The Psychology of Optimal Experience", Harper and Row.

Cullen-DuPont, Kathryn, (2002) "American Women Activists' Writings: An Anthology 1637-2002" Cooper Square Press.

Damasio, Antonio R., (1994), "Descartes' Error: Emotion, Reason and the Human Brain", G.P.Putman's Sons.

Darwin, Charles, (1859), "On the origin of species by means of natural selection", John Murray. (Reprinted in 1964 by Harvard University Press.)

Darwin, Charles, (1871), "The Descent of Man, and Selection in relation to Sex'

Darwin, Charles, (1872) "The Expression of the Emotions in Man and Animals" and "The Descent of Man, and Selection in Relation to Sex" (1871) in "From So Simple a Beginning: The Four Great Books of Charles Darwin" Ed., Edward O. Wilson, W.W. Norton, 2006.

Dawkins, Richard, (1976), "The Selfish Gene", Oxford University Press.

Dawkins, Richard (2004) "The Ancestor's Tale: A Pilgrimage to the Dawn of Life", Houghton Mifflin Company.

Dawkins, Richard, (2006), "The God Delusion", Bantam Press.

de Beauvoire, Simone, (1989) "The Second Sex", Knopf.

Dennett, Daniel, (1991) "Consciousness Explained", Little Brown & Co.

Dennett, Daniel, (2003) "Freedom Evolves" Viking Press.

Dennett, Daniel C. (2006), "Breaking the Spell", Viking

Derkx, Peter, (2013) "Humanism as a Meaning Frame" in "What is Humanism and Why Does it Matter?" Ed. Anthony B. Pinn.

De Waal, Frans and Frans Lanting (1997) "Bonobo: The Forgotten Ape", Univ. Calif.

Press.

De Waal, Frans, (2013) "The Bonobo and the Atheist: In Search of Humanism Among the Primates", W.W.Norton & Company.

De Waal, Frans (2014), "One for All" in Scientific American, vol 311, pp 69-71

Dewey, John, (1908) "Ethics", reprinted in John Dewey: The Middle Works, 1899-1924, Ed. Jo Ann Boydston, Southern Illinois University Press.

Dewey, John, (1932) "Ethics", reprinted in John Dewey: The Later Works, 1925-1953, Ed. Jo Ann Boydston, Southern Illinois University Press.

Dewey, John, (1939) "Theory of Valuation" vol. II, International Encyclopedia of Unified Science, Otto Neurath Ed.

Dewey, John, (1934), "A Common Faith", Yale University Press.

Diamond, Jared, (1998), "Guns, Germs, and Steel", W.W. Norton & Company.

Drucker, Peter, (1973) "Management: Tasks, Responsibilities, Practices", Harper & Row.

Drucker, Peter, (1990) "Managing the Nonprofit Organization", Harper-Collins.

Duhigg, Charles, (2012) "The Power of Habit: Why We Do What We Do in Life and Business", Random House.

Duncan, Otis Dudley, (2004), "The Rise of the Nones" Part 1, Free Inquiry, Dec. 2003

and Part 2, Free Inquiry, Feb. 2004.

Durkheim, Emile (1921) "The Elementary Forms of Religion".

Dutton, Denis, (2000) "Art and Sexual Selection", Johns Hopkins Univ. Press.

Eagelman, David, (2011) "Incognito: The Secret Lives of the Brain" Pantheon Books.

Eagelman, David, (2015) "The Brain: The Story of You" Pantheon Books.

Edmonds, David and John Eidinow (2001) "Wittgenstein's Poker", Harper-Collins.

Edwards, Paul (2004), "Heidegger's Confusions", Prometheus Books.

Edwords, Frederick, (1984), "The Humanist Philosophy in Perspective" The Humanist, Jan/Feb vol. 44.

Eller, David, (2004) "Natural Atheism", American Atheist Press.

Ellis, Albert, (1961), "A Guide to Rational Living", Wilshire Book Co., 1997.

Ellis, Albert (1962) "Reason and emotion in psychotherapy" Citadel Press.

Emerson, Ralph Waldo

Epstein, Greg M. (2009), "Good Without God: What a Billion Nonreligious People Do Believe", Harper-Collins.

Ferguson, Niall, (2008) "The Ascent of Money", Penguin Press.

Finch, Robert D. (1992) "What We Owe to Others: Humanist Ethics and Systems", Essays in the Philosophy of Humanism, Eds. M.Hillar & H.R. Leuchtag 1, 41-54.

Finch, R. D., (1994), "The Philosophy of Sir Karl Popper", Essays in the Philosophy of Humanism, Eds. M.Hillar and F. Prahl vol.3, 133-152.

Finch, Robert David, (1997) "Are Corporations Meeting Their Ethical Responsibilities?", Essays in the Philosophy of Humanism, vol. 5, pp 113-116, Eds. Marian Hillar and F. Prahl

Finch, Robert D., (1998) "The Humanist Lifestance: Important Issues in the Lives of Individuals" in Essays in the Philosophy of Humanism vol. 6, Eds., R.D. Finch, Marian Hillar and Frank Prahl.

Finch, Robert D.(1999) "Humanist Futures" in Essays in the Philosophy of Humanism, vol. 7, 30-57, Eds. Robert D. Finch, Marian Hillar and Frank Prahl.

Finch, Robert D. (2000) "Evolution, Adaptive Systems and Humanism"

Essays in the Philosophy of Humanism, Eds. R.D. Finch, M.Hillar & F. Prahl 8, 28-51.

Finch, Robert, D., (2001) "The Evolution of Religion" in Essays in the Philosophy of Humanism, Eds. R.D. Finch and Marian Hillar, 19, 1-24.

Finch, Robert David, (2002) "Economics and Humanism", Essays in the Philosophy of Humanism, vol. 10, pp 57-79, Eds. Robert D. Finch and Marian Hillar.

Finch, Robert D., (2008) "Ethical and Moral Systems" Essays in the Philosophy of Humanism vol. 16 part 1, Marian Hillar, editor

Finch, Robert D. (2009) "Humanist Ethology", Essays in the Philosophy of Humanism, Ed.M.Hillar 17 (2) 43 – 66.

Finlayson, James Gordon, (2005), "Habermas: A Very Short Introduction", Oxford University Press.

Fisher, R.A., (1915) "The Evolution of Sexual Preference." Eugenics Review, 7, 184-192.

Fletcher, Joseph (1966) "Situation Ethics: The New Morality", Westminster Press.

Flew, Antony (1967) "Evolutionary Ethics".

Flew, Antony (1971) "An Introduction to Western Philosophy".

Flynn, Thomas R., (2006), "Existentialism: A Very Short Introduction", Oxford University Press.

Frank, R.H. (1988), "Passions Within Reason: The Strategic Role of the Emotions", Norton.

Frankel, Viktor (1972) "Why Believe in Others?" Internet.

Frankel, Viktor (1997) "Man's Search for Ultimate Meaning", Insight Books.

Friedrich, Carl J., (1949) "The Philosophy of Kant" Random House.

Fromm, Erich, (1947) "Man for Himself: An Enquiry into the Psychology of Ethics", Owl Book Edition, 1990.

Fulcher, James, (2004) "Capitalism: A Very Short Introduction", Oxford University Press.

Fuller, Steve, (2003), "Kuhn vs Popper", Icon Books.

Gazzaniga, Michael S. (2008) "Human: The Science Behind What Makes Us Unique", Harper-Collins.

Geer, James, Julia Heiman and Harold Leitenberg, (1984), "Human Sexuality" Prentice Hall.

Gell-Mann, Murray, (1994) "The Quark and the Jaguar: Adventures in the Simple and the Complex", W. H. Freeman and Co.

Gensler, Harry J. (2013) "Ethics and the Golden Rule", Routledge.

Gleitman, Henry, (1986) "Psychology", Norton.

Goldstein, Rebecca Neuberger, interviewed by Andy Norman (2014) in "The Machinery of Moral Progress" The Humanist Magazine, September/October pp 28-31 referring to "Plato at the Googleplex" (2014).

Goodell, Edward, (1994) "The Noble Philosopher: Condorcet and the Enlightenment", Prometheus Books.

Goodenough, Ursula (1998), "The Sacred Depths of Nature", Oxford University Press.

Gore, Al (2006) "An Inconvenient Truth", Rodale.

Gore, Al (2007) "The Assault on Reason", The Penguin Press.

Graffin, Gregory W. and William B.Provine, (2007) "Evolution, Religion and Free Will" Am. Scientist, 95, 294-297.

Graybiel, A.M. and K.S. Smith, (2014) "How the brain makes and breaks habits". Sci.

Am., Jun 2014

Grayling, A.C. (2003), "What is Good? The Search for the Best Way to Live"

Weidenfeld & Nicholson.

Grayling, A.C. (1996), "Epistemology" in "The Blackwell Companion to Philosophy", Nicholas Bunnin and E.P. Tsui-James, Eds., Blackwell.

Greenblatt, Stephen, (2011) "The Swerve: How the World Became Modern" W.W.

Norton & Co.

Habermas, Jürgen (1984) "The Theory of Communicative Action," Beacon Press.

Haidt, Jonathan (2006), "The Happiness Hypothesis" Free Press.

Hampden-Turner, Charles and Alfons Tropenaars, (1993), "The Seven Cultures of Capitalism," Doubleday.

Hare, R.M. (1963) "Freedom and Reason" Oxford University Press.

Harris, Lee, (2007) "The Suicide of Reason: Radical Islam's Threat to the West", Basic Books

Harris, Sam (2004), "The End of Faith", W.W. Norton.

Harris, Sam (2010), "The Moral Landscape: How Science Can Determine Human Values", Free Press.

Hauser, Marc D., (2006) "Moral Minds: How Nature Designed our Universal Sense of Right and Wrong", Harper-Collins

Hawkins, Jeff, (2004) with Sandra Blakeslee "On Intelligence", Times Books.

Haydon, A.E. (1929) "The Quest of the Ages", Harper and Bros.

Hayek, Frederich, (1944) "The Road to Serfdom" University of Chicago Press.

Held, David, (1980) "Introduction to Critical Theory: Horkheimer to Habermas", Univ.

of California Press, Berkeley.

Hibbert, Christopher, (1979) "The Rise and Fall of the House of Medici" Penguin Books.

Hibbert, Christopher, (1987) "The English: A Social History 1066-1945" Guild Publishing London

Hickman, Larry A. (1990) "John Dewey's Pragmatic Technology" Indiana University Press.

Hillar, M. and Claire S. Allen (2002) "Michael Servetus: Intellectual Giant, Humanist, and Martyr" University Press of America.

Hillar, Marian, (2007), "Servetus and the Switch to the Humanistic Social Paradigm", Essays in the Philosophy of Humanism, Eds. M.Hillar and Robert D. Finch vol.15, 91-116.

Hitchens, Christopher, (2007), "God is not Great", Hachette Book Group

Hoffer, Eric (1951) "The True Believer", Harper & Row

Howe, Fisher, (1997) "The Board Members Guide to Strategic Planning", Jossey-Bass Publishers.

Humanist Jan/Feb 2003, "Prostitutes as Slaves and Entrepreneurs".

Humanist Manifestos I and II, see for example Appendix to Corliss Lamont's "Philosophy of Humanism", Ungar, 6th edition 1982.

Hume, David, (1748) "An Enquiry Concerning Human Understanding", Edited by Eric Steinberg, Hackett Publishing Company, 1977.

Hume, David, (1777) "An Enquiry Concerning The Principles of Morals" in "Enquiries", Edited by L.A. Selby-Bigge, Third Edition with notes by P.H. Nidditch, Clarendon Press, 1975

Hume, David, (1777b) "Essays: Moral, Political and Literary", The Liberty Fund, (1985)

Hume, David, (1739 & 1740) "A Treatise of Human Nature", with Introduction by Michael P. Levine, Barnes & Noble, 2005

Huxley, Julian, (1957) "Knowledge, Morality, and Destiny" Mentor Books.

Huxley, Julian, (1957) "Religion without Revelation" Max Parrish.

Huxley, Julian, Ed., (1961) "The Humanist Frame" George Allen & Unwin.

Huxley, Julian, (1964) "Essays of a Humanist", Penguin Books.

Huxley, Julian, (1964) "Evolutionary Humanism" Prometheus Books Ed. 1992

Inwood, Brad, L.P. Gerson and D.S. Hutchinson (1994), "The Epicurus Reader", Hackett Publishing Co.

Jackson, Arthur M. (2010), "How to Live the Good Life: A User's Guide for Modern Humans" AMJ Mentor Press.

Jacoby, Susan, (2004) "Freethinkers: A History of American Secularism" Henry Holt &

Co.

James, William (1890) "Principles of Psychology", Henry Holt.

James, William (1902) "The Varieties of Religious Experience", Modern Library Ed.

(1936).

Jamieson, Dale, (1991) "Method and Moral Theory" in "A Companion to Ethics", Ed.

Peter Singer, Blackwell Publishing.

Johanson, Donald C. and Kate Wong (2009) "Lucy's Legacy: The Quest for Human Origins", Harmony Books.

Kant, Immanuel, (1783) "Prolegomena". First English edition 1902 Open Court Publishing Company.

Kant, Immanuel, (1785) "The Metaphysical Foundations of Morals"

Kant, Immanuel, (1788) "The Critique of Pure Practical Reason"

Kant, Immanuel, (1790) "Critique of Judgment". Oxford University Press edition published in 1945.

Kelly, Kevin (2010) "What Technology Wants", Viking.

Kerr, Michael E. and Murray Bowen (1988), "Family Evaluation: The role of the family as an emotional unit that governs individual behavior and development", Norton.

Jacobs, Robin and Roy Speckhardt, "What Do We Do Now that the Sexual Revolution is Over?" Humanist Nov/Dec 2004

Johanson, Donald C. (2009) "Lucy's Legacy: The Quest for Human Origins", Harmony Books.

Kidder, Rushworth M., (1995) "How Good People Make Tough Choices", Simon &
Schuster.

Kinsey, Alfred C., Wardell B. Pomeroy & Clyde E. Martin, (1948), "Sexual Behavior in the Human Male", Saunders.

Kinsey, Alfred C., Wardell B. Pomeroy, Clyde E. Martin, & P. Gebhard (1953), "Sexual Behavior in the Human Female", Saunders.

Kirkegaard, Soren (1843), "Either/Or," 1987 edition Princeton University Press.

Kitcher, Philip (2011), "The Ethical Project", Harvard University Press.

Kitcher, Philip, (2013) "Experiments of Living: An Ethical Stance for the Human Future", The Humanist Magazine, January/February pp 12-15

Kohlberg, Lawrence (1981), "Essays on Moral Development, Vol. 1: The Philosophy of Moral Development", Harper and Row.

Kolenda, Konstantin (), "Cosmic Religion: The Autobiography of the Universe", Kuhn, Thomas S., (1962), "The Structure of Scientific Revolutions", Second Ed. 1970, University of Chicago.

Kurtz, Paul (1980), "Does Humanism have an Ethic of Responsibility?" in "Humanist Ethics", Morris B. Storer, Ed., Prometheus Press.

Kurtz Paul (1983), "A Secular Humanist Declaration", in "In Defense of Secular Humanism", Prometheus Books.

Kurtz, Paul (1988) "Forbidden Fruit: the Ethics of Humanism," Prometheus Books.

Kurtz, Paul (1989) "Eupraxophy," Prometheus Books.

Kurtz, Paul (2006) "Creating Secular and Humanist Alternatives to Religion" in Free Inquiry, vol. 26, No. 5, pp 4-8.

Kurzweil, Ray, (1999) "The Age of Spiritual Machines: When Computers exceed Human Intelligence", Viking Press.

Kurzweil, Ray, (2005) "The Singularity Is Near", Viking Press.

Kurzweil, Ray, (2012) "How To Create A Mind", Viking Penguin.

Lamont, Corliss, (1977) "A Humanist Funeral Service", New Ed., Prometheus Press.

Lamont, Corliss, (1990) "The Illusion of Immortality", 5th Ed., Continuum.

Lamont, Corliss (1982), "Central Propositions of Humanism" from "Philosophy of Humanism", Ungar, 6th edition and see also Humanist Manifestos I and II, in the Appendix.

Lamont, Corliss (2001), "Philosophy of Humanism", Ungar, 8th edition, Humanist Press.

Larue, Gerald A. (1996) "Freethought Across the Centuries", Humanist Press.

Leuchtag, Alice "Sex Trafficking & Prostitution," Humanist Jan/Feb 2003, Humanist Sept/ Oct 2010

Levinson, Daniel J., (1978) ""The Seasons of a Man's Life", Ballantine Books.

Lieberman, Gin Kohl, (2002) "From Arm-Chair Philosophy to Social Agency" PhD Dissertation, Department of Communication, University of South Florida.

Livingston, Ken (2006) "God, Aristotle and the New Science of Happiness", in Free Enquiry *26*, 32-38

Livingston, Donald W. and James T. King (1976)) "Hume: A Re-evaluation", Fordham University Press

Locke, John, (1666), "The Second Treatise on Civil Government" in "John Locke on Politics and Education" with introduction by Howard R. Penniman, Walter J.

Black, 1947.

Locke, John, "Essay on Human Understanding"

Locke, John, "Essay on Toleration"

Machiavelli, Niccolo, (1532) "The Prince", Mentor Books (1952)

MacIntyre, Alasdair, (1984), "After Virtue", 2nd Ed., Univ. of Notre Dame Press.

Mackie, J.L., (1977) "Ethics: Inventing Right and Wrong", Penguin Books.

MacIntyre, Alasdair (1981) "After Virtue" 2nd Edition, 1984

Marx, Karl, (1867) "Das Kapital". Abridged edition, Oxford University Press, (1995)

Maslow, Abraham H., (1971) "The Farther Reaches of Human Nature", Viking.

McCready, Stuart, Ed., (2001), "The Discovery of Happiness", Sourcebooks Inc.

Mill, John Stuart, (1859) "On Liberty".

Mill, John Stuart, (1861) "Utilitarianism".

Mill, John Stuart, and Harriet Taylor (1869) "The Subjection of Women".

Mill, John Stuart, (1873) "Autobiography".

Miller, Geoffrey, (2000) "The Mating Mind: How Sexual Choice Shaped the Evolution of Human Nature", Anchor Books.

Miller, Stephen A. and John B. Harley (1999), "Zoology", 4th Edition, McGraw-Hill.

Mursell, James L., (1953) "How to Make and Break Habits", Lippincott Co.

Munn, Norman, (1962) "Introduction to Psychology", Houghton Mifflin.

Nietzsche, Friedrich (1886), "Beyond Good and Evil", Penguin Books edition, 1973

Nietzsche, Friedrich (1887), "The Birth of Tragedy" and "The Genealogy of Morals", Anchor Books edition, 1956

Nozick, Robert (1989), "The Examined Life", Simon & Schuster Paperbacks.

Nye, David E., (2011) "Getting Better All the Time?" Am. Scientist vol. 99, 156-158.

Paine, Thomas, (1791) "Rights of Man", Parsons, Talcott, (1982) "On Institutions and Social Evolution" Selected Writings, Edited and with an introduction by Leon H. Mayhew, University of Chicago Press.

Patrick, Bethane, (2011) "An Uncommon History of Common Courtesy: How Manners Shaped the World", National Geographic.

Peden, W.C. (1992), "The Philosopher of Free Religion, Francis Ellingwood Abbot", Peter Lang.

Peden, W.C. (2006), "A Good Life in a World Made Good, Albert Eustace Haydon, 1880-1975", Peter Lang.

Peirce, Charles Sanders, (1896) "The Scientific Attitude and Fallibilism" see "Philosophical Writings of Peirce", Ed. Justus Buchler, (1940), Dover Ed. 1955

Pennock, Robert T. (1995), "Moral Darwinism: Ethical Evidence for the Descent of Man" Biology and Philosophy 10: 287-307.

Phillips, David, (2011) "Sidgwickian Ethics", Oxford University Press.

Pinker, Steven (2011), "The Better Angels of Our Nature: Why Violence has Declined", Viking.

Pinn, Anthony B. Ed., (2013) "What is Humanism and Why Does it Matter?' Acumen.

Plato, (2004) "The Republic", Barnes and Noble Classics.

Pojman, Louis P., (1990) "Ethics: Discovering Right and Wrong", Wadsworth.

Popper, Sir Karl R. (1934), "The Logic of Scientific Discovery" first published in English 1959. Harper Torchbook Ed. 1965

Popper, Sir Karl, (1957), "The Poverty of Historicism" Routledge & Kegan Paul.

Popper, Sir Karl, (1963), "Conjectures and Refutations: The Growth of Scientific Knowledge", Harper & Row.

Popper, Sir Karl, (1966), "The Open Society and Its Enemies", Princeton University Press, 5th Ed.

Popper, Sir Karl, (1972), "Objective Knowledge: An Evolutionary Approach" Clarendon Press.

Popper, Karl R. and John C. Eccles, (1977), "The Self and its Brain: An Argument for Interactionism", Routledge and Kegan Paul.

Posner, Richard A., (2009) "A Failure of Capitalism" Harvard University Press.

Postrell, Virginia (1998) "The Future and its Enemies", The Free Press.

Quine, W.V.O., (1953) "Two Dogmas of Empiricism" in his "From a Logical Point of View", Cambridge University Press.

Rachels, James, and Stuart Rachels (2007) "The Elements of Moral Philosophy", 5th Ed., McGraw-Hill.

Radest, Howard B., (1987) "Toward Common Ground: The Story of the Ethical Societies in the United States", 2nd Ed., Fieldston Press.

Radest, Howard, (1998) "Felix Adler. An Ethical Culture", Peter Lang Publishing.

Rand, Ayn (1943), "The Fountainhead", Bobbs-Merrill.

Rand, Ayn, (1963) "For the New Intellectual", Signet Books.

Rand, Ayn (1964), "The Virtue of Selfishness", New American Library.

Rand, Ayn, (1967), "Capitalism: The Unknown Ideal" with additional articles by Nathaniel Branden, Alan Greenspan and Robert Hessen. Penguin Books.

Rapoport, Anatol (1986) "General System Theory: Essential Concepts & Applications", Abacus Press.

Rawls, John, (1972) "A Theory of Justice" Oxford University Press. Revised Ed., 2003, Belknap Press of Harvard U.P.

Rawls, John, (2001), "Justice as Fairness" Harvard University Press.

Raymo, Chet, (2000), "A New Paradigm for Thomas Kuhn", Sci. Am. 104-105.

Rees, Sir Martin (2003) "Our Final Hour" Basic Books.

Reese, Curtis W., (1926) "Humanism," Open Court Publishing Company.

Reeves, Richard, (2008) "John Stuart Mill: Victorian Firebrand" Atlantic Books.

Restak, Richard, (1984) "The Brain", Bantam Books.

Ridley, Matt, (1993) "The Red Queen: Sex and the Evolution of Human Nature", Harper Perennial.

Ridley, Matt, (2010) "The Rational Optimist: How Prosperity Evolves", Harper-Collins.

Rifkin, Lawrence, (2008) "Evolutionary Humanism for a New Era" Free Inquiry, June/July, 44-46.

Roe, M.F.H. (1975) "Letters From Afar" The Quatrefoil Press.

Roe, M.F.H. (1990) "Ethical Issues" Brittania Press.

Russell, Bertrand, (1929) "Marriage and Morals", Liveright Paperbound Ed., 1970.

Russell, Bertrand, (1945) "The History of Western Philosophy", Simon & Schuster.

Ryan, Christopher, and Cacilda Jetha (2010) "Sex at Dawn", Harper-Collins.

Penguin Press.

Sachs, Jeffrey (2005) "The End of Poverty: Economic Possibilities for our Time", Penguin Press.

Sagan, Carl, (1980), "Cosmos" Random House.

Said, Edward, (2004), "Humanism and Democratic Criticism," Columbia University Press.

Samuelson, Paul A. (1976), "Economics" 10th edition, McGraw-Hill.

Sartre, Jean-Paul (1943), "Being and Nothingness", Citadel Edition 1984

Sartre, Jean-Paul (1945), "Existentialism Is A Humanism," 2007 English translation, Yale University Press.

Schultz, Bart (2004), "Henry Sidgwick: The Eye of the Universe", Cambridge University Press.

Schneewind, J. B. (1977), "Sidgwick's Ethics and Victorian Moral Philosophy", Clarendon Press.

Schelling and Frank Science, (2 October 2009), Vol 326, Special Section on Ardipithecus ramidus.

Searle, John R., (1996), "Contemporary Philosophy in the United States" in "The Blackwell Companion to Philosophy", Nicholas Bunnin and E.P. Tsui-James, Eds., Blackwell.

Seidman, Barry F. and Neil J. Murphy, (2004), Eds., "Toward a New Political Humanism" Prometheus Books.

Seigel, Jeremy, (1998), "Stocks for the Long Run" 2nd Ed. McGraw-Hill.

Seligman, Martin (1990) "Learned Optimism" Vintage Books.

Seligman, Martin (2002) "Authentic Happiness" Free Press.

Shermer, Michael (2004) "The Science of Good and Evil", Owl Books.

Sidgwick, Henry (1902) "Outlines of the History of Ethics" reprinted in 1988 Hackett Publishing.

Sidgwick, Henry, (1874) "The Methods of Ethics", 7th edition 1907, republished by Hackett Publishing Co., 1981

Simon, Herbert A., (1969), "The Sciences of the Artificial" 2nd Ed., MIT Press, 1981.

Simpson, Lyle L., (2003) "A Humanist Perspective: Maslow's Purpose for Your Life" in Essays in the Philosophy of Humanism vol. 11, Marian Hillar Editor.

Simpson, Lyle L., (2005) "What is the Purpose for Your Life: A Sequel to A Humanist Perspective: Maslow's Purpose for Your Life" in Essays in the Philosophy of Humanism vol. 13, Marian Hillar Editor.

Singer, Peter, (1975), "Animal Liberation: A New Ethics for our Treatment of Animals,"

Random House.

Singer, Peter, (1981), "The Expanding Circle: Ethics, Evolution, and Moral Progress", Princeton University Press, Second Edition, 2011.

Singer, Peter, Ed., (1991), "A Companion to Ethics", Blackwell, See especially Parts VI and VII.

Singer, Peter, (1993), "Practical Ethics", Second Edition, Cambridge University Press.

Singer, Peter, (1993), "How Are We to Live?" Prometheus Books.

Smiles, Samuel, (1859) "Self Help".

Smith, C.M. (2005), "Origin and Uses of Primum Non Nocere --- Above All, Do No Harm!" The Journal of Clinical Pharmacology 45 (4): 371-377.

Soros, George, (2008), "The Credit Crisis of 2008 and What It Means" Perseus Books.

Spencer, Herbert, (1862), "First Principles of a New System of Philosophy".

Stanford Encyclopedia of Philosophy, "Positive and Negative Liberty" (2009)

Stearns, Peter N., (1990) "Be a Man! Males in Modern Society", Holmes and Meier.

Sterba, James P. (2005) "The Triumph of Practice over Theory in Ethics", Oxford University Press.

Stoesz, Edgar, and Chester Raber, (1994), "Doing Good Better", Good Books.

Storer, Morris B., Ed., (1980) "Humanist Ethics," Prometheus Press.

Stout, Harry S. (2007) "Upon the Altar of the Nation: A Moral History of the Civil War", Elsevier.

Streit, Clarence K., (1940), "Union Now" Harper and Brothers.

Stringer, Chris and Peter Andrews, (2005), "The Complete World of Human Evolution", Natural History Museum, London.

Tate, Jeffery L., (2007) "Habermas for Humanists" in Essays in the Philosophy of Humanism, Ed. M. Hillar. Vol. 15, 58-75.

Tattersal, Ian, (1998), "Becoming Human", Harcourt Brace & Co.

Tegmark, Max, (2014), "Our Mathematical Universe", Alfred A. Knopf.

Thucydides (431-400 BCE), "History of the Peloponnesian War". Barnes and Noble Edition ((2006)

Tooby, J., and Cosmides, L. (2001) "Does beauty build adapted minds? Toward an evolutionary theory of aesthetics, fiction and the arts" Substance 30:6-27.

Van Doren, Charles (1991), "A History of Knowledge", Carol Publishing Group.

Van Praag, Jaap (1982), "Foundations of Humanism", Prometheus Books.

de Waal, Frans and Frans Lanting (1997), "Bonobo: The Forgotten Ape, University of California Press.

Wade, Nicholas, (2006), "Before the Dawn: Recovering the Lost History of Our Ancestors", Penguin Press.

Wade, Nicholas, (2009), "The Faith Instinct: How Religion Evolved and Why It Endures", Penguin Books.

Walters, C. Kenneth and Albert Van Helden, (1992) "Julian Huxley: Biologist and Statesman of Science", Rice University Press.

Warnock, Mary (2004), "The Intelligent Person's Guide to Ethics".

Watson, James D., (1968), "The Double Helix", Atheneum Publishers.

Werth, Barry (2009) "Banquet at Delmonico's: Great Minds, the Gilded Age, and the Triumph of Evolution in America", Random House.

Weismann, August, (1893) "The Germ-Plasm: A Theory of Heredity" Charles Scribner's Sons. Online Electronic Edition, Electronic Scholarly Publishing.

Wikipedia, "Kinsey Reports", http://en.wikipedia.org/wiki/Kinsey_Reports

Wikipedia, "Neuroscience of sex differences", http://en.wikipedia.org/wiki/Neuroscience_of_sex_differences

Widrow, B., and S.D. Stearns (1985) "Adaptive Signal Processing", Prentice Hall.

Williams, Bernard, (1995), "The point of view of the universe: Sidgwick and the ambitions of ethics" in "Making Sense of Humanity" Cambridge University Press.

Williams, Bernard, (1996), "Contemporary Philosophy: A Second Look" in "The Blackwell Companion to Philosophy", Nicholas Bunnin and E.P. Tsui-James, Eds., Blackwell.

Willson, Jane Wynne, (1995), "Funerals Without God", British Humanist Association.

Wilson, E.O. (1975), "Sociobiology: The Abridged Edition" Harvard University Press.

Wilson, E.O., (1978) "On Human Nature", Harvard University Press.

Wilson, E.O. (1994), "Naturalist", Warner Books.

Wilson, E.O. (1998), "Consilience: The Unity of Knowledge", Alfred A. Knopf.

Wilson, E.O. (2012), "The Social Conquest of Earth", W.W. Norton & Co.

Wilson, E.O. (2014), "The Meaning of Human Existence", W.W. Norton & Co.

Wilson, James Q., (1993), "The Moral Sense", Simon and Schuster.

Wolff, Jonathan, (1996), "An Introduction to Political Philosophy" Oxford University Press.

Woolman, John, (1961) "Journal", Citadel, New York.

Woolstonecraft, Mary (1792) "A Vindication of the Rights of Women"

Wright, Robert (1994), "The Moral Animal: Evolutionary Psychology and Everyday Life" Vintage Books.

Zahavi, Amotz (1975), "Mate selection: A selection for a handicap". J. Theoretical Biology, 53,205-214.

Zimbardo, Philip, (2007), "The Lucifer Effect", Random House.

Index

Printed in the United States
By Bookmasters